Marie Lloyd

MARIE LLOYD

MARIE LLOYD

The One and Only

❧

MIDGE GILLIES

VICTOR GOLLANCZ

LONDON

The right of Midge Gillies to be identified as the author of
this work has been asserted by her in accordance with
the Copyright, Designs and Patents Act, 1988.

First published in Great Britain in 1999 by Victor Gollancz
An imprint of Orion Books Ltd,
Orion House, 5 Upper St Martin's Lane,
London WC2H 9EA

A CIP catalogue record for this book is
available from the British Library.

ISBN 0 575 06420 X

Typeset by
SetSystems, Saffron Walden, Essex

Printed and bound by
Clays Ltd, St Ives plc.

Dedication
To my old man

Contents

Acknowledgements   ix

Prologue: The Funeral of Marie Lloyd   1

1 Early Life in Hoxton (1870–85)   5

2 Playing the Halls (1885–7)   20

3 Developing an Act (the late 1880s)   33

4 A Proper Pantomime (1890–91)   43

5 Celebrity Status (1891–2)   58

6 Twiggy Voo, My Boys? (1891–2)   65

7 Maid of London (1893–6)   77

8 The Battle for the Empire (1894)   85

9 Charges of Immorality (1895–6)   96

10 Taking the Empire Abroad (1897)   109

11 Alec Hurley and the Family Years (1898–1900)   122

12 A Measure of Indistinctness – Australia (1901)   132

13 Bella's Troubles (1901–2)   141

14 Changing Tastes (1902–5)   148

15 Trouble Brewing (1906–7)   160

16 Strike (1906–7)   170

17 Alice Lloyd's Sister Goes to New York (1907)   185

18 Marriage Problems (1908–11)   199

19 Horse-racing (1911)   211

20 Disgrace (1912–13)   221

21 Moral Turpitude (1913–14)   236

CONTENTS

22 War (1914–18)   249

23 A Crowded Hour of Life (1918–21)   263

Epilogue: Who Killed Marie Lloyd?   276

Note on Sources   283

Notes   285

Bibliography   304

Who's Who   313

Index   327

ACKNOWLEDGEMENTS

At several points during the research for this biography I have been aware of historical events and characters colliding with contemporary settings and people in a remarkable way. The most eerie example of this was when I took Alice Lloyd's daughter, Mrs Tomme (Grace) Thomas, to No. 10 Downing Street to try to establish whether the Sickert painting hanging there, *The Sisters Lloyd*, was indeed of her mother. John Major, whose father had been one of the early members of the Variety Artistes' Federation, was then Prime Minister. If people do turn in their graves, surely both Marie and Oswald Stoll must have been stirring restlessly at the thought of Marie Lloyd's niece being invited to No. 10 and that she would be visiting the home of the son of a music-hall militant.

The Sisters Lloyd shows two young girls in white dresses and large yellow hats. They have long blonde hair and are standing in front of a gloomy stage backdrop that many critics of the time mistook for a real room. The way they were dressed reminded me of a photo I had seen of Bella Orchard. But Tomme dismissed the painting with the directness of her family: 'They're much too ugly to be Lloyds,' she said bluntly. She conceded, though, that another version of *The Sisters Lloyd*, which appeared in the *Idler* in 1895, bore a resemblance to Marie's sister Grace when she stood with her hands clasped in front of her body.

Tomme is one of several members of the Wood clan who have shown me both hospitality and kindness in my search for Marie, and kept me entertained along the way. I have also enjoyed meeting Johnny's grandson, Dick Mott, and his performing dog, Tessa. I spent a fascinating afternoon with Alec Hurley's great-nephew Colin Devereaux, who is one of Britain's most successful pantomime dames and who carries on the music-hall tradition with his portrayal of Dockyard Doris. Fred McNaughton's granddaughter, Lindy Rawling, was particularly encouraging at the start of the project.

Bernard Dillon's nephew Mick and his wife Brenda were also

generous with their time and encouragement. Mick has inherited his Derby-winning uncle's charm but not his vices; he started his working life in horse-racing, but later became a double for movie stars – most notably Ringo Starr in the Beatles' film *Help!*. Old posters for the film show Mick as one of the Fab Four, the only apparent difference between him and the real thing being the groove in Mick's fingers left from years of gripping reins.

Several actors have shared their impressions with me about what it feels like to perform music-hall songs: Elizabeth Mansfield, who starred in *Marie*; Helen Fraser, who still performs *Vesta* (about Vesta Victoria) and *Vitality* (about Cicely Courtneidge); and Robert Lister, who wrote and performed a one-man play about Alec Hurley called *Mr Marie Lloyd*.

Music-hall experts who have studied the subject for decades have been most generous with their knowledge and encouragement. I am particularly grateful to the British Music Hall Society and to its Study Group Administrator, Terry Lomas, and BMHS historian, Max Tyler. Max, in particular, has always been ready to share his immense knowledge with me and has been tireless in his willingness to answer my countless music-hall queries with great good humour. Likewise, I value the suggestions made by Professor John Stokes and Lucie Sutherland and am grateful for the time they devoted to reading the manuscript.

Dr Peter Bailey, of the University of Manitoba, has offered me encouragement from afar and, on several occasions, pointed me in the direction of interesting articles about the subject. John Diamond has shared his knowledge of the political content of music-hall songs, and David Kenten provided me with the great thrill of seeing Marie 'in action'. Other people who have shared their expertise include: Jill Craigie; Dr Peter Fryer; Viv Gardner, Department of Drama, University of Manchester; Rt Hon. Lord Jenkins of Hillhead, OM; Professor Joel Kaplan; Paul Mathieu; Rosy Thornton; and Norman Wisdom OBE. The staff of No 10. Downing Street were also kind enough to enter into the spirit of my trip in search of *The Sisters Lloyd*.

Many librarians around the world have helped me forage for information. I am particularly grateful to: the Cancer Research Campaign; Joanna Corden, Local Studies and Archives, Hendon Library; Robert A. McCown, Special Collections and Manuscripts Librarian, University of Iowa Libraries, University of Iowa; Graham Dalling, local history officer in the London Borough of Enfield; Jill Kelsey, Assistant Registrar, The Royal Collection Trust, Windsor Castle; and Birgit Boehme of the Zentral und Landesbibliothek, Berlin. I am especially grateful to Eddie Trigg and Gae Diller Anderson in Australia for their long-distance help.

I am indebted to the K. Blundell Trust for their generous financial assistance which allowed me to pursue my research in America. The Society of Authors has also been most helpful.

I am grateful for permission to reproduce various lyrics. 'A Little Of What You Fancy', words and music by George Arthurs and Fred Leigh © 1915 Francis Day & Hunter Ltd and Redwood Music Ltd, lyric reproduction by kind permission of Carlin Music Corp., Iron Bridge House, 3 Bridge Approach, London NW1 8BD; 'Piccadilly Trot', words and music by George Arthurs and Fred Leigh © 1913 B. Feldman & Co. Ltd and Redwood Music Ltd, lyric reproduction by kind permission of Carlin Music Corp., Iron Bridge House, 3 Bridge Approach, London NW1 8BD. I am grateful also to David Bateman, Ada Beresford, Michael Hankins and Patricia Thomas for allowing me to reproduce lyrics. 'Blighters' is reproduced by kind permission of George Sassoon, copyright Siegfried Sassoon.

The short extract from George V's diary, the correspondence between Alfred Butt and Sir William Carington and the provisional bill for the first royal command performance in chapter 20 are reproduced by the gracious permission of Her Majesty The Queen.

My thanks to Richard Bonnett for bringing to my attention several rare photographs of Marie.

From the very start of this project, Marie Lloyd has been supported by a strong bill. At Victor Gollancz my editor Sean Magee has provided wisdom and inspiration and proved to be an old-fashioned publisher – in the nicest possible sense of the word. My agent, Faith Evans, has lived up to her name and, as well as constant encouragement, has offered sound advice throughout every stage of the book's development. As copy-editor, Hazel Orme provided patience, thoroughness and encouragement. Although I was never fortunate enough to meet her, the late Liz Knights was supportive of the book in its early stages, for which I will always be grateful.

My friends and family have stood by me throughout my growing obsession with Marie. My mother, Renee Gillies, has acted as an unpaid research assistant and secretary and my father, Donald Gillies, has provided the blind belief in me that only a father can supply. I am particularly grateful to Bridie Pritchard and Veronica Forwood for reading early drafts of the book and to Veronica for guiding me round Paris. As well as providing constant emotional support, Ann-Janine Murtagh and Richard Scrivener stepped into the breach with a replacement computer when mine blew up a fortnight before I was due to deliver the manuscript.

Finally, thanks to Jim Kelly for his forbearance and for his unstinting belief in the book.

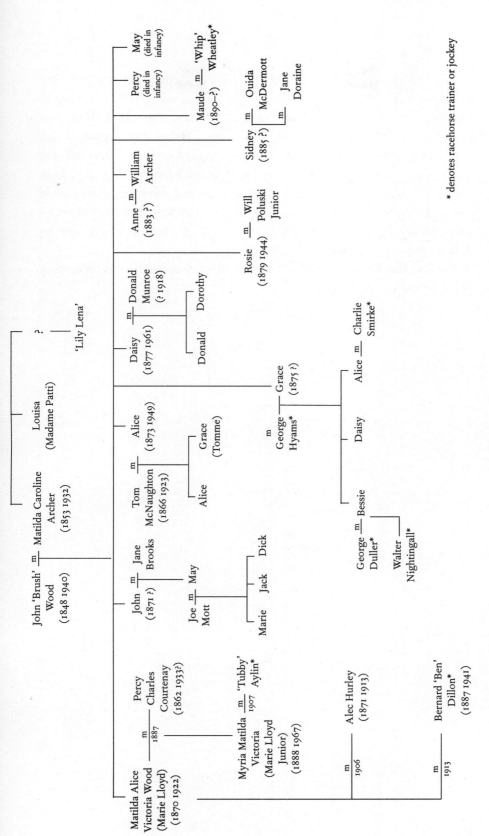

Marie Lloyd
Family Tree

THE FUNERAL OF MARIE LLOYD

*'It is questionable if a more spontaneous and sincere display
of public grief has ever been seen in London . . .'*[1]

Crowds started to gather at Hampstead cemetery as early as seven o'clock on the morning of Marie Lloyd's funeral on Thursday, 12 October 1922. As the numbers grew, police were called in to control the mourners who pressed in on her grave until they stood twelve deep in the roped-off area around the gaping hole that would receive her coffin. So great was the crush that the gates of the cemetery were shut an hour before the interment.

There were crowds, too, in Woodstock Road, Golders Green; the road, pavement and neat gardens of the suburban street were a sea of faces turned towards the door of number 37. Marie's house was full of her extended family and her many music-hall friends; they stood or sat restlessly among the four hundred floral tributes that had arrived at the house. Outside men removed their hats when the tiny coffin appeared at the door and the funeral cortège of twelve cars left at 11 a.m. Mounted police cleared a way through the mass of people. One of Marie's most famous props, an ebony cane, lay wreathed in orchids on top of the hearse, which was followed by the chauffeur-driven car that had taken her to so many performances. A rug tossed over her empty seat was just visible through the car's half-closed blinds.

The cars were heaped high with wreaths from stagehands, dressers, managers and fellow artists. Her agent had sent a model stage with red roses in front of the curtain, while from her 'jockey pals' had come a horseshoe of white chrysanthemums decorated with spurs, a whip, and a cap of blue flowers. A floral representation of an empty bird cage with its door open was a reminder of the 'old cock linnet' of 'My Old Man Said Follow The Van', and a copy in flowers of her favourite armchair represented her as a home-lover. There were more wreaths, from boxers, Piccadilly posy-sellers, the Costermongers Union and London taxi-drivers. Music-hall comic Kate Carney sent flowers in the form of a broken pedestal with the message, 'To a real white woman from her oldest friend',[2] and a laurel wreath inscribed 'In memory of a great artist. She gave lightness of heart to many a heart bowed down' arrived from the Shakespearian actress, Ellen Terry. The mass of flowers wrapped the procession in the sweet, heady musk that normally only accompanies funerals and weddings. Later it took four hours to unload them.

On the day of the funeral Golders Green was a place of lowered blinds. Police stopped the traffic as the procession made its way to St Luke's Church in Kidderpore Avenue, Hampstead. Onlookers showed 'remarkable demonstrations of public sympathy'[3] and photographs and newsreels of the day reveal men and women bemused by grief. Most are wearing black armbands. A window-cleaner, steadying himself against the side of a building, strains for a better view.

Nearly a hundred thousand people were estimated to have turned out to pay their respects. 'Old Kate',[4] a racecard seller and familiar figure at Newmarket, was reported to have walked the seventy-five miles to attend. Max Beerbohm believed Marie's funeral was the biggest London had seen since the death of Wellington. The family firm of funeral directors, A. France & Son,[5] who made the arrangements for Marie, claims to trace its business back to the undertaker responsible for Nelson's state funeral. The *Era*, a weekly theatrical newspaper that had charted Marie's career from its very start, commented on 19 October 1922: 'Marie Lloyd, "Queen of Comedy", had an almost royal progress to her last resting place . . .'

At the church the Reverend Daniel Bartlett 'took the opportunity of addressing the cosmopolitan congregation in his own direct and impressive style'. The mourners sang 'Onward Christian Soldiers', 'Peace, Perfect Peace' and 'Nearer My God To Thee'. The cortège then wound its way slowly to the cemetery, crossing the route that, seventy-five years later, would be taken by the funeral procession of Diana, Princess of Wales. Indeed, many of the contemporary descriptions of Marie's funeral could just as easily have been written about Diana's; the Queen of Hearts and the Queen of Comedy tapped identical wells of public emotion, and prompted similar outpourings of clichés.

> It is questionable if a more spontaneous and sincere display of public grief has ever been seen in London. That Marie was beloved of everybody, rich and poor, stalls and gallery, was plainly visible from the wave of emotion that ran through the huge and mixed crowd as the cortège passed. Moist eyes were the rule rather than the exception, and she whose life's mission was to make people smile, took her 'last curtain' amid the tears of her public . . .
> . . . The sun shone bright and warm as the cortège passed through the cemetery gates. It seemed almost as though it had emerged from its autumn reticence to pay a last glowing tribute to one who had brought sunshine to the lives of so many careworn and toiling mortals.

At the cemetery in Fortune Green Road, West Hampstead, Marie's elderly parents clung to each other for support while her estranged husband, Ben Dillon, stood slightly apart from the family group. The face of the former champion jockey, heavy-jowled but still handsome, looks out from photographs contorted with grief. His appearance prompted groans from some sections of the crowd, who knew of his reputation as a wife-beater. However, Marie's reputation and ebullient character were such that they gasped with surprise at the sight of the coffin, whose diminutive size belied the force of Marie's personality. Unknown to all but her immediate family, Marie's mother had placed a gold locket[6] inside the coffin; it had been frequently pawned to buy props and costumes at the very start of her career.

At the graveside the ululations of grief were so great that Mr Bartlett paused to allow the crowd to recover itself.

Hampstead Cemetery is full of grandiose graves, such as a mock-Egyptian temple and a seven-foot-high stone organ with seat and sheet music. But Marie's grave is short and squat, its simple Celtic cross now overshadowed by the statue of a tall, willowy woman belonging to the next plot. The inscription on her gravestone, composed by Catherine

3

Geere, principal of Clarence House School, Brighton, which Marie's daughter attended, reads:

> Tired she was, although she didn't show it,
> Suffering was she, and hoped we didn't know it,
> But He above – and understanding all,
> Prescribed "long rest", and gave the Final Call.

Mourners continued to visit Marie's grave for three days after her funeral. Around 120,000 people were said to have visited the spot, which was guarded by police, and which today is still occasionally adorned with fresh flowers and faded photos of Marie, placed there by admirers.[7]

Chapter 1

EARLY LIFE IN HOXTON

(1870–85)

The boy I love is up in the gallery.
The boy I love is looking now at me.
There he is. Can't you see?
Waving his handkerchief,
As merry as a robin that sings on a tree.
'The Boy I Love Is
Up In The Gallery' by George Ware

Matilda Alice Victoria Wood was born on 12 February 1870 at 36 Plumber Street (now Provost Street) in Hoxton in the East End of London – although music-hall legend has it that Marie's birthplace was 'Peerless Street'. It was in one of the most densely populated parts of the wider district of Shoreditch, and in 1871 some houses in Hoxton Square were home to seven or eight families.

Marie's father, John Wood, was a maker of artificial flowers. His parents had left their home in the countryside – where his father was a willow-cutter and his mother a willow-weaver – in search of work in the fast-expanding East End. They were part of a much larger exodus, from rural parts and from famine-riddled Ireland, which helped transform the area into a neighbourhood inhabited by a transient and cosmopolitan population. Between 1801 and 1861 Shoreditch, which at 640 acres was a comparatively small parish, saw its population soar from 34,000 to 129,000 – one of the largest bursts of growth in such a district at that time.

John met his future wife, Matilda Caroline Archer, whose parents were bootmakers, in Bethnal Green. They married in April 1869, when John was twenty-one and his bride just sixteen. Marie, their first child, was conceived within weeks of their wedding.

Like most of their neighbours in Hoxton, the young couple moved frequently: they were always on the look-out for a better deal to meet their constantly changing circumstances. John appears either to have escaped the census of 2 April 1871, or to have moved on, as his family is not listed then as living at number 36. Perhaps as his wife worked at home, helping her husband, and there was another baby on the way, it had become necessary to find larger lodgings.

Although the Woods had quit Plumber Street, the details listed in the census give some idea of the cramped conditions endured by those families living in the brick houses that lined the narrow streets of Hoxton. The records also show the diversity of employment and the number of 'cottage industries' that existed in this teeming area of London. Fourteen people lived at number 36, Plumber Street: a carpenter, his wife and four children; a cigar-maker, his wife and daughter; a flower-maker and his two sons, engaged in the same profession; and a female boxmaker and her daughter. Their neighbours in the street included a glass-cutter, a scholar, a porter, a cabinet-maker, a cravat-manufacturer, a flower-maker, a bricklayer and a French polisher.

During the early years of Marie's life, Shoreditch's population was squeezed into ever smaller living spaces. Residential buildings were gobbled up by workshops, warehouses, the North London Railway link between Dalston and Broad Street and what was later known as the Bishopsgate Goods Station. The thirst for land led to evictions and those made homeless found their new quarters overcrowded and often hazardous. Furniture-making, followed by boot and shoe production, was the dominant trade in the area, in the so-called 'slaughterhouses' clustered around Curtain Road. The Regent's Canal provided a direct link to the docks and a ready supply of imported wood. Like most trades in the area, cheap labour meant that much work was sub-contracted and it was not uncommon for one chair to pass through the hands of several tradesmen.

The manufacture of artificial flowers, principally for use in hats, burgeoned in Marie's youth and John Wood earned thirty shillings a week working for an Italian called Luigi Corti in Bath Street, off the City Road. Although he and his employer got on well throughout the thirty-six years they worked together – and Mr and Mrs Wood later visited the Corti family in Italy – it remained a niggling source of irritation within the Wood family that John received neither sufficient financial reward nor recognition of his inventiveness. Marie's sister, Anne, writing in her notes for memoirs that remained unpublished, attributed the success with which Marie later blended shades of material in her lavish stage costumes to a keen eye for colour inherited from her father. She also credited John with solving the problem of how to produce a realistic-looking field daisy, and other members of the family have described his success in inventing a flower with a fragrant centre.

John was a reserved man, whose nickname 'Brush', or 'Brushie', reflected the pride he took in his appearance and that he carried a clothes brush everywhere with him. Family photos show him staring unsmilingly from beneath a lush, walrus-like moustache. As well as his ingenious way with artificial flowers, his other notable gift was for mental arithmetic – a talent he honed supplementing his income as a waiter in some of Shoreditch's many music halls and pubs.

Matilda was a strong, if not domineering character. As well as helping Brushie, she brought in extra money by producing bead ornaments. However, unlike her husband, she was illiterate, able only to make her mark on her children's birth certificates. She and Brushie had eight, although two, Percy and May, died in infancy, one from a childhood illness, which was probably mumps, the other, according to family legend, accidentally smothered in an overcrowded bed. After Marie and Johnny came Alice, on 20 October 1873, then two years later – almost to the day – Grace. Daisy followed in 1877 and Rosie in 1879. Later on, the ranks were swelled by another three.

As the eldest, Marie – or Tilley, as she was called – had many of the responsibilities and chores of a surrogate mother. It was a role she enjoyed. She liked bossing the others about and they proved both a ready-made cast and a captive audience for her performances. Later, aged twenty-five, she said, 'I remember, as a youngster, while engaged in attending to the domestic concerns of my mother's house, I used to steal odd intervals in order to practise my singing and dancing. Whenever I found myself alone for five minutes, away went the broom or the duster, and I would proceed to "knock" an imaginary audience with my rendering of the latest popular ditty, accompanied, of course, by a few "steps" of my own improvisation.'[1]

The image may be of a Walt Disney-style Cinderella, ready to burst into song at the drop of a duster, but Marie enjoyed housework. She lacked the patience to do it regularly, but she found the physical effort therapeutic, a welcome outlet for her excessive nervous energy. By nature Marie was brash as a girl, and grew up with the confidence of the first-born, which even Johnny's arrival failed to dent. He, like his father, was quiet and submissive, easily dominated by his older sister, but their mother was strong and outspoken; Marie and her string of sisters took after her.

Marie made friends easily: she enjoyed talking to strangers and she had the healthy disregard for authority endemic to her area of London, which had its own rules and even its own language of rhyme and backslang. From an early age she knew how to flirt – both for fun and as a means of getting her own way. She had a quick temper, too, but soon forgot a quarrel: she was always impatient to get on with life.

Both Marie and Alice went to school in Bath Street, which was where their father worked. The school, a tall, forbidding, church-like building, was close to a vinegar factory on City Road. It had a high reputation for both singing and elocution, attributes the school inspectors found particularly noteworthy in such a poor neighbourhood.[2] Marie loathed school: she could not bear to sit still for long and she hated being told what to do. She frequently played truant although when she became well known she invented a past[3] in which she had been a model student: winning prizes for elocution and only narrowly escaping becoming a teacher.

Today, Marie would probably be described as precocious: she liked showing off and she liked being in charge. She also enjoyed the drama and ritual of funerals. Frequently, she took her siblings to the graveyard where she coached them in the art of mourning until they could sob uncontrollably in a tableau of perfect Victorian grief.

Burials were not the only way in which religion offered an outlet for Marie's insatiable need to show off. Hoxton was well endowed with churches, chapels and other religious institutions dedicated to saving local souls from drink and non-educational entertainment. Just as Victorian explorers in Africa brought with them the message of the Gospel, so moral reformers sent missionaries into the wilds of the East End where music halls, pubs and 'free-and-easys' represented the main targets of their assault. One way to spread the message was to use a variant of the devil's weapons of song and sketches. Marie attended a Sunday school in Nile Street, at which youngsters were encouraged to perform their own moralistic tales. Marie snatched this God-given opportunity to appear on stage and formed her siblings into a troupe called the Fairy Bell Minstrels. She coached them for weeks beforehand and gave them explicit directions both on and off stage. Alice could recite the melodramatic poem 'The Dead Doll', with expansive gestures to show that the doll had died from the double complication of a broken heart and a 'dreadful crack on the head'. Johnny sold programmes and Marie sang 'Throw Down The Bottle And Never Drink Again', which she later claimed caused a man in the audience to hurl a bottle of whisky at his wife, declaring that that was the last time he would ever touch it. Temperance was also the theme of a sketch in which Marie played an alcoholic man who had sworn to eat his hat if he ever touched drink again. Alice was his wife, seen preparing a stew of the hat as she awaited his return in the early hours of the morning. The set consisted of a kitchen table, two chairs, a candle and a heavily symbolic bottle of water.

The performances might have remained no more than childhood memories, except that Marie found it difficult to hold down a job once she left school. She barely lasted a week at the jobs her mother lined up for her, whether at a small factory making babies' boots or bead trimming, or curling feathers. The work bored her and she was too often a bad influence on the other workers: productivity dropped off sharply with her arrival because Marie had to be the centre of attention. Just as modern comedians often discover their gift at school when covering up their own insecurities – of being too fat or too clever – so Marie could not resist trying to entertain the other girls when the supervisor's back was turned. Her desire to be at centre-stage seems to have stemmed from a need not to be lost in a crowd, such as the one she lived in at home. At one job she was sacked for dancing on a table, at another for imitating a supervisor.[4] Eventually, she gave up trying to stick to a conventional job and announced that she wanted to perform in music halls.

Later she recalled, rather pompously, the glamour that had first attracted her:

It was always my ambition to become a music-hall artiste, and long before I had ever trodden the boards of the variety stage, I was an eager aspirant for what the professional papers term 'vocal and terpsichorean' honours ... The dazzling lights, the gilded mirrors, the crowded audience – all these things had attractions for me, but the enchanting region beyond the imposing proscenium, with its background of classic terraces and shady groves, exercised a still greater fascination over my youthful fancy, and I determined at the earliest opportunity to gratify my ambition.[5]

Initially her parents offered a few weak protests, but they knew their daughter well enough to realize that she was too stubborn to take no for an answer. She lacked the patience for the eye-straining tedium of the work most young girls were offered, and she would never be content in a job that did not allow her to show off. John and Matilda, struggling to bring up their large family, were also pragmatic enough to accept that, within reason, it did not matter how their daughter earned money so long as she made some contribution to the household. And the stage did not hold for them the terror it might have induced in middle-class parents.

Marie's family was well acquainted with music hall and later Marie claimed that her mother had been a performer before she married.[6] By the time Marie first appeared in a music hall, her mother was sufficiently reconciled to the idea that she even helped make her costume. There was another family connection in that Matilda's sister Louisa was a dancer, Madame Patti, and her niece became a comedian, Lily Lena. Louisa was a particularly strong influence on the young Marie, and took her to the halls where she was performing. Alice said later that it was this that had left Marie irrevocably 'stage-struck'. Aunt Louisa, who had worked 'on the continent' and who dressed up in exotic clothes for a living, must have seemed deliciously glamorous to a teenage girl who had known only the streets of Hoxton and did not even have a dressing-up box of cast-off clothes to rifle through.

It was hardly surprising that the stage appealed: Marie lived in an area of London that bristled with theatres and the like. Shoreditch boasted the Alhambra Music Hall, the Britannia Theatre, the City of London Theatre, the Grecian Theatre and the Eagle Tavern,

McDonald's (also known as Hoxton Hall), the National Standard Theatre and the Variety Theatre – and these were only the best-known venues. At the bottom end of the market 'penny gaffs' entertained audiences by candlelight in rooms that were little more than small shops, the attractions ranging from a garbled melodrama to glorified freak shows such as 'the tallest soldier in the world'. From Tudor times impresarios had looked to Shoreditch as conveniently close to the City of London but just beyond its authority. In 1576 Richard Burbage, head of the Earl of Leicester's company of actors, set up the Theatre in the south of the parish following a ban on plays within the City. In the late nineteenth century, Shoreditch's theatres were still attracting attention: the Britannia, in particular, run by the colourful performer and manageress Sara Lane, was well known for its extravagant pantomimes.

It is impossible to say exactly when and where Marie made her début, but it seems most likely to have been at the Eagle Tavern, or the Grecian Theatre, in 1885, when she was fifteen. The two buildings were in the same complex at the corner of Shepherdess Walk and City Road, on the western edge of Shoreditch, and their names were frequently used interchangeably. Marie maintained, ten years later, that she made her début at the Grecian Theatre but quoted the manager's name as Broom when, in fact, Thomas Broom had been the manager of the Eagle. Alice Lloyd gives the date for her sister's début as Saturday, 9 May 1885.[7]

Assuming that Marie's version of events was accurate, she made her début at one of the most famous halls in the East End. She was aware of the Eagle's high reputation for entertainment, which attracted audiences from beyond Hoxton, and grew up with tales of the shows that had been staged there; she probably passed the building on her way to school and would have been struck by its imposing architecture.

Thomas Rouse, credited with importing the term 'vaudeville' to England from France where it was used to describe musical shows with satirical content, had rebuilt the Shepherd and Shepherdess tavern at the beginning of the nineteenth century and renamed it the Eagle. His ambitious programme of entertainment, which included balloon ascents, concerts and wrestling, was matched by the theatre's architecture: it was a great wedding cake of a building with vast eagle statues perched on the roof gazing down at the arriving audience. Pleasure gardens and a rotunda, the Grecian Saloon, completed the exotic atmosphere.

After a visit in 1836, Dickens described a typical visit there in *Sketches by Boz*:

> There were the walks, beautifully gravelled and planted – and the refreshment-boxes, painted and ornamented like so many snuff-boxes – and the variegated lamps shedding their rich light upon the company's heads – and the place for dancing ready chalked for the company's feet – and a Moorish band playing at one end of the gardens – and an opposition military band playing away at the other. Then, the waiters were rushing to and fro with glasses of negus, and glasses of brandy-and-water, and the bottles of ale, and bottles of stout; and ginger-beer was going off in one place, and practical jokes were going on in another; and people were crowding to the door of the Rotunda; and in short the whole scene was, as Miss J'mima Ivins, inspired by the novelty, or the shrub, or both, observed – 'one of dazzling excitement'.

The writer J. Ewing Ritchie, a staunch opponent of music hall, was more critical: in *The Night Side of London* (written in 1857, the same year that Gladstone saw *The Hunchback* at the Grecian) he warned of the temptations of street-walkers and drink and of 'questionable sausage rolls and bottled beer'. He described the audience as those who would 'be drowned rather than get up and walk into the ark'. The Eagle, he continued, 'is situated in an appropriate locality in the City Road, not far from a lunatic asylum, and contiguous to a workhouse'. Its reputation as a place of great temptation is reflected in the nursery rhyme:

> Up and down the City Road
> In and out the Eagle
> That's the way the money goes,
> Pop goes the weasel.

Although interpretations vary, the last line probably refers to the way in which tailors 'popped', or pawned, their flat-iron, or 'weasel', an essential tool of their trade, for beer money. Other readings translate 'weasel' as 'watch', or 'coat' from the Cockney rhyming slang 'weasel and stoat'.

When Rouse retired in 1841 Benjamin Conquest took over and, with his son George, made the Conquest name famous for pantomime.

George, a writer and acrobat, peopled his plays with fantastic creatures: giant crabs with human eyes, an octopus, apes and assorted goblins. In 1878 he sold up and moved to the Surrey Theatre in Blackfriars Road where he gained a reputation for productions featuring flying ballets and acrobatics (in one panto he used thirty different trapdoors) and for discovering Dan Leno.

His departure sparked one of the most acrimonious squabbles between moral campaigners and East End music hall. General Booth of the Salvation Army[8] earmarked the Grecian and Eagle as a base behind enemy lines from which to hit back at the devil and his works, and the site was sold to the Salvation Army in June 1881 for £16,750 via an officer acting *in cognito*. But the battle did not prove straightforward and as a thousand Salvation Army members marched from Finsbury Square to the Grecian and Eagle for its official opening on 21 September 1882 as a place of worship they were jostled by a crowd estimated at thirty thousand.

A rearguard action was fought in the courts over the terms of Rouse's original lease, which stipulated that the Eagle should be used as a public house. General Booth tried to circumvent this by retaining the licence and running a temperance hotel with seventy beds, providing food but not selling alcohol. A cartoon in 1883 shows him with wild hair, staring eyes, a hooked nose and a bushy beard crouched over the money he had amassed to buy the Grecian and Eagle. The caption read: 'And now that you have collected all this money, Mr Booth, what do you intend to do with it?' Eventually the Salvation Army decided that a former London Orphan Asylum at Clapton would make a more sensible headquarters and moved there in 1884.

The assault on so prestigious a local institution as the Eagle and its subsequent recovery enhanced its standing among local people: it came to symbolize an independence of spirit in the face of outside interference. When Marie made her début there it was a nerve-tingling experience for the whole family. For the seven children left at home it was the most exciting night of their young lives and marked the culmination of the obsessive preparation that had transformed their cramped home into a place of noisy rehearsal and frantic dress-making. Marie's costume consisted of a figure-hugging bodice that tapered into a full skirt left open to show off a flurry of pretty petticoats. On her head she wore a mantilla of black lace that made her look like a fifteen-year-old widow.

But if her début at the Eagle was an evening of nerve-racking anticipation for Marie, it was simply another night out for the crowds in search of a good time. The bills stuck to the pub's grimy windows enticed customers with promises of exotic entertainment: 'Mdlle Clairi – Chansonette Française'; 'La Petite Amaros – The Graceful Gymnast'; 'Miss Florrie Forde – Burlesque Artiste'; 'The M'Naughtons – Grotesque Comedians'; 'Nellie Farrell – The Glittering Star of Erin'; 'Ada Lundberg – The Gem of Comedy'; and 'Miss Kate Harvey – The Simple Country Maid'. For most people, though, who climbed the narrow stairway to the barrier and rough pay box that led to the hall the main draw was the chance to be with friends in a warmer, more exciting atmosphere than their drab homes.

Even before they reached the barrier, the customer was hit by a blast of noise, heat and the smell of warm bodies that funnelled out of the music hall and down the stairway. The room where Marie performed measured sixty feet by thirty-two; it was nineteen feet tall and linked at one end to a rowdy saloon. Officially, it held three hundred people, although more squeezed in on a busy night. Performance starting times meant nothing to customers, who came and went as they pleased – usually while an act struggled to be noticed on the raised platform that served as a stage. There were rickety benches for the audience to sit on but these were usually backless and without cushions, so that the need to stand up and shift numb buttocks or stretch aching limbs transformed the room into a maelstrom of milling people.

The heavy, multilayered clothes of the Victorian audience meant that the hall soon stank of sweat, and the odour grew stronger as the night wore on. There was nowhere to leave coats or jackets, and most members of the audience did not trust their neighbours enough to risk leaving a valuable possession on the back of a chair from which it might vanish. Their clothes accumulated stains and splashes of beer from the inevitable and frequent collisions. Boys hung over the hall's balconies whistling to each other or at the person on stage. They munched their way through whelks, shrimps and nuts, spitting out the debris on the audience below, or firing missiles aimed at the hats of their elders.

Reports of fire casualties at music halls show that a large proportion of the audience was female, of whom only a few were prostitutes, and that they were mostly young. There were also many children: reformers were particularly worried by their presence – they felt sure the atmosphere would transform them into hooligans. This concern reappeared in the early days of cinema when campaigners saw a link between the concentration of youth in confined, night-time spaces and the urge to commit criminal offences.

Music-hall customers had little respect for performers. Applause was hard-earned and rarely allowed to interfere with the serious business of eating, drinking porter or smoking long, clay churchwarden pipes. Waiters like Brush Wood dashed, sweating, from table to table, their bottles chained to the trays for safety, a napkin over one arm. Performers had to compete – without, of course, the aid of a microphone – against the noise of pewter on pewter, glass on glass, as well as the hubbub of conviviality and catcalls. The glare from the gaslight was intense and undimmed when the performance started, and gilded mirrors added a distorted *Alice in Wonderland* effect. Tobacco smoke and the packed-in bodies gave the hall a fetid atmosphere hardly conducive to entertainment: today's purveyors of comedy recommend that the best way to warm up an audience is to keep them slightly chilled, and American television producers put the ideal temperature for a studio audience at something like 13.3°C (57°F).[9]

In the middle of the chaos was the chairman. He perched, usually with his back to the performer, on a table placed at an angle to the stage and close to the hall's musical instruments – a piano, perhaps, or a harmonium. He was there to keep order and to encourage beer consumption, but the best chairmen enhanced the appeal of a particular hall with the force of their personality. They were known for their witticisms in introducing or commenting on acts, for their banter with the audience and, often, for their sartorial elegance. Also, they might be called upon to perform a song if a gap in the programme required it. Baron Courtney, at the South London Palace of Varieties in Lambeth, sang, drank, wore large diamond cufflinks, diamond studs in his dress shirt and loaded his fingers with rings. John Watkins, chairman at Gatti's – also in Lambeth – sported a huge buttonhole, a red silk handkerchief overflowed his breast pocket, and his moustache was fiercely waxed into two five-inch spikes.

Since the Eagle was so close to her home, Marie probably walked there. There were no dressing rooms, and performers either changed in a cab on their way or used makeshift rooms under the platform. As the timing of the music-hall bill was tightly controlled there was no time to chat with other performers, and since there were plenty of young girls desperate to work the halls Marie's nervous figure lingering near the stage would have elicited little sympathy. Nor was there anyone to offer support or consolation after her appearance: the best performers had to hurry off to their next booking while the worst did not want to remain at a scene of humiliation.

There was no proscenium arch and often no backdrop. Marie had to burst through a curtained archway and plunge straight into the rowdy auditorium. There was a row of footlights but, apart from this, nothing to draw a line between audience and artist. As she searched for a pair of eyes to lock on to, she would have found herself competing with alcohol, food and conversation. Some people even flicked languidly through penny dreadfuls.

Confident though Marie was, it must have been a terrifying ordeal for her to stand in front of an audience of noisy, distracted drinkers impatient for a good time. Her small stature, the lack of any rake to the stage and the constant shifting of the crowd meant it was difficult to make contact with the customers. If an act was lucky enough to begin in silence it was usually only by coincidence rather than politeness on the part of the audience. Since she was local to the area Marie may have known a few faces, but even this was no guarantee of support: the criticism of friends and acquaintances is usually more painful than the censure of strangers.

At her début, Marie – appearing as Matilda Wood – sang two sentimental songs. Her only experience so far had been of serious temperance songs and she did not know then that she could make people laugh. Her first performance was emphatically as a 'serio': a singer of serious songs. Bizarrely, given her youth, she chose 'In The Good Old Days' (or 'Time Is Flying' – accounts differ) and followed it with a song Aunt Louisa used to sing, 'My Soldier Laddie'. She finished with an Irish jig. She must have been a strange sight in her hybrid costume with her brilliantly white, prominent teeth, her long blonde hair and sparkling blue eyes.

Just because Marie was young and new did not mean that the audience would be kind to her. Once an audience had decided a performer was good only for target practice, the odds were inexorably weighted against them. Audiences were imaginative in their choice of missiles – which often took on regional characteristics: iron rivets in Glasgow, trotter bones, rotten fruit, vegetables and eggs in the East End. A woman in the audience at the Parthenon music hall in Liverpool threw a pair of boots at a turn then demanded that the stage manager return them so that she could use them again. Dead animals, such as cats, were occasionally hurled at the platform and in Chester in the 1870s an audience dismantled the stage because they were not happy with a dioramic depiction of a Zulu war and demanded a refund. Pewter pots were easy to throw and could cause considerable injury from close range. If the hall had a band it might be protected by a metal grid from flying missiles, and sometimes the performer was 'wired in' by a screen that shielded them from an over-enthusiastic audience.

Marie's début went unremarked by the press but she did well enough to secure a second booking. Her self-confidence meant that she was shocked that her first appearance had not caused a greater stir, but this was forgotten when she moved on to the next challenge. After the Eagle she played the Sir John Falstaff Music Hall in Old Street, which – with a capacity of 250 – was smaller than the Eagle. Again, Marie was on home territory: the hall was close to her former school, and the knowledge that her father was serving drinks to the audience gave her a – probably misplaced – sense of security. She sang treacly romantic ballads about searching for a 'charming figure, manliness, and grace . . .'.

The Falstaff used a number of visiting chairmen to introduce the turns. Most were local to the area, and while Marie was performing George Belmont, who ran Sebright's Music Hall in Coate Street, Hackney, was in charge. He was immediately impressed by her lively personality and the way she 'connected' with the audience by capturing their attention and even engaging some of the boys in flirtatious repartee. He took her mother to one side and suggested a contract. The news sent a charge of excitement through the Wood household, but even this was not enough for Marie: she was greedy for every opportunity to appear in public, both for the money and for the thrill of being on stage. She instantly broke her contract by appearing at the rival Hoxton

Theatre of Varieties, a hall with a particularly rough reputation known locally as the Flea Pit. George was furious, but Marie calmed him down by pleading ignorance and smiling sweetly. Perhaps in retaliation, he claimed later that her appearance at the Sebright Music Hall on 3 February 1886 marked her music-hall début.

Sebright's was much larger than the Eagle and could hold just over seven hundred people. In this respect it was a step up and, for the first time, took Marie outside Hoxton. She started to expand her repertoire to include songs that required a more expressive treatment and adding 'The Boy I Love Is Up In The Gallery', which is still associated with her name. It is unashamedly sentimental and played on her appearance as a sweet young girl who needed looking after. Marie was 'over from the country' and had fallen in love with a cobbler called Johnny. Demure and submissive, she wanted nothing but him:

> Now if I were a duchess and had a lot of money,
> I'd give it to the boy that's going to marry me;
> But I hav'nt got a penny so we'll live on love and kisses,
> And be just as happy as the birds on the tree.

To add to the song's pathos Marie planted her brother Johnny in the audience to wave a handkerchief in her direction at the appropriate time:

> There he is. Can't you see?
> Waving his handkerchief . . .

The innocence of the lyrics, however, did not reflect Marie's sense of honour. Impetuous and anxious to make an impact, she performed 'The Boy I Love' without the permission of Nelly Power, who had originally sung it. She had also purloined 'In The Good Old Days' from Jessie Acton. These thefts were more serious than they would be today since songs then were a performer's bread and butter: a popular number might secure him or her weeks of bookings. Marie managed to placate the owners of both songs with the excuse of naïveté.

It was while she was appearing at Sebright's that the music-hall agent and composer of 'The Boy I Love', George Ware first saw her and decided to take her on. At the time her stage name was Bella Delmeyer – or variations of it – which sounded cosmopolitan to a girl who had never left Hoxton. However, George said Bella was not memorable enough and had to go. They found a suitable replacement simply by looking around them: 'Lloyd' appeared everywhere, on railway bridges and walls to advertise a range of products including a popular newspaper. She opted for 'Marie', simply because she liked it and pronounced it *Mar*-ee as in 'starry'.

Chapter 2

PLAYING THE HALLS

(1885–7)

~⁊

My Harry's a sailor
On board of a whaler.
I love my Harry,
And Harry loves me.
When he comes home from sea
'Tis married we will be.
Composer unknown

Now that she had a name, an agent and was groping her way towards an image that would make her famous, Marie settled down to the task of playing as many halls as George could book for her. The work was as different from the jobs she had toyed with in the past as she could have wished. She loved the uncertainty of her new life and thrived on the prospect of meeting complete strangers each evening.

She soon found that each audience was unique and each hall had a separate identity. Managers at the larger halls put more thought into the programme and designed a bill to keep the audience happy throughout the various stages of the evening's entertainment. Performances usually started at about seven-forty-five and went on until around eleven-thirty; the big names appeared between nine-thirty and eleven. Usually the show began with a musical overture, which did not require much concentration on the part of the listeners and would not be ruined by late arrivals. The early acts settled the audience before a comic came on to wake them up. A 'name' would appear about three-quarters of the way through to build up anticipation for the real star. The evening ended with another undemanding act.

Each performance required precision timing: Marie had to make an impact within seconds of appearing on stage and had to hold her audience for fifteen minutes. It was then a matter of dashing on to a

new hall in time for her next slot; there was no room for running late
or loitering on stage to wallow in a good reception. The work was
physically punishing, but a mixture of adrenaline and the occasional hint
that an audience was there for the taking was enough to propel her
through an evening's work.

She learned to project her voice above the cacophony of the audience
and to silence hecklers, but her vocal cords, already strained by singing,
were further battered by the relentless tobacco smoke and the fumes of
the gaslights. As late as 1893 Katie Lawrence, famous for songs like
'Daisy, Daisy, Give Me Your Answer Do', complained that performers
came home so 'saturated with foul tobacco smoke as to be intolerable –
such an atmosphere cannot be good for the voice'.[1]

Marie's first mention in the *Era* was on 20 June 1885, when she
appeared in an advertisement for the Eagle. She was at the Star in
Bermondsey for the August bank holiday and earned her first 'notice' in
the *London Entr'acte*, which said her contribution had been 'well
received'.[2] She was still concentrating on earnest ballads. At the Royal
Holborn in September, the *Entr'acte* commented that she 'must be
regarded as a youthful vocalist of promise',[3] and the *Era* said she 'kept
it briskly going'.[4]

The Holborn booking was significant because it took her out of the
East End for the first time and gave her a chance to sample a slightly
different audience, with whose customs she was not so intimately
acquainted. She was beginning to enjoy the freedom of working away
from home and the opportunities this brought to dally with admirers at
the bar after her turn. She was also becoming more conscious of her
own sexuality: she looked younger than her fifteen years and had a
baby-fresh complexion that men found attractive. A certain awareness
began to inform her act when she incorporated into it a schoolgirl
character, a common Victorian pornographic icon. The costume allowed
her to emphasize her figure when she slung her satchel over her shoulder
so that the strap crossed a breast that was slightly too prominent to be
prepubescent.

In October 1885 she was at Collins's on Islington Green, in north
London, in a special performance to celebrate its refurbishment with a
bigger bar and lounge, and handrails fitted to the staircase. The hall,
nicknamed 'the chapel', was another milestone because it expanded

Marie's circuit of experience north. By December she was at the Hammersmith Temple of Varieties in west London, then rushing across town to appear at the Royal Cambridge Hall of Varieties in Commercial Street, Shoreditch, and Collins's on the same night.

She finished 1885 at the Middlesex Music Hall, in Drury Lane, which was also known as the 'Old Mo' after the Mogul tavern, which shared the site. The hall was a large, rowdy place with an unpredictable crowd. It attracted a range of customers, including medical students, who were quite different from the audiences Marie had experienced in the East End. Their short attention span was acknowledged in the hall's advertisement which promised: 'The quickest and grandest programme in London . . . Always something new and novel to be seen, Look, look, look.' Marie was on the same bill as a boxer, who brought along his trophies for display, and 'Sir Roger Tichborne', who delivered an address on his memorable trial and lengthy imprisonment. Marie was learning that the competition was varied and continually changing. A childhood spent in the culturally diverse East End meant that she was rarely perturbed by the often strange acts with whom she shared the bill, but she was impressed by the glamour of the larger music halls with their gilt and red plush. The audiences, too, were better dressed: the men wore top hats that they tipped at a jaunty angle if they cared to attract the attention of a prostitute. Each night Marie took tales of these strange creatures back to her siblings, who thrilled to their sister's new world.

Sir Roger's appearance on the music-hall circuit gave a helping hand to a new acrobat and comic singer learning his trade at the same time and in the same halls as Marie. Harry Relph was originally nicknamed Little Tich after the 'Tichborne Claimant' because as a baby he resembled the twenty-eight-stone butcher from Wagga Wagga, Australia, who turned up on Christmas Day 1866 claiming to be the Tichborne heir and whose courtroom battle for the estate became a Victorian *cause célèbre*. Harry grew into a tiny man, much shorter than Marie, with an extra finger on hands that were slightly webbed and devoid of the usual lines. As she was struggling to find her stage identity, Little Tich was touring the halls as one of the many black-faced dancing acts, as yet unable to identify a turn that would set him apart.

At this time, George Galvin, known professionally as Dan Leno, was performing in London for the first time as an adult after years of touring as a child in an act called 'The Great Little Lenos'. Offstage, and without his make-up, his appearance was almost girlish: he had a wide, thin-lipped mouth, perfectly plucked, sweeping eyebrows, hair neatly parted in the middle and hooded eyes that made him seem haughty. On stage he was a darting, manic character, with a sense of humour surreal enough to belong to the next century. He had a grasp of detail and feel for language that allowed him to create complex characters such as the Shopwalker or an orator in *The Midnight March*. Halfway through a meandering monologue he would pause and say, 'There's a postman mixed up in all of this', or start his act by rushing on stage shouting, 'Don't be stupid, now!'

The late 1880s was a propitious decade for an aspiring performer. It was boom time for music hall and every manager was on the look-out for fresh new talent to pep up his bill and attract a loyal following. According to figures quoted in a House of Lords debate on regulation of entertainment in June 1888 there were 50 theatres, 35 concert halls and a staggering 473 music halls in London in which some £4 million had been invested. However, the true figure for music halls was certainly much higher since countless smaller rooms would have fallen outside this calculation.

As early as the 1830s publicans had spotted the commercial potential in allowing amateurs to try their luck with local audiences in the back room of a pub. The natural progression from this event, known as the 'free-and-easy', was the 'singing' or 'music saloon' held at the pub but staffed usually by professional performers. In London there were plenty of precedents for this type of entertainment, most notably the 'glee clubs', exclusively male gatherings, 'song-and-supper' rooms, such as the Cyder Cellars in Covent Garden where fashionable men met to carouse late into the night, and the 'judge-and-jury' clubs, such as those held at the Coal Hole in the Strand, where mock trials were staged to lampoon well-known public figures. The capital's pleasure gardens, open-air venues such as the area surrounding the Eagle, or the Vauxhall gardens, where the audience could mingle and enjoy a range of entertainment, was yet another stage in the progression towards the concept of music hall. By the 1850s more publicans or 'caterers' were exploiting this new form of entertainment and either built halls for the shows, accommodated them in adjacent derelict schools or chapels, or even converted workshops, pub gardens, stableyards or urinals. Entry was by cash or token, known as 'wet money', which entitled the bearer to refreshment. Usually the patrons sat at marble-topped tables arranged at an angle to a raised platform at one end of the room and a bar at the other, but in more modest halls they perched on wooden benches. The room was oblong and had at least one balcony, like the bulbous cast-iron one at McDonald's Music Hall in Hoxton.

The best-known of this new breed of pub entrepreneur was Charles Morton, a grandfatherly figure with bushy side whiskers who later became known as the Father of the Halls and lived to be eighty-five. He opened the Canterbury in 1851 in Lambeth, south London, over a pub's skittle alley, but it became so popular that in 1854 the whole site was rebuilt to hold 1500, and, as an early nod to respectability, its own library and picture gallery. He went on to open the Oxford Music Hall in 1860, in London's Oxford Street, which had its own stage, fixed stalls, a reputation for pretty barmaids and susceptibility to fire.

The distinction between theatre and music hall was accentuated by the Theatres Act of 1843. This forced anyone who wanted to put on entertainment to choose between staging plays, which was subject to the authority of the Lord Chamberlain, but refraining from selling food and drink in the auditorium; or to opt for a magistrate's licence for music and dancing, permission to sell food and drink, and to allow smoking. This legislation, together with the new, sweeping thoroughfares of Charing Cross Road and Shaftesbury Avenue, paved the way for the development of the Theatreland of the West End of London. Leicester Square and the Strand became centres for a version of music-hall entertainment that was watched by tourists and wealthier patrons in much grander settings than the public-house prototypes.

Music hall was viewed with suspicion, if not hostility, by the 'respectable classes'. Anyone who was not poor yet visited music halls did so because they were in search of an experience that bordered on the dangerous, or as an experiment in social anthropology. William Gladstone falls into the latter category: in his diary of 21 July 1877 he records 'cooling his head' after a hard day's work of letters and meetings with a walk followed by half an hour at the Metropolitan Music Hall, commenting, 'The show was certainly not Athenian.' Later that year, on 25 September, he spent an hour at the Alhambra at

Leicester Square with 'Mrs Th', 'where there was the prettiest & best ballet I ever saw'.

Walter Richard Sickert regularly trudged the ten or so miles from performances in Hoxton to his bed in West Hampstead. A tall man, who wore a loud checked coat reaching to his ankles and carried his drawing equipment in his bag, it is perhaps not surprising that on one occasion some girls he encountered fled screaming, believing him to be Jack the Ripper. A former actor, he was drawn to paint the halls because they were dark and dangerous, far removed from the polite subjects chosen by most of his British contemporaries but akin to the urban nightlife depicted by Manet and Degas. He became sucked into the music-hall world, following female performers from hall to hall and jotting down snatches from comic songs, such as Minnie Cunningham's 'It's not the hen that cackles the most, that lays the largest eggs,' to help him recapture the atmosphere when he was back in his studio. He studied the faces of audiences, chairmen and performers then brought them together on one canvas in a sea of expectancy against smudged reds and browns. His paintings depicted the performer from the audience's viewpoint, at odd angles or reflected in mirrors, making the audience seem all-powerful, the artist stranded on a vast stage. His *Minnie Cunningham at the Old Bedford*, which showed a long-limbed young girl in vivid red dress and hat, was condemned because it was assumed that the scarlet hat meant she was a prostitute.

Jerome K. Jerome, the comic writer and author of *Three Men in a Boat*, remembered a trip to a music hall in the early 1870s with a fourteen-year-old boy's thrill of the first taste of forbidden fruits. An aunt had given him five shillings for Christmas to spend on a 'high-class and improving entertainment' – specifically *Coriolanus* – but Jerome's accomplice, Skegson, suggested they should head for the halls. Jerome recalled:

I gasped for breath. I had heard of Music Halls. A stout lady had denounced them across our dinner table on one occasion, fixing the while a steely eye upon her husband, who sat opposite and seemed uncomfortable, as low, horrid places, where people smoked and drank, and wore short skirts, and had added an opinion that they ought to be put down by the police – whether the skirts or the halls she did not explain. I also recollected that our Charwoman, whose son had lately left London for a protracted stay in Devonshire, had, in conversation with my mother, dated his downfall from the day when he first visited one of these places: and likewise that Mrs Philcox's nursemaid, upon her confessing that she had spent an evening at one with her young man, had been called a shameless hussy, and summarily dismissed as being no longer a fit associate for the baby.[5]

They purchased massive cigars and set off for Sadler's Wells in Rosebery Avenue, Finsbury, north London. Jerome remembered the night out through a fug of nicotine:

We sat at a little marble table. I know it was marble because it was so hard and cool to the head. From out of the smoky mist a ponderous creature of a strange, undefined shape floated heavily towards us, and deposited a squat tumbler in front of me containing a pale yellowish liquor, which subsequent investigation has led me to believe must have been Scotch whisky. It seemed to me then the most nauseous stuff I had ever swallowed. It is curious to look back and notice how one's tastes change.

He reached home 'very late and very sick': 'I can remember to this day standing in the middle of the room in my nightshirt, trying to catch my bed as it came round.'

Most of Marie's audiences in the East End were of ordinary working people, hungry for entertainment to break the drudgery of their daytime existence. Many were first- or second-generation families who had moved from the countryside to the city and whose lives were now governed by the rigid routine of factory or sweatshop rather than by the changing seasons. Leisure was set apart from work, rather than seeping into it. Folk songs and traditions jarred with the new urban industrialized backdrop. By 1850 a national railway network existed and cities, especially London, faced a population explosion that transformed urban life. By 1871 a seventh of the total population of England and Wales lived in London. Leisure became an activity you paid for, and it was supplied by professionals.

The demand for entertainment took Marie to parts of London she would otherwise not have visited, and by 1886 her performances were winning regular, if unspectacular, credits. In January, at Collins's, she was 'pleasing and promising' and there were 'indications of ability' that should 'encourage her to further study'.[6] She was at Sebright's in February, as well as at the Metropolitan on the Edgware Road in Paddington – another long-established hall that could hold 2,000 people. Dan Leno took her place at the Metropolitan when she moved on to the South London Palace of Varieties in London Road, Lambeth.

At Easter she was at the Oxford Music Hall, which stood at the corner of Oxford Street and Tottenham Court Road and on the site of the Boar and Castle pub. It had already been rebuilt twice after fires, and was the most glittering music hall outside Leicester Square. For Marie it was the height of luxury compared with the cramped chaos of the East End halls: rows of fixed seats replaced its original supper tables and its stage and auditorium were lit by electricity – a significant luxury in the warm summer months. Walter Sickert's 1888–9 painting of the Oxford shows a brightly lit proscenium arch with a tiny figure in a dress just below her knee picked out centre stage and captured leaning confidentially towards the audience, who are tiny smudges portrayed mostly as chatting to one another. It would be pleasing to believe that this is Marie, but art experts think otherwise.

At the Queen's Palace of Varieties, High Street, Poplar, Marie shared the bill with 'Herr Marvelle and His Wonderful Educated Cockatoos'. In the summer her bookings included the Bedford in Camden Town and the South London Palace, where she appeared with Signor Felise Napol, the Great Italian Hercules, and Charlie Chaplin's mother, Hannah,[7] who was known as 'Lily Harley', at the start of her brief, unsuccessful music-hall career. Marie followed these bookings with trips to the Hammersmith Temple of Varieties, which was featuring a grand naval spectacle based on the death of Nelson, and at Collins's, where she was third on the bill, appearing at eight-fifteen and performing for fifteen minutes. Her act included dancing a hornpipe and singing three songs including 'Who'll Buy My Flowers?'

September saw her on the same programme as Professor Harvard and his Famous Disappearing Lady at Royal Forresters, Cambridge Road, Mile End, and at the Middlesex. Later that autumn she was at the Parthenon in Greenwich and the Paragon Theatre of Varieties, Mile End Road, alongside Dan Leno and Little Tich.

A review of her performance at Greenwich showed Marie's growing success was having repercussions on the rest of her family. Her songs and dancing were 'cordially appreciated; while the Wood family, who are successful throughout London, are not less so at this establishment'.[8] Although the report does not expand on which members of the Wood family, Alice and Grace are the likely candidates, and in the following year, 1888, the *Era* carried several references to the Sisters Lloyd.

In 1887 Alice, the second oldest daughter, was thirteen and Grace eleven. It was common for girls as young as this to perform on stage, and as they worked together they could look after each other as their parents were too busy to accompany them on late-night jaunts. Brushie was working and their mother was still producing babies: Annie was born in 1883 and Sidney in 1885. Perhaps, prompted by tales of Jack the Ripper who was prowling around Whitechapel at this time, their mother persuaded an aunt, neighbour or grandparent to accompany the girls. Either way, Marie had eased Alice and Grace's progress on to the halls: if their parents had any qualms about their work, Marie's growing success was enough to silence them. To her younger sisters, Marie's life must have seemed infinitely glamorous: getting up late then disappearing with her costumes into the night; hurtling between halls by cab in which she changed and adjusted her make-up. However, Alice and Grace soon discovered the truth behind the apparent glamour and glitz: dressing rooms – if they existed – were badly lit, damp and often lacked running water. Rats thrived on greasepaint and were a constant hazard. The social reformer Charles Booth noted that the music-hall lifestyle was so exhausting that performers rarely lived beyond fifty.

By the end of 1887 Marie was described increasingly as a 'serio-comic' due to the inclusion of more light-hearted songs into her act. She knew now how to move around the stage to best effect and her innate confidence was backed by two years of solid work on the London circuit. Her dancing skills were frequently praised, although they took the form of subtle movements, between verses, designed to emphasize partly hidden curves. She had learned how to use her neat little hands and feet to make calculated gestures; she was 'agile', 'clever', 'genial' and 'nimble'.

But what was beginning to set her apart from the countless other female singers was her personality. Audiences watched a young girl with tumbling blonde hair, sparkling blue eyes, a large mouth and a trim figure. She was pretty, rather than beautiful, and Alice and Grace were generally thought better-looking than their elder sister. Marie's teeth were too big for her mouth, but served to draw attention to her lips and gave the impression that she was more attainable than the average Victorian woman – and that she might even enjoy the attention. She was fresh and girlish, but appeared more knowing than she should have been at her age. Much of the time her stage appearance mirrored exactly how she felt off-stage: she had found her true vocation and she was bubbling with enjoyment at the attention she was attracting. She lived a carefree existence, too absorbed in the excitement of each night's performance to worry about tomorrow.

At a time when women were usually quiet and docile, Marie had the audacity to look the audience straight in the eye and, an even greater feat, to make them laugh. Unlike many of the other turns, who performed to a formula, Marie gave the impression that she was communing with an audience for the first time. Her act was unpredictable and, as a result, they were forced to pay attention. At Collins's, in April 1887, she wore a pretty black costume and 'adopted a coquettish back kick in her dancing which brought down the house'.[9] A steaming hot August saw her at the Oxford, where the word 'saucy' was first linked with her name when she sang a song about young men and their ways of courting. Even when she dressed up as an older, plainer woman her appearance was titillating because it stressed the real character hidden beneath the drab exterior.

George Foster, who later became a successful music-hall agent, remembered Marie's performance on Boxing Day 1887, at Collins's, when she was 'the sauciest, most alluring little creature' he had ever seen. She was dressed as a sailor in a blue satin blouse, short white skirt and white socks, and wore on her head a hat 'cocked at the pertest of angles . . . Her flashing eyes were full of deviance and devilment' as she sang of 'her Harry' who was far away on a whaling ship but whom she would marry as soon as he returned home. From Marie's mouth, marriage sounded like something daring and naughty. By the second verse she had forgotten her lines. She stopped dead, laughed, leaned over the footlights and whispered to the conductor, who ordered the band to strike up a hornpipe to which she danced. As George noted later, 'It was not because Marie was especially brilliant. Actually she never achieved what she set out to do. Marie Lloyd triumphed by sheer personality and charm.'[10]

But sheer personality was not enough. Marie's rise to a certain level had been meteoric, but she was in a firmament crowded with other stars. Staying put was just as hard as getting there in the first place. Victorian audiences were as difficult to please as any latterday television viewer, and bills were handpicked to appeal to crowds that demanded to be shocked, dazzled by glamour, moved by pathos, reduced to tears of laughter and held on the edge of their seat by a good drama or acrobatic feat all in the space of an evening. An act might be flavour of the moment one night only to be replaced by some equally fleeting sensation the next. In December 1887, for example, Marie shared the bill at the Oxford with the 'Strongest Woman in the World' and some 'droll darkies'.[11] By January the competition had increased to include Tholen and His Singing Dog.

Music-hall audiences had a thirst for the bizarre and freakish and acts sprang up to capture the public's imagination briefly before subsiding into obscurity. The Victorians lived in an empire that was expanding fast geographically and scientifically, and there was a genuine desire to explore and assess developments. But more often the quest for knowledge was the excuse for the prurience that lay at the heart of some of the biggest music-hall draws.

Animals were particularly popular and the most successful acts were those that included a human element remarkable in its own right. In 1888 a group of performing wolves caused 'a profound sensation'[12] in Manchester, helped by their German trainer Mollie Wallenda, 'a splendid specimen of her race, standing nearly six feet high' who persuaded her lupine colleagues to pick up whips, jump over her head and balance on the trapeze. That same year Marie performed at the Royal Forresters, Mile End, with 'Cyrus and Maud, Musical Grotesques, With Their Performing Donkey, Bess' and at the Old Mo with 'Capt. Pike's performing Fish, Literally and Actually a Fish Out of Water'. She missed Professor Frederick's potentially lethal cocktail of a dozen each of cats, rats, mice and canaries, who also appeared that year at the Middlesex. In the first month of 1890 she shared the bill at the Royal Holborn with Lockhart's Performing Elephants; at the Pavilion with

Herr Wallender's Pack of Enormous Boarhounds and at the Alhambra with 'Rags, the Canine Wonder'.

The public never tired of animal acts or of hearing about animals. Gorilla songs had their vogue and in 1870 Alfred Vance helped popularize the word 'zoo' with his song 'Walking In The Zoo'. In 1894 the Prince of Wales was moved to visit the Royal Aquarium to see the Boxing Kangaroo who earned £340 a week – more than the combined income of the Prime Minister, the Chancellor of the Exchequer and the Home Secretary.

Animals were a hazard to other performers not only because they were stars in their own right, but because if they were dangerous enough to watch as a spectacle they had to be avoided backstage. Performers played cruel tricks on each other: if a bear was waiting in the wings, one would creep behind a performer on stage and scratch the scenery to ensure that he or she finished in record time. Animals added to the unpleasant odours of sweat and damp that pervaded the area behind the gilded arch, and menstruating women were warned to keep away from them.

Victorians were unashamedly fascinated by human freaks, especially if their oddness was accompanied by some sort of record. Among the attributes that qualified someone to appear on a music-hall bill size was among the most important. A giant baby, who at a year old weighed fifty-eight pounds, stood three feet tall and had a chest of thirty inches, was exhibited at the Albert Palace in London in 1886. The following year Herr Winkelmeier, an Austrian who claimed to be the tallest man in the world at eight feet nine inches, caused a sensation at the London Pavilion where he performed for at least six months. Winkelmeier was said to top Chang, the Chinese Giant, by a foot. He toured the audience, shaking hands with the tallest man there, whom he always dwarfed, and allowing those who were six foot tall to walk, without stooping, under his outstretched arms.

The fascination extended to the other end of the spectrum: the smallest married couple in the world appeared at the Canterbury in November 1888 with nothing more to recommend them than their height. The Bon Accord Music Hall, Aberdeen, staged a special Hogmanay wrestling match in 1889 between Snowball and Figg, 'champion Boxing Midgets of the World'. Snowball won.

Joseph Merrick, more commonly known as the Elephant Man, made his first London appearance a year before Marie's official début in a seedy back room of a shop at Whitechapel Road. Merrick blamed his condition – which made people recoil at the sight of him – on a fall his pregnant mother sustained in front of a runaway elephant in Leicester. He was exhibited at music halls in the Midlands by a syndicate of impresarios who included Sam Torr, himself a well-known performer.

The boundaries of good taste had started to shift by the late 1880s, but not enough to prevent headlines such as 'Una, the Human Fly Killed in a Fall'.[13] In this case, 'Una' was a boy called Sydney Bird, who made a living from descending a ladder head first using a technique known as 'ceiling walking'. The ladder was suspended above the stage and, usually, a safety-net was ready to catch him should he fall – although he had never had an accident. On the fateful day at the Prince of Wales's Theatre, Great Grimsby, however, there was no room for a net and Una's father stood ready to catch him. When his foot slipped, though, Una plunged head first on to the stage and his father was unable to break his fall. He died from skull fractures. At the inquest the coroner condemned such dangerous performances, which he said were taking place all over the country. The more dangerous the act, he noted in disbelief, the more people it attracted.

Science, too, offered an excuse for 'prurience', by Victorian standards. Scantily clad strong men[14] like Eugene Sandow, who had a long and distinguished international career that included marketing his own corset and a fitness club, was measured and moulded[15] in the name of science and his bulging biceps stroked backstage by well-to-do female members of the audience. It was not just women performers who attracted ardent admirers.

Chapter 3

DEVELOPING AN ACT

(the late 1880s)

~~❧~~

Say, boys, whatever do you mean,
When you wink the other eye?
'Wink The Other Eye' by George le Brunn and W. T. Lytton

Marie, too, had her admirers. Her teasing character, and the very fact that she appeared on stage, made her sexually alluring. Music-hall performers were viewed as a particularly vulgar strain of the Victorian actress, and everyone knew what a bad influence an actress might be. Marie and her ilk were the very antithesis of the Victorian ideal of femininity, 'the angel in the household'. The word 'actress' was often used as code for 'prostitute', and both the actress and the music-hall artist cropped up in pornography. And prostitutes were often to be found as music-hall performers.

Female performers were suspect on several fronts: they made a living from showing off and their work demanded the removal of clothing away from the privacy of the home. Deception, in that they assumed different characters, was an important skill of their trade, and they worked side by side with men, usually on equal terms. Numerically, too, actresses were a force to be reckoned with: the 1881 and 1891 censuses show that marginally more women than men worked in the theatre in England and Wales. In the 1890s there was a 74 per cent increase in the number of actresses.

There were isolated instances of music-hall women marrying into the aristocracy, but they were so rare as to be the stuff of dreams for young performers – and of nightmares for wealthy dowagers. In July 1889,

33

when Belle Bilton, of the serio-comic vocalists and dancers the Sisters Bilton, married Viscount Dunlo, eldest son of the Earl of Clancarty, at Hampstead register office the event was so noteworthy that the *Era* reproduced the marriage certificate. Less than eight months later the Viscount was suing for divorce. Soon after the wedding, and under pressure from his father, Viscount Dunlo left for Australia. His father engaged a detective to follow Belle in the hope of unearthing grounds for divorce. The *Era* was disgusted and ran an editorial to say so:

> The conduct of these two persons should serve as a lesson to profession-
> als to be very careful how they entrust their happiness to the hands of
> members of the aristocracy ... The 'dirtiness' − there is no other word
> for it − of the scheme which the father appears to have originated would
> excite the disgust of the poorest public performer.[1]

Belle had audiences on her side too: when her sister Flo appeared at the Trocadero music hall she drew large crowds who shouted, 'Bravo,' and 'Good old Sister Flo!' Belle's appearance in the box to watch her sister prompted chants of 'He lost it.' Eventually the couple were reunited and Belle, now Countess of Clancarty, after the death of her disapproving father-in-law, announced her retirement from the stage to assume a quiet life at the ancestral seat in County Galway. Her retirement coincided with the news that another performer who had married well, the Countess of Orkney, formerly the teenage burlesque dancer, Connie Gilchrist, was to leave the boards for good.

The nearest Marie came to nobility was an 'eccentric admirer in the person of a coloured gentleman, who was nicknamed the Shah',[2] who regularly took a private box at the Oxford to deluge her with flowers. He disappeared without warning, and Marie found out later that he was serving a three-year prison sentence for embezzlement. Other suitors got nearer their target. Gus Leach, the son of a local music-hall manager in Hoxton, started to court Marie in earnest, and George Foster claimed that he and Marie had become engaged, that he had even introduced her to his parents − although this may have been the sort of teenage 'engagement' shared only by the two of them. Brushie repelled all attempts to court Marie with the fierce protectiveness of a father reluctant to acknowledge that his little girl had become an object of desire and that she was now leading an independent life. Her suitors were not allowed to cross the family threshold and she was forced to conduct her trysts on the doorstep.

At the halls, though, Marie was her own woman and Brushie was helpless to protect her from the men whom Marie played off against each other. George, a well-dressed young man in a suit, made the mistake of introducing her to his friend, Percy Courtenay, a silver-tongued, good-looking fellow who enjoyed hanging around music-hall bars. They soon became lovers, doubly humiliating for George as the turn of events inspired a new music-hall song by the coster-singer Gus Elen, 'Never Introduce Your Donah [sweetheart] To A Pal!', which showed just how well known Marie was becoming. George, though, found it hard to conceal a whiff of relief that she had slipped through his fingers: 'Naturally I was very cut up about losing my wonderful sweetheart, but it did not take me very long to realise that temperamentally we should have been quite unsuited to each other.'[3]

George described Percy as 'a young blood and racing man with plenty of money and an attractive personality', and Alice remembered him as 'nice looking'. Marie's friend and early biographer Macqueen Pope said he had the 'air of a gentleman'; he has also been described as a 'stage-door johnny' or 'racecourse tout'. However, Percy remains a maddeningly elusive figure. He was a good talker and he made Marie laugh. He also made her pregnant — which was the most convincing reason why, aged seventeen, she married him.

The realization that she was pregnant stopped Marie dead in her tracks: suddenly the world was not such a welcoming place. Her parents were furious and there were bitter rows and recriminations. Her career was just beginning to take off, she had completed her first brief tour, including Birmingham, Hull and Chatham, she was enjoying a freedom her mother had never experienced and earning good money, too. Percy was the ideal person to have a laugh with but, as marriage material, he had little going for him — not that marriage had ever been uppermost in Marie's mind.

They married in what Alice termed a 'walking wedding' at St John the Baptist church, Hoxton, on 12 November 1887. Even to Marie, who was not easily intimidated, the grand Georgian church, with its fancy clock-tower and yellow Bathstone brickwork, must have brought home the seriousness of what she was doing. The entrance was framed by huge Egyptian-style doors, which leaned in at a precarious angle, as if bearing down on anyone considering escape. Marie's unease about what she was doing showed in that she lied about her age, adding a year when she told the vicar she was eighteen; Percy said he was twenty-five and described himself on the marriage certificate as a 'general dealer' from Bow, the son of Captain Edwin Courtenay. Marie left blank the space for her profession. Given the circumstances, the wedding must have been a sombre affair. Afterwards the couple left for their first home, two rooms in Arlington Street, New North Road, a solid Victorian square near to the Grand Union Canal and less than a mile from where Marie had been born.

Despite her sudden marriage, her routine changed little: the following year, Marie played the Oxford, Collins's, the Foresters and the South London Palace. As the shock of finding herself a wife and expectant mother wore off, she emerged from her black mood. She had never been one to dwell on a setback, or to suffer much from guilt. Her immense reserves of energy enabled her to carry on as before and she was determined not to lose the reputation she had built for herself over the previous two years. Looking to her mother as a role model, she realized that it was possible to lead an active life and cope with impending motherhood. Her smock-like costume and the fashions of the day allowed her to hide her bump and she was able to continue work until April, when her name stopped appearing in the professional press. Despite her natural restlessness, her routine of rushing round London halls and standing in fetid, smoke-filled rooms cannot have made for an easy pregnancy.

In May Marie's details were noted in the *Era* 'letterbox' for forwarding mail, and Myria Matilda Victoria was born on 19 May 1888 at home. On the birth certificate Percy's occupation was given as 'commission agent'. By the time the birth had been registered, two months later on 9 July, the family was living at 55 Graham Road, a tall, Victorian house in Hackney.[4] Marie had also moved her parents and siblings to nearby Powerscroft Road in Clapton. Although it was still in the East End, the area was less cramped and its occupants had pretensions beyond the usual 'coster' dreams.

Marie grew up surrounded by a distinctive group of East Enders known as costermongers, who sold mainly fruit and vegetables from trolleys that they wheeled around by hand – the name probably comes from the word 'costard' for a type of apple. They were known for their distinctive style of dress – bell-bottomed trousers, flat cap and wide scarf – and for their cheerful, but tough, demeanour. They even had their own secret rhyming language, frequently used to fool the police. Many music-hall performers incorporated the coster in their act.

The arrival of her first child triggered in Marie nesting instincts that had lain dormant ever since childhood. She enjoyed trying out new brands of paint in her home, decorating it in garish pinks, reds and blues and constantly rearranging the furniture, almost as if she was designing a stage set. However, these dual interests made poor companions: she was often too impatient to allow the paint to dry before shifting the furniture, with the result that beds and chairs were frequently found stuck to the walls.[5]

By October Marie was back at work and the couple's new home proved well suited for Marie's role as Princess Kristina in *The Magic Dragon of the Demon Dell, or The Search for the Mystic Thyme*, staged at the Britannia in Hoxton. The pantomime ran from Boxing Day until the end of February, and gave Marie two months' work close to home and her mother. Sara Lane had run the theatre since the death of her husband, Sam, in 1871 and was sixty-five when Marie worked for her. She continued to don tights to play Principal Boy until she was well into her seventies.

When Charles Dickens visited the Brit, as it was known, in 1858, he compared its stage to those of La Scala in Milan and the Grand Opera in Paris.[6] He was particularly impressed by the purity of the air. The theatre also had a reputation for the amount of food its audience could consume: burly men sold thick sandwiches, saveloys, pasties, fried fish, jellied eels, oranges and beer from huge baskets.

Sara was known for employing music-hall performers, such as Charles Coborn, famous for singing 'The Man Who Broke The Bank At Monte Carlo' and who starred as King Addlepate at the end of 1881. Pantomime was a popular option for music-hall performers: it provided the rare security of a long period of employment. Marie played the Principal Girl, Princess Kristina, in late 1888, sharing the bill with several members of the Lupino family, a large, theatrical clan descended from an Italian puppeteer who emigrated to England in the seventeenth century. Harry Lupino married Sara's niece and was uncle to Barry and

Stanley Lupino,[7] who went on to become panto stalwarts in the West End. Marie's time at the Brit gave her valuable experience of playing a huge theatre – it could hold nearly 3,000 – and of pantomime. The *London Entr'acte*'s assessment of *The Magic Dragon* that 'There's plenty of scenery to accompany the action of the story' may sound damning by faint praise, but when a sense of spectacle was even more important in a pantomime than it is today, it was probably meant as a compliment.

Sara treated her pantomime cast like a close-knit family, which gave Marie a period of stability in what had been a tumultuous couple of years. Like her mother, Sara was a potent example of a strong woman; she was one of several Marie encountered who wielded an influence within their own sphere that was in sharp contrast to the rule of order outside the music-hall world. Others were Sam Collins's widow, Anne, who took over the Islington hall for three years after he died, and Ellen Poole, who managed the South London Palace of Varieties after she had seen off three male Pooles.

The established female music-hall stars who inspired Marie were also formidable women. Jenny Hill was at her peak when Marie was just starting out and in many ways Marie was her natural heir. She was known as 'The Vital Spark' because of her effervescent personality and annoyed managers with her off-the-cuff asides to the audience; she had a strong appeal to women and knew how to throw a good party. For Marie, though, she was a powerful example of what a female performer could achieve.

Jenny, a small, bird-like woman, with a pointed nose and thin lips, had built up a phalanx of convincing stage characters: 'The Coffee Shop Gal' enjoyed impersonating her customers; a landlady reminisced about life; there was a servant girl, and a costerwoman out with her sweetheart. Jenny's act included singing, dancing the hornpipe and 'Cellar Flap', male impersonations and monologues, such as 'The City Waif'. The daughter of a Marylebone cabbie, her early life was hard. She began working in a pub where, so the myth goes, for seven years she rose at dawn and continued until nearly midnight. She had a child early in life and was married to an acrobat, Jean Pasta, who beat her up. Desperate for money she trudged from hall to hall looking for work, until one manager sent her to a rival with a note purporting to recommend her for work but in fact telling the recipient she was a talentless time-waster

– which he ignored. An early break came when she was chosen to play the legs of Mother Goose in the pantomime.

This image of the down-trodden skivvy, though, is belied by contemporary reports that she punched a pub manageress, and threatened a newspaper with legal action: its readers had voted her Smartest Actress on the Stage but the proprietors deemed her ineligible to take the prize, a diamond brooch, because she was a music-hall performer. 'I have instructed my lawyer to take such steps as he may deem necessary to vindicate my professional status from what I consider to be an unwarrantable attack,' she said loftily.[8]

She was one of the first women to adopt the heady lifestyle of a 'star'. She bought a racehorse called Vitality and aped the habits of her social betters with garden parties at her home, The Acacias, in south London where guests watched fireworks and played lawn tennis, badminton and quoits. When the American impresario Tony Pastor visited Britain, she hired a steamboat for a river party – an unfortunate choice, given his fear of water.

Another role model for Marie's early years was Elizabeth Ann Mahony, whose stage name was Bessie Bellwood. She was a comic singer who could handle the roughest audience and silence the most persistent hecklers. Born in Ireland, she spent her early life as a rabbit-skinner in Bermondsey. Her most famous song was 'What Cheer, Ria!', which, it has been argued, was delivered to sound like 'Watch your rear!' – and she portrayed such characters as a 'light-hearted, befeathered factory girl in garish coloured skirts'.[9] A contemporary review of one of her performances commented: 'Great cheering followed the announcement of Bessie Bellwood, who justified her reception by the exhibition of her low comedy powers. We cannot say that Miss Bellwood gives us fun without vulgarity; but the fun is decidedly there and laughter is a matter of compulsion.'[10] The exact terms Bessie used to silence a boisterous crowd were too vulgar to be recorded, but an 1882 description by Jerome K. Jerome of a verbal battle between a coal-heaver and a female singer is thought to refer to Bessie:

She announced her intention of 'wiping down the bloomin' 'all' with him, and making it respectable; and, metaphorically speaking, that is what she did. Her tongue hit him between the eyes, and knocked him down and trampled on him. It curled round and round him like a whip, and then it uncurled and wound the other way. It seized him by the scruff of his neck, and tossed him up into the air, and caught him as he descended, and flung him to the ground, and rolled him on it. It played around him like forked lightning, and blinded him. It danced and shrieked about him like a host of whirling fiends, and he tried to remember a prayer, and could not. It touched him lightly on the sole of his foot and the crown of his head, and his hair stood up straight, and his limbs grew stiff. The people sitting near him drew away, not feeling it safe to be near, and left him alone, surrounded by space, and language.[11]

With models such as Bessie, Jenny, Sara and her mother around her the concept of a forceful woman would have been commonplace rather than exceptional to Marie.

In 1889 Marie played halls such as the Paragon and Royal Foresters in Mile End, as well as old favourites like the Oxford, the Holborn Royal, the Middlesex and the Canterbury. She started to secure bookings in the more Bohemian venues such as the Empire and Alhambra in Leicester Square, the Trocadero Palace of Varieties in Great Windmill Street, off Shaftesbury Avenue, and the Royal Standard in Victoria. The Sisters Lloyd were following in her footsteps by appearing at the Middlesex and the South London Palace. They 'provided [sic] conclusively that they have profited by the example, and, possibly, the teaching of clever sister Marie. They sing well, and their dancing is of a very nimble and finished order.'[12]

The Woods now had three successful daughters on the stage, which made the family's life much easier – especially as by 1890 Matilda was expecting her eleventh child, Maude. Marie's home was at the centre of the Wood universe and she filled it with her own ménage of friends and hangers-on. Her obsession with never being alone might have pointed to an unhappy marriage, but being surrounded with people was normal to her. Sunday afternoons meant open house at Marie's to music-hall performers, both famous and not so famous. Little Tich, Dan Leno, Lottie Collins, renowned in the 1890s for her multi-petticoated rendition of 'Ta-ra-ra-boom-de-ay', the romantic singer Marie Kendall, quick-fire American comedian Richard G. Knowles, Cockney funny-man Joe Elvin, comic Harry Randall and Gus Elen turned up to exchange gossip and try out new routines. Like her, Marie's closest friends were on the way up and brimming with excitement at the possibilities in front of them. Their constant chatter bubbled away while they gorged themselves on the buffet of cold ham, chicken and tongue that was laid out first thing in the morning and topped up during the day.

Percy felt excluded from this close circle of music-hall camaraderie and resented sharing Marie with her extended family – it was bad enough that the whole of London could eye her up every night. His only role in these gatherings was as Marie's husband, which he hated. He took to escaping from the chaos of his home to spend more and more time in the West End with his betting buddies. Marie's work meant that she finished late at night then needed a few hours at the bar of whichever hall she was playing to 'come down' from the buzz of being in the limelight. Percy, though, was not prepared to tag along from hall to hall, sharing her with thousands of strangers.

The couple's strained relationship was dealt a further blow in January 1890, when snow, fog and influenza dented music-hall attendance. On the twenty-fifth amid the usual ragbag of items about indisposed performers and a charity hundred-yards' piggy-back race the *Era*'s gossip column announced: 'Miss Marie Lloyd (Mrs Courtney) [*sic*] was prematurely confined of a dead baby on Monday last. The indefatigable little lady's condition gives no cause for anxiety.'

The matter-of-fact tone of the announcement is more an indication of Victorian attitudes to death, than of callousness, and Marie tried to mirror the *Era*'s breeziness. Infant mortality was nothing new to her: she had seen her own mother cope with the death of two children. A month later she appeared at the Alhambra in Leicester Square on the same bill as a new ballet entitled *Asmodeus*; a grand naval and military spectacle, *Our Army and Navy*; and Rags, 'the Canine Wonder'. She continued to play a range of London halls until the end of April when she was taken ill one morning and sent to bed for a few days. After recovering briefly her name disappeared from the pages of the *Era* for several weeks. Perhaps she had been fooling herself into believing that the stillborn baby had not affected her, or perhaps the tragedy had come to symbolize her fast-decaying marriage.

By late June she was back at work, appearing at the Pavilion in Pall Mall – which claimed to be the 'coolest place in London' by virtue of its sliding roof. In early August, though, Lottie Collins was called upon to deputize for her at the Tivoli. No reason was given for Marie's indisposition.

By September she seemed fully recovered. On the twentieth her card, now to be found in a regular slot at the top left-hand corner on the back page of the *Era*, announced in effusive tones that jarred with the succinct advertisements that surrounded it:

Miss Marie Lloyd sails today from Liverpool per SS *Wyoming* for New York, specially engaged by Messrs Koster and Bial, to play ten weeks at their theatre in New York. Kind regards to old friends. P.S. Anybody wishing to buy copies of the most successful song on record entitled 'Wink the other eye' (one guinea for each turn) kindly communicate to Marie Lloyd, 55 Graham Road, Dalston. Entirely new business and wardrobe for America. Sole agent, dear Old George (fifth year).

Chapter 4

A PROPER PANTOMIME

(1890–91)

~*~

While toffee and tarts were the joy of their hearts,
And they drank nothing stronger than tea.
'That Was Before My Time, A Long While Ago' by
T. W. Connor and Ernest Symons

It must have been bewildering for an exuberant young woman who made her living by rushing from music hall to music hall, and who had rarely left London, to find herself limited to the cramped conditions of a ship and out of sight of land for the week or so that it took to cross the Atlantic. New York, a bustling port and funnel for emigrants from all over the world, was strangely similar to the East End of London Marie had just left, yet completely different from anything she had ever experienced. She must have been awed by the Statue of Liberty, which in 1890 had been gazing grimly at arrivals for a mere four years.

Marie's visit to New York, before she had completed a major regional tour of Britain, was prompted by the sudden popularity of English music-hall performers on the other side of the Atlantic. Her friend and fellow artist Little Tich had toured North America and appeared in New York in 1887. He had confidently expected to encounter marauding Indians during his visit and it had only been the reassurances of New York impresario Tony Pastor that had convinced him there was no need to purchase a large Colt revolver. Pastor had signed up Little Tich after seeing him at the Pavilion in London during the first of what were to become annual tours of Europe in search of music-hall talent.

Antonio Pastor was to American vaudeville what Charles Morton was to British music hall: a founding father who broadened the appeal of his particular form of entertainment by attracting the moneyed middle classes. Born in New York, he had been entranced by the world of entertainment from an early age. He made his singing début aged fourteen at Barnum's 'museum' – a term used to give an educational gloss to what was essentially a freak show. Next he ran away to the circus, then a mainstay of the American entertainment business bringing light relief to far-flung communities. He learned tumbling and how to handle horses, but only found his forte when the ringmaster died and he was forced to step into his boots. He grew a moustache for gravitas and this, with his top hat, shiny patent leather boots and tails, became a trademark image he retained for life. During the Civil War he carved out a successful career as a serio-comic singer through his rabidly patriotic songs such as 'The Star Spangled Banner'.

In 1865 he opened Tony Pastor's Opera House at 201 Bowery, named to suggest a more polite form of entertainment than the so-called 'variety' that had grown out of concert saloons. The Bowery district of New York on the Lower East Side was well known for its dime museums, dance halls and beer gardens, which catered for a tightly packed immigrant population.

Dime museums usually had a 'professor', who performed the role of the music-hall chairman by introducing the exhibits and cajoling patrons into parting with cash. The auditorium was often known as the 'lecture room'. One New York museum in the 1870s offered free admittance to the first five children who arrived with a mouse to be fed to the rattlesnake inside, and Phineas T. Barnum tested his audience's credibility with exhibits such as George Washington's 160-year-old black nurse, a mermaid and the midget General Tom Thumb, whom he introduced dressed in Napoleonic costume to Queen Victoria. Vaudeville took strands from these Bowery styles of entertainment, from the circus and from burlesque, which started to emerge in the late 1860s. The latter was a form of entertainment divided into three sections: the first was made up of chorus numbers, monologues and comic sketches; then came the 'olio' – named after a kitchen product advertised on the curtain – in which variety turns performed while the stage was prepared for the final sketch, a travesty on politics or a parody of a current theatrical success.

Variety's growing respectability can be clearly charted by the addresses of its venues: the further north the halls moved in Manhattan the greater their acceptability. In 1875 Pastor took over the Metropolitan Theater at 585–7 Broadway, which was well placed for hotels and transport links. Pastor's New Fourteenth Street Theater began trading on 24 October 1881, the day often claimed as the birthdate of vaudeville. Ironically, for a man credited with 'cleaning up' variety, the theatre was based in Tammany Hall, which was synonymous with political corruption. Pastor banned smoking and drinking in the auditorium and curbed the more vulgar elements who appeared on bills. He was highly successful in enticing women to his shows, wooing them with bouquets and candy and allowing unescorted females in free for matinée performances. So successful was he that some mothers began to view his theatres as a sort of informal creche where they could leave their children unattended for a few hours. Although one of Pastor's nicknames was 'Tony the Puritan', and he was a devout Catholic, his main impetus for cleaning up entertainment was to boost ticket sales. As the actor Fred Stone put it, Pastor made vaudeville a place 'a child could take his parents'.[1]

The word 'vaudeville' was only just becoming common currency when Marie made her first trip to New York. There are two theories about the origins of the word: that it is a corruption of Vau (or Val) de Vire, meaning '[songs of the] Vire Valley' and that it alludes to the practice in fifteenth-century Normandy of singing satirical ballads aimed against the English lords who ruled the area at that time; or that it derives from *voix des villes* (voices of the city streets). Either way, the term's sophistication suited those like Pastor who wanted entertainment specifically aimed at respectable family audiences.

Including European performers on the bill gave an establishment sophistication and in 1889 Pastor enticed the male impersonator Bessie Bonehill and the singer Lottie Collins to New York. They proved so successful that British performers were suddenly in great demand. Bessie was popular enough for Pastor's wife to present her with a diamond bracelet of nine solitaires as a birthday present, and she returned to New York at the same time as Marie made her début in the city.

Talent scouting abroad became an important part of the vaudeville manager's job. When Marie arrived in New York she had just missed Charlie Chaplin's father, who had been appearing at the Union Square Theater. Koster & Bial's Music Hall at the corner of West 23rd Street and the Avenue of the Americas, where Marie made her début, was particularly well known for its European acts and had a bohemian air similar to that of the Empire, Leicester Square. John Koster, who had emigrated to America from Hamburg in 1863, had formed a joint venture with Albert Bial to run restaurants and a beer-bottling business before moving into variety. One of their earliest coups was when they presented the Spanish dancer, Carmencita, at Koster & Bial's in February 1890 to great acclaim and helped to attract polite society to see what all the fuss was about from within their safely curtained boxes.

Marie took with her to Koster & Bial's the first song that became linked with her name. 'Wink The Other Eye' was written by George le Brunn, a prolific songwriter whom Marie had met at one of her parties. George started his career playing the piano at a music hall in Brighton, then toured in W. Hamilton's diorama to Preston as pianist, harpist, organist and choir-master before returning to Brighton. His London début was at Harwood's Variety Theatre in Hoxton, again playing the piano and later as musical conductor.

He teamed up with John P. Harrington, who provided the words, to produce hundreds of songs for a range of performers including the male impersonator Vesta Tilley, Dan Leno and Charles Chaplin senior. George came up with the idea for Marie's first big hit when she caught him winking at someone while making fun of her.

> Say, boys, whatever do you mean,
> When you wink the other eye?
> Why, when you tell where you've been,
> Do you wink the other eye?
> You preach your wives such stories,
> You can tell them just a few –
> Just met an old acquaintance.
> Or the train was overdue,
> And when the simple wife believes
> That every word is true,
> Then you wink the other eye.

Marie sang it dressed in a tight, sleeveless bodice with a deeply plunging neckline and bow falling over one shoulder. She wore her hair down, in tumbling curls, topped with an extravagantly plumed floppy hat that made her look like a circus bareback rider. It was her most figure-hugging and provocative costume to date. 'Wink The Other Eye' also gave Marie her trademark gesture: a conspiratorial wink. Her other songs at this time included 'After The Pantomime', in which she wore an 'elegant get-up', and 'You Should Go To France And See The Ladies Dance', which allowed her to mimic French dancing – probably a tame version of the can-can – and to include a few steps of her own. With songs like these she was on safe ground in New York since London characterizations, such as the costergirl, or local dialects, baffled the audiences. When Jenny Hill appeared in New York the year after Marie, Tony Pastor was so worried that his customers would not be able to understand her patter that he distributed a Cockney dictionary among them.

The management of Koster & Bial's was pleased with Marie's performance, which was satisfactory rather than spectacular, and in early December the *Era* reported that she had been 'beguiled by flattering offers from numerous American managers, but expects to return to her native land for Christmas'. A farewell dinner, attended by sixty people, was thrown in her honour, and Koster and Bial gave her a nine-piece monogrammed silver tea service. A salver bore the inscription: 'Marie Lloyd, from Koster and Bial, Friday December 12th, 1890, New York'. A contract for a future New York engagement was placed in the teapot.

She returned to a fog-bound Liverpool 'with happy reminiscences of success' and nightly engagements at the Oxford, Collins's, the Pavilion and the South London. An advertisement she placed in the *London Entr'acte* proclaimed: 'Miss Marie Lloyd made the biggest hit ever known at Koster and Bial's variety hall, New York.' The American visit had restored her confidence after the baby's death, as the *Entr'acte* commented: 'Miss Marie Lloyd is now sailing on a strong tide, and her songs are quite household words. Her success here [at Gatti's] is very great.'[2] The Alhambra in Leicester Square engaged her from February 1891 to the end of 1892, refusing to release her when the Gaiety made an approach, and Sir Augustus Harris asked her to be in a Drury Lane pantomime.

As was customary with music-hall songs, Marie immediately capitalized on the winking phenomenon with a follow-up in 1891, 'Listen With The Right Ear!' It starts with some advice:

You wink the other eye, when you don't wish to see,
Sometimes it's very useful, it's been so to me,
So all take my advice, and you need never fear,
All you see is not real, and not half of what you hear.

The subsequent verses describe situations in which it is advisable to turn a deaf ear: you should catch every word if your husband offers to buy you a cloak, but feign deafness if it's nothing more than a hat; if a rich man describes you as a 'charming creature' and asks to be introduced you should hear straight away; if, however, you are described in less than glowing terms you 'close up both ears tight!'; an offer from your 'masher' [sweetheart] to lend you a thousand pounds should come through loud and clear, while Jennie Juggins's request for 'a little loan' should pass unheeded. There was also a topical allusion in the final lines of the last verse:

Only prove that 'black' is 'white', like people of *that ilke* –
It's easy, if you copy good old Charley Dilke.

It was common for music-hall singers to update their lyrics to take advantage of the latest fashion craze or scandal and the choice in this case was particularly salacious. Sir Charles Wentworth Dilke was MP for Chelsea, president of the Local Government Board under Gladstone and a radical with republican undertones. He became embroiled at the centre of one of the most juicy scandals of the 1880s, which lingered into the next decade – which was littered with the corpses of high-profile men fallen foul of public opinion. In 1885 Dilke was named in the divorce case of Donald Crawford as having taken a string of lovers, including a maid who, it was alleged, participated in a three-in-a-bed romp with Dilke and Mrs Crawford, and of having taught Mrs Crawford 'every French vice'. Although Dilke pleaded his innocence – and a band of his supporters published a pamphlet providing him with convincing alibis and damning evidence against Mrs Crawford – he never again held high office.

'Listen With The Right Ear!' is a silly song, but in it Marie acknowledges to the women of the audience that life is a game and offers advice on how to play it. Not only does she hold herself up as a woman of the world, and a canny one at that, but she establishes a conspiracy of knowingness with the audience. The choice of a wink as her leitmotif represents just this: it suggests a shared secret and is the emblem of someone who knows how to have a good time.

The title of another of Marie's songs 'No Flies On Me' confirms this image of the worldly-wise young woman. At the South London Palace in January 1891 she was again in schoolgirl mode, singing either George Ware's 'Whacky, Whack, Whack' — the sheet music shows her as a schoolgirl in front of a backdrop bristling with canes — or le Brunn's 'I Was Slapped'. Marie wore a 'pretty hood and frock, satchel on back and slate in hand' and confided how 'she and "little brother Jackie" dislike the rigour and routine of the Board School, where they whip you "ha' of a minute" but you feel it "ha' of a day".' As an encore she gave, with a 'sly humour, an exposition of the whole art of captivating a curate. No doubt the curate would find all but the dénouement that "leaves him lonely, sets him free", with a select dinner to pay for, greatly to his taste.'[3]

Marie's slyly seductive songs were in keeping with the morally ambiguous late nineteenth century, in which scandal was rife, fuelling concern among reformers that the population was in danger of being contaminated by the cavortings of public figures. The Royal Family was unpopular and the Prince of Wales a figure of fun. His name had already been associated with the Mordaunt divorce case in 1870, following which he was booed when he visited the theatre, and in 1891 his dissolute lifestyle was paraded for all to see in the Baccarat or Tranby Croft scandal. A cartoon in the London Entr'acte depicted the heir to the throne hiding behind a row of lawyers. Coincidentally, a line drawing in the same issue showed Marie in her schoolgirl costume with the caption, 'She winks the other eye.'

The Baccarat case centred around a house party given by the newly rich shipping tycoon Arthur Wilson at his home, Tranby Croft, after the St Leger horse race. Bertie's friend, Sir William Gordon-Cumming, a colonel in the Scots Guards, was accused of cheating at baccarat and forced to sign a document saying he would never gamble again in return for reassurance that the entire incident would go no further. But the story leaked out and in February 1891 Sir William decided to take legal action. The Prince of Wales was subjected to six days' cross-examination. He was booed again, this time at Ascot.

The incident followed the Cleveland Street scandal in September 1889, in which Lord Arthur Somerset was accused of offences with telegraph boys at a homosexual brothel, and the downfall of the Irish national leader Charles Stewart Parnell who, in the same year, was named as a co-respondent in the O'Shea divorce case. Oscar Wilde was hitting new heights of controversy and *The Picture of Dorian Gray*, which was published in April 1891, was banned by W. H. Smith bookshops. At the same time the London County Council had been established under the Local Government Act of 1888 to replace the haphazardly run Metropolitan Board of Works, itself the subject of accusations of financial impropriety. The LCC was made up of 126 councillors, who were elected every three years, and sobriety was its keynote. The councillors – many of whom were austere, God-fearing men – saw their mission as saving London from corruption. Music hall became caught in the zealots' cross-fire when the LCC set up a committee to replace the law courts' authority to license the capital's venues. Its vice-chairman was George Russell, also chairman of the National Vigilance Association, which had been established in 1885 to fight vice and public immorality. Frederick Charrington, another NVA supporter who distributed anti-music hall leaflets and who had renounced the fortune his family made from brewing, was also on the committee, as was the staunch Methodist, John McDougall. In fact, according to one estimate, a third of the licensing committee's twenty-one members were either members of, or sympathetic towards, the NVA.

The LCC was determined to root out the evil in music halls and to provide attractions such as libraries and parks to replace taverns and theatres. The Metropolitan Building Act of 1878 had already imposed measures aimed at reducing the risk of fire and accident, but this had been irregularly enforced. A hall had to pass an engineering inspection to ensure it was structurally safe before the LCC committee would recommend a licence and this was sufficient to close many halls: several – especially the smaller ones – could not afford to make the necessary alterations.

Halls that cleared this first hurdle still had to have their application for a licence passed at a special hearing. LCC councillors could speak for or against; police might be asked to give their opinion of a hall's 'morals'; and hired inspectors were sent out incognito to report back on the respectability or otherwise of a hall and its performers. Managers took this threat very seriously: notices appeared in halls warning performers to moderate their material. The music-hall establishment recognized that it was under threat and immediately drew up battle lines to try to discipline its foot soldiers. The *Era* did its best to promote discipline among performers:

> Notwithstanding the hostile action of a certain section of the LCC at the last licensing meeting, and the warnings then given, we regret to find that there are still sundry performers whose wheezes are only dirty and not funny. The other evening at a well-known West End hall, a certain member of the 'Ethiopian' persuasion delivered himself of something very objectionable in connection with a parody he undertook to recite. The watchful manager, we are pleased to be able to add, made punishment follow swift upon the offence by giving directions that the offender should not again be permitted to go upon the stage. Artists who play into the hands of McDougall & Co. are their own enemies and the enemies of the profession.[4]

The *London Entr'acte*'s cartoonist portrayed McDougall,[5] the most outspoken critic, who was also known as MuckDougall or The Grand Inquisitor, as a grim, bearded man wearing pince-nez. His fellow reformer, Mrs Grundy, depicted as a masculine harridan with thick eyebrows, brandishing a handbag and umbrella, asks: 'Why don't you give the theatres a turn with your purifying remedy? They would repay a little attention.' Mr McDougall replies: 'We shall have 'em by-and-by.'

But the newspaper also exposed the hypocrisy of the situation in an exchange that might easily have referred to Marie:

> 'A brazen minx!' said one lady to another as they freely criticised the character of a female who was announced to contribute to the entertainment which they had come to see and hear. 'I wonder she has the impudence to appear before a respectable audience,' replied Number Two. Just then was posted up on the walls a notice to the effect that, owing to regrettable indisposition, the so-called 'brazen minx' would be unable to appear, whereupon the lady critics ejaculated: 'What a burning shame! We ought to have our money back.'[6]

The tenacity of the moral reformers soon became evident in 1890 over the celebrated case of Zaeo's armpits. Zaeo was a young acrobat who, despite her name, had been born near London. She had been apprenticed to a circus-owner since the age of twelve and had perfected an act in which she performed death-defying stunts on horseback, the trapeze and the high-wire. Audiences were thrilled by the culmination of her act in which she returned to earth with a back somersault and a 54-foot free fall from her trapeze.

The LCC inspector took exception to her work at the London Aquarium in Tothill Street, Westminster, because the design of the music hall meant she had to perform above the audience's heads, offering them an unexpurgated view of her body flying through the air. Placards, pamphlets and postcards showing Zaeo, a plump performer in tights and an ill-fitting bodice that revealed her armpits, were banned as a condition of the Aquarium's licence renewal. In 1891 the LCC was itself criticized after reports in the press that inspectors, who claimed her descent on to the net below was harming her back, demanded to examine her torso. The *Financial Times* applauded the case as an adroit way of boosting takings at the Aquarium.

But even while the social reformers were doing their best to curb the influence of music hall, its tentacles were extending further into society. An editorial in the *Era* defended the use of twenty- to thirty-minute sketches at music halls, which so incensed Henry Irving, who thought they degraded legitimate drama, that he threatened to withdraw his advertisements from the newspaper.

The middle classes had been exposed to music-hall stars through pantomime, one of the oldest forms of entertainment. One of the driving forces behind the movement to bring music halls to a wider public was the theatre manager Augustus 'Gus' Harris, whom *Punch* dubbed 'Druriolanus' because his forceful character dominated Drury Lane. His productions were grand spectacles and generally featured large casts – sometimes as many as five hundred actors – a grand procession and some feat of engineering such as a ship that filled the stage. Once, a massive rock became stuck and had to be smashed to pieces. He also enjoyed presenting dancing spectacles, and in 1889 when Marie was providing the variety entertainment at the Empire, Leicester Square, he was producing its 'grand ballet' *Diana*.

Gus had been born in Paris and had tried his hand early on as a foreign correspondent. He had also dallied with serious acting – only a great showman could appreciate the alliterative potential of playing Malcolm in *Macbeth* at Manchester, as he did in 1873 – and light comedy. Eventually, though, he realized his true skills lay in management. He was knighted, because he happened to be sheriff of the City of London when the German emperor visited, and took over Drury Lane in 1879.

Vesta Tilley, who appeared as Captain Tralala in the 1882–3 Drury Lane production of *Sinbad*, remembered him on the opening night, rushing around in full evening dress with a flowing black Inverness cloak, finally retiring to his private box to watch the performance and hiss stage directions through a speaking tube to his team backstage. In 1889 *Vanity Fair* honoured him with one of its famous Spy cartoons, which portrayed him as a rotund man balancing on delicate, pointed black shoes with bows, a white flower in his buttonhole, flowing cloak, white-gloved hands, his huge bulk encased in a black waistcoat. His neat moustache and beard made him look a little like the future Edward VII, but his red-faced balding head cocked to one side is much more reminiscent of a somewhat surprised oversized pigeon.[7]

Later Marie admitted that when Gus first asked her to appear at Drury Lane she pretended to think he was referring to the Old Mo.[8] When he explained to her that he was talking about *the* Drury Lane Theatre she is said to have exclaimed that she had been under the impression that it was a prison because of the way it was guarded by sentries wearing busbies. Secretly, though, she was thrilled at the offer. She was to take the part of Princess Allfair in *Humpty Dumpty* in a cast that united some of her closest friends. Herbert Campbell was the King of Hearts, his booming voice and nineteen-stone bulk providing a perfect foil to Dan Leno's emaciated Queen of Hearts, which he delivered with quicksilver movements. Little Tich, who was Humpty-Dumpty, clowned and turned acrobatic tricks like a court jester, and George Lupino played an equally foolish Twirley-Whirley.

Humpty Dumpty, or The Yellow Dwarf and the Fair One epitomized one of the main complaints levelled against Gus's form of pantomime: that it did away with traditional storylines. On 2 January the *London Entr'acte* commented: 'The pantomime is designed rather with the intention of rejoicing adults than of giving satisfaction to the young, many of the references requiring a mind educated in the most modern slang and scandals of the period to understand them.' It was also four and a half hours long.

Pantomime had been moving steadily away from its earlier reliance on ballet and the story-telling dances of the Harlequin, and from classical to fairy tales. Old-fashioned plots were squeezed and manipulated to accommodate alluring actresses, grand spectacles and a mixture of music-hall talent that ranged from slapstick to romantic songs. The confused 'mix-and-match' formula gave rise to the expression a 'proper pantomime', meaning a 'state of mayhem or confusion' – in 'I'd Like To Live In Paris All The Time', or 'The Coster Girl In Paris' (1912), Marie delights in a city that is a 'proper pantomime'.

The 1891–2 Drury Lane pantomime was no exception. The new-look Humpty Dumpty was the arch-rival of Dulcimar, King of the Gold Mines, for the hand of Princess Allfair, daughter of the King and Queen of Hearts. The Princess at first detests Dulcimar, played by Miss Fanny Leslie, but a cup of magic tea makes her fall in love with him and they marry. Humpty Dumpty, however, kidnaps her and takes her 'evidently by the underground railway' to a very terrible place, 'Steel Castle'. Eventually Dulcimar and his wooden-headed soldiers rescue her and allow her to enjoy 'The Dream of Bliss', in which six nymphs appear from a classical fountain containing real water and ascend into an opaline sky from which bands of glittering tissue fall. This 'transformation scene' was an important part of the new-style pantomime in which the set was instantaneously and ingeniously transformed to take the audience's breath away.

If *Humpty Dumpty*'s reviews are anything to go by, the storyline was purely incidental to the night's enjoyment. Marie had to deliver the first song, which may have made her nervous. *The Times* described her as 'playful in gesture, graceful in appearance, but not strong in voice'.[9] she was also at the centre of one of the pantomime's setpieces in which Princess Allfair summoned an assembly of dolls that put the best-stocked nursery to shame. They came in all colours, nationalities and hairstyles, and included pierrots and giant baby dolls, who stared at the audience with big blue eyes and flaxen curls escaping from their hoods. They walked with stiff wooden limbs, their joints cracking audibly, or bounced along on indiarubber legs.

The orange-grove scene relied similarly on costume for effect. Each dancer carried a lily, and their dresses were decorated with flowers. As they pranced about in the moonlight the foliage above their heads lit up and their lilies were transformed into electric lamps. The third setpiece consisted of the Procession of Nations paying their respects to Princess Allfair, bedecked in white trimmed with orange blossom and a long train. The richly costumed representatives of twenty-four countries, including India, Arabia, Dalmatia, Tartary, Cochin-China, Persia, Lapland, Montenegro and Timbuctoo, offered an insight into the Victorian worldview: Russia and Germany met with hostility from the audience, America was cheered, but the pit and gallery went wild over England.

Little Tich, who evolved from Humpty Dumpty to the Yellow Dwarf, was hardly outdone in the costume department, switching from a nautical outfit to sporting wear to Scottish dress and then a 'ballet girl with a *pas seul* that would send a hypochondriac into fits of merriment'.[10] 'He has a funny little body, funny little legs, a funny little face, a funny big smile that stretches right away from the footlights to the topmost gallery.'[11] The *Saturday Review* described him as 'a veritable imp, with the wizened face of a fiendish old man and the body of a boy . . .' and Marie as 'a lovely princess'.[12] The *London Entr'acte* said she 'delivers her text quite pungently, and sings and dances with spirit too'.[13] The *Saturday Review* concluded, rather superciliously, 'There is plenty of music-hall foolery in this pantomime, but very little wit or boisterous fun.' The *Times* mentioned a 'witty, but vulgar song'[14] that contained allusions to false hair and false teeth and a later joke about a surgeon who successfully made use of half a column of Gladstone's speeches in place of an anaesthetic.

But for all the fine costumes, and the presence of the Prince and Princess of Wales, the Duke of Clarence and other luminaries in the royal box, it was Marie and her fellow music-hall artists who injected a new atmosphere into pantomime. The audience in the cheap seats was squeezed in tight, 'ready to shout itself hoarse upon the slightest provocation in an orchestral suggestion of a music-hall chorus'. Those above yelled, 'Get your hair cut,' to those below, who answered, 'Wink the other eye.' There was an impersonation of Albert Chevalier's hit 'Knocked 'Em In The Old Kent Road' and Marie herself sang 'Whacky, Whacky, Whack' dressed in a white frock with a pinafore and sun bonnet. She performed it 'with much kicking up behind and before [and] seemed to give immense satisfaction to the gods, who cheered her to the echo'.[15] With her energetic performance she was probably capitalizing on Lottie Collins's success with 'Ta-ra-ra-boom-de-ay', which had become popular in the halls that autumn. *Dwarf* was particularly impressed by her athleticism: 'Miss Marie Lloyd [is] clever, decidedly clever. If the loftiness of this lady's salary is measured according to the height she kicks she is an expensive luxury. But again I say it, she is clever.'[16]

The pantomime gave Marie a chance to forget that she was a wife and mother. Gus's lavish budget allowed her to wear the sorts of sumptuous outfits she revelled in and she was surrounded by people with whom she chose to spend her free time anyway. Pantomime was less physically demanding than music hall because she did not have to rush around London.

Compton Mackenzie, author of *Whisky Galore*, remembered Marie's antics vividly. His old nurse took him and his brother and sister to see *Humpty Dumpty*. They sat in a box on the prompt side of the stage.

Marie Lloyd was doing the high kicks which punctuated the singing of the chorus with glorious verve and revealing a great display of amber silk petticoats and long amber silk drawers frilled below her knees.

I turned to Harry Paine [the pantomime's clown who was in the box with them] in surprise and said, 'She's showing her drawers!'

From the surprised ejaculation of mine do not suppose I was shocked. If I had been shocked I should have said nothing and surrendered to a puritan's private enjoyment of the display while pretending to be shocked. No, I was not shocked, but I *was* greatly surprised that any girl should have the courage to let the world see her drawers as definitely as Marie Lloyd.

Harry Paine laughed so loudly that Marie Lloyd heard him and with a wink turned towards the stage-box and gave a terrific high kick almost into it.[17]

After the show Harry took the children backstage to meet Marie, who was already dressed to leave the theatre, 'trim and tight-laced, bustled and bonneted'. Harry introduced Compton as 'the young gentleman who was shocked by seeing your drawers, Marie'. The Principal Girl took in his awkwardness and gave him a kiss and a hug – a strange way, perhaps, to ease a young boy's embarrassment.

Ernest Shepard, illustrator of the *Winnie the Pooh* books, was also taken to Marie's first Drury Lane pantomime. The family had been lent a box at short notice and he and his brother Cyril were plucked from school to attend the matinée. Their excitement was such that, for once, they did not mind putting on their best velvet suits. The fog was so bad that boys with flaring torches guided people along the streets and traffic crawled along at walking pace. Outside the theatre, Drury Lane was packed with cabs and carriages, the horses' coats steaming in the damp weather. When they were finally ensconced in their box Cyril gave way to his nerves and was sick, but even this did not distract Ernest from the stage: 'I remember a gay young woman with prominent teeth and a flaxen wig who sang and danced bewitchingly. She could only have been Marie Lloyd, the unforgettable, aged seventeen and in her first Pantomime at "the Lane".'[18] He was also impressed by the Principal Boy. 'Ample-bosomed, small-waisted and with thighs – oh, such thighs! – thighs that shone and glittered in the different-coloured silk tights in which she continually appeared. How she strode about the stage, proud and dominant, smacking those rounded limbs with a riding crop! At every smack, a fresh dart was shot into the heart of at least one young adorer.'

Pantomime opened the eyes of a new generation to the addictive jollity of music-hall songs. For Marie, her first Drury Lane pantomime was a lark; she enjoyed working with Little Tich, Dan, Herbert and George, and her central role in the pantomime's big spectacles just about offset the trial of playing second fiddle to a band of dancers dressed as dolls.

Chapter 5

CELEBRITY STATUS

(1891–2)

~≈

And when the darling looks at him in a very Frenchy way,
You can bet a monarch's ransom
That the fellow calls, 'A hansom!'
Well, actions speak louder than words, so they say.
'Actions Speak Louder Than Words' by George le Brunn and Harry Leighton

In many ways, 1891, which culminated in her pantomime success, was the year in which Marie 'made it'. She had a string of hit songs, and was seen as a star draw at West End halls such as the Alhambra. When she appeared at the Oxford in June 1891 the audience clamoured so long and hard for her return that the following act could not be heard. By September she was described as 'the favourite of the hour'.[1]

The songs with which she bombarded her public painted her as someone apart from the moral strictures that confined the rest of the population. 'That Was Before My Time (A Long While Ago)', by T. W. Connor and Ernest Symons, stressed how far removed Marie's lifestyle was from 'the goody-good days of the past' when:

> For girls to wear dresses their figures to show
> Was reckoned an awful crime.
> They went to tea meetings along with their Ma's [*sic*]
> And filled up their time darning socks for their Pa's [*sic*] . . .

'Madame Duvan', by Joe Tabrar and Tom Costello, poked fun at actresses with social pretensions and 'Don't Laugh' (George le Brunn and Richard Morton) took a gentle swipe at the curate with a crush. Like other music-hall performers, she made much of the fads of the moment as in 'Mischief', by Thomas and George le Brunn, which the sheet music described as an 'invitation negro song and dance' and which is written in the 'coon' style of the time. The (excruciating) lyrics tell the story of a mischievous girl who causes trouble through pranks such as stealing peaches and does not care who knows it.

> Isn't it funny, when you see a gal
> Up to mischief all the blessed day?
> Old Nigs holloa, whack her, too, as well,
> When her games on dem she starts to play
> When a piccaninny – wid not hair –
> Aunti Cloa to wash her would not dare,
> For she'd kick de water off de chair –
> Hold me! for I use gwine to laugh!

'Actions Speak Louder Than Words', by George le Brunn and Harry Leighton, was a rollicking number that tackled honeymoons, one of Marie's favourite themes, 'Lovebirds honeymooning, hang the price!', and a French girl in London. France was glamorous and sexually enticing and anyone 'abroad' might find themselves in a situation where anything could happen:

> And when the darling looks at him in a very Frenchy way,
> You can bet a monarch's ransom
> That the fellow calls, 'A hansom!'
> Well, actions speak louder than words, so they say.

George claimed he regularly churned out thirty melodies a week for Marie and his other customers, freely admitting that he rarely spent more than three or four minutes on each composition, 'dotting down the melody in the first place on a little slip of paper, and subsequently rectifying the notes, if necessary with the aid of a piano'.[2] Of these, he said, no more than half were ever heard of again. Of his performing customers, George commented, 'Although very few music-hall artists have any real musical knowledge, and generally learn their melodies parrot-fashion, they are remarkably quick at acquiring a tune.' He added that Marie was particularly adept at this: she could learn the words and music of a song and sing it within an hour and a half.

Now that she had an astute agent and a prolific songwriter she was equipped to enter the game of tag that top-flight music-hall performers played with each other's work. Artists were always on the look-out for a song or theme that became suddenly popular and, while they could not steal a song wholesale, they could take an element — the tune, character or theme — and mould it to suit their own performance style. Thus a popular song could go through several evolutions until it had burned itself out. Usually the original artist was quite happy for this to happen: it was seen as a compliment and it helped to keep their own song in the public eye.

Marie's song ''Arriet's Reply', by Joseph Tabrar, was one of these ricocheting songs. It was a response to Jenny Hill's ''Arriet's Answer', which in turn parodied Albert Chevalier's hugely popular 'Coster's Serenade'. Albert was a former character actor who made a good living from singing coster songs, such as 'Knocked 'Em In The Old Kent Road' and the poignant 'My Old Dutch' about a couple forced to live apart after forty years together when they enter a workhouse where the sexes are segregated. Albert's portrayal of the cheerful, good-hearted Cockney evolved into a caricature that has left traces in characters like Dick Van Dyke's chimney sweep in *Mary Poppins*. His version of East End life was reassuringly safe: he took it to afternoon concerts and gave recitals at fashionable drawing rooms.

The 'Arriet Marie portrayed is a Cockney girl seduced away from her childhood sweetheart, 'Arry, by a 'pearly toff' — a 'bit of stuff in blue'. The two East End lovers are eventually reunited by a 'flag of truce' in the shape of a 'Sunday "stuke"', which, one newspaper explained to its readers, 'we believe is Whitechapel for a small necker-chief'. The story was a cautionary tale of the dangers that befall anyone who trespasses outside their immediate social milieu, but appealed to the women in the audience as a straightforward romance.

Marie took her strong repertoire of songs on tour in the summer of 1891 to the Grand Theatre of Varieties, Liverpool, the Empire, New-castle, the Cardiff Empire, the Palace Theatre of Varieties, Manchester, and the Gaiety, Birmingham. At Manchester she was so popular that she abandoned a trip to Paris to stay on an extra six nights; she also awakened the city to the possibility of a new breed of woman for, as one newspaper noted, 'Miss Lloyd possesses that excellent but uncommon thing in a woman, a sense of humour, and as she is a past mistress of winking and waggling, her songs obtain an added piquancy which is very refreshing after the dead level of dullness reached by the ordinary music-hall comedienne.'[3]

Her elevation to the top rank of the music-hall establishment also meant that she became more involved in high-profile charity events: singing at a Music Hall Benevolent Fund event in January and appearing in a ladies' charity cricket match in Dulwich with other stars, who included Jenny Hill. Philanthropy was important to music-hall artists because it gave them status in an age when charity was seen as a cornerstone of society, and also because those at the top knew how precarious the profession could be. Marie's charity appearances were an acknowledgement that she had been accepted by the other music-hall stars and set her apart from the lower echelons of the profession.

Her growing success qualified her for a 'complimentary matinée' one Monday afternoon at the Oxford early in November 1891. Benefit performances represented another strand of the music-hall mutual-support system in which stars turned out for each other or at least lent their name to an event. In Marie's case the matinée turned into a family affair. She started the afternoon's entertainment by singing ''Arriet's Reply', in a blue costergirl's dress and feathered hat. Then, apparently ignoring demands for an encore, she left the stage. She returned with Alice, Grace and fourteen-year-old Daisy in the Sisters Lloyd. They performed a dance arranged by Marie with music by Joe Tabrar. Wearing Kate-Greenaway-style emerald dresses, the sisters each sang a solo, and finished kneeling with their dresses over their heads in the can-can fashion of the day.

Marie was deluged with flowers from the audience but when asked to make a speech the natural fluency ever-present in her singing escaped her and she was unable to string a sentence together. She introduced George Ware, and said that he had raised her weekly wages from thirty shillings (£77 today) to £30 (£1,541). George begged to differ, saying it was nearer £75 and would go even higher. Then she lifted up her three-year-old daughter to show to the audience. The toddler, who had started life as Myria, had become subsumed by her mother's personality and was now known as Marie. One hundred and twenty acts were due to appear that afternoon in Marie's honour, including Albert Chevalier and Dan Leno, but there was time for only a third of them.

The event had all the ingredients designed to make Marie feel she had truly 'arrived'. Her peers turned out to acknowledge her success, and her own position was magnified by the growing popularity of her sisters. She had a baby she could show off and her agent had boasted of her financial pulling power. Marie had everything a woman could want and much more than most could expect. The only thing missing was her husband.

Percy did not enjoy his wife's success. Music hall's anti-social hours made it difficult to sustain relationships and the most successful marriages were those in which both partners were performers or where a whole family was involved in a single act, which meant they could share its success and failure and maximize their time together. Percy did not understand the music-hall world and resented that Marie was solely responsible for their comfortable standard of living, which had allowed them to escape from the East End. They had moved from Graham Road to 54 Lewisham Road, New Cross, with four uniformed maids and a St Bernard dog called Bob. The house was on a hill and afforded views of South London; it had a large garden and stables for Marie's carriage and horses. But even in this grand residence Percy was unable to escape the source of their new-found wealth: one of the reasons Marie had chosen the area was that its close proximity to several halls in south London, combined with its gentrified air, had made it a ghetto for music-hall performers.

The whole Wood family had moved in with Marie and Percy and the house was run like an informal hotel, not just for Marie's relatives but for anyone else who needed a bed for the night. Unable to communicate with Percy, Marie increasingly sought solace with her sisters and other female friends. She became particularly close to a teenager called Bella Orchard, a gawky young singer whom Alice and Grace befriended when all three were in panto at the Pavilion in Whitechapel Road, Stepney. One evening they asked Bella, whose stage name was Ella Lane, to come home to meet Marie. They hit it off instantly: Marie liked Bella's sense of humour and her no-nonsense approach to life, and suggested she move in with them. As Bella was later proud to say, she came for tea and stayed ten years.

Although Bella had come second in a beauty contest at the Whitechapel Theatre she was not conventionally pretty. She appears in photos as rather awkward and long-limbed; her nose is a little too large, her eyes a little too small, and she has the confused air of someone who has temporarily mislaid their glasses. Alice's daughter, Tomme, remembered her affectionately as you might an eccentric aunt whose name always raises a laugh – although no one is ever sure why.

Bella Orchard had been born Leah Belle Orchard in New York and was seven years younger than Marie. Her father, a solicitor, had emigrated with his wife and five children to America where he had two brothers. Bella's mother returned to England after the death of her husband with five-year-old Bella and a second daughter, leaving her two boys with relatives, a third daughter having died aged three. Her mother remarried when Bella was ten and the couple set up as Venetian-blind makers in Leytonstone, east London.

Bella slid easily into the chaotic Lloyd household; she shared the family's East End roots and their nomadic lifestyle. Since Bella knew the business of music hall, the importance of costume and quick change, and because she understood Marie's moods, it made sense for her to become Marie's dresser. She was widely referred to as Bella Lloyd and as late as 1922 Alice described her as 'my sister Bella'. Bella enjoyed being part of the family, and during the night she often found herself rolled over in her bed to make room for a stranded female performer Marie had brought home with her. Sometimes it was even Marie, tired of waiting for Percy to appear, who crept into Bella's bed.

This cosy nest of women did not suit Percy and a fortnight after the start of *Humpty Dumpty*, on 14 January 1892, his resentment spilled over into a bout of public violence. He and Marie had gone to a masked ball[4] at Covent Garden Theatre with Marie's parents and Alice. It was a theatrical party that sounds, in retrospect, like a publicity event for a Lewis Carroll fantasy. One guest, for example, went as 'Tea-time': his mask consisted of a clock face, tea cosy, spout and strainer, his torso was covered in a willow pattern, his legs were sugar tongs and he carried a French loaf under one arm.

It was the early hours of the morning before Marie decided it might be time to leave, but rather than make the trek back to New Cross, and with the logic born of excessive drinking, Marie felt that now was the time to take her mother to see Alice's sweetheart in his rooms – even though he would be asleep. The women would go ahead and they left Covent Garden in two cabs. However, Brushie felt it improper for his wife to go unchaperoned to a young man's rooms. Percy, stung by his father-in-law's assertion of authority, protested that Marie should not go unaccompanied either. An ugly slanging match spluttered into life and eventually Marie and Alice were left sitting on a doorstep in Drury Lane listening to Percy haranguing them.

Marie decided to ignore him and went back into the deserted theatre to rest in her dressing room on a couch. Percy followed her inside, swearing and accusing her of being a slut. He reached for a sword hanging on a wall and, according to *The Times*,[5] threatened to 'cut her throat and serve her as Pollie Newberry was served' in a reference to an artist recently butchered by her husband. Marie tried to get away from him but he kicked the back of her leg and the small of her back. By now it was seven o'clock in the morning and Marie dragged herself, sore and drunk, round the corner to Bow Street police station. After that episode she went to a hotel with Alice.

The full story emerged when Percy appeared in court to answer the charge of assault. His counsel tried to suggest that Percy had been provoked. Under cross-examination, Marie defended herself against this but gave the impression she had tried to stand up to him. *The Times* reported: 'She did not say anything offensive to him, nor smack his face. His hat fell off as they went through the stage door, but she was sure that she did not knock it off. The door swung to as she went through it.' It is probably true that Marie, who enjoyed a slanging match, did her best to defend herself.

The court's presiding officer, Mr Lushington, noted that Marie had been well enough to appear at both the afternoon and evening panto-mimes. He also seemed to think that Marie had provoked Percy in knocking off his hat, but conceded that this would not 'justify the defendant in acting as he had done'. Percy was bound over in the sum of £25 to keep the peace towards his wife for six months.

The whole sordid tale was reported in *The Times*,[5] including humili-ating details such as the fact that Marie provided her husband with an allowance of three pounds a week and that he was in the habit of forwarding his accounts to her for settlement. Her public, who watched her as Princess Allfair enact a fairy-tale existence, read of the nightmare that was her private life. The incident brought a subtle shift in her persona: she was still a good-time girl, but she also had her own, private monsters to grapple with.

Chapter 6

TWIGGY VOO, MY BOYS?

(1 8 9 1 – 2)

_~ᵗ_

Twiggy voo, my boys? Twiggy voo?
Well, of course, it stands to reason that you do;
All the force and meaning in it you can 'tumble' in a minute,
Twiggy voo, my boys? Twiggy voo?
'Twiggy Voo' by George le Brunn and Richard Morton

Marie's unhappy home life might have remained little more than a lurid court case read about by a small percentage of music-hall goers – except that she and her songs had become public property. Technological advances, such as the railways and safer theatres, which became less susceptible to fires as electric lighting replaced gas, aisles were widened, and fireproofed scenery was introduced, enabled her to build a following that reached far beyond her class and also transformed her into an entertainer with a much higher profile than her predecessors. At the very top of this list of technical advances was something that today is taken for granted: the piano.

In Marie's day music was all-pervasive. In the street could be found the German band, the barrel-organ and the hurdy-gurdy; most parks had a bandstand, while towns and cities were dotted with concert and music halls. However, the piano took music into the home on a scale never seen before. This was only possible because improved metallurgical skills meant that pianos could be made smaller and more robust, so that they fitted into modest homes. Their reduced size also meant that they did not require as much wood, which was expensive, and they were no longer made exclusively by craftsmen. Increased competition, especially from Germany, helped push down the price. In 1851 they were still a luxury item,[1] and an upright piano cost between fifty and a hundred guineas – equivalent to the annual income of a clerk or schoolteacher. By 1900, though, output had jumped ten-fold and pianos were priced at the much more affordable equivalent of three months' income for a clerk or teacher. As Marie's career took off the piano was becoming a must-have item and by the 1880s some piano-makers offered a monthly payment plan. In the early twentieth century one Englishman in every 360 bought a new piano every year – three times more than in 1851 and a figure only exceeded in the USA, where it was one in every 260.[2]

Pianos carried social cachet. Queen Victoria bought a Steinway for Balmoral, and the New York manufacturers made sure the world knew about it. London makers John Brinsmead also advertised their royal endorsement, describing themselves as 'pianoforte makers to HRH the Princess of Wales'. As the total number of pianos in circulation expanded so the second-hand market developed and ownership cascaded down the social ranks. For Charles Pooter, the socially aspiring clerk and hero of *The Diary of a Nobody*, first published in 1892, the cottage piano purchased on the 'three years' system' and 'manufactured by W. Bilkson (in small letters), from Collard and Collard (in very large letters)' put the final touch to his domestic bliss. In an article in *Lloyds Sunday News* Alice remembered that as soon as Marie started to earn a decent living one of the first things she did to flag her family's new social status was to buy a piano. 'She made Mother give up home work, she bought a piano on the hire system, and she bought new furniture.'

But piano music meant much more than new-found entertainment to fill the Saturday half-holiday that became widely observed in the 1870s. As with most things Victorian, it carried a moral imperative too. In 1886 the Reverend Hugh Reginald Haweis, MA, gave a lecture before a crowded audience at the London Institution on 'The Anatomy of Musical Notes' using a gong, small bell, penny whistle, tuning fork, piano and violin. 'Music,' he said, 'is the great art of the present age . . . By dissecting the notes of music they would find that music was related to and affected the senses; the senses were related to the emotions, and the emotions to conduct and conduct being related to morals, morals must be related to music.'[3]

Music, it was thought, should be a civilizing influence and as such should be taught in the newly emerging school system. The fiendishly difficult tonic sol-fa system, which used the liturgy of doh, ray, me, fah, etc., of learning to sing by sight, without the *aide-mémoire* of a Hollywood ditty, was designed to help the ill-educated appreciate music. Playing the piano was a required accomplishment for the middle-class young lady, but music was a peculiar mixture of pleasure and endurance. In 1886 crowds gathered to watch a piano teacher in Stockport play for twenty-five hours without a break, beating the previous – Indian – record-holder who used one hand to eat with during the feat. The triumphant teacher, a Mr N. Bird, sucked only ice for refreshment. The piano symbolized endurance and application – as strongman Sandow demonstrated in his act when he carried a pyramid of pianist, piano and piano stool off-stage.

The exalted position of the piano prompted much debate in the mid-1880s and early 1890s over whether or not music-hall songs were unworthy of the new instrument and ought to be more edifying. George Bernard Shaw, who visited the Empire in 1892 to keep himself up to date with the latest trend in entertainment as more theatres went over to variety, was critical of Marie's latest hit, 'Twiggy Voo?' by Richard Morton and George le Brunn. The song combined a suggestiveness, reinforced by the French flavour of the title, with a conspiratorial tone that is at its most blatant in the chorus:

> *Twiggy voo, my boys? Twiggy voo?*
> Well of course, it stands to reason that you do;
> All the force and meaning in it you can 'tumble' in a minute,
> Twiggy voo, my boys? Twiggy voo?

The verses home in on common music-hall scenes of embarrassment: the sudden arrival of a baby, a furtive visit to 'Uncle's famous shop' – the pawnbroker's, a woman out of control on the top of a windy London bus with her 'gamp' or umbrella (from Sarah Gamp, the umbrella-toting nurse in *Martin Chuzzlewit*), an impending honeymoon and an illicitly spooning couple.

> Now a lover and his lass
> Were exchanging spoony gas,
> And I thought they'd keep it up till all was blue;
> For I heard him, plain and clear,

Say, 'Sit closer to me, dear' –
Twiggy voo, my boys? Twiggy voo?
Then I heard a kick and bark,
And a scuffle in the dark,
And the father gave the girl a welting, too;
'I'll teach you to play at shops!'
And the bulldog licked his chops –
Twiggy voo, my boys, twiggy voo?

While Shaw acknowledged that probably half the audience had come specifically to hear Marie sing this one song, he believed it unworthy of her:

> Miss Marie Lloyd, like all the brightest stars of the music hall, has an exceptionally quick ear for both pitch and rhythm. Her intonation and lilt of her songs are alike perfect. Her step-dancing is pretty; and her command of coster-girls' patois is complete. Why, then, does not someone write humorous songs for her? 'Twiggy Voo' is low and silly; and 'Oh, Mister Porter', though very funnily sung, is not itself particularly funny. A humorous rhymester of any genius could easily make it so.
>
> I am greatly afraid that the critics persisted so long in treating the successes of music-hall vocalism as mere impudent exploitations of vulgarity and indecency (forgetting that if this were more than half-true managers could find a dozen Bessie Bellwoods and Marie Lloyds in every street) that the artists have come to exaggerate the popularity of the indecent element in their songs, and to underrate that of the artistic element in their singing. If music-hall songs were written by Messrs. Anstey, Rudyard Kipling, W. S. Gilbert, etc., our best music-hall singers would probably be much more widely popular than they can ever become now. Twiggez-vous, Miss Lloyd?[4]

But 'Twiggy Voo' was wildly popular. At the Trocadero it was impossible for the eighteen-year-old Princess Pauline, who was eighteen inches tall and weighed seven pounds, to appear after Marie because the audience was clamouring for her song and would only settle down when she reappeared to explain that she had to be at another hall.

Shaw does not comment on Marie's other success of 1892, 'G'arn

Away' by E. W. Rogers, but if he thought 'Twiggy Voo' 'low' he would have been unimpressed by this song about a Cockney girl whom various men try to dupe. Verse two is typical of its style:

> Once a chap walk'd me out as was considered quite a nob,
> Whiskers on his face so werry fierce and black;
> Well, he kidded me to lend 'im 'arf a dollar, Whitsun week,
> And I 'ad to punch 'is 'ed to git it back.
> Then 'e got a month in quad and said as 'ow 'e 'ad been ill!
> I says, 'Who cut all yer 'air orff?
> Why you've been up on the mill! [treadmill, prison]
> Do yer think I'd have a "tea-leaf", [thief]
> You must take me for a fool,
> What say? Doctor cut your 'air orff just to keep yer noddle cool!'

Songs like 'Twiggy Voo' prompted a surge in demand for sheet music of all kinds, partly fuelled by the piano-buying boom. Technology was refining this aspect of the music industry, too: although songs and ballads had been printed for sale in England since the fourteenth century, the invention of lithography and a sudden interest in typography gave sheet music a sort of comic-book appeal. Covers outlined the story of each verse of a music-hall song in detailed vignettes that encircled a drawing or, later, photo of the performer. The cover of 'Buy Me Some Almond Rock', written and composed by Joseph Tabrar, has a cameo picture framed in a pink heart of a winsome young Marie Lloyd with long golden locks, blue eyes and an elaborate white-flowered hat. She is surrounded by an unlikely set of suitors, who each appear in the lyrics. An austere Gladstone, instantly recognizable in his oversized collar and frock coat, kneels to declaim with an outstretched arm, 'Say you'll be mine and I'll renounce everything – even my Home Rule Bill.' A caption, dripping with irony, reads: 'The GOM [Grand Old Man] gets excited.' The two other scenes show Marie having 'A nice cup of tea with "Labby"', the radical politician Henry Labouchere, and a boy dressed in top hat and tails, 'Randy Pandy [the sexually wayward Randolph Churchill] waits on me with Sugar-de-Candy'.

Certain illustrators became associated with different music publishers and helped to reinforce a performer's image in much the same way as record-album and compact-disc covers do today. A popular song, helped by piracy, could sell as many as eighty thousand sheets and 'The Lost Chord' sold half a million copies between 1877 and 1902.[5] Sheet music took music hall into households that had not experienced it at first hand.

Newspapers were also helping to make music hall and its stars a part of everyday life, rather than just something to think about on a night out. The popular press, which emerged in the 1880s and 1890s, began to pay music hall more attention. Cheaper paper and the abolition of stamp duty made newspapers more affordable, while improved printing presses, faster communication through the railways and greater literacy provided a wider audience. The illiterate were read to or could grasp the talking-points of the day through cartoons and line drawings. In January 1898 the *News of the World* started to publish the words and music of a music-hall song every week.[6] A piano was installed in the paper's offices near Fleet Street and performers like Marie or George Robey dropped by to try out their new songs. Robert Berry, a newshound with a particular nose for what would now be called celebrity stories, toured London music halls on the look-out for promising new singers.

As the cult of the personality grew, music-hall performers were anxious to protect their image from contamination through cheap imitation. There are countless cases of audiences being duped into believing that they were about to see the real thing. Dan Leno, in particular, suffered from this and perhaps the most audacious example was a man billing himself 'Don Leno' in a bid to confuse the less vigilant theatregoer. On another occasion, in late 1900, 1,400 people turned up expecting to see Dan Leno to discover they had fallen for a hoax.

Marie became increasingly bitter about lesser performers whom, she claimed, were stealing her material and making capital from her success. She could not resist the chance to take a swipe at them in advertisements and interviews: 'PS: Warning to proprietors & C. I have been informed that a man is going about representing himself as my Secretary and Manager. The person is nothing whatever to do with me, or have I ever heard of him'; 'Another song for you all to copy'; or 'An artiste of originality creates, an artiste without talent imitates.'[7] Her concern stemmed from more than arrogance. She was now in her early twenties and the blind optimism of her teenage years was gradually being replaced by a niggling insecurity as she realized how fickle the music-hall world was. While she had remained in relative obscurity she had everything to go for and nothing to lose; but once she turned the corner into fame she became aware of just how easy it was to miss her footing. And, because of her unhappy marriage, she knew that tomorrow had to be taken care of, after all.

George Foster recalls an incident concerning Marie's appearance on the Isle of Man, probably in June 1892, that perfectly illustrates her sensitivity about her status. They met at Douglas pier and hailed a cab to take them to Derby Castle, where rehearsals were due to start. As a precaution the cab driver pointed out that the fare was likely to be steep. George recalls that Marie 'turned on him like a tigress' at the implication that she might not have the means to pay him. She hailed another cab and ordered him to drive her to the theatre; she then told him to wait while she and George drank champagne inside. The trip backwards and forwards, including the refreshment stop, was repeated four or five times.

Marie visited the Isle of Man during her second provincial tour. These long, out-of-town excursions – usually in the summer months when London was hot and the theatregoing public turned to outdoor pursuits – began to punctuate her annual routine. In the summer of 1892 Marie visited, in chronological order: the Isle of Man; the Empire, Swansea; the Gaiety, Birmingham; the Palace Theatre of Varieties, Manchester; the Empire, Cardiff; the Gaiety, Glasgow, and the Alhambra, Brighton. In April she had visited the Grand Theatre, Liverpool. She zigzagged around the country in an exhausting itinerary that defied geographical logic, consolidating the impact of the previous year's tour and incorporating new venues. She scored a notable hit at Glasgow, which was viewed as a difficult venue: 'Miss Marie Lloyd with her very "taking" songs, "fetching" style, and ravishing "frocks" is certainly "knocking" them in the little Sauchiehall Street house, which is crowded every evening.'[8]

Trains made touring possible, but it was the growth of newly industrialized centres, such as Birmingham, Glasgow, Cardiff and Manchester, that made it worthwhile. Long, tedious Sunday rail journeys, accompanied by theatrical props, small animals and carefully packed costumes, became a regular feature of a performer's lifestyle. The tedium was eased by the chance to catch up on gossip, discuss routines and try out songs with other artists and musicians while waiting to make rail connections, which were notoriously poor on Sundays. Trains took Marie through countryside that no one in her family had ever seen before and opened her mind to different ways of living, which is perhaps why she was rarely judgemental of others. According to one estimate, by 1900 there were 142 special trains every Sunday in England and Wales transporting touring companies of actors and musicians.[9] Gatherings of theatricals on railway platforms became a spectacle in themselves and star-spotting by locals was a sport. Star performers had their own reserved carriage – a printed label on the window continuing the billing system even while they were in transit.

Railways featured in several of Marie's songs. They represented adventure and escape, their carriages fraught with the possibility of romance, especially when a tunnel threatened to plunge passengers into darkness. In 1892 'Oh! Mr Porter', by George and Thomas le Brunn, was hugely successful: ostensibly the song is about an *ingénue* who visits her aunt in London but arrives late for the train and, in her confusion, boards the wrong one.

> Oh! Mr Porter, what shall I do?
> I want to go to Birmingham and they're taking me on to Crewe,
> Send me back to London as quickly as you can,
> Oh! Mr Porter, what a silly girl I am.

An elderly gentleman urges her to have the guard stop the train but in attempting to do so she nearly falls out of the window and is only saved when the old man pulls her in by the leg. In the third and final verse, it is not clear who is taking advantage of whom:

> On his clean old shirt front then I laid my trembling head,
> 'Do take it easy, rest awhile,' the dear old chappie said.
> 'If you make a fuss of me and on me do not frown,
> You shall have my mansion, dear, away in London Town.'
> Wouldn't you think me silly if I said I could not like him?
> Really he seemed a nice old boy, so I replied this way:
> 'I will be your own for life your imay doodleum little wife.
> If you'll never tease me any more, I say.'

The song is one of Marie's most famous numbers, and to sing it she wore a long, Empress-style dress, with puffed sleeves, and a floppy Wee-Willie-Winkie hat perched on a mass of tight curls.

Touring also became more viable as music-hall groups emerged, run by powerful businessmen – most notably Oswald Stoll, Richard Thornton and Edward Moss – around the country and in the suburbs of London.[10] They raised money through the stock-market as the financial press promoted theatres as a good investment. The Australian-born Oswald Stoll started at the Liverpool Parthenon where, aged fourteen, he helped his widowed mother to run the business. He moved to Cardiff, at that time the centre of the world coal industry, and expanded into Wales then took on the Midlands. At Cardiff he introduced the two-houses-a-night system and, spurred on by his experience of rowdy audiences, determined to make music hall more genteel.

But well-bred customers wanted clean air as much as clean acts and they finally got it – as well as comfortable seats, excellent sightlines and gaudy, exotic decorations – from architect Frank Matcham, or 'matchless, magnificent Matcham', as he was called. His name became a byword for comfort and safety and was used in the slogan to advertise theatres, 'You can't match Matcham.' He combined practicality with sumptuous design, but his greatest achievement was the invention of the 'sunburner' in the roof, which caused hot air to rise and thus improved the ventilation. The Paragon Music Hall in Mile End, where Matcham perfected this system in 1885, advertised itself as 'the best ventilated theatre in London'. This was no idle boast since, only a year before, a report had declared that air taken from a theatre was fouler than that found in a sewer. Some larger music halls, such as the Pavilion, had sliding roofs, which they opened when the atmosphere became too much to bear. The increasing use of electric lighting in the late 1880s and 1890s made theatres pleasanter to visit and lessened the threat of fire – especially welcome after the tragic blaze in 1887 at the Theatre Royal in Exeter in which an estimated 186 died.

In 1892 Moss commissioned Matcham to build the Edinburgh Empire and in 1895 Stoll asked him to work on the Cardiff Empire. Most big towns outside London eventually had an example of his extravagant gilt work and sweeping rows of cantilevered seats. Matcham's theatres were luxurious pleasure domes decorated in a riot of styles: from Oriental to military, to baroque and Louis XIV. Although a quiet-mannered man, Matcham himself became a celebrity. He was one of the first to own a Daimler Benz, and *Vanity Fair* and the *London Entr'acte* both honoured him with cartoons.

By now the chairman was disappearing: instead an artist's number would appear on the proscenium arch or on an easel so that the audience could consult their programme to see who was about to perform. The disappearance of the chairman, combined with fixed seats and growing opulence in music halls, meant that there was little difference between the atmosphere of the venues Marie routinely played and her second Drury Lane pantomime. Officially called *Little Bo-Peep, Little Red Riding Hood, and Hop O' My Thumb*, it strayed even further from the traditional format. The show was five hours long and the harlequinade did not appear until the end, which meant that anyone who had to catch a train to their suburban home missed it.

Gus again delivered the sort of spectacle that had come to be associated with his name. Critics who carped at the music-hall content marvelled at the Watteau ballet of shepherds and shepherdesses, like scenes from Dresden china brought to life, the hall of mirrors that reflected the dancers' every movement giving the impression of a huge room of swirling ballerinas. The procession of thirty-nine nursery rhymes and the woodland scenes in which fairies cavorted with electrically lit stars in their hair also brought gasps of delight. Some of the subtlety of the sporting parade was lost on the Cockneys in the audience, who were dumbfounded by the lacrosse and polo representatives and confidently confused a punting pole with a golf club.

The three interweaving fairytales were criticized for being 'muddled and mutilated',[11] but Gus used the contrived plot to introduce as many music-hall performers in star roles as possible. The glamour element was provided by Marie Loftus as Little Bo-Peep, Ada Blanche as Little Boy Blue and Marie as Little Red Riding Hood. Dan Leno played the woodman Daddy Thumb next to Herbert Campbell as his wife, Goody Thumb. Their seven children included Hop O'My Thumb (Little Tich), whom Goody Thumb bathed and put to bed, when he discarded his feeding bottle for a brandy and soda.

Gus's script, co-written by Wilton Jones, was designed to put music-hall stars in comic situations – Leno and Campbell pragmatically discussed their predicament as they were strung up for roasting before a great fire — but also offered them the chance to do a 'turn'. Dan Leno delivered a monologue in the character of a mob orator eventually smothered by a pile of refuse thrown by the crowd he is addressing; Little Tich produced a comic version of the popular 'skirt dance' in which he tried to use the voluminous folds of his frock to weave an elegant Terpsichorean display in a way that only a genuinely nimble performer could carry off.

Marie was praised for her 'quaint fun' and the *Stage* enjoyed her singing and dancing. But she was becoming uncomfortable with a dramatic form that demanded a mixture of acting skills and the ability to perform side by side with other music-hall stars, each of whom was vying for attention. Her elevated status meant she no longer enjoyed appearing in a show in which she lacked absolute power over her own performance and the long waits backstage bored her. However, she had the satisfaction of hearing 'Oh! Mr Porter' played throughout the pantomime. It was also incorporated into the opening orchestral arrangement, alongside music-hall hits such as 'The Man Who Broke The Bank' and 'The Rowdy Dowdy Boys'. The gods joined in the medley with gusto — only to be wrong-footed by the orchestra, which moved determinedly on to the next song after a few bars, while the audience persisted to the end of the chorus they were singing.

This was all too much for some of the more serious publications. The *Athenaeum* denounced Gus as a pantomime villain out to rob children of their innocence:

By the all but exclusive employment of music-hall 'artistes' the action gains in spirit, but loses in delicacy and charm. Pretence to poetry or grace of sentiment is no longer made. What is worse, the stories in which childhood delighted are vulgarized. To see Little Red Riding Hood or Little Bo-peep presented by a young lady with the pronounced style of the music-hall, to hear her talk of nothing but kissing and hugging, and to watch Little Boy Blue tipping a knowing wink to his sweetheart for the time being, is nothing short of desecration. Oh, Sir Augustus! most lavish of caterers, most skilful of organizers, most inspired of managers, leave our children their fairy tales. Though our maids and matrons may confine their studies to the society papers;

though, to the quintessential delight of elderly admirers, they dance skirt dances in our drawing-rooms; though they dine and sup in public, and find the music-hall better fun than the theatre, leave us the nursery and the cradle ... For your admirable ogres, for your comic woodcutters, for your superb ballets, we are thankful, but your little shepherdesses of the music-hall, with their vulgar fancies and style, have nothing to do with pantomime nor with childhood![12]

Max Beerbohm, though, like most of the audience, was captivated by Little Red Riding Hood. Writing to Reggie Turner in January 1893 he commented wistfully: 'Isn't Marie Lloyd charming and sweet in the pantomime? I think of little besides her – except Marie Loftus and you and so forth.'[13]

Chapter 7

MAID OF LONDON

(1 8 9 3 – 6)

~⁊

Maid of London, ere we part, ere we part!
Give, oh, give me back my heart, back my heart!
Since thou has gone from my breast, from my breast,
Keep the stick with a silver knob,
Given by a certain snob, give me back my thing-a-my-bob,
and you can keep the rest!
'Maid Of London' by Joe Tabrar, George le Brunn and J. P. Harrington

Judging from Marie's photograph in the society magazine, the *Sketch*,[1]
Max Beerbohm's breathless adoration is understandable. For a rare
moment in her life, her features appear in balanced harmony. Her face
is full and sensual, but not overblown as it became in later years. She
looks confident and assured, the jaunty plumed hat fitting her character
perfectly rather than seeming to try to disguise something.

Eighteen ninety-three was a year of workmanlike consolidation for
Marie. Having finished her pantomime season she played the major
London halls in the first half of the year: the Bedford, the Oxford, the
Royal Cambridge, the Empire, Leicester Square, the Royal Canterbury
and the Paragon. Vesta Victoria, a cheeky comic singer from Leeds,
was causing a sensation in London and New York with 'Daddy
Wouldn't Buy Me A Bow-Wow' by Joseph Tabrar. Marie, whose songs
that year included 'Keep Off The Grass', 'Silly Fool', 'The Same Thing'
and 'The Naughty Continong', was searching for a new hit. 'The
Naughty Continong' describes the wanton behaviour of the French, as
characterized by the can-can, and demonstrated in various settings, such
as by the seaside and at a ball.

A lady friend took me to a ball – *one*, that's all!
Oh! they're terribly warm you know! yes, they're terribly warm, you know,

A lovely sight to see, but the dance you would call
Well a terribly 'leggy' show! Yes, and terribly warm, you know.
For the mamzelles fair, throw their limbs about in a reckless way,
And the young men there get a special seat for the grand display,
At *these* little bits, I could give them fits,
But I give 'em best, when they begin to do the splits.

Marie was now a celebrity whom journalists sought out. She enjoyed
every minute of the attention: a reporter who visited her home for 'A
chat with Marie Lloyd' was unable to take control of the interview and
became irritated by her habit of laughing out loud at his serious
questions. When asked whether she had been lucky with her songs she
replied, 'Well, yes; you may say that I have not made many failures, if
any. But there's a good deal of picking and choosing to be done first.
You can't say to yourself that you want a new song and just buy it. I
suppose I spend more than a hundred pounds a year on songs, and buy
an immense number that I cannot sing. I have quite a large collection of
songs that I shall probably never sing. You may take it that one has to
buy ten songs before one finds a really good one.'[2]
    She discussed music-hall songs and the 'censors', meaning the Licens-
ing Committee, and their ability to find hidden obscenity where none
was intended while overlooking dubious lyrics. She recalled her challenge to a 'certain eminent authority' to sing 'Home Sweet Home',
'provided she received a guarantee that her audience should be as
morally unimpeachable as her songs'. Asked whether her challenge had
been met, she merely winked at the interviewer.
    This cryptic comment is probably the origin of the story that Marie
confounded the Licensing Committee by singing one of her supposedly
filthy songs, such as 'She'd Never Had Her Ticket Punched Before',
with all the demureness she could muster and none of the gestures or
intonations that made it popular. She went on to sing a worthy Victorian
song – 'Home Sweet Home' or 'Come Into The Garden, Maud' –
which she transformed into a raunchy pothouse performance. The story
tries to show that the apparent rudeness of her songs was all in the mind
of the listener, but also revels in the triumph of the humble performer
over authority. The tale, which became a Marie Lloyd legend, reveals

her obvious delight at causing deep embarrassment in those who seek to judge.

There were plenty of cases in which members of the Licensing Committee tied themselves in knots in their attempts to explain why a song was disreputable while avoiding revealing their own minds as anything less than pure or repeating the lyrics in question. If a reformer wanted to criticize the use of a term such as 'Almond Rock' he had two choices: either he could say it was disreputable without explaining why – and, of course, the music-hall managers would feign ignorance – or he could point out that it was rhyming slang for 'cock' and be uncovered as a man with an unhealthy knowledge of obscene terms, and the managers would still appear mystified.

The blatant sexuality that lurked behind Marie's early representation of schoolgirls and younger sisters was becoming more pronounced in the lyrics of her songs and the accompanying winks and knowing glances. But she always veered away from saying anything explicit and stories that suggest the opposite show merely how adept she was at leading on her audience. In his 1972 biography, the late Daniel Farson repeats two such stories. In the first Marie struggled to open a parasol, and when finally successful gasped, 'Thank God, I haven't had it up for months.'[3] In the second, she picked up a banana skin from the stage and said, 'If the man who threw this wants his skin back, he can come to my dressing-room afterwards.'[4] Both stories were told to Farson long after the event and are in sharp contrast to anything that was written, or hinted, about her by contemporaries. The reviewers of the time were unable to describe something so crude, but it is unlikely that it would have gone unnoticed by, say, Max Beerbohm, Arnold Bennett or Bernard Shaw – even if only in a private diary or in correspondence.

Marie relied on subtle innuendo – which was much more subtle than some of the *double-entendres* in Shakespeare. An audience that 'discovered' something rude, rather than having it spelt out to them, was much more likely to enjoy the joke because they felt partly responsible for creating it. As Arnold Bennett said, it was the silence presented to the audience to fill with their own imaginings that was deadly. The laugh was even more satisfying if the customers felt it had been won at the expense of the music-hall manager: the audience was in conspiracy with the joke-teller and anyone else who 'got' the joke. That Marie was rumoured to be saying much more explicit things elsewhere only added to the sense of illicit fun. Another line often attributed to her, and sometimes to Jenny Hill, is, 'She sits among the lettuces and peas', or 'She sits among the cabbages and leeks', but there is no written proof that Marie ever said this. It was far easier to make people laugh by singing 'Give Me Back My Thingamybob', as in 'Maid of London' (1896) – which may or may not have been rude – than with anything more overt. Many of Marie's songs used slang for body parts and sexual acts, and some of her audience would have appreciated it. Others suspected something risqué and laughed, while the rest were carried along by the atmosphere and the sheer silliness of words like 'thingamybob'.

The songs that included Cockney rhyming slang would have been meaningless outside London at a time when the inhabitants of some parts of the country found it difficult to understand an accent other than their own. But Marie adapted her lyrics where necessary, and in the summer of 1893 chose songs with fewer London references for her now customary provincial tour. This year the trip took in The Folly Variety Theatre, Manchester, the Gaiety Concert Hall, Glasgow, Barnard's Theatre of Varieties, Chatham, and the Empire, Portsmouth. Marie was starting to show signs of what became a hallmark of her personality: an almost reckless generosity. She gave her time and her money: in February that year she dressed up as an Italian organ woman at the Covent Garden Theatre fancy dress ball to collect £9.10s. for the Central London Throat and Ear Hospital, and in November she gave two hundred pairs of 'stout winter boots' to the children of Hoxton.

Comedians are not generally well known for their generosity – in fact, many of the most successful ones, such as W. C. Fields, Max Miller and Charlie Chaplin, have gained a reputation, sometimes unjustly, for being 'careful', if not downright mean. Sometimes the stinginess is part of a stage persona that seeps into the public image; at others it reflects childhood poverty. Marie was most susceptible to cases in which she could see herself – the performer who had suddenly fallen from favour, or the Hoxton child who needed warm boots. Her generosity increased in proportion to her fame, though not only through the formalized conduit of committees and charity events.

Vesta Tilley's charity work doubtless improved her credentials for becoming Lady de Frece when her husband, a music-hall impresario turned Tory MP, was knighted. Her calculating approach to giving is evident in her pompous autobiography: 'from the earliest day Providence enabled me to bring succour to the weak and suffering, it became to me not only a duty but a delight to assist'.[5]

By comparison, Marie was impulsive, and anyone who had any dealings with her remembers her generosity. She pressed five pounds into the hands of a newly married couple who met her briefly backstage 'for their honeymoon'; she bought a drink and slipped cash to a turn who had fallen from favour; her name was usually on the list of famous people asked to contribute to a particular cause. She was also capable of grand gestures: she provided 150 beds for homeless children in the East End; she bought her father the Albion Hotel in Hastings, and gave both her parents a pub in Wardour Street in London's Soho.

Her reputation for generosity went before her. Music-hall manager Billy Boardman described her dresser as her 'almoner', handing out money to anyone who came asking. 'A minor artiste would perhaps creep into her dressing room and say, "Miss Lloyd, do you remember that old circus clown who was in the bill at Barnsley? He's out of a shop – not done a handspring for six months, and his wife and kiddies are living on air." And Marie, without turning from her mirror, would call to her dresser, "Give the old cockalorum a tenner to be going on with – and let me know how he's making out." '[6]

The comedian Arthur Roberts remembered how she used to ask him to wait for her after a performance to protect her from the crowds of people ready to press her for money at the stage door.[7] So constant were the demands on her that she sometimes failed to discriminate between the sponger and the genuine appeal for help. One story handed down within the Lloyd family tells of a visit from a man who tried to persuade her to back his new invention. It sounded so outlandish that even Marie knew where to draw the line, and Mr Marconi had to look elsewhere.

In November 1893 Marie enjoyed another benefit performance, this time at the Canterbury. The tribute was even more effusive than the previous one at the Oxford. The historic hall symbolized the very heart of the business and the artists who turned out for her represented the cream of the profession. The floral 'double step-ladder' sent by Jenny Hill, who had sailed for South Africa in search of health, was particularly gratifying since it came from the most successful female performer of her day. When 'The Naughty Continong' was played, flowers rained on to the stage and, finally, manager George Adney brought Marie out. She appeared tongue-tied: 'I thank you all for your kind reception of me this evening, and – well, you know what I mean.' Her daughter struggled on-stage laden with flowers before the braying audience and the actors, some of whom she recognized, dressed in strange costumes and garish face paint. It must have been quite an ordeal for a five-year-old.

It was not a sanctimonious evening: Marie was fully prepared to make a fool of herself. The main part of the entertainment was an elaborate skit on the Dahomey Amazon Warriors, 'the most perfect example of muscular womanhood extant' the *Era* remarked, who were proving a big draw at the Oxford. The troupe of about sixty 'dusky ladies' performed blood-curdling war dances in which they pretended to cut up their victims. The Marie Lloyd version of the act, the Amazing Worriers, saw her dressed as the warrior queen, Gumma, in an outfit designed by the famous costumier and wig-maker Willy Clarkson that included a fur muff round her ankle and a huge German sword. Other music-hall stars who blacked up to join the Amazonian dance were Little Tich, Eugene Stratton and Alice. George Robey appeared as a policeman to chase another man in uniform round the stalls. Near the wings, someone – rumoured to be Richard C. Morton, serving penance for writing 'Ta-ra-ra-boom-de-ay' – kept up a rhythmic beat on a toy drum. After the burlesque, a string of about forty music-hall turns, including Alice, Daisy, Vesta Victoria, Lockhart's Elephants and two Cockney singers, Gus Elen and Alec Hurley, paid tribute to Marie.

There was more than a hint of riotous behaviour, too, in Marie's third and final Drury Lane pantomime. Daniel Defoe would not have recognized his original story in Gus's version of *Robinson Crusoe*, but the plot was far less convoluted than it had been in recent Drury Lane pantos. It was no less spectacular, though. *A History of England in Twenty Minutes* took a sort of *1066, and All That* scamper through antiquity and included William the Conqueror landing at Hastings; Henry I dying of gluttony; a ballet of the Wars of the Roses; Richard I setting off for the Crusades and John being forced to sign the Magna Carta. Essentially it was an excuse for spectacular costumes.

One reviewer complained that the rocking-boat scene before Robinson Crusoe's shipwreck was too realistic and made him feel seasick, but most critics were won over by the Fish Ballet. This took place on the seabed and showed molluscs and other crustacea dancing side by side with oysters, who were followed by waiters carrying vinegar, salt and pepper, whelks whirling, crabs pirouetting next to shrimps, and busty, finned ballet girls in tight costumes. The only criticism of this part of the performance came from the *Stage* reviewer, who pointed out that, strictly speaking, the lobster, as yet unboiled, should have been black rather than pink. This nicety was lost on most of the audience.

Marie played Polly Perkins, true love of Ada Blanche's *Robinson Crusoe*, for which she earned a massive £100 (£4,836) a week – a sum that was widely reported and added to her glamorous appeal.[8] Polly was a sweet-faced innocent, and wore a costume that highlighted a nipped-in, unfeasibly tiny waist. A lacy frill covered her shoulders, her long curly hair was brushed to one side, and she wore a wide-brimmed hat tilted at a jaunty angle. The part had been written to allow Marie to sing 'The Barmaid' and 'The Naughty Continong'. She also showed off her dancing, including a mazurka with Dan, who was Mrs Crusoe, a widow desperate for a replacement husband and who is carried off in error by Will Atkins (Herbert Campbell) intent on capturing Polly. Little Tich was Man Friday.

Many critics felt that the predominantly music-hall cast had succeeded in turning Drury Lane into 'an 'all' and erudite reviewers were ill equipped to deal with this unfamiliar terrain. The *Sketch*'s representative described the theatre as so packed that the galleries looked like 'successful fly-papers' and in the pit there was hardly standing room for a 'Euclidean line'.[9] You can almost see the journalist turning with a mixture of disdain and curiosity as a man behind him urges a singer with a weak voice to 'Chuck it off yer chest!' and describes one of the ballet dancers as 'an eye-skinner'. The *Era*'s reviewer noted that one of the cast, Lily Harold, wore a 'central garment' – probably a tunic – that seemed to have shrunk in the wash and brought surprised stares from the audience.

Marie might have been, in one critic's words, 'dainty, arch and exquisitely attractive' – but not in combination with Little Tich. One night he decided to spice things up by shouting from the wings, 'Look under the bed!', prompting Marie to search for a chamber-pot. The audience knew what she was doing and the *ad lib* brought the house down.[10] But it was not the sort of antic Gus had envisaged for his spectacle show.

Chapter 8

THE BATTLE FOR THE EMPIRE

(1894)

~✦~

Tol, loll, then, Poll, until tonight! the Empire?
See you there? all right
I never knew a lady wink so,
Awf'lly jolly girl, don't you think so?
'The Barmaid' by E. W. Rogers

By 1894 Marie and Percy were living apart. They had moved from Lewisham to Brixton, another music-hall ghetto, but eventually relations between the two became so strained that Marie left for 73 Carleton Road, a large, rambling brick house on the corner of a quiet, leafy road in Tufnell Park, north London. People were openly gossiping about her private life and even the *Era* let its readers know, if rather coyly, what was going on through an item in its music-hall gossip column that could only have referred to Marie:

> There has been much fluttering in the domestic dovecotes of the music-hall world of late, and the air is thick with preliminary preparations for matinées at the Divorce Court. A serio-comic member of a celebrated family which has given several sisters to the stage seeks to cut the shackles that bind her to a gentleman who gained his reputation on the turf and elsewhere.[1]

Marie was not in the best health, and towards the end of *Robinson Crusoe*'s run an understudy took over for a few days. In May she suffered a bout of laryngitis, no doubt brought on by a punishing workload. By the summer she was appearing at five venues daily, in a schedule that demanded precision timing if each hall was to be reached on time – as her advertisement shows:

Sadlers' Wells	8.00
Empire	8.30
Middlesex	9.15
Belmont's	9.40
Paragon	10.40

Among these venues the Empire was like no other. It sat on the north side of Leicester Square, the Moorish façade, domes and half-moons of the Alhambra Theatre of Varieties flanking it to the east. To outsiders the two theatres were dark and menacing, places of temptation and misrule. Lurid stories circulated about the things that happened to the unsuspecting visitor: one man was taken home by a painted lady but fled after catching sight of a corpse slumped in her wardrobe. The probably apocryphal Pearl was seen as typical of the young women sucked into Leicester Square's black hole of corruption. She was 'once the gayest, youngest, and most attractive of the bedecked and painted crowd that nightly thronged the promenades of the Alhambra and the Empire. After two or three months of being the transient darling of bad men, and leading a "gay" life, she succumbed to the effects of much drink, late hours, excitement, and fatigue, and became very thin, pale, and hysterical.'[2]

For the mainly male audience, the Empire had a club atmosphere. It was a place for pruning and strutting in evening dress, top hats – carefully tilted to just the right fashionable angle – were worn at all times, smoking was common and the popular drink 'fiz' or champagne. Prostitutes paraded along the promenade and homosexuals were also known to gather there. Variety acts were a backdrop to the incessant hum of talking and laughing generated by the audience. Marie found the Empire similar to the rough East End halls of her youth, and, despite her skills, the audiences harder to 'read': it was difficult to predict what they would enjoy.

Ballet was the main attraction at both the Alhambra and the Empire – each of which had their own in-house companies – and was used as a vehicle for spectacles. It was common for a ballet girl to spend her whole career at either theatre and the company included many mothers working side by side with their daughters. The programmes promised scantily clad dancers, but in reality the performers wore 'fleshings' – thick flesh-coloured fabric – to cover their legs, arms and abdomen. The range of body sizes and shapes, and the fact that the one or two hundred dancers in the spectacles usually had to carry a shield or a lamp meant that athletic gestures were impossible. The journalist F. Anstey described the dancers' movements as 'galloping', which gives some idea of the disparity between the Leicester Square spectacles and modern notions of ballet.

While she was appearing at the Empire one of Marie's most popular songs was 'The Barmaid', which tells the story of a girl at the Rose and Crown who, although a 'rorty bit o' cracklin'', is tough enough to maintain control over a range of customers, from the swell to the sportsman and the coster.

Percy found Marie's success intolerable and was convinced that she was cheating on him. Her nightly cavortings as a barmaid in front of a Leicester Square audience of toffs and prostitutes only confirmed his suspicions. He again chose to attack her at her place of work.

On 10 May Percy appeared at the stage door at 9 p.m., just as Marie was about to leave for her next hall. As before his attack was a mixture of violence and threats. The *Era* reported that he lunged after her with a hooked stick in one hand, shouting, 'You are not going into that brougham tonight. I will gouge your eyes out and ruin you.' She turned and fled back to the stage door, while Bella, her dresser, and another woman tried to bar his way. Percy continued his tirade for another ten minutes before Marie made a dash for her cab. Percy ran to the other side, pushed his stick through the window and hit the hapless Bella before the cabbie drove off.

Marie struggled through her remaining engagements that night. Around midnight she returned to her parents' pub where she knew she would find refuge after a hard evening's work, made more gruelling by her husband's ugly behaviour. Perhaps she was looking forward to her favourite drink, a brandy and soda.

But Percy was waiting for her. The stream of obscene language began again, probably centring on the two men with whom Percy believed Marie was having an affair. 'I am going to – well, murder you tonight. I will shoot you stone dead, and you will never go on stage any more,' he yelled, according to the *Era*.

Marie's uncle, George Archer, who was living at the pub, stepped in to restrain Percy while Marie fled home in her brougham.

The Empire, which made its money by peddling the promise of sexual adventure, refused to tolerate real-life domestic violence on its doorstep and the next day Marie was sacked. This confirmed to her that her grip on stardom was precarious and that the biggest threat to it was her husband.

Percy, then thirty-one, was arrested and charged with threatening his wife 'whereby she went in danger of her life or of some bodily harm'.[3] When the case came to court in June, she was performing in Dublin and sent a letter saying she did not want to see Percy punished, but the court ruled that she had to attend.

The later hearing was humiliating. Marie confirmed that she was financially independent of Percy. Bella was called as a witness and told the court: 'They used to quarrel because he was so frightfully jealous of his wife.' Under cross-examination, Marie was asked if she had attacked Percy at Datchet, on the Thames, where many music-hall stars had houseboats and where he had accused her of conducting her affairs with two men. She replied, said the *Era*, 'Since the warrant was issued I did not strike my husband with a horsewhip and if I did so it was in self-defence to protect myself because he threatened to shoot me.'

Percy's defence was that he had gone to the Empire to remonstrate with his wife about the men, who would be made co-respondents in a forthcoming divorce case. The judge ruled that the case was 'all one way' and that something serious must have gone on that night for Marie to have been dismissed from the Empire so promptly. Percy was ordered to pay two sureties of £50 (£2,499) as a guarantee of keeping the peace for six months. The case confirmed that, on the rare occasions they were together, Marie and Percy led a cat-and-mouse existence: Percy was convinced that Marie was cheating on him and Marie was not prepared to submit to him – whatever his threats.

The Empire suffered a much greater scandal later that year when the formidable vigilance campaigner, Mrs Laura Ormiston Chant, turned her attention on it. The fiercely bonneted Mrs Chant was often mistaken for an American – which, to her detractors, made her interference even more irksome. Her career had included roles as assistant manager of a private lunatic asylum and marshalling nurses for the Greek front, for which she received the Order of the Red Cross from Queen Victoria. She wrote poems, pamphlets, short stories, and was founding editor of the National Vigilance Association's paper, *Vigilance Record*. She also enjoyed billiards.

Mrs Chant homed in on the Empire as a symbol of the corrupting powers of music halls. She believed that dormant desires were ignited by the stage cavortings of the partially clad ballet girls and informed the LCC that the dancers' tights were so close to flesh colour that she had been forced to use opera glasses to make sure they were not barelegged. The audience's desire was fuelled, she believed, by the evil combination of alcohol with prostitutes. She succeeded in blocking renewal of the Empire's licence until a screen was erected between the auditorium and the promenade where prostitutes gathered.

The *Daily Telegraph* hit back with regular pieces attacking 'Prudes on the Prowl' and *Punch* lampooned her. But the issue was far from clear-cut. Several churchgoers, particularly Methodists, praised Mrs Chant's opposition to alcohol, while others felt the debate was really about free trade. The Empire's management warned that if the theatre closed seven hundred people would lose their jobs.

Herbert Campbell mocked Mrs Chant in the music-hall song 'New Women', in which he wore a hermaphroditic costume, which suggested that Mrs Chant's approach was unnatural because of her stridently mannish *modus operandi*. Wearing a lady's short tweed coat, with a collar and tie, skirt hitched up, boots, gaiters and a Homburg while brandishing a walking-stick, he sang the refrain:

> Oh! a woman is an artful card
> If she mayn't promenade
> If Mrs Ormiston has got to chant
> Let her chant in her own backyard.

When the young Winston Churchill visited the Empire with other cadets from Sandhurst, a walking-stick was poked playfully into the canvas screen that was meant to hide the promenade and the scene turned to one of mass destruction. Winston mounted the pile of rubbish to deliver his maiden speech, a moment he compared to the storming of the Bastille or the death of Julius Caesar.

By this time, Marie was safely on the other side of the Atlantic for her second visit to New York, this time playing at the Imperial Music Hall on Broadway and 29th Street. She had spent the summer on a provincial tour that took in seaside resorts such as Newport, where she experienced a mishap. Marie loved swimming and frequently took the opportunity for a quick dip. Crowds would form around her on the beach. In June she went swimming with a female friend at the public baths at Newport, but suffered the indignity of being fished out after she got into difficulties.

In September she set sail with her sister Grace on the *Etruria*, a Cunard ship, which operated a weekly service between Liverpool and New York and which had won the Blue Ribbon six years previously for the fastest crossing of the Atlantic. Lord Curzon, who was on board the ship during his honeymoon six months after Marie had travelled on it, found it dirty and cramped. It ran out of champagne, and when they hit bad weather, a roast chicken became wedged under the bunk occupied by Curzon and his new wife, a refined American socialite.

For Marie, who revelled in living at close proximity to lots of people, the week-long voyage was a rare holiday from the halls. It also offered some respite from Percy, who had decided to file for divorce, claiming he had witnessed his wife committing adultery with two men at Datchet and at 73 Carleton Road between 13 May and 3 June that year. If she was worried by the scandal, it did not show in the bullish advert she placed in the *Era*:

> The Droll
> Marie Lloyd
> Instantaneous success,
> Pronounced hit
> Imperial Theatre
> New York . . .[4]

It went on to add, in a chatty postscript that was longer than the main advertisement,

> PS. In spite of all my successes being sung here by English artists who cannot make a success with their own songs, I have made a genuine success with my latest, which would have been sung, no doubt, should they have wanted them. How is it 'Oh! Mr Porter' has not been sung in America? Now there was a dead cert, for some of you. Am singing the following nightly:

'Keep off the grass'

'Bird in the hand'

'Tale of a pretty sole'

'Oh, Mr Porter'

'The Barmaid'

'Spanish Senora, or the Naughty Continong'

Exquisite floral tributes nightly. Nevertheless shall sing some of my old successes during my stay here, to show them the way they should be sung. I read a lady's advertisement last week about her wig being copied. Wasn't that wig copied from Marie Lloyd's – slight difference, a shade darker? Ask Mr Clarkson. Kind regards to all friends.

Marie may have been referring to Madge Ellis, a singer who was also appearing at the Imperial, and whom she claimed had copied one of her songs. It was an intimation that this might not be an entirely happy visit to America.

At this time the entertainment industry was dominated by enterprising showmen willing to try anything to keep audiences turning up although America was in the grip of a severe depression. Frederick Francis Proctor's 23rd Street Theatre in New York was pioneering 'continuous variety', which meant keeping the theatre open from noon until midnight. The big stars, or 'headliners', appeared twice a day, but other performers might find themselves on-stage up to five times.

There was a strong turn-out to see Marie at the Imperial, which seated 1,200 and operated a variety bill that ran from eight o'clock until midnight. She was 'dainty', 'bewitching' and 'beautiful', while her costumes were praised and her songs said to have 'swing' and 'go'. The newspapers were also impressed by her boast to be the highest paid vaudeville performer, 'the peer even of the famous Vesta Tilley'. Marie was reported to be earning $500 (£5,139) a week. The *New York Mail and Express* even commented: '. . . chiefly, the songs that she sings are not couched in the more or less offensive terms that one has almost learned to expect from imported music-hall talent. She combines excellently well the French and English methods to be found at the Concert de Paris and the Alhambra without "going the limit" of either place.'[5] Either she had toned down her act considerably for New York audiences or the reviewer had missed the point.

But after the initial euphoria subsided a few weeks into her run at the Imperial, she was fired abruptly by the manager George J. Kraus because she had 'violated the rules of the house' and refused to attend rehearsals. Marie's side of the story was that he did not want to pay her and was looking for a way out:

> Eleven o'clock was the time for my act and Kraus put up a notice in my dressing-room commanding me to be there at eight. I had my friend Ada Alexandre to come in and sit with me. I was humming a snatch of music in an undertone, when a porter brought a bit of a dirty note into me from Kraus. It said he didn't allow strangers on his stage, nor did he allow me to try my voice in my dressing-room, as it annoyed his audience. I sent for him, and said I wanted to know what he meant, and he cried out that he had a lot to worry him, and that he was liable to write anything when he was wild.
>
> On the 8th. inst., I was standing in the café, and a good-humoured chap – Jim, the checktaker – came to me and said that Kraus had discharged him because he had admitted me by the front door when Kraus had ordered me to go by the sub-cellar way. Subsequently, I got a note from Kraus, saying that on account of my unladylike behaviour I was dismissed. It asked me to take my clothes away, but said nothing about salary for last week.[6]

Clearly there had been, in today's management term, a 'personality clash'. And Kraus's attacks hit home at Marie's most sensitive spots. In banning her friend from her dressing room and ordering her to use the back door he had failed to treat Marie as a 'headliner'. In another account Marie complained that her dressing room smelt of stage animals because cages of monkey and dog acts were left outside it. Kraus criticized her professionalism: she was made to turn up ridiculously early and he accused her of 'unladylike behaviour' – elsewhere he had ticked her off for being drunk. Lastly, he undermined her relationship with her public in implying that her voice had 'disturbed' the audience, and he sacked the checktaker for paying her too much attention.

Kraus might have been desperate to let her go, but another theatre was prepared to take legal action to secure her talents. Koster and Bial, who had booked her in 1890, claimed she had failed to fulfil a contract signed the last time she was in New York which carried a thousand-dollar penalty clause. Presumably this was the contract stuffed unceremoniously into the teapot with which they had presented her at the end of her tour. Both Kraus and Marie were served with a 'writ of attachment'. Deputy Sheriff McGuinness delivered Marie's to the rooms where she was staying at Manor House, and two trunks of her stage costumes, together with $500 of back salary due to her from Kraus, were handed over to him.

Marie was most upset by the loss of her costumes. She told the *New York Sun* tearfully that she had been offered work in Buffalo, but could not accept without her dresses. She claimed the whole thing had been a misunderstanding: she had been willing to fulfil the engagement but had been prevented by her London managers from appearing in New York when Koster and Bial wanted her. The solution was that she agreed to spend her final fortnight in New York performing at Koster & Bial's Music Hall on 34th Street, which was then being managed by Oscar Hammerstein, a German immigrant and grandfather of the lyricist of musicals such as *Oklahoma*, *Carousel* and *The Sound of Music*.

Koster & Bial's had been redecorated in the August before Marie arrived, giving it a white and gold entrance and a hundred new incandescent electric lights in the ceiling of its main vestibule. An extra twenty private boxes had been added, making sixty-five in all, transforming it into what was supposedly the largest place of amusement in the USA, and a new lounge held 800 people. A wax image of a well-dressed woman was placed next to a railing that guarded the opening; at least one man misread her steady gaze and sent over a card of introduction.

Hammerstein was perhaps the greatest showman of his day and it was not the first time that Marie had come across him. His early money had come from a cigar-making invention and from property speculation, and he continued to dabble with inventions throughout his life, usually selling a patent too soon because he needed the cash for his latest scheme. He was passionate about the theatre and took a keen interest in the design of the thirteen he built, which were renowned for their good acoustics.

He was a neat little man with a meticulously trimmed goatee beard that made him look like Victor Hugo. He always wore a top hat — perhaps to give the appearance of height — and was known to the public, who read about his countless legal battles and other escapades, simply as 'Oscar'. Although he enjoyed spasmodic periods of wealth he lived a spartan lifestyle, as if the countless schemes in his head allowed little room for the practicalities of life. His sons made sure that he always had a five-dollar bill in his pocket as he frequently ran out of cash and had to leave his coat as surety for a meal. He lived in two small rooms above his Victoria Theater and preferred to travel by streetcar.

Oscar took a keen interest in the acts who performed at his theatre, and was well known for paying them good money. He liked to include European artists and at one time had ten agents scouring the continent for new faces to bring to New York. Cissie Loftus, Albert Chevalier and Anna Held were among the most famous names he presented to America, as well as Iberian dancers, and acrobats from Berlin. In February 1894 Bessie Bellwood was reduced to tears by dollars hurled at her at Koster & Bial's as the audience mimicked their British counterparts by poking fun at her legal proceedings to recoup money owed to her by her lover, the Duke of Manchester.

Oscar had a talent for gimmickry and publicity. If a bat made its way into the theatre, as it did in September 1894, the chances were that it would alight on the shoulder of Venus, a central figure in a 'living picture' on display at that time, and the chances were that the papers would be told. In the year that Marie appeared at Koster & Bial's it became the first music hall to allow patrons to check in their bicycles with the box office, and in the summer a twelve-foot square blackboard showed the temperature in the auditorium and the building's roof garden in a bid to persuade passers-by to leave the dusty sidewalk. The roof garden, too, became a feature of the building where patrons could gaze out across Manhattan and where Koster and Bial could use field-glasses to check business on their rivals' roof gardens.

Returning to England must have seemed like escaping from an asylum for Marie after the machinations and intrigue of New York. While she had been away, she discovered, Percy had dropped the divorce proceedings, but even better was the roar of welcome that erupted when her number went up at the Oxford, the last hall she played in an evening of her usual hectic routine:

Middlesex	8.30
Canterbury	9.10
Cambridge	10.10
Oxford	10.45

At Christmas she travelled to the Shakespeare Theatre in Liverpool, where she appeared as Principal Boy. She took the starring role in *Pretty Bo-Peep, Little Boy Blue, and the Merry Old Woman who lived in a Shoe*, dressed in tight breeches. Although Marie's was the only big name on the bill, the production was not dissimilar to a Drury Lane pantomime: it lasted until midnight and the sets were so lavish that the scenic artist was called to take a bow three times during the course of the show. Marie's singing, acting and dancing were praised as being 'delightfully easy, graceful and self-possessed'.[7] After her tussles in New York a Liverpool panto audience was just what she needed.

Chapter 9

CHARGES OF IMMORALITY
(1895–6)

~≈

I've been fêted, feasted, photographed . . .
'Tricky Little Trilby' by J. P. Harrington and George le Brunn

Marie's growing reputation for winks and risqué songs allowed her to capitalize on the craze of the moment: a new play called *Trilby*.[1] The stage version of George du Maurier's novel opened at the Haymarket Theatre on 30 October 1895 and thrilled audiences with its delicious mixture of melodrama and sexual tension bubbling below the surface. The play was primarily a vehicle for Herbert Beerbohm Tree – half-brother of Max – who played Svengali, the evil hypnotist who captures the mind of the play's heroine, Trilby O'Ferrall. The cast included a small part for the author's son, Gerald du Maurier, whose daughter Daphne produced her own distinctive brand of suspense in the next century.

Trilby, the daughter of a barmaid, earns money by sitting as a nude model for artists to the chagrin of her admirer, the insipid 'Little Billee' who meets her when he is living the Bohemian life in the Latin quarter of Paris. Trilby and Little Billee decide to marry but Svengali kidnaps her and, by hypnosis, transforms her into a singing phenomenon who captivates audiences across Europe and makes Svengali rich. Eventually Little Billee rescues her and Svengali expires suddenly from a heart-attack. The scene is set for a happy Christmas-time ending when an anonymous present is delivered to Trilby. She opens it to discover a picture of her tormentor and falls into Billee's arms in a fatal swoon from which she never recovers.

The play is a surprisingly sensuous work. Trilby scandalized audiences by appearing with bare feet – for the first time ever in a Victorian theatre – and smoking, but Svengali has all the best lines. Take this exchange with two of Little Billee's artist friends:

LAIRD: Svengali, you are destined to be hanged!
SVENGALI: (*laughing*) That's more than can be said for your pictures, my friend.
TAFFY: And when you're on the gallows – I – I'll come and make a sketch of you.
SVENGALI: (*laughing*) You add a new terror to my death, my friend.

The story captured imaginations on both sides of the Atlantic and provides one of the earliest examples of a marketing bonanza, complete with merchandising spin-offs. In America, where it was first serialized in 1894 by *Harper's*, there were Trilby sausages, Trilby ice-cream, Trilby cocktails, Trilby shoes and Trilby cigars, as well as the hat whose popularity has outlived that of the play. In Florida the town of Trilby built a Svengali Square, presumably not the ideal meeting-place for a blind date.

In Britain, too, the play's success sparked a craze for hats, for society women to take up smoking – behind closed doors – and for music-hall performers to seek out Trilby songs. J. P. Harrington and George le Brunn produced 'I'm Looking For Trilby' for Vesta Tilly and 'Tricky Little Trilby' for Marie, and other composers churned out a Trilby barn dance and waltz[1]. Many songs focused on Trilby's bare feet for titillating detail.

The subject was particularly appropriate for Marie since, like Trilby, she was capable of shocking people, she came from a poor background and eventually made her fortune through her voice. A picture in the *Sketch* of 25 December 1895 shows a bare-headed, thick-waisted Marie, with beefy washerwoman's arms, dressed in the flowing robes of someone who looks as though they have just escaped from an Eastern harem. Her costume mimics exactly the illustration from the original novel, which depicts Trilby singing in a theatre at Svengali's behest.

Her new song, though, was not universally appreciated: when Marie performed 'Tricky Little Trilby' in the East End her audience, which was unfamiliar with the play, was bewildered at her lack of shoes. But the lyrics put Marie on the side of the less educated audience; they depicted an actress asked to take the lead in the play with no idea who Trilby is. She confides that she will take any part for money and plays on her reputation for brashness:

> I'm a modern actress, and I play
> All the uptodatey parts today.
> Serious or gay, not one is miss'd,
> Trilby is the latest on my list.
> 'Twasn't in my line I thought because
> I had no idea who Trilby was;
> But the pay of course, cured my disgust
> So I thought I'd play the part or bust,
> They said Trilby modest ought to be,
> Modest Trilby, what a part for me.
> Quiet and prim, me?
> Eh, no jolly fear!
> So I made Trilby quite a new idea.

In the final verse the Trilby melodrama turns into a story that includes familiar music-hall people. Her Svengali 'does this for fun,/ Something in the style of George le Brunn'. She concludes by bringing the tale even closer to home:

> At my Trilby many folks have laughed,
> I've been fêted, feasted, photographed,
> Been in all the papers, tho' of course,
> Trilby's not yet been in a divorce.

Marie's Trilby song, like other music-hall numbers, helped audiences to explore new phenomena, facilitating debate about the many changes going on around them – whether the introduction of X-rays, London Zoo or a new fashion accessory. Another hotly debated arrival was the bicycle: which Marie wheeled on in more than one song. 'Salute My Bicycle' was the most popular and, like her songs about railways, the seaside, and foreign places, it was based on the themes of escape and independence. A form of transport that involved a woman mounting a new-fangled gadget also gave her plenty of scope for suggestiveness.

Cycling offered women a unique chance to take off under their own steam and escape their chaperone. It also provided a rare opportunity for physical exertion in public. For these reasons the new pastime caused much consternation in both Europe and North America. Also, some Parisian doctors suggested that cycling might damage the female sexual organs, while other 'experts' worried that it might cause a mother's milk to dry up – or at the very least damage a woman's nerves, which were susceptible to upset under the best of circumstances.

Women agonized over what to wear for cycling: the voluminous skirt with the brutally nipped-in waist was viewed as more hygienic and safer, although it was liable to catch in the spokes and collected all the dirt of still primitive roads. There was, though, the daring 'bifurcated nether garment', also known as bloomers or 'The Rational'. American cyclists were the first to adopt this practical option in the spring of 1893, and a year later a hundred New York women were said to be cycling in 'trousers' – although mainly after nightfall. In England, the Rational Dress Society tried to encourage the wearing of bloomers.[2]

In 1896 Marie cut through these worries with 'It Was A Good Job I Had These On', about a young girl who is relieved that in certain situations, such as climbing down a ladder to escape a fire, she was wearing her bloomers or 'mare's nests'. Marie's Rational dress for 'Salute My Bicycle' was a neat pair of bloomers under a long coat that fitted snugly at the waist and had leg o' mutton sleeves. She also wore a dainty hat and wheeled a bicycle on stage. The *Sketch* reported that some of the women in the audience seemed dismayed: 'I overheard one buxom-looking lady observe to her escort her firm resolve not to adopt the fashion.'[3]

As the first verse shows, the female cyclist keeps her cool and is determined to enjoy her independence – despite the taunts of passers-by. She flaunts her confidence in her own sexuality – to the dismay of the confused males she encounters:

> You see I wear the Rat'nal Dress –
> Well, how do you like me? Eh, boys?
> It fits me nicely more or less.
> A little bit tasty! eh, boys?
> When on my 'bike' I make a stir,

Girls cry, 'My word!' Men cry,
'Oo-er!' And in this garb
They scarce can tell whether I'm a boy or 'gel'.
The fellows all 'chike' when they see me on my 'bike',
But I'm as cool as any icycle;
They can chaff me all they like,
But I never get the 'spike'.
I only say 'Salute my bicycle!'

The song's daring flirtatiousness appealed to men, but a certain type of young woman liked it, too, for its defiant tone and glamorous costume. These women were among a growing number of female admirers who looked up to Marie for her heady lifestyle and free-spiritedness. As she travelled in her carriage between halls she was frequently deluged with presents from young girls thrust through the window. A journalist who had been commissioned to interview her for one of the New York dailies at the end of 1895 noted how, as she travelled between five halls in one night, she was greeted with shouts of 'Bravo, Marie!' and 'Wot cher, Marie?'[4] In the Mile End Road a bevy of small girls suddenly appeared at the window of her brougham shouting, 'Good luck, Marie!' and hurled a huge box of sweets at her. Typically, since she was remarkably accident-prone, the gift 'unfortunately hit Miss Lloyd and cut her mouth, though not severely'. Luckily, she was stationary when another group of East End girls presented her with a huge cut-glass bottle of perfume at the stage door of the Varieties in Hoxton.

Another hit of 1895 was 'It's A Jolly Fine Game Played Slow!' (Harrington and le Brunn), which tells the familiar story of spooning couples caught in awkward situations. The second verse describes a common scenario and allowed Marie to flirt with the audience:

To sit with a girl, on her sofa, for a spoon,
Is a jolly fine game played slow,
You don't need much light save the radiance of the moon,
It's a jolly fine game played slow.
You kiss the girl, and she kisses you,
And your mouths they go like so!

For her ma and pa are both out, ha! ha!
It's a jolly fine game played slow.

Till some saucy little loafer
Cries, from underneath the sofa,
'That's a jolly fine game played slow.'

She went even further with 'What's That For, Eh?' which was also known as 'So I Know Now' and 'Johnny Jones'. In the song, by George le Brunn and W. T. Lytton, a schoolgirl pesters her parents with awkward questions. They refuse to help her so her friend, Johnny Jones, enlightens her. Even without Marie's interpretation, the words are immediately liable to *double entendre*. For many of the audience the very title 'What's That For, Eh?' was suggestive. We can only guess at the gestures and inflection she added to lines such as: 'I want to know the in and out . . .'

The third verse, in which the young girl is taken to town by her father, is less opaque, and there is a sense that perhaps the singer is not as innocent as she pretends:

Oh! how the ladies made me stare,
They nearly all had yellow hair,
And one of them – oh! what a shame! –
She called Pa 'Bertie' – it's not his name –
Then went like this [kissing sound] and winked her eye –
And so I said to Pa, 'Oh, my!' –

The schoolgirl threatens to ask her mother what it all means, but as usual Johnny Jones obliges.

The song was a hit and Marie performed it at the rather more genteel venues, such as the Tivoli, in November 1895. The Tivoli frequently carried a notice saying: 'The Management will feel obliged to any persons who will bring to their notice any item in the Programme that they consider objectionable.' This may have been because it wanted to be seen to support the fight against impropriety rather than actually charge into battle.

When in October 1896 the Oxford Music Hall applied for the renewal of its licence 'Johnny Jones' was cited as evidence that it should be withheld; the reformers were also worried about prostitution and drinking that centred around the promenade. The third and fourth verses of Johnny Jones – in the latter the schoolgirl's mother is obviously preparing for the arrival of a new baby – were deemed 'quite improper'. However, the reformers who objected to the licence renewal classed 'Johnny Jones' as less offensive than a song by Lady Mansel. This told the story of various mishaps: an elderly lady who goes for a walk in a high wind and trips over a stile; a female bather who stumbles into a men's bathing machine by mistake, and a dancer whose tights split on stage. Each verse was followed by the refrain: 'What I saw I must not tell you now.'

One witness at the licence hearing, Miss Carina Reed, a follower of Mrs Ormiston Chant and secretary of the social purity section of the British Women's Temperance Association, which campaigned against prostitution, also objected to a scantily clad man dressed as a woman who, when he was thrown over the shoulder of the second man, was left 'entirely exposed'.

Another witness, Mr Charles Cory Reed, a temperance campaigner from Wood Green in north London who was no relation to Miss Reed, valiantly made several trips to the Oxford to monitor its morals. When pressed he said it was the 'gestures and suggestions' that accompanied 'Johnny Jones' that he found offensive. But, the *Era* continued, Marie was far from alone in upsetting him; he also objected to the patter of another performer who concluded a piece about two young people with the line, 'And then let nature takes its course'. 'The effect of that was very demoralizing,' Mr Reed said.

He was upset by a diagram of a woman's feet under a nightdress next to a policeman's feet, but was unable to explain exactly what form the diagram took. He took offence at a song about the 'new photography' (X-rays) and someone's picture being taken in bed. And the singer – Madge Ellis – whom Marie had accused of plagiarism in New York – he said, appeared as a schoolgirl singing a song about bruises, 'You Show Me Yours, First' and made 'an objectionable raising of the skirts'.

Mr Reed also complained that he was accosted on several occasions by prostitutes, which prompted the Oxford's manager to ask, 'Have you much spare time for looking after the morals of other people?'

Mr Reed replied, 'No; I did it at personal inconvenience.'

Mr Reed's wife also put herself out for the cause of morality by visiting the Oxford, only for an elderly man to lean against her and ask her why she did not look more cheerful. Mrs Reed said she had an appointment and rushed off, only to bump into the same man later and hear him say, 'He has not come; he's a blackguard. Won't you come and have a drink with me?'

But Mrs Reed was no match for the Oxford manager who made her wandering off alone sound more morally reprehensible than anything she had seen on stage. Cross-examined about why she felt 'Johnny Jones' had 'evil tendencies' Mrs Reed could only say that while it was being sung the women in the audience looked at the men more often than was normal. In a pattern that was repeated several times in the West End the Oxford's licence was renewed, but it was warned to be more careful in its selection of songs.

There was further embarrassment for the reformers when Madge Ellis threatened to sue Mrs Reed for her allegations that she had appeared without tights. Mrs Reed had been convinced Ellis was barelegged because she could see the texture of her skin, which was 'very red all over', but the case was settled out of court, Ellis winning costs, damages and an apology for the slander.

Marie's songs, then, were not outrageously risqué compared with what was being sung around her. Nevertheless, she made capital out of her growing reputation in her memoirs, *Marie Lloyd's Blue Book*. The music-hall press referred to it in their pages and the *Era* even reviewed it. Marie claimed the title was simply borrowed from the term used for parliamentary reports. She was obviously being disingenuous. The book sounds as though it was a lightweight account of carefully fabricated 'celebrity' – the *Era* actually uses the word – tales: the autograph hunters, the original Johnny Jones and the many suitors for her hand in marriage. It also, apparently, contained her axioms, stories from America and a comedy in one act called *The Broker's Man*. 'Apparently' because – if it ever existed – no copy of the book has survived.

In March 1895 Marie suffered congestion of the lungs and her younger sister, Daisy, stepped in to fill her place at the Middlesex. She was seven years younger than Marie and pretty in a sweet, innocent way that eluded the rest of the family. She was the only sister to retain the Wood name professionally. More than Marie's other sisters, Daisy carved out an independent career for herself and became a popular Principal Boy in pantomime.

Alice and Grace were still doing well and had been praised for their 'nimble dancing' which was 'high in favour'[5] The Lloyd brand was always a key ingredient in their success, but they began to develop their own style, singing of 'lovers and their vows',[6] and dancing 'very prettily' in their 'tasteful dresses'. In 1892 they appeared in Glasgow, shortly after a visit from their elder sister, and were described as being nearly as popular as her and 'exceedingly pretty and clever young ladies'.[7] The partnership began to peter out after Alice married Tom McNaughton of the cross-talking, knockabout act, the McNaughton Brothers, in 1894.[8]

Unlike Percy, Tom fitted in easily with the Wood tribe. He came from a theatrical family, had first performed at the age of four, and had three brothers who were also on the stage. He was tall and slim with a constantly animated face in which each feature seemed to operate to its own agenda. On and off stage he was always dapper: white-gloved hands resting on a cane, regimentally starched shirt collar, buttonhole, bowler hat at a jaunty angle and sometimes even a monocle. All in all he looked like a well-dressed will-o'-the-wisp. Tom's long-limbed elegance was accentuated by the short, stout stature of Fred, his 'feed'.

Earlier they had appeared as Irish comedians, the Two M'Naughtons, before perfecting a type of quick-fire act rare in Britain but which became common in America. It was a difficult act to pull off and required perfect diction and spot-on timing. The routine was built around a conversation held at cross-purposes; the trick was to play the routine at the right speed for the audience just about to follow what was going on – as well as to enjoy the mounting misunderstanding between Fred and Tom. Each line could deliver a laugh but the act was played at such high speed that realization of the joke was only triggered by the next remark, which in turn propelled the audience ever deeper into the conversation's murky levels of confusion. The following gives some hint at the surrealism of the exchange:

TOM: What in blazes, Philip, did you mean by not putting my money in
the bank?
FRED: What are you talking about? My name is not Philip.

TOM: Ah-ha! You even deny your name, but you can't deny you have
   my property. It's in your possession now. I see it.
FRED: What nonsense is this? What property?
TOM: My handkerchief. But don't worry, Philip, I have every confidence
   in you; you may use it.[9]

Off stage, Tom played his life at quick-fire speed. Like Marie, he was
accident-prone: he was once badly injured on walking into a glass door[10]
and on another occasion wrapped his car round a lamp-post.[11] Even in
court, over the motoring offence, he could not resist trying to engage
his lawyer in a bit of cross-talk. He enjoyed practical jokes: he would
hide herrings under tables or pieces of ripe cheese behind pictures in
lodgings that had been overpriced or cold. He was the sort of person
who could be at turns infuriating or hilarious to live with, depending on
your mood. Yet despite the relentless round of wisecracks and gentle
put-downs, Tom worried about the future, was always anxious to 'do
the right thing' and not let his friends down.

After they married, Alice made every effort to appear on the same
bill as the McNaughton Brothers. When she and Grace performed in a
benefit at the end of 1895 it was for the first time in a year. Their double
act was finally laid to rest when Grace married the jockey George
Hyams in 1896. George raced for Baron Hirsch in Austria and the
couple moved to a new home near Vienna. Alice was forced to
concentrate on a solo career. In March the following year her song 'I
Was On The Safe Side' at the Holborn was censured in an inspector's
report;[12] three years after that she was described in a programme for the
Tivoli music hall as 'Miss Alice Lloyd, serio and dancer'.

Rosie was also in a double act from 1893, with her cousin Alice
Archer, the two appearing as another version of the Sisters Lena. She
was the sixth child in the Wood family and after her birth Mrs Wood
had enjoyed a gap of four years before the next baby arrived. Marie was
nine when Rosie was born and she enjoyed a longer period as 'baby' of
the family than any of her older siblings. In fact she never managed to
shake off this image and was an awkward and easily embarrassed girl.
While the sisters were living with Marie they regularly met in the
morning to discuss the gossip of the night before but if the talk became
racy Rosie would draw up her knees to hide her blushes. Marie would

shout, 'Take your feet down, I can't hear the story!' so that she could see Rosie's red face.[13] The two youngest Woods, Sidney and Maude, also appeared together. Only Anne had no direct contact with the stage. It may have been her safe remove from theatrical jealousies that allowed Marie to declare her the most talented singer of the family.

Eighteen ninety-five was a year of indulgence for Marie – revealing that she felt secure enough in her own standing to relax slightly. In June she visited Ascot midweek in a 'four-in-hand' but was late back, missing her performances that evening. The slip in professionalism made the gossip page of the *Era*. Towards the end of the year she took a trip to Paris, cementing her association with a city whose reputation was similar to her own.

The next few months were marked by personal tragedies. George Ware, who had been Marie's agent for nearly ten years, died in December 1895 after a brief illness. He was known as 'Old Reliable' and had learned the entertainment trade in the army before striking up a comedy double act with his wife. It was a bitter blow for Marie, since George represented a direct link with her roots in the East End. He had even written her first, purloined hit, 'The Boy In The Gallery'. Gus died in June 1896, followed the next month by Jenny Hill and Bessie Bellwood in September. They were all under fifty and were mourned at large public funerals that suggested the passing of an institution.

That the music-hall world could boast such well-known public figures shows that it had become an institution itself, with its own hierarchy and traditions, which was moving steadily away from its public-house roots. And, just as music-hall was becoming old enough to have a 'hall of fame', so signs were emerging – that went unnoticed at the time – that entertainment was on the cusp of something new. In 1896 Lord Northcliffe founded the *Daily Mail*, which was to become the most popular daily newspaper of its time; Marconi arrived in London to try to sell his wireless; motorists no longer needed someone to walk with a red flag in front of their car and *The Times* noted the first cinematographe film show at the Polytechnic in Regent Street on 20 February but failed to cover any subsequent cinematography for another eight years. The first 'newsreel', also in 1896, featured the Prince of Wales's horse, Persimmon, winning the Derby. An electrical engineer, R. W. Paul, stood at the finishing line to shoot the film. The snowy footage was shown in a one-and-a-half-minute slot at the Alhambra the following evening.

As well as the passing of key figures in her life, Marie had to deal with several trying incidents that year. In March 1896 she was called to the witness box after her twenty-four-year-old coachman, Herbert Norton,[14] was charged with stealing a gold Geneva watch and a half-hoop diamond ring from her home in Carleton Road.

Norton had been working for her for two and a half years before suddenly leaving without notice. Following a tip-off from her housemaid, Marie went upstairs to discover that a ring was missing. It was eventually found at a pawnbroker's in Seven Sisters Road, along with the watch, which had been pledged by Norton. The two items together were worth £8 10s and the pawnbroker revealed that the watch had been in his shop for over a year. Presumably Marie had so much jewellery by now that two items could be overlooked.

Marie was reluctant to prosecute Norton, although it was the second time he had stolen from her. She sent a telegram to his Brixton address, saying that if he did not return the items before six o'clock she would be forced to call in the police. She heard nothing that day, but eventually his brother-in-law arrived with Norton's uniform breeches, a new tie and the two pawn tickets. Marie returned the package and called in the police. In court she still seemed uneasy about prosecuting him, appealing to him directly from the witness box: 'If you had asked me to forgive you I would have done so.'

When the magistrate inquired whether she 'desired to recommend him to mercy now', she replied, 'Oh, yes, please.' The magistrate ordered Norton to carry out two months' hard labour, the minimum sentence he felt able to hand down, given that it was not the man's first offence. He added that the theft represented 'an outrageous breach of trust' against a 'kind mistress' and that he had been 'no doubt, well paid'. The watch and ring were returned to Marie.

The episode shows Marie's unease with the mistress/servant relationship. She might fly into a rage if she thought someone was copying her on stage and threaten to sue them, but when a trusted member of her household made off with her jewellery she was reluctant to see him punished. Drivers and maids, who shared her social background, were part of her extended family rather than servants. In her will she left £100 to her maid, Maud Wilson, one of only three named beneficiaries.

In April Marie had one of those cab accidents to which certain female performers were susceptible. Perhaps she and Bessie Bellwood were both unlucky with transport – or were the subsequent bruises that kept them away from work man-made? Daisy stood in for Marie, who was ill again in May, but still managed the summer tour of the provinces, taking with her a new song 'The Geisha Girl' in which she travels to Japan in search of work and is seduced – but not quite unwillingly. 'Maid Of London' was a parody of 'Maid Of Athens', which was written by that pillar of respectability, the Poet Laureate Alfred, Lord Tennyson. As was now expected in her songs, there was plenty of innuendo. When the girl's swain asks for his heart back, she replies: 'Give me back my twiddly bits and you can take the rest.'

Chapter 10

TAKING THE EMPIRE ABROAD

(1897)

~⁊

Though far from home, across the foam,
You can't stop a girl from thinking.
'Though Far From Home' by Joe Tabrar,
J. P. Harrington and George le Brunn

In 1897 Marie was described by one newspaper as 'the most popular
artiste of modern times'[1] and as such she was given a huge send-off for
her first visit to South Africa, which suggested that she was emigrating
rather than spending a few months abroad. Joe Lyons heped her to
organize a dinner and ball for two hundred of her closest friends at the
Trocadero on Piccadilly Circus for the Sunday before she was due to
sail from Southampton.[2] The restaurant was an upmarket establishment
owned by J. Lyons & Co. to capitalize on the expanding leisure industry
in that part of London. Lyons had launched its first teashop in Piccadilly
in 1894 but did not open its first Corner House until 1907.

Guests included Marie's parents, her brother Johnny, Alice and Tom,
Grace and George, Daisy, Bella and Rosie, as well as music-hall friends
such as Sandow, Joe Elvin, the coster singer Alec Hurley, Herbert
Campbell, Harry Tate and songwriters George le Brunn and J. P.
Harrington. George Adney Payne, an important director of one of the
leading London music-hall syndicates, led toasts to Marie's health and
prosperity. It was exactly the sort of occasion Marie revelled in – a
party thrown in her honour and attended by everyone she loved or
respected. However, when called upon to speak, Marie – stripped of her
songs – could not find the words. Once before she had refused
pointblank to make a speech, saying she could not 'speak for nuts';[3] at

the Trocadero she turned to poetry. The rather sickly piece, written for her by J. P. Harrington, parodied one of her recent songs 'You Can't Stop A Girl From Thinking'. She declaimed it in her husky speaking voice, which has, with some justification, been compared to Ellen Terry's.

> I am leaving dear old England, and my heart of hearts sinks low
> When I think of it!
> I see so many friends here I've scarce got the heart to go
> When I think of it!
> Familiar faces all around are very dear to me,
> And you will think of 'Marie', though I'm far across the sea.
> I will not say 'Farewell', my friends, but simply 'Au revoir',
> I – I – Well, you can guess the rest, I can't say any more
> I couldn't tell you what I mean!
> When I am in a far-off scene
> Moments like the present long will live,
> Our hearts together linking,
> I cannot say a single word
> Of how my inmost soul is stirred;
> Though far from home, across the foam,
> You can't stop a girl from thinking.

Dan Leno played for laughs rather than sentimentality. Glancing down at the evening's commemorative menu, the cover of which carried a drawing of Marie dwarfed by a Matabele chief carrying assegai and shield, he said he hoped Marie would be happy with her new manager. After further speeches, including one from her real manager in South Africa, Edgar Hyman – who said he had expanded one of the halls Marie was to play to meet the expected demand for seats – the guests adjourned to a reception room where Marie, Daisy and Alec Hurley gave an impromptu concert while the banqueting hall was cleared for dancing. The Tivoli orchestra led the dancing, which continued until the early hours with only a minor hiccup when, at about two o'clock in the morning, Marie slipped on the highly polished parquet floor and was only just rescued by a male dancer from crashing into a fountain.

The train taking her and her entourage to Southampton was due to leave Waterloo station the following Saturday. There was a sense that Marie was going on a great voyage, and there was more than a streak of imperialism in the notion that 'the most popular artiste of modern times' was set to conquer a foreign country. About five hundred people, a mixture of fellow performers and fans, turned up to see her off; like ancient retainers they presented her with choice gifts to send her on her way and those who could not attend sent flowers, presents, keepsakes and messages of good luck. George Ware, son of her original agent, gave her a lady's companion set and silver pin-box; Joe Lyons presented her with a gold locket, some turquoise jewellery and pearls; Willy Clarkson offered a gold-mounted crocodile purse with a little gold watch, and the principal members of the Drury Lane pantomime provided a silver writing-desk. Ada Lundberg, another performer, sent an emotional message: 'God bless you, dear, and bring you safe home again.' Brother-in-law Tom sent two barrels of oysters and another friend presented a box of red herrings 'as a specific cure for sea sickness'.

The only sour note was that Percy was unable to allow his wife's biggest triumph so far to slip by without interfering. Like a Victorian villain he appeared from nowhere to assert his paternal rights and refused to allow their daughter to travel to South Africa. Rather than risk an ugly scene, Marie set off for Southampton without her.

Three first-class saloon compartments were reserved on the train to transport fifty guests, including Marie's parents, Grace and Alice, George le Brunn and his wife and Harry Tate to Southampton, where railway staff lined the platform as if a royal personage were about to alight. There were more well-wishers at the docks and, in a year when patriotism was running high due to Queen Victoria's diamond jubilee, Union Jacks were everywhere. Meanwhile Marie's brother, Johnny, arrived at the port with her daughter and her maid. The little girl was smuggled on board the ship, while Marie posed for the cameras. Lunch was served aboard *The Moor* and telegrams read, including one from George Belmont who had given Marie her first big engagement.

Despite the presence of her daughter, Rosie and Bella, Marie immediately felt homesick and burst into tears as the ship left port. Once land was out of sight, however, she tried to distract herself by working on a new pierrot costume for South Africa with Rosie and Bella. The dressmaking circle was a disaster: the three women fell out and Marie hurled the outfit into the sea, where it billowed in the waves like a drowning mime artist.

It is clear from the press coverage of Marie's arrival in South Africa that her reputation had gone before her and several knowing allusions were made to 'winking' and 'knick-knacks' – the latter referring to her song 'Among My Knick-knacks'. The Empire Palace of Varieties in Johannesburg announced her arrival in newspaper advertisements that used the sort of hyperbole an old-style music-hall chairman would have been proud of:

> . . . the Leading Music Hall Artiste of the World.
> Engaged at enormous expense for 6 weeks only.
> The Great and only
> MARIE LLOYD
> Direct from London, in the height of her popularity,
> in all her Greatest and Latest Successes.

Rosie and Bella, who were to perform as The Sisters Lloyd, were: 'A chip of [*sic*] the old block. Charming Duettists and Dancers.'

As Marie travelled through the foreign countryside, which was unlike anything she had ever seen before, she began to suffer a growing unease as to how she would be received. Her anxiety was increased by the knowledge that she was at the top of her profession. Interviewed on a train heading for Johannesburg, she confessed that she was anxious about her first appearance in the new country:

> Do you know that I am very nervous? . . . It is perfectly true, and tomorrow, for instance, from when I rise to when I take my exit from the platform I shall be in a tremble the whole day long. I am very foolish, I know, but it is natural to me. Even now I always have the horrible sensation of feeling that the people don't want me . . . After the first plunge I feel better, but can never plead guilty to feeling over-burdened with confidence.[4]

When she arrived in Johannesburg on the Cape train, crowds gathered and *South Africa* reported, 'our only Eye-Winker . . . looked her very self, and becomingly, even demurely, dressed in a blue serge travelling costume'.

In the late nineteenth century South Africa had a Wild West feel to it. The discovery of diamonds at Kimberley in 1867 and the world's largest deposits of gold near Johannesburg in 1886 had tranformed it from a sleepy, rather awkward colonial backwater into a fermenting cultural mix. As with any discovery of natural riches, prospectors flocked from all over the world in the hope of taking advantage of the new-found wealth. Engineers, lawyers, money men, labourers, tradesmen and pure chancers came to South Africa hopeful of using whatever skills they possessed to reap their own rewards from the precious harvest.

Barney Barnato was one such man. His notoriety became such that legends and stories grew up around him in such profusion that it is difficult to separate truth from fiction. He was born in the East End of London and, like Marie, was attracted from an early age to the halls. According to which source you believe, he made some sort of a living as a conjuror, boxer or clown. Later, when he was wealthy enough to be able to lunch at the Savoy Hotel in London, a woman at a nearby table could not resist leaning forward to ask if it was true that he had been a clown. Barney's response was to remove his jacket and walk round the dining room on his hands.

Barnett Isaacs – Barney Barnato was his stage name – was persuaded to sail for South Africa in 1873 by his elder brother, Harry, who had already settled there. When Barney arrived, having travelled steerage with only a box of cigars that he hoped to sell, he found a brother who confessed that he may have overstated the country's prospects. Barney, ever the optimist, began to assemble a business empire by tactics that sailed close to the edges of propriety and built himself a reputation as a wily, if not downright dishonest, entrepreneur.

He made money from trading in diamonds, buying and selling investments in goldfields, which sometimes turned out to be far removed from the main mining seams, from a water company, banking, real estate and playing the stock market, both in South Africa and abroad. It was whispered that he located rich diamond and gold seams by nefarious means. He was unpopular with many of his fellow businessmen, who feared his ruthlessness and despised him for the humble roots he made little attempt to hide and which many of them shared. He once bought a Sydney Cooper painting simply because he said one of the sheep in it looked just like him; Lord Rothschild spoke of his 'unspeakable vulgarity'.

Business was paramount to Barney but he also enjoyed mixing it with his hobbies, which included billards, acting, horse-racing, and boxing. The Barnato family, which soon included Barney's nephews, Solly and Woolf Joel, also invested in the Empire Theatre, and Barney took a box there. Under such wealthy patronage the Empire was able to attract star names willing to make the long trek to Johannesburg. New-found wealth had transformed the town into the bustling heart of the region populated by a cosmopolitan, sometimes unruly set of people. The large numbers of males employed by the mining industry had to be entertained, whether by prostitutes, cheap beer, the music halls erected near their canteens or at the Empire. Pay-day saw them flocking in to spend their money at the Empire's bar; cashing cheques that left them with banknotes spilling out of their hands, later collected from the floor by barmaids. There were frequent fights; on one occasion a shoot-out left the instigator dead and the barman injured while the turn on the stage played on. Independence Day was an excuse for Americans to let off fire crackers, while a riot of chair throwing erupted at a theatre near to the Empire when the manager refused to play the American national anthem.

Even before open hostilities broke out between the Boers and Britain, there was tension among the sombre, God-fearing, mainly rural burghers, the wild, disparate *uitlanders*, and between the ethnic divisions within this last group. Queen Victoria's jubilee was celebrated in areas that seemed as remote and un-English as the set of a Spaghetti western but in which official buildings were decked with bunting and huge paintings of Britannia. Many of the newly rich clung to their British heritage and to English fashions in clothing and how they lived.

Like Marie, Barney was intensely superstitious, and avoided making a permanent home for himself in one building: he preferred to rent accommodation, although he owned houses in London's prestigious Park Lane. When he was finally persuaded to build a mansion, he designed it to be as grand as an English country house. Barnato Park had thirteen acres of garden filled with fountains, an artificial lake, rustic bridge and a 'Ladies' Mile' for exercising horses. The house had ten bedrooms and other, oak-panelled chambers. Barney died before he could ever live there and Solly, to whom he left it, also avoided it.

Alice suggested in *Lloyds Sunday News* that Marie was drawn to Barney, who was short and moustachioed, because he reminded her of their father.[5] But it seems more likely that she appreciated how much they had in common – which was not simply their East End background, their love of gambling and parties. Both were outsiders and insecure about their success to the extent that they could allow suspicion to get the better of them, making them appear ruthless – if not cruel. By the time he struck up his friendship with Marie Barney was a millionaire, but he repeatedly asked her for cash. When she asked the Empire's manager why this was, he replied that Barney rarely carried money with him as he was concerned not to be taken advantage of by the less wealthy.

Unlike some music-hall stars, such as Vesta Tilley and George Robey, Marie did not like to surround herself with people who were grander, richer or higher up the social pecking order than herself. She felt at home with Barney because she could understand him and the way he operated; he was simply an East End boy who had done well. Barney, despite being short of change, lavished diamond jewellery on Marie and offered her betting tips that proved wildly successful. They went unheeded, though, because her perverse financial logic told her to ignore the advice of a rich man and listen instead to the yarns of hard-up conmen. In one instance he urged her to put her week's salary on a horse but she refused and missed out on winnings of £2,000. She was not entirely without luck at the races, though, and in May 1897 she won £1,000.[6]

Johannesburg represented a version of London music hall in which Marie did not have constantly to look over her shoulder for the disapproving syndicate owner or licensing inspector. The atmosphere was more relaxed. The Empire was well known for its musical conductor, Dave Foote, dubbed 'the Jimmy Glover of the Goldfields' after his famous English counterpart, who affected an air of insouciance and would casually nod to minor acquaintances throughout the performance. A boxing match usually followed the official programme and performers drank into the small hours at the Parisian-style cafés opposite the theatre. The racing journalist Percy Swaffer remembered taking Marie to the races and how she held court at the Empire bar, which performers used as an informal club, half an hour after she had been on stage.[7]

Barney was among the handful of millionaires who attended the famous tea parties Marie held at her bungalow. She said hotels were too impersonal, although others suggested she preferred rented accommodation because it worked out cheaper and the food was better. Barney was the first to recognize Marie Junior's gift for mimicry when he spotted her impersonating him at one of these parties. While her mother was set to pack her off to bed in disgrace for being rude to a guest, Barney suggested she appear at the Empire — which she did. She earned £50 per week and joined Rosie and Bella on the bill.

Marie was highly successful in South Africa, earning about £200 a week and extending her tour by a fortnight. 'The Geisha Girl' capitalized on a growing interest in things Japanese and was particularly popular: it 'knocked the audience pretty considerably'. The free-spending prospectors helped her net £1,000 from her benefit performance, at which 'standing room was not to be had for love or money'.[8] Marie Junior also performed at the benefit before her mother appeared for over half an hour, during which time she performed ten songs. The stage was covered with flowers and Marie thanked the audience for their warm welcome and the management for treating her 'downright well'. She might have stayed even longer, but she missed kippers too much — although Solly had some specially imported for her.

Interest in her continued after her departure and *South Africa* reproduced an extract from an interview she was supposed to have given in London, but which it acknowledged must have been a spoof:

I saw President Kruger at Pretoria, and we had quite a nice chat. There's a general notion out there that our little interview has settled all international difficulties. I asked him how he was, and he replied, 'Oh, going strong,' or words to that effect. Then I tried to get out of him why he didn't do the square thing by the *uitlanders*, and give them their Aliens Immigration Act and close their Drifts and things, or whatever it was the *uitlanders* wanted, and he said if I asked Johnny Jones I should know, see? He rather got back on me, didn't he?[9]

Shortly after Marie set sail for home, Barney was also on his way back to England. Rumours were circulating that his many-layered financial empire was on the point of collapse, and that he was beginning to lose his mind, that he had been spotted counting imaginary banknotes and picking diamonds out of walls. As he sat on the ship's deck he asked his nephew the time, but before Solly could answer Barney made a dash for the side. Solly managed to grab a leg, but could not hold him. An inquest reached a verdict of death by drowning while temporarily insane, but the rumours that had surrounded him all his life persisted in death. In a foretaste of the speculation that surrounded the death of the late-twentieth-century tycoon Robert Maxwell, Barney's demise was regarded variously as suicide, murder or an accident. He was buried in the Jewish cemetery in Willesden, north London. Solly's brother, Woolf, was shot the following year by a German adventurer who had tried to involve him in a plot to kidnap President Kruger.

Marie returned to a country basking in the glow of Queen Victoria's diamond jubilee. On the actual day, 22 June, London theatres shimmered with coloured lanterns, hanging baskets, crowns, stars, royal initials and portraits picked out in fairy-lights. Just two months after the celebrations Marie was appearing at the Berlin Wintergarten on yet another foreign tour. She was billed as 'Londons Liebling' (London's darling) and – with Anna Held ('Etoile de Paris'), Emilia Persico ('Italiens *grosste* Soubrette'), and the American Biograph – opened the new season at a venue that prided itself on being able to attract a raft of big international names. Performers who were visually appealing – no matter what their nationally – did well at the Wintergarten in the 1890s and far into the 1920s. Magicians and jugglers, acrobats, dancing girls and pretty singers were particularly successful. When it celebrated its fortieth birthday in 1928 the Wintergarten included among its hall of fame Marie Lloyd, Paul Cinquevalli, Harry Houdini, Chung Ling Soo, W. C. Fields, the Tiller Girls and Little Tich. After a month in Berlin Marie travelled to Bremen and then to Southampton, from where she set sail for New York.

The immigrant population of the United States, like Canada, Australia and South Africa, made a lucrative touring circuit for music-hall performers, although the audiences were not always Union Jack-toting admirers of Britannia. Overseas audiences could be difficult to 'read': not all immigrants, of course, were British, and those who were not were mystified by songs about costergirls and Piccadilly johnnies. Others had been keen to leave Britain emotionally, as well as physically, far behind: in May 1897, for example, Dan Leno was hissed by Irish Americans because of a patriotic reference he made during a performance in New York.

When Marie arrived in America the city was dominated by English female performers. On one night she shared a box with the male impersonators Bessie Bonehill and Vesta Tilley and the singer Marie Loftus. The *Era* was astounded by the concentration of talent in such a small space: 'The earning power per week, too, of this quartet would stagger a Rothschild or a Morgan – if they had to face the bill.'[10] But, despite their financial clout, the conversation between the women might have been a little stilted. Vesta was never a close friend of Marie and did her best to distance herself from her own modest upbringing as one of twelve children born to a china painter in Worcester.

Vesta was highly successful in America where she was reported to be earning, $1,500 a week, and adapted her act to incorporate local types, such as the Wall Street stockbroker in her song 'The Man Who Broke The Brokers'. Audiences appreciated the attention to detail that went into her lavish costumes and the mystique with which she imbued them. She made sure that the public knew that a particular favourite – a pearl grey frock-coat suit, with silk hat and vest of delicately flowered silk – had once belonged to the late Marquess of Anglesey. Then, as now, a title worked wonders in America.

Most of her outfits were made in Bond Street and she never took shortcuts: all her costumes were buttoned, laced or tied as appropriate. Her following was such that her appearances often sparked fashion crazes and one particular trend was set by accident. Rushing off to change from her Eton schoolboy impersonation to her American 'dude', the meticulous Vesta was dismayed to find that her maid had forgotten her cufflinks. In desperation she snatched the ribbons from her hair to use as makeshift ones. The new way of securing shirtsleeves became all the rage. Vesta Tilley boaters, waistcoats, cigars and cigarettes were also marketed. Her popularity was such that while she was at Weber and Fields in November 1897 a man called Don Leno (*sic*) was thrown out after he was spotted jotting down the lyrics of Vesta's songs on his cuff. The offending sections of his shirt were also confiscated.

Shortly after her arrival in America Marie gave a disarmingly honest interview with an American journalist, Jessie Wood, from the *Evening World* in which she assessed her own marketability.[11] In particular, they discussed a new song, 'What Did She Know About Railways' or 'She'd Never Had Her Ticket Punched Before' (by C. G. Cotes and B. Scott). On the face of it, the song is the tale of a 'regular farmer's daughter' who travels up to Euston by rail but repeatedly gets into trouble because she does not understand the etiquette of train travel. It is full of *double entendres* such as:

> The man said, 'I must punch your ticket,' spoke sharp, I suppose,
> Said she, 'Thou punch my ticket and I'll punch thee on thy nose!'

Eventually, police seize her 'rolling stock'.

In the *Evening World* interview Marie defended the song's innocence:

> ' "There's nothing in that," said Marie, and added rather inconsistently, "Think they'll let me sing it here?"
> ' "I don't know," I replied. "We're very particular. We permit our music-hall favourites to be wicked off the stage – in fact we encourage it – but on – " '

Marie went on to describe a discussion she had had with Anna Held. The account shows how she enjoyed the intimacy of a friendship with a fellow female star, as they weighed up each other's physical attributes like two schoolgirls getting ready for a party. Marie's account of their conversation also shows that, off stage, any characters in a story she told spoke with her own East End voice.

> ' "Anna Held told me I would have a rival at Koster's," interrupted Marie, irrelevantly. "Who?" said I.
> ' "Why she's the greatest French beauty – after me," says Held. (Good, wasn't it?)
> ' "Does she sing?" says I.
> ' "No, she dances, but not enough to hurt," says Held.
> ' "Well, thank God she don't sing," I said.
> ' "A dancer," continued Miss Lloyd, "should never be tall. Anna

Held is tall enough but she hasn't good legs – she knows she hasn't. She said to me, "Marie, I'd be perfect if I had your legs – give me your legs."

'"Lord," I said, "my legs are the only good thing about me."'

Marie's answer to the question 'How long will you stay here?' was: 'Two months if you like me, two minutes if you don't.' Her lack of confidence in herself – probably coloured by her last visit to America – emerged when she confided to her interviewer that she had 'brought no mother with her and no dog'. New York audiences certainly liked her, but her critical reception was not an unalloyed success – as an advert she placed in the British trade press shows:

> Many thanks to the kind creature who took the trouble to send a copy of a two cent newspaper, with an adverse criticism of myself, to all the proprietors in London, no doubt thinking it would injure my reputation. My position has been of too long a standing (and got through hardwork, not a fluke) to be injured in that way. I am sorry my wellwisher has been disappointed. – Marie Lloyd.
>
> I know who did it.
>
> What a dreadful complaint 'Jealousy'.

It never became clear who the 'kind creature' was and it may well have been that Marie was simply being paranoid. On the other hand, and despite its apparent camaraderie, the music-hall profession could be jealous and vindictive; it was too insecure a business for things to be otherwise.

The criticism bit even deeper than Marie's outburst suggests, as the following letter shows. Music-hall performers did not keep diaries and rarely wrote letters. This was not only because they had had limited formal education; it was because they lived for the moment and had little sense of posterity. Marie frequently threatened to fire off letters but as this seems to be the only hand-written one to have survived perhaps her anger had burned out before she put pen to paper. It is addressed to the journalist, Epes Winthrop Sargent, who wrote under different pseudonyms and perhaps produced the unfavourable review that irked her enough to place the advertisement:

77 West 68 Street

October 12th 97

EWS

Sir

I can see by your notice in today's issue of the Morning Telegraph that you were not present last night at Koster & Bials and if you were you are the best representative of an . . . s [can't read] I have ever heard of, your report is a *lie* from start to finish.

You can *roast* me as much as you like, I only laugh. The Public are my judges and supporters.

Marie Lloyd

P. S. I never dreamt that American reporters were so prejudiced against English artistes.[12]

Marie's bitterness and hurt are searingly evident in the short letter. Her only consolation was that – for her – the public's opinion was all that mattered.

It was ten years before she returned to New York.

Chapter 11

ALEC HURLEY AND THE FAMILY YEARS
(1898–1900)

~*

And ev'rything in the garden's lovely
Ev'rything in the garden is absolutely grand,
Ev'rything in the garden is great, you'll understand
'Ev'rything In The Garden's Lovely' by George le Brunn and J. P. Harrington

Alec Hurley was brought up less than two miles from where Marie was born.[1] He was a year younger than her and came from a family as dominated by men as Marie's was by women. His father, John, was an Irish sea captain and Alec had three brothers and a sister. Their mother ran a boarding-house for sailors from their home in Wellclose Square, near the docks in Wapping. Like Marie, he lived in an area studded with music halls. One of the most famous was Wilton's, which was also known as the Old Mahogany Bar after its central feature, and was situated down an alleyway by Wellclose Square. The raucous hall, which could squeeze in 1,500 people, was closed after a serious fire when Alec was six.

Working in the docks was an obvious choice of employment for Alec, but he earned extra money by singing at smoking concerts during the winter months. His first professional engagement was as an actor in the play *Harbour Lights* in the East End. He was spotted by an agent and made the transition to mainstream music hall with songs such as 'The Strongest Man On Earth (Up Came Sandow)' which capitalized on his own physique. Then he joined up with his brother to experiment with a double act, which, like Tom and Fred McNaughton's early efforts, had an Irish flavour.

By 1891 Alec had settled into the character of the coster singer that made his name. His style was similar to Albert Chevalier's and many of his songs appear rather maudlin to modern sensibilites. 'A Little Mother', for example, tells the story of a ten-year-old girl who keeps her family going after the death of her mother.[2]

Although many singers assumed East End credentials as part of their act, few had the affinity for the area that Alec and Marie shared. They met early in their careers when they played the same halls, and they started to attract attention at around the same time. Certainly, they were both at the Middlesex and South London Palace in October 1892; their paths crossed again at the Royal Cambridge in November and December that year, and Alec sang 'Mary Had A Little Lamb' at Marie's benefit at the Canterbury in December 1893. He gave her permission to sing 'No More Up At Covent Garden Market' or 'There Goes The Bloke Who Dunno Where 'E Are' when she appeared in the *Pretty Bo-Peep* pantomime at the Shakespeare Theatre, Liverpool, and she thanked him publicly through her advert in the *Era*. They probably became lovers in the mid-1890s.

Alec was as solid and dependable as Percy was shadowy and unreliable. He was tall and well-built, with a thick neck and bullet head – a sort of kindly Bill Sykes figure. In a surviving 'flicker-book' of photographic frames he has the appearance of a sinewy workman, downing his pint with the relish of someone who has just completed a job of hard manual labour. He retained the physically imposing stature of a docker all his life and kept fit by running on Hampstead Heath when he lived at nearby Jack Straw's Castle. Well into his thirties he enjoyed sculling and taking out his frustrations on a punch ball. This, together with his love of professional boxing and horse-racing, is enough to qualify him as 'a man's man'. It also seems fitting that the file containing photos of him in the Theatre Museum, London, was at one time erroneously labelled 'Burley'. Appearance was important to Alec and he was always immaculately turned out: a perfectly tailored suit, starched collars, a slightly rakish waistcoat and tiepin, sparse but neatly swept-back hair and a bowler hat. He and Marie were a handsome couple; two Cockneys made good – and proud of it.

Alec's physical bulk made his style of performance all the more surprising. For such a big man, he had a quiet, gentle voice that compelled the audience to pay particular attention. Bud Flanagan, of the famous Flanagan and Allen double act, modelled his style on Alec's, whom he had heard as a child: 'His voice was like silk, he never shouted – but you could hear him at the back of the hall. Instead of going out to them, he made them come to him.'[3]

Alec was also unusual in that reviews of his appearances concentrated on his technical abilities, and in particular on his well-controlled tenor voice: his 'neat, unobtrusive style'[4] was 'in distinct contrast to the aggressive manners adopted by some comic singers' and 'his quiet, unassuming method, capital enunciation and tuneful voice are all in his favour . . .'[5]

Very slowly, Marie and Alec became recognized as a couple and gradually they, with Marie Junior, became a family. News of their relationship seeped out into the general public and when Marie made a surprise appearance in a crowd scene at a Britannia pantomime, she was bustled off by the police protesting, 'Don't you push me, I'm a respectable married woman.'[6] The audience knew just how 'respectable' she was.

If any period in her life could be described as a time of relative calm, this was it. Her family adored Alec, who was kind, generous and a stabilizing influence. As a couple, he and Marie presided over a dynasty that looked to them for guidance. In September 1898 Marie moved into Granville Lodge at 98 King Henry's Road. The new home, in St John's Wood, was a few hundred yards from Primrose Hill yet at a convenient distance from the West End halls. Long since replaced by a block of flats, it was known for its grand furniture, particularly the Chippendale in the dining room.

She also followed the fashion among music-hall performers for houseboats and kept two on the Thames at Laleham, near Staines: *Moonbeam* to sleep on and *Sunbeam* for use during the day. The boats were used to put up friends and families after weekends out in the country and were also conveniently close to Ascot for trips to the races. But, given Marie's tendency to clumsiness, they did not make an ideal base. She often picked her way to the boats at the dead of night after several hours' socializing and it is hardly surprising that more than once she ended up in the river.

Alec and Marie also enjoyed Romano's, a tall, narrow Bohemian restaurant in the Strand with oak parquet floors where sportsmen, singers, dancers and journalists met after their day's work.

Although Marie was playing the head of the household at home, her stage persona was still a combination of the glamorous singer in beautiful gowns and the knowing young girl who spies on her courting sister, as in 'There They Are – The Two Of 'Em – On Their Own'. On Boxing Day 1897 she made her first ever appearance at the Palace in Cambridge Circus, on the edge of Soho, a move described as a 'daring experiment'. There was speculation that she would have to tone down some of her material in deference to the genteel audience. In the event, though, she was 'just as daring as ever'.[7]

She was the main attraction at the Royal Cambridge Music Hall in Shoreditch, which reopened in late 1897 after being destroyed by fire in 1896. The building, which held 2,500, was a lavish example of how far removed from the original music hall the new theatres were becoming. The East End had never seen anything quite like it. Mindful of the blaze that had destroyed its predecessor, the building contained eight wide entrances and exits in Commercial Street, roomy aisles within, fire hydrants on every floor, under the stage and in the flies, a fireproof curtain and behind it a sprinkler 'always fully charged with water'. The doorway and façade were Moorish in style and surmounted by richly coloured stonework, the vestibule was decorated in Venetian red, deep blue, cream and terracotta, there was tiling to match, and electric lamps. The *Era* noted that the 'garish decoration, which in the olden days was considered *de rigueur* in an East End music hall, is conspicuous by its absence'. The boxes were hung with rich red plush; the tip-up chairs in the grand circle and stalls helped to 'give the house a warm and cosy look'. There were saloons for refreshments on both floors, good ventilation and radiators. Each of the nine dressing rooms was heated with a radiator and there were 'retiring rooms' for both sexes on each floor.[8]

1898 was taken up with Marie's one and only experiment in musical comedy. In *The ABC Girl*, written by Chance Newton, Marie played a waitress, Flossie the Frivolous. The show's title referred to the Aerated Bread Company, whose café Flossie worked in, but 'ABC' was also a term for the facts of life. The show followed the fashion of the day for comedies about girls, as in *The Girl Behind the Counter, The Girl in the Taxi* and *The Girl in the Train*. These young women, like the characters Marie portrayed in her songs, were independent girls-about-town who knew how to have a good time. But, unlike in most of Marie's songs, they were ultimately unthreatening types who normally settled down to married life. Perhaps the fact that Marie could not meet this image contributed to the show's lack of success. Its tour was limited to Wolverhampton, Dublin, Nottingham, Stratford East and Sheffield. Apart from the confusing message of Marie's portrayal, her own brand of acting skills did not flourish in a conventional format.

Marie's domestic calm was briefly jolted in 1898 when Daisy was struck down with typhoid, which it was thought she had picked up in Liverpool and which was 'the cause of serious anxiety'.[9] Her mother nursed her back to health and the pair went to the genteel Victorian resort of Ventnor on the Isle of Wight to convalesce. Daisy's recovery was completed with a visit to her sister Grace in Austria.

By Christmas 1898 Marie and her little sister were reunited at the Crown theatre, Peckham, for the pantomime *Dick Whittington*, the first of three at Peckham that would include several Lloyds. Marie played the title role and wore a dangerously short tunic that revealed a figure much trimmer than in her *Trilby* days. Daisy was engaged to the handsome young director of the Crown Theatre and the Pavilion in Whitechapel, Donald Munro. He had money and Daisy was pleased to have found a husband who was not a performer, but who was still 'in the business'.[10] Like the showgirls who married peers, she planned to retire after her marriage, and Marie grumbled that she started to affect airs once she became 'Mrs Munro'.

The wedding took place in 1899 at the nearest church to Granville Lodge, St Mary the Virgin, and Marie presided over a day of April weather that oscillated between sunshine and showers.[11] Daisy wore duchesse satin, a lace train with orange blossom and a Brussels lace veil over a small coronet that her future mother-in-law had worn at her own wedding thirty years before. Alice, Rosie, Annie, Maude and Marie Junior were bridesmaids in empress dresses and Kate Greenaway bonnets. Marie Senior ignored any etiquette about leaving the limelight to the bride and chose to wear a 'cream lace and chiffon costume over apple green silk, with a wide-pointed collar of green moiré velours. A handsome maize-coloured tulle toque, with a paradise feather at the side, completed this bright and versatile artiste's attire.' Perhaps she did not want to be outdone by a younger, prettier sister, but it seems more likely that she simply enjoyed dressing up.

Several of music hall's biggest names attended the ceremony and the wedding gifts smacked of the *nouveau riche* anxious to show off. Most items – whether a cribbage board, fruit bowl or toast-rack – were silver or silver-plated. Marie gave her sister a diamond, sapphire and ruby ornament for her hair, tortoiseshell and silver glove and handkerchief boxes, a silver salver and a cheque. The groom gave his bride a gold and pearl necklace with the message 'My last gift as a bachelor'.

Marie did her best to promote her father's hotel in Hastings, the Royal Albion, advertising it through the card she placed in the *Era* for her own act, and brother, Johnny, became its general manager. The hotel was close to the Empire Theatre of Varieties, an elegant building that looked out on to the seafront and claimed to be one of the first buildings in England to use a special terracotta facing by Doulton's of Lambeth that helped to prevent corrosion by the salty air. The Royal Albion's proximity to the theatre, and its connection with the Lloyd family, helped to make it popular among music-hall stars such as Kate Carney. The future Edward VII was also rumoured to have stayed there.

Marie topped the bill at the Empire's grand opening on Saturday, 1 April 1899 when there was standing room only and she faced such a barrage of bouquets that she had some difficulty in dodging them. Herbert Campbell and Alec whom, the *Hastings Standard* said, 'is correctly described as a "melodious" coster comedian, which many are not',[12] were among the other star attractions.

Her new song, 'Hulloah! Hulloah! Hulloah!', was particularly appropriate for Hastings. In it, Marie takes the standpoint of the voyeur; she can see through the tricks and social conventions and really knows what is going on. The verses offer little vignettes: the fellow at the garden fête who disappears with Kate into the conservatory; when they reappear her face is all aglow and his coat is covered with powder – 'Hulloah! Hulloah! Hulloah!' Other verses tell of the wife who finds a dainty pink silk bootlace in the portmanteau of her commercial-traveller husband, and of Harry and Connie, who disappear during a picnic only to emerge with her hat looking 'rather rocky'. The final verse describes Marie's stay at a 'big hotel down by the sea' and how she watches couples arrive and sign themselves in as 'Mr and Mrs Brown', only to display their true relationship by revealing that they do not know how the other takes tea. The choice of setting showed that public knowledge of Marie's private life – the fact that she had installed her family in their own hotel – now regularly informed her songs.

During the last years of the century, her songs had titles such as 'Not For The Very Best Man That Ever Got Into Trousers/Breathing' (1897), which tells – if obliquely – about certain things a lady would not do for a man. In 'Bathing' or 'Should The Sexes Bathe Together?' (1898) she wore 'decidedly French' pretty blue bathing bloomers and tackled the issue thrown up by the popularity of seaside resorts. She was certainly not alone in her penchant for innuendo, and at her benefit night at Peckham in February 1899 Marie Kendall sang 'If I Could See This For 1s.6d., What Could I See For A Quid?'

The *Era* felt Marie's 'Everything In The Garden's Lovely' too sophisticated for an East End audience. Her targets in the song, though, are familiar: a 'dosy youth', whose foppish outfit is ruined when he is hit by a decorator's paint pot; 'a tasty little titbit,/Yes, a breach-of-promise case', who ends up in court with his sweetheart whispering their secrets to a judge; a group of men spying on women bathing in the sea who catch sight of a 'nice fat lump: a slap-up sort of gel' who turns out to be one of their wives.

The only verse that jars is the last, in which Marie makes an uncustomary foray into foreign affairs referring to the late-nineteenth-century preoccupation with China, and Europe's keenness to slice up parts of Pacific Asia.

> There's a handy bit o' China far away across the sea,
> And ev'rything in the garden's lovely,
> Possessors of that tea-set all the powers want to be,
> Because ev'rything in the garden's lovely,
> Japan said, 'China looks well on a Japanesey tray,'
> France tried to hold the sway,
> Ev'rything in the garden's lovely,
> Till John Bull barred the way,

He said: 'You want the whole set?
Oh! where do I come in, eh?'
And ev'rything's in the garden's lovely
[*Chorus*] They want sixteen millions cash,
Else the China goes to smash,
And ev'rything in the garden's lovely.

It was difficult to escape the repercussions of foreign affairs and Marie was on the bill at the Palace Theatre of Varieties in November 1898 when a thrill went through the audience upon the realization that they were sharing an evening's entertainment with the hero of Khartoum.[13] Only weeks before, Kitchener had been responsible for defeating the Dervishes in north Africa and occupying Khartoum in an act that at least avenged the death of General Gordon in 1885. Now the steely-eyed, ramrod-straight soldier with the luxuriant moustache was at a music hall. The band played 'Rule Britannia' in the interval and the audience sang 'See the Conquering Hero Comes'.

The Boer War, which started on 11 October 1899 between Britain and the Afrikaner republics of Transvaal and the Orange Free State and in which Kitchener played a notorious part, aroused the strongest feelings of jingoism.[14] The conflict represented a new brand of struggle not fought by anonymous cannon fodder in places so far off that no one had heard of them. Hand-held cameras operated by experienced photographers such as Horace W. Nicholls and faster communications meant that the public could plot the progress of the war from the comfort of their parlours. The soldier, or 'Tommy', was a real person and the public wanted to know all about him. Journalists like Winston Churchill, who sent back a report of his heroic escape from enemy hands, turned the war into a tale of derring-do that was reinforced through moving-picture images shown at music halls.

The manufacturers of cocoa and Bovril claimed that they were helping to win the war by sustaining the Tommies. Newspapers raised funds for the troops and the *Era* published details of individual donations. At Peckham, where Marie was performing in *Cinderella* with Alice and the McNaughton brothers, twenty pounds was collected in one week in February 1900 for the *Daily Mail* Fund. However, the fund-raising was low-key compared with the effort that went into

Marie's benefit performance, which took place in the same month. Marie was secure enough in her own professional standing to feel comfortable playing Prince Heliotrope next to Alice as Cinderella, and the benefit had the feeling of an intimate Lloyd family party. And, as at any Lloyd party, the participants lost all sense of time: the benefit started at six-thirty and ended six hours later.

So great was the deluge of bouquets that Tom commented that the stage smelt like Covent Garden flower market. The evening's entertainment included very few extracts from the pantomime although a scene entitled 'Beecham The Waiter' was featured in which Alice poured custard over the conductor's head. Stars such as Vesta Tilley, singing 'Piccadilly Johnny', and Ada Blanche, with 'Somebody Had To Stand In Front', needed little persuasion to make the long trek to south London. Marie, who had been suffering from bad colds throughout the pantomime's run, was presented with two silver bowls, 'big enough to be soup tureens', and wisely decided against a speech, given that by then most of the audience would have been in danger of missing their last bus home.

Marie's benefit was a rare breath of frivolity in an otherwise predominately earnest bill of music-hall fare. Military spectacles, such as the 'Soldiers Of The Queen' at the Alhambra, became popular and Sebright's included a sketch (which was illegal, strictly speaking, because it fell outside the form of entertainment allowed at a music hall) called 'Ladysmith' about the beleaguered British garrison that had finally been relieved in February 1900 at the fifth attempt. Marie was in a difficult position. She needed a war song, but her lyrics usually relied on making fun of someone, typically a figure of authority, but this approach did not sit comfortably with the mood of patriotism stirred up by the war. In the end she turned her song into a fashion statement: 'The Girl In The Khaki Dress' (1900).

> I am a girl who's rather larky,
> Always dressing myself in khaki,
> Just the same as men who claim to fight for their home and Queen;
> Now they're winning a nation's praises,
> You all know what the latest craze is – khaki this, and khaki that!
> Well, I'm in on that scene!

Khaki boots and stockings on either leg,
And, every morn, at breakfast time, I have a khaki egg!
Khaki cuffs and collars, yes,
And khaki 'dicky dirts',
And I've got khaki bloomers on, underneath my skirts!

Although Marie's repertoire failed to capture the sudden surge in patriotic feeling, she nevertheless joined in 'Mafekinging', the near hysteria that erupted with news that the siege of Mafeking was over and British troops were no longer in danger. When the news reached London Marie was on stage at Collins's and Rosie appeared in the middle of her act brandishing a Union Jack. Eugene Stratton, Harry Tate and Will Dalton joined them for an impromptu dance.[15]

The country collapsed into a mellifluous binge of self-congratulation. At the Tivoli in June Marie was 'not in her most audacious mood' when she sang 'The Girl In The Khaki Dress'. It must have seemed rather flippant, compared with other acts on the bill, which included a specially written poem, 'Something To Remember' recited by Leo Stormat:

They said old England was worked out –
Our Empire couldn't last, our army was degenerate –
Our fighting days were past!
In the kennel of the nations the bulldog stands alone
But our gallant boys have shown we still know how to hold our own
Let them read how British soldiers smiled in the face of death!
And dying cheered their comrades on with every gasp of failing breath!
In all the world's long history no braver tale is told –
That's something to remember as you're growing old.[16]

This is not to say that Marie did not care. The next time she visited South Africa she was found sobbing in a train carriage. Asked why, she pointed to the row upon row of earthy mounds, which she had taken to be the graves of fallen Tommies. They were anthills.[17]

Chapter 12

A MEASURE OF INDISTINCTNESS
Australia (1901)

~✺

It's a place where costers seldom go
Look on us as low, stuck-up lot, you know
I said, Come, girls, we'll upset the show
So, off we started for the day, With all our blokes in tow.
And they haven't got over it yet, you bet
We livened up the town . . .
'Folkestone For The Day' by George le Brunn and Edgar Bateman

When Marie and Alec set sail for Australia in February 1901 they left behind them a country in mourning for a queen who had been on the throne for over thirty years when Marie was born. Most legitimate theatres closed on hearing of her death, but many music halls stayed open. The front page of the *Era* was framed with a black border for several weeks. The halls argued, with little justification, that since the Queen had never been to a music hall and had found incomprehensible the words of a music-hall song she once overheard, it was what she would have wanted. Marie, Alice, the McNaughton brothers, Dan and Herbert were among sixty artists who sent 'a small token of loyal and devoted affection' for 'the dear departed Queen'. The 'small token' that arrived at Windsor was a four-foot-high floral tribute in the shape of a harp; its strings were of Parva violets – one string symbolically broken – and its frame was of lilies of the valley and cattleya orchids.

Preparations for the Australia trip threw the house at King Henry's Road into a flurry of excitement. It was Marie's most exotic destination to date and the trip was even more significant for Alec, who was far less travelled. The house was bombarded with parcels containing fabric and other bits and pieces for Marie's costumes, and there was an endless round of dress fittings. Messrs White Brothers of Nottingham were commissioned to make especially large dress baskets to hold the fifty or sixty stage dresses, the frills, hats, shoes, stockings, sunshades in 'every colour of the rainbow', evening dresses, street gowns, indoor dresses, silk blouses, Parisian hats, petticoats and laces she intended to take with her. Two hundred letters and telegrams arrived to wish her well and the housemaid constantly answered the door to visitors, while the telephone bell trilled incessantly in the background. There had been the usual farewell party, and again Marie declined to say more than a few lines herself, claiming overwhelming emotions and a bad head cold as excuses.[1]

Alec's preamble to their Australian visit was just as hectic, but for less pleasurable reasons. He was called to Westminster County Court to answer a summons by Messrs Skinner & Co., tailors of Jermyn Street, who sought to recover £25. 13s. (£1,257) for two suits and an overcoat supplied to him. Alec, who took great care in his appearance, claimed that the overcoat and trousers Skinner had made for him were of poor quality and overpriced. The tailors countered that they had been charging the same price for thirty years and that seven guineas for an overcoat and £2. 6s. for a pair of trousers was not exorbitant. Alec produced the clothes and said he had taken them on tour with him but had been forced to visit tailors in Birmingham, Manchester and Liverpool to have them altered. He had given away one item because it would not fit.

As with her trip to South Africa, a streak of imperialism lurked behind the warm send-off Marie and Alec enjoyed. The *Era* commented, patronizingly, that they were 'going to our kith and kin beyond the sea – to a new Commonwealth, to a generous-souled, loyal-hearted people, who love the Motherland, and there should be no fear for her welcome'.[2]

A huge ivy horseshoe that had followed Marie from hall to hall during the previous week proved particularly troublesome when she left St Pancras station for Tilbury, with the usual entourage of friends and family assembled on the platform to wish her well. The railway porters had difficulty loading the horseshoe on to the train but eventually it was squeezed in alongside her twenty-one trunks. It was hardly surprising that, in the chaos of the departure, she confided to a reporter that she needed 'a little drop of you know what, mixed as you know how'.[3] The train departed on time with Marie waving and blowing kisses.

Marie and Alec were signed up to appear together on the same bill, with Marie at the top, of course. She was earning £250 a week, while his weekly wage was £100.[4] Alec's brother accompanied them[5] and Alec, who was paying his fare, bought him a second-class ticket for the journey – when Marie found out she paid for him to be upgraded. This does not prove that Alec was mean: he may have felt his brother would be more at home in second class, or perhaps his lowly background could not allow him to justify the expense. However, he did not take offence at Marie's generosity.

They travelled as man and wife, although still unmarried. This flouting of convention went largely unremarked upon, although Marie was frequently mistaken by young dock labourers in Australia for Edward VII's mistress, Lillie Langtry.[6] As she bore no physical resemblance to the actress with the hourglass figure the case of mistaken identity must have been due to a similarity of reputation.

Marie soon discovered that the *Era*'s imperialist assessment of Australia was not entirely up to date. True, most local newspapers had given extensive, black-edged coverage of Queen Victoria's death, and the visit of the Duke and Duchess of York and Cornwall was also celebrated with copious pages of print, line drawings and photographs. But patriotism towards Britain was mingled with growing pride in Australia. By the turn of the century most of the top public jobs – except in the army and railways – were held by men born or brought up there and there was an increased respect for local products: efforts were made to serve only Australian fare at public dinners.

By the early twentieth century Australia had 3.8 million inhabitants, about 85 per cent of whom were native-born. Immigration had slowed to a halt and between 1898 and 1900 the number of people leaving the country was greater than the number of arrivals. The population was concentrated in two states: about 1.36 million people lived in New South Wales, with its principal city of Sydney, and 1.2 million in Victoria, dominated by Melbourne. At the end of 1900 Australia had been declared a commonwealth and federalism was starting to take hold when Marie visited. By the time she left in September the new Australian flag was flying over Melbourne. In 1902, Australian women won the vote – sixteen years ahead of Britain.

Marie arrived in the middle of a severe drought that had started in 1897 and which coincided with a shift in agricultural production.

Australia was still the world's leading producer of wool but farmers were starting to diversify and production of wine, dried fruit and dairy products was on the increase. The sheep population fell from 106 million in 1890 to 70 million by 1900.

Given the concentration of the human population, it is hardly surprising that Marie's tour of 'Australia' homed in on the south-east of the country. She arrived in Adelaide on Monday 25 March 1901 – having left Tilbury on 15 February – and a reporter from the *Register* was there to greet her.[7] He found her playing with and kissing some children who had been travelling on the ship and took the opportunity to interview her on the launch transporting her to the port. The reporter's question of which song first brought her 'into prominence' prompted a remarkable outpouring of resentment, coupled with an edginess at arriving in an unfamiliar country where she had, once again, to prove herself:

> 'Winked [*sic*] the other eye', but it didn't keep me there. I have winked myself almost blind since. I can't open my mouth or wear a dress without all the matinée birds being present. In America or Australia you don't mind your songs being sung because you don't hear much about it, but in London it is different. You make a success of a certain song and the following week you will hear it almost word for word. I can tell you that they sail perilously close to the wind so far as the copyright laws are concerned.

She also let the reporter know about British censorship: 'If there is anything objectionable in a song they stop it at once. Nowhere is the censorship as severe as it is in London, on account of the London County Council. They run you like sharks.'

Sharks may have been uppermost in her mind since she and Alec had fished for them from the ship's deck during a delay in the journey. Marie eventually caught one but decided to throw it back.

Asked how long her engagement was due to last she replied, with a fierceness that was perhaps indicative of nervousness and which echoed her comment on arriving in New York for her previous tour: 'It is for six months, but it's for six nights if I don't catch on; I get the very next boat back.'

Marie had been reluctant to leave England for the other side of the world but Harry Rickards, the impresario organizing the tour, persuaded her by offering a three-month contract with a clause that allowed her to cut the visit short if she was not happy but still be paid for the full period. He ran the Tivoli music halls in Adelaide and Sydney and wanted Marie to star at the new Opera House in Melbourne, which was due to open in May 1901. Harry had once been a comic singer himself, which may have helped persuade Marie. He had left for Australia after he was declared bankrupt in Britain.

Harry was a supremely optimistic person who liked to have his photo taken dressed as Napoleon and was consequently known as 'the Napoleon of vaudeville'. He made regular trips to Britain to sign up performers whom he brought back to Australia for extensive tours. Marie was following Lottie Collins, who had been well received at the Tivoli in Adelaide. During the course of his career Harry persuaded the English magician Chung Ling Soo, strongman Sandow, comedian Harry Tate and escapologist Harry Houdini to appear in Australia. W. C. Fields made his longest ever appearance as a juggler in 1904 when he performed at the Tivoli in Sydney on his second Australian tour.[8]

Marie and Alec were well received in Adelaide, but Sydney and Melbourne represented a far bigger challenge. Visitors ranging from Mark Twain to Beatrice Webb, who both toured Australia at the end of the nineteenth century, had been impressed by Adelaide, its wide streets, graceful public buildings and lush foliage. Sydney was quite different. Beatrice Webb described the women of Sydney as 'Dressy, snobbish and idle, and whilst they are willing enough to companion the men on the racecourse, they apparently think it "unwomanly" to take an active part in public affairs ... The clothes are fresh and flashy: powder and paint ruin complexions and the women age rapidly. The women of Australia are not her finest product.'[9]

But Marie conquered Sydney when she opened at the Tivoli and received thirteen encores after singing five songs on a bill that included the Soukes Brothers' three bears, who were trained to wrestle and waltz, and the singer 'dainty Irene Franklin'. One review was a strange mixture of lavish praise about her skills as a mimic counterbalanced with the assertion that Marie could not sing: 'She has no claims to be considered a singer, but her vocal powers are pleasantly sufficient for the development of her character sketches. The latter are new, bright, and clever; her mimicry and general acting are admirable, and the humour of her "lines" piquant and meritorious [*sic*].' She was '"'Arriet" not alone in dress – though that was a faithful reproduction in paisley and violet of the genuine article – but in voice and action, and apparently in thought and temperament. Her narration of a descent of 40 costers on Folkestone to give the "toffs a turn" was exquisitely comical, both in construction and treatment.'[10]

But Melbourne was a different matter; it was more pretentious, and more elegant, than Sydney. Even in the intense heat men and women insisted on wearing the most formal outfits and approached Marie, and Rickards's new Opera House, warily.

It had been a rush to finish the Opera House in time and, as a result, there was a slight hitch with the electric lights on the grand opening night. The building was overcrowded. Most critics described it as 'elegant' and 'comfortable', although a few were not so sure about some of Harry's innovations. The backdrop was painted to represent a Parisian boulevard, or 'the casino of a continental watering-hole' – no one was quite sure which – and during the course of the evening members of the company strolled around dressed as though they were attending a carnival, which some members of the audience found distracting. The extreme slope of the dress circle was designed to 'minimize the inconvenience of the matinée hat'; but not everyone appreciated this concession to ladies' fashion. One reviewer noted cuttingly: 'Building a theatre in order to beat the matinée hat is rather like burning down a house in order to boil an egg.'[11]

Like an anxious football manager who selects himself to play in an important game, Harry was on the bill for the opening night; his daughters Noni and Madge also performed and his wife helped to make the costumes. Mademoiselle Celina Bobe, an expert xylophone player and violinist from Paris, and a 'coon ballet' of twenty girls were promised. But, as the programme proclaimed, the real attraction was:

First appearance in Melbourne of London's Idol
MISS MARIE LLOYD
Absolutely the Most Marvellous Artist the World has ever seen.
She will appear in Selections from her own Original Creations.

A few months later the wording was amended to read 'Absolutely the Most Marvellous Artiste in the Universe'. Harry's advertisement, too, spoke of 'The Marie Lloyd boom'.[12]

Few knew who Marie was, and reviews of her performance are unencumbered by the weight of her reputation. Reading them is like seeing her act afresh. One newspaper said she was 'as much at home with her audience as if they were her intimate girlfriends, and has, seemingly, the same certainty that it will not be shocked'.[13] It added, though, that she had not yet mastered the new theatre and her words were consequently a 'trifle indistinct'. However, she interpreted each song with 'an archness and meaning that few female singers know how to infuse, and if some of the incidents she described were not such as would meet the approval of the prim, there are not many patrons of the music hall who come within that definition, and therefore there was nothing, as far as could be judged, in Miss Lloyd's repertoire on Saturday night which the audience would have cared to be omitted'.

Another paper was not sure quite what to make of her, and eventually decided she was beyond the pale. She was a

> dainty, although somewhat peculiar figure, a fascinating laugh, and some extraordinary creations in the way of dress, were the impressions which Marie Lloyd left on most of the audience ... The songs, however, were for the most part irredeemably vulgar, and sung by anyone else would probably have been ill received. Coarseness may at times be associated with wit, but the songs to which the audience was treated on Saturday night had not even the saving grace of humor. Apparently they pleased a number of those present, but the laugh and applause were often gained by double entendre.[14]

The *Australasian* was a wholesome weekly publication that counted farmers and wealthy citizens among its readership and carried articles on such themes as how to build the perfect hen coop. Its reviewer, who had been so arch about matinée hats, was unequivocal about Marie:

> Miss Marie Lloyd, a character vocalist of much ability, could be heard with extreme distinctness. Directors of Sunday-schools might be led, indeed, to believe that the acoustic properties of the house were a bit too good during some of Miss Marie Lloyd's songs, and that a measure of

indistinctness would not be amiss. Miss Marie Lloyd sails close to the wind, and her ditties about the bicycling girl, the barmaid and the bather were frankly of the smoking-room type. Exuberant spirits, vivacity, and assurance are the stock-in-trade of the successful vocalist of this class, and Miss Marie Lloyd is fully equipped.[15]

By the end of her Australian visit, though, she had won over some of the *Australasian*'s readers and 'Everything In The Garden Is Lovely' had become so popular that string quartets were forced to add it to their repertoire.

Alec's reviews, which were shorter and usually tucked on to the end of a long discussion of Marie's performance, are muted by comparison. He was 'capable of putting in the light and shades of both comedy and tragedy'[16] and was praised as a 'very clever coster singer'.[17] He was 'cordially received' and his song 'I Haven't Told Him' 'has a certain merit'.[18] Two reviews even got his name wrong, calling him Alen and Alex, and another described him as Marie's husband.[19] More annoying than any of this was that the band parts for his 'big number' – 'The Lambeth Walk' (not to be confused with Lupino Lane's later hit of the same title) – went missing on the way to Melbourne, robbing him of the chance to perform it at the Opera House's grand opening.

The piece was a parody of Eugene Stratton's 'Cake Walk', itself the product of a craze for a certain style of song. Alec's 'scena' was a sort of sketch that involved special scenery with three men and three women in Cockney dress.

> Talk about the cake walk, just a bloomin' fake walk
> Wot the niggers do upon the plantee-ation.
> Come the Surrey side, boys,
> Keep your peeper wide, boys,
> The Lambeth Walk'll beat creation . . .

He was unable to sing his most successful song at the biggest date of the tour – which the critics did not fail to point out. Yet while the loss of his band parts made Alec furious, he did not begrudge Marie her success. He was secure enough in his own talents to share her triumphs and he knew that as a coster singer of sentimental songs he could never make it to the dizzy heights that Marie, with her range of characters and sparkling humour, could command.

The Australian tour was extended from three months to six but it was not the great financial success it should have been for its two key players: both Alec and Marie found the local racecourses too great a temptation. They bought a horse and called it Marie Lloyd, although it turned out to be male. It did not win a single race during their ownership and Alice believed it was this that contributed to their lack of funds. 'As a matter of hard fact, they came back broke to the wide!'[20]

Nevertheless, Marie was in high spirits, as this letter written on 10 September to the *Era* shows. It also revealed that she had no hesitation about linking her name with Alec's:

> Just a line to let you know my most successful engagement is drawing to a close. I will sail on September 24th on the Himalaya, due home about November 3d. We are playing twelve nights farewell here, then sail. Our last night in Sydney was a great affair. I had no end of flowers and presents; and we were entertained at supper by the World's Entertainers of the Palace Theatre. They were all Americans, except Arthur Nelstone, so I took it as a great compliment. Mr Rickards gives me a farewell banquet the last night here, at which 200 guests are invited. My visit has been most successful and enjoyable. Mr Hurley joins me in kindest regards.[21]

Chapter 13

BELLA'S TROUBLES

(1901–2)

~✦

Over the tea-cups, strange stories we hear;
Things we are learning,
Mostly concerning
Neighbours – fond neighbours – whom we hold so dear!
Time, somehow, always seems to go
So pleasantly,
Running down other folks, you know . . .
'The Bond Street Tea Walk' by George le Brunn
and J. P. Harrington

At the end of October 1901 Bella married the former prize fighter Dick
Burge at Brixton Road register office. Marie and Alec were on their way
back from Australia, but they were represented at the wedding by
several other members of Bella's adopted family: Marie's parents, Alice
and Tom, and Bella's former music-hall partner, Rosie, who was a
bridesmaid. The couple's honeymoon was short-lived.

The following month a twenty-nine-year-old bank clerk, Thomas
Peterson Goudie, disappeared after his employer, the Bank of Liverpool,
realized that £160,000 (£7.7 million) had gone missing. Goudie, who
was originally from the Shetlands, was said to demonstrate 'regular
habits' and was 'never overdressed'. When James Mances, an unemployed American, and Laurence Abraham Marks, a bookmaker, heard
of the manhunt they immediately fled the country. Mances told friends
he was leaving England for a 'continental tour'[1] and was never heard of
again. Marks appears to have committed suicide by jumping overboard
from a Channel ferry.

Dick, who was friendly with both Mances and Marks, was at home in
Brixton when Detective Sergeant Goff arrived unannounced. He had
noticed the policeman in the audience at the Tivoli music hall in the
Strand a few weeks earlier and had also spotted him at various
racecourses. The policeman's sudden appearance must have alarmed

Bella – especially given the huge publicity surrounding what quickly became known as the 'Liverpool Bank Frauds' and, later, the 'Goudie Scandal'. Shortly after their wedding she had opened an account with the London and South Western Bank and during the weeks that followed she deposited amounts varying in size from £1,000 (£48,360) to as much as £16,000 (£773,760) in it. Detective Sergeant Goff arrested Dick for conspiracy to defraud the bank and for forging cheques, and left with him and some of Bella's jewellery as security.

As soon as news of Dick's arrest hit the evening papers Marie issued a statement:

> Miss Marie Lloyd's attention having been called to the statement in the daily press that she is a sister of the wife of Richard Burge, who is remanded under a charge in connection with the Bank of Liverpool forgeries, she desires to state that she is no relation whatever either to Richard Burge or his wife. The latter, whose professional name is Bella Lloyd, appeared for some time at the halls in partnership with Miss Rosie Wood, a younger sister of Marie's, as the Sisters Lloyd, and this fact has given rise to the erroneous report.[2]

A front-page item that appeared in the *Daily Express* under the headline 'Marie Lloyd and Mrs Burge' appears slightly less callous. After repeating the formal statement, a less officious voice emerges:

> 'I am no relation whatever to Mrs Burge,' said Miss Lloyd last night, 'though she is a very dear friend of mine.
>
> 'Yes, at one time she was my dresser, and when she went on the "boards" took my name and appeared in "turns" with one of my sisters. Since then she has appeared "on her own".
>
> 'She has been only married to Dick Burge about a month. We all liked Dick, as everyone does.'[3]

She added, cryptically, 'No, there was never any idea of my going with the Burges to Egypt this winter.'

Marie's description of Dick in the past tense was ominous, as was the fact that she made no attempt to protest his innocence with her usual verbose spontaneity. Bella must surely have had her suspicions about the sudden rush of money that poured into her new bank account and, given their sisterly closeness, Marie must also have suspected that Dick was involved in something not entirely above board. But Marie and Bella were in a profession where gifts and favours came in all forms and it was not in their natures to ask too many questions where money was concerned.

At thirty-five, Dick was ten years older than Bella. He was born in Cheltenham but spent much of his early life in Newcastle. As a professional boxer he became popular for taking on big men and for remaining dignified in defeat. In 1896 he challenged the French-Canadian fighter the Saginaw Kid for the world championship. Like Alec, who became a close friend, he was a fastidious dresser and also enjoyed horse-racing.

By the turn of the century his professional boxing days were over and he made a living by public exhibitions in which, dressed in his boxing silks, he thumped a punchball in time to music. Bella first caught sight of him when she was waiting with Rosie to go on at Gatti's music hall in Lambeth, south London. Dick was the act before and he smiled at her as he came off. He invited her to Romano's that evening, and a few months later they were married.

Marie's cold denial of any blood relationship to Bella appears a betrayal, given how close they had been for so long, and her efforts to distance herself from a financial scandal, when she had lived so long in the shadow of sexual notoriety, also seem hypocritical. Perhaps being seen to be above criticism when it came to money was important because her wealth was part of her star appeal. Her background and trade meant she could never be fully accepted in the upper classes of society, but her money gave her a certain standing. Fraternizing with criminals was not good for her image. Perhaps, too, she was a little afraid of money: her business acumen was negligible – money was there to be spent, to have a good time with or to help a friend out.

Maybe she was simply intimidated by the size of the fraud: Marie knew how to deal with a violent husband or sexual transgressions but financial impropriety was harder to cope with because the rules were more strictly defined. Bella and Dick were similar to Alec and herself: all four had used a talent to entertain to drag themselves out of poverty. Dick and Bella, though, had taken too many risks. And financial ruin so close to home reminded Marie of just how precarious her own lifestyle was.

The shock of Dick's arrest and the spectre of his trial in the new year cast a shadow over Marie's return to England. Although she was warmly welcomed home with flowers and poems from her public, she missed several performances through colds and a weak voice she blamed on the thick London fog. At the Oxford in November she stopped abruptly and said, 'It's no good – I can't go on.'[4] By January 1902 Marie's cold had developed into bronchitis and Katie Lawrence deputized for her at Collins's. Under doctor's orders, Marie limited her performances to two turns a night and cancelled her scheduled appearances at the Oxford.

Dick's trial took place at the Old Bailey at the end of February in a crowded courtroom. Members of the horse-racing world had come to see how their industry had proved the spur for such a huge scam. Viscount Falmouth and Leonard Brassey, stewards of the Jockey Club, were joined by the Marquess of Cholmondeley, Sir Edgar Vincent, the Duke of Westminster and Lord Crewe. Dick, 'well-groomed and clean-shaven and anxious-looking',[5] stood alone in the dock after the judge ordered Goudie, who was to be called as a witness, to leave. Alec was in court to hear his friend face charges, to which he pleaded not guilty, and to relay each tortuous day of the trial to Marie and Bella at home. Marie was working at the Crown, Peckham, and was able to comfort and reassure Bella between performances.

Goudie had been employed by the Bank of Liverpool for eight years as a hardworking, efficient ledger clerk when his betting debts forced him to look for a quick way of making money. Since he was in charge of the accounts of customers whose surnames began with H and K, Mr Robert Hudson and his company, the well-known Liverpool soap manufacturer, were the obvious targets for his fraud. Having perfected Mr Hudson's signature, Goudie started to cash cheques on the account. He then destroyed them before they could be entered in the bank's ledger and made sure the books tallied at the end of the month.

In the early years his gambling debt was manageable – the most he lost in a year was £400 (£18,736), which was still a substantial amount for someone on an annual salary of £150 (£7,026) – but he increased his betting in a bid to meet his mounting debts. Word got round the close-knit horse-racing community that a Liverpool bank clerk had access to a lot of money and allowed commission agents a free hand in placing bets on his behalf. Presented with such a gullible client the agents could not resist pocketing the money for themselves rather than wasting it on a bet.

Mances and Marks, who had an office close to the Charing Cross Hotel in Adelphi Terrace, decided Goudie was ripe for picking. Dick, who before he married Bella lived in the Hummums Hotel in Covent Garden, knew Mances and Marks through various betting transactions. According to the prosecution, Dick went to Newmarket races to try to find out the clerk's identity. It was customary for the Post Office to keep original telegrams for three months and Dick left a paper trail of incriminating evidence behind him. He and Mances visited Liverpool and Mances tracked down Goudie and told him of a jockey called Ballard who had good inside information. On their second meeting Mances told Goudie he knew a bookmaker who would accept a bet as large as £5,000 only an hour before the race. Over the next three weeks Goudie placed bets on Mances' advice, the amounts expanding with his desperation. On average he was betting up to £25,000 (£1.2 million) a week.

Once, by some strange fluke, Goudie even backed a winner; he wired Marks to put £10,000 on Sansome, which was due to run in the one-thirty at Leicester. The horse came in first after starting with odds of 5–2 against – which would have netted Goudie £25,000. But at 1.35 p.m. Dick sent a telegram from Marks saying, 'Not doing any business today.' All in all Goudie forwarded cheques worth £91,000, which went straight into Marks's Credit Lyonnais account to be divided between the three men.

Dick spent four and a half hours in the witness box and managed to tie himself in knots during the cross-examination. Several times after making elaborate notes the judge, Mr Justice Bigham, put down his pen pointedly when Dick appeared to contradict what he had said earlier. He claimed that he had earned £30,000 from boxing and betting in the previous eight years, but it emerged that he had had nothing in his bank account the year before. He admitted eventually that he had pawned Bella's jewellery to raise money. His main defence was that he did not know that the customer was Goudie and that the money had been stolen. Goudie said that he had never met Dick.

As the jury left to make up their minds the judge told them he thought there had been a gross swindle and that Dick had been at the centre of it – but that that was only his opinion. Earlier in the trial when Dick's defence counsel had pointed out that an expert had wrongly identified his handwriting the judge had commented, 'The best of us make mistakes.'

The jury took five minutes to find Dick guilty. He accepted the verdict quietly, but when he returned to court after the weekend for sentencing he was described as entering the dock with a 'sprightly' gait. He had agreed to hand over £39,000 (£1.8 million) in money, furniture and jewellery, and was confident that repaying this would help to reduce his sentence. Many people felt that he had been indulging in a fraud that was widely practised in betting circles: he could hardly be blamed for not demanding details of where his client's money came from. He was also standing as a scapegoat for Mances and Marks. Alec told Bella and Marie that he thought Dick might get away with two or three years.[6]

The court was packed on the day of sentencing; sportsmen and bookmakers were there in force, as well as the novelist Zangwill and the actor Seymour Hicks. The tension was prolonged by an angry exchange between the judge and a defence lawyer after Justice Bigham asked how many more speeches he would have to listen to then took offence at the barrister's reply.

At last judgements were passed. Goudie's punishment must be exemplary, the judge said, and gave him a sentence of ten years. Next he turned to Dick who, he said, was as bad as Goudie. He had no doubt that Dick knew where the money had been coming from and that he had cheated Goudie in claiming to put bets on horses. His sentence was a total of ten years – of which two were to be spent in hard labour. There were cries from the gallery and a deep sob from Dick, who turned pale and collapsed. He was immediately forced to sign cheques and documents handing over everything he owned.

Bella received several letters of sympathy and there was talk of a petition to the Home Secretary to reduce Dick's sentence. As soon as the trial was over a short item appeared in the gossip columns of the *Era* saying that Bella Lloyd 'will in future style herself professionally as Miss Ella Lane' and would be appearing at the Empire, Liverpool. The only way to keep going, financially and emotionally, was for her to return to the halls, which she knew as well as Marie and Alec. Although they had not spoken out in Dick's defence, they immediately helped her

The sheet music for 'Oh! Mr Porter' with Marie shown between two pictures depicting scenes from the song, 1892.

Marie in a provocative pose typical of many of her early performances. c. 1890.

Marie seated next to her parents. In front of them, from left, are: Anne, Maude and Sidney. Standing at the back, from left, are: Daisy, Rosie, John, Grace and Alice. Date unknown.

Marie, aged thirty-three, and her fifteen-year-old daughter Myria in what is thought to be the only surviving picture of them taken alone, 1903.

Alec Hurley and Marie on their wedding day, October 1906.

The Music Hall strike: the strikers' head office in Wellington Street, London, with Marie sitting by the window, February 1907.

Marie and Alec leaving Liverpool for America: local members of the Variety Artistes' Federation present them with a floral arrangement that includes white flowers picking out the words, 'Our Marie's Heart', September 1907.

Marie and her friend and fellow performer Victoria Monks indulge in the 'rinking', or rollerskating, craze, November 1909.

Bernard Dillon on Lally after the 1906 Derby; although he was the favourite he failed to win.

The view from the stage at the Canterbury on a Saturday night in June 1912.

Marie sitting on the terrace at 'Oakdene' next to the wife of Sime Silverman, editor of *Variety*. Behind them, from left, are Marie Junior, Bella Burge and Alice Lloyd.

Marie with her new 20hp Austin car outside her home, 'Oakdene', in Golders Green, north London, July 1914.

Alice Lloyd, 1921.

Marie in costume for 'It's A Bit Of A Ruin That Cromwell Knocked About A Bit', October 1920.

Marie and her husband Bernard Dillon: a picture of apparent domestic harmony, 1922.

Marie's coffin leaves the home in Woodstock Road, Golders Green, which she shared with her sister Daisy, October 1922.

A rare picture of Marie out of costume and without a hat. Date unknown.

to rebuild her life: George le Brunn wrote several songs especially for her and she started to tour the country, staying with Alec and Marie when she was in London. Years later, when Dick bumped into the judge at a Turkish bath, Justice Bigham told him that the case might have gone differently if the Court of Appeal had existed then.[7]

Bella's troubles were not over. Marie was making extensive alterations to Granville Lodge and had decided to put many of the most valuable possessions belonging to her and Bella in storage. In September she and Bella lost them all in what the *Era* referred to as 'a calamitous fire' at Dixons' repository in the Harrow Road. The next month Alec, who had recently been robbed of some valuable jewellery, had to cope with his mother's death.

Chapter 14

CHANGING TASTES

(1902–5)

~♫

By correct manipulation, she her figure can display,
And her ankles, and, er, well, it's hard to turn your eyes away
When, there's half a yard of 'open work' about.
'The Tale Of The Skirt' by Fred W. Leigh and George le Brunn

The early years of the twentieth century were marked for Marie by a series of firsts and lasts indicative of subtle changes in public taste and her changing position as a performer.

In June 1902 she had tried her hand at revue, a form of entertainment that first came to London in *Under the Clock* in 1893 at the Royal Court Theatre as part of a longer show. Revue's main distinguishing feature was that it consisted of a series of items, sketches, monologues, songs and dances – often of a topical nature – performed by a single cast of actors. In the Tivoli revue Marie played Sarah Bernhardt, Cecilia Loftus as Marguerite in *Faust*, Olga Nethersole in *Sappho*, and Prehistoric Woman. Little Tich, the other main star of the production, also played a range of characters, including Faust, the Terrible Greek and Ben Hur.

Scene one was set among 'the chimney-pots of London at night' and contained allusions in 'the Spirit of the Strand improvement' to the building works that were transforming London, to pirated music (in March a music publisher had raided a building where 15,000 illegal versions of a song had been found), and to 'Shamrock Homes, the detective'. The second scene took place in 'Grand Coronation Stand in the Strand' and included 'Macaroni, the wireless wonder'. In the final scene, set in the courtyard of the House of Commons and Ludgate Circus, 'Pinpoint Moregain' (a thinly veiled reference to the American millionaire, John Pierpont Morgan) and Dr G. W. (*sic*) Grace were among the characters.

The programme's cover, with its photo snapshots of the main characters, most of whom are pulling faces or standing in exaggerated poses, and the six glum-looking women holding a letter each to spell out the word 'TIVOLI' has a surreal feel to it. It certainly appears to have been ahead of its time – revue took off just before the First World War – and even some members of the cast were confused by the convoluted 'plot'. By July the production had been cut back and Marie and Little Tich replaced. Later Alice blamed its failure on the enormous payroll, which she said ran to four figures a week, and on the Tivoli's small capacity – in 1900 seating had been increased to hold a thousand people, but the recently opened Hackney Empire held three times this number. Removing its two stars propped up the production's ailing budget, but robbed it of its main attractions.

Marie, like other music-hall stars, was also experimenting with 'scena'. This was a form of sketch that was still, strictly speaking, forbidden under the original definition that separated music hall from theatre. Her new song, 'The Bond Street Tea Walk', was performed in front of specially designed scenery reminiscent of the set for the first act of *The Wilderness*, a play being performed at the St James's Theatre, and she had a cast of female dancers to accompany her.

The song can be interpreted on several levels. It was a gentle dig at the sort of people who enjoyed a play like *The Wilderness* and taking tea in a genteel way. It was also an obvious parody of the popular 'Cake Walk':

> The cake walk's the rage, at present, on the stage,
> But the Tea-Walk takes the tea-cake ev'ry time!

But this was not simply a comedy of manners: the first verse could easily be describing a brothel, rather than a tearoom:

> They've lots of spoons! Parisian
>   confections.
> Elaborate complexions.
> When you walk in those up-to-date salons!

The final verse confirms the tone of moral impropriety:

> Lovers, each week, get
> Meeting in secret,

Find this a really ideal rendez-vous,
Ladies with ennui,
Travel a long way
Just to be meeting – your husbands?
Not you!
No girl, without a chaperon,
Would ever go!
All on their naughty little own,
They never go!
A male thing, bright and merry
Is very necessary,
To pay the bill and give the thing a tone!

'The Bathing Parade' was introduced, after several delays, in June 1902. It relied on the newly fashionable vogue for seaside resorts and the public's fascination with mixed bathing. Marie played a character called Lady Di: she and six 'lovely nymphs' wore peignoirs, which they eventually discarded to reveal bathing costumes. Charles McNaughton played a 'dude' who flirted with Marie. At the end she was drawn off-stage in a bath-chair. But the sketch sparked a bitter exchange of letters over its originality, which piqued Marie's professional pride and showed that she was still highly sensitive about being copied.

Sir, – I notice you stated in your issue of the 9th inst., that Miss Minnie Palmer was producing a new sketch at the Metropolitan Music Hall, entitled 'Mixed Bathing'. For fear I should be accused of copying, allow me to make an explanation. On June 9th last I produced at the above mentioned hall a sketch, entitled 'The Bathing Parade' by E. W. Rogers, dealing with the subject. The original title of my sketch was 'Mixed bathing', but this title was objected to. The sketch was received by the public and the Press in a most flattering manner, and is extensively booked.

Perhaps those in charge of the new(?) sketch may like to borrow the manuscript of mine to complete their task?

Yours faithfully, Marie Lloyd.

Clifton Hotel,

Blackpool.

August 13th.[1]

A week later the *Era* printed a reply, which showed that Marie's sketch was simply latching on to a well-established trend.

Sir, – Re Miss Marie Lloyd's letter in your issue of the 16th inst., wherein, by some extraordinary stretch of the imagination, she claims to be first in the field with a bathing sketch. I shall be obliged if you will allow me to state a few facts which, I think, will prevent any further argument on the subject.

Miss Lloyd produced 'The Bathing Parade' at the Metropolitan in June this year. Miss Palmer, in the present month, followed at the same hall with 'Mixed Bathing'. Edwin Brett and Emmeline Orford, nearly twelve months ago, viz, in September, 1901, produced at the same place of amusement a sketch entitled 'On the Quiet', or 'Mixed Bathing'. The said title was extensively advertised – see the *Era*, April 26th, 1902. Then followed a tour of the Livermore halls in 1901. Moss Empires, spring 1902; and lastly, four weeks at the Tivoli, Strand, in April of this year. You see all this was before the production of Miss Lloyd's 'first and original'[?] bathing sketch. These facts clearly prove that Edwin Brett and Emmeline Orford's 'On the Quiet', or 'Mixed Bathing' saw the footlights ten months before Miss Lloyd's 'seaside episode'.

Yours faithfully, Edwin Brett
Oxford Music Hall, London W.

Marie was on safer ground with 'The Wedding March' or 'The Coster Wedding', a gentle and affectionate story of a mass Cockney wedding. The song, an original recording of which still exists, has a catchy, lilting melody:

> There's bin a reg-lar How-de-do-di-do this morning boys,
> For such a splicing up of pairs you never saw!
> Just seventeen of us got wed for bett' or wuss
> And not none of us had never been spliced before.

Its tone is chatty – 'We live in Befnal Green – that's near the Old Red Church, you know' – and perked up by appropriate sound effects, 'dicky birds' singing and church bells ringing. A sequel, 'The Coster's Christening', followed, which re-creates the chaos and heightened emotions of a Cockney celebration to wet the baby's head: a spread of 'lovely pig's 'ead, or "trimmins" and bread' and the men going for a 'liv'ner'.

> An' the baby 'e was cryin' like an angel,
> And Mother Jones was moppin' up the gin;
> An' they came from near an' far on the new electric car,
> To see the christ'ning party goin' in.
> My old mother she was weeping in the doorway;
> When the parson came the kid began to sing;
> Then we finished up wiv fightin',
> So it got a bit excitin'
> At the Coster Baby's christening ...

Other songs were more daring, acknowledging that Edwardian audiences had a greater tolerance of titillation. 'The Tale Of The Skirt' allowed Marie scope to manipulate the voluminous garment in a way that revealed a glimpse of ankle and, to an audience well versed in the signals of the time, showed whether Marie was portraying a 'proper lady' or a prostitute. The jaunty melody suits the teasing words.

> By correct manipulation, she her figure can display,
> And her ankles, and, er, well, it's hard to turn your eyes away
> When, there's half a yard of 'open-work' about.
> 'Parlez-vous français? No? Très bien.
> Goodnight, Charlie, uh? Naughty boy!'

In a recording of the song Marie delivers the last two lines, designed to give her a cosmopolitan sheen, in an excruciating French accent. Most of her audience, however, would have been unfamiliar enough with the language not to find fault with Marie's pronunciation.

'Customs Of The Country' was a romp round the world and its conventions in dress and marriage. Persian men had at least 'three score and ten' wives, 'In far away Samoa, They ought to wear *some more!*' and 'There's the playful Hottentot – you know, he plays the game,/ Though he isn't civilized, he gets there just the same.'

The inclusion of Scotland in this roll-call of exotic places demonstrates, too, how parts of Britain were still viewed by Londoners as a distant country.

Up in Scotland, they're fond of wedded bliss, and they're not a bit
   afraid, no fear! . . .
Courting – marriage, honeymoon, other things occurring, soon
That's the custom of the country, here! . . .

'What, What' was another 'nudge, nudge, wink, wink' song. Take the
second verse, about a young girl who claims to be entirely innocent:

> And she's always talking baby,
> Though she'll be twenty-two.
> She asked her eldest sister
> About her honeymoon.
> She said, 'I always wonder
> If they are nice or not.'
> But I'll bet she won't die wondering.
> Eh? what – what – what – what – what!

'And The Leaves Began To Fall' (1904) was Marie's most erotic song
to date. It played on the fact that overcrowding and the moral
restrictions of the time meant that a lot of clandestine sexual encounters
took place in the open air. Marie half sang, half spoke the lines,
accompanied in her recording by a tinkling piano. The first verse
describes a courting couple who miss their train home.

> Said the maiden, pretty maiden,
> 'I'm so glad that we can get home after all!'
> And they both felt just as good
> As the two babes in the wood
> When the leaves began to fall!

The next verse is less subtle and describes a multi-millionaire who
decides to fill the garden of his mansion with classical statues:

> And old connoisseurs, you see, used to rub their hands with glee,
> When he planted Venus 'neath his chestnut-trees!
>
> (*Chorus*)And the statue – classic statue! –
> Stood beneath the trees 'mid nodings' on at all,
> It was lucky, when a pair

Of young lovers wandered there
That the leaves began to fall!

Marie made her first recordings in 1903 when the Gramophone and
Typewriter company produced single-sided versions of 'That's How
The Little Girl Got On', 'There Was Something On His Mind' and
'You Needn't Wink – I Know'.[2] Thomas Alva Edison had invented the
tinfoil phonograph as long ago as 1877 but it had failed to fulfil its
potential. Some had dreamed of fitting phonographs inside the statues of
dignitaries so that they could recite their most famous speeches, or of
using the instrument to reproduce edifying music, but this proved
impossible because the cylinders played for barely a minute and the
sound quality was irritating.

By the late 1890s there was some improvement, and American
listeners could hear recordings of military bands and dramatic recitations
through the medical-looking rubber ear-tubes and, eventually, the more
elegant metal horn. The new form of entertainment was slower to take
off in Europe, where phonograph equipment remained expensive.

Marie recorded at least six songs with the Pathé company in 1904.
Since 1894 Charles and Emile Pathé had been churning out cylinder
blanks in France and the 'Le Coq' instrument to play them on. (The
brand became so popular that the crowing bird became the trademark of
the Pathé newsreels.)

These early recordings took place in bleak rooms decorated with little
more than posters advertising gramophone equipment and uncluttered
by modern technology. The singer and musicians were arranged so that
the maximum sound made its way into a metal recording horn that
jutted out of the wall. A performer, like Marie, who was particularly
short stood on a wooden box so that their mouth was nearer the horn.
Likewise, the piano and piano stool were placed on a platform, giving
the impression that both musician and instrument were levitating.
Performers often sang in full stage costume, including hat, as if they
were performing before a live audience. But they had little idea of the
ways in which the recording might pick up extraneous elements of their
act. In 'You Needn't Wink' it is possible to catch a tantalizing snippet
of the 'real Marie' as she turns to the band with the husky aside 'Last
verse of the song'. The recordings that survive also show how she

tinkered with the lyrics to make them more up to date because she preferred a new version.

Although she had hit a rich seam of songs in the early part of the century, Marie was let down by her health. At the end of 1902, she took the title role in Aladdin at Peckham and was 'very sprightly . . . full of go'.³ Rosie was Orange Pekoe and there was a small part for Tom's second brother Charles; it was the last of Marie's eight pantomime performances. In March 1903 she went to the South of France to recover her voice, but continued to be plagued by sore throats. The following year she visited Ostend and Switzerland in July. In January 1905 she had to miss an appearance at the Hackney Empire due to catarrh, which she blamed on being driven between halls in an open car. Her condition worsened and a specialist was brought in, who told her to rest for six to eight days. An evening paper carried an alarming account of her illness and she announced that she was going to Brighton with a nurse for some fresh air.

As well as her hectic round of performances, she was also leading a full social life. She missed a performance in 1904 because she was not back in time from the Derby. In May 1905 the *Era* carried a picture of her and seven men, including Alec and Eugene Stratton, when she hosted a trip to the races at Kempton. In June there was a family outing, which included Alec, Bella, Alice and Tom, and Sam Poluski. Motoring, like golf, was becoming a popular pastime among music-hall stars, partly because of its social cachet. Performers, including Marie, liked to be pictured in or near their motors. In 1906 Gus Elen was caught breaking the twenty-mile-an-hour speed limit in Balham, and Fiat gave Vesta Tilley one of their models in 1910. Marie owned a series of cars and used to carry a chamber-pot with her in case she was caught short.⁴ One of her vehicles had such a small petrol tank that it was necessary to drive up hills backwards to provide the engine with sufficient fuel.

Unlike Marie, Dan Leno had few outlets to help him escape from the pressures of being a top performer. He once said, 'The Leno System of Philosophy regards the world as a football, kicked about by higher powers with me somewhere hanging on to the stitching with my teeth and toenails.'⁵ As the new century dawned, his grip on the ball was loosening. He had reached the height of his powers: his popular appeal was undisputed – a comic was named after him and he had even edited a newspaper for a day (with the rotund Herbert Campbell as his deputy) – but he had also received recognition among the upper classes through his invitation to perform before the King at Sandringham in 1901. This made him the first non-circus comedian in the post-Georgian era to receive a royal command and endorsed the social acceptability of music hall, but some of his friends felt the honour went to Dan's head and that he set too much store by the tiepin the King had given him.

Dan Leno is probably best remembered as a pantomime dame, but his humour – on and off stage – was as surreal as anything a modern comic might deliver. When the journalist Henry George Hibbert first visited him at his home he was ushered by a servant into a yellow and green drawing room filled with bronze figures, marble vases and flowerpots on bamboo tripods. The room was so cluttered and so dimly lit that Hibbert fell headlong over the skull of a tigerskin hearthrug. Then Dan stepped out from behind a screen and, smiling, said, 'They mostly does that.'[6]

George Formby Senior and Dan were the only performers Marie watched for pure enjoyment rather than from professional politeness.[7] Dan's patter in the song 'Detective Camera', by George le Brunn and J. Newland, about a blundering investigator, shows a skilful manipulation of language and an astute feeling for the absurd:

Kissed her right before my face. Well, I never! 'Pon my word, I never heard a kiss like that since I was vaccinated. It came so sudden on me that, for the moment, I didn't know whether I'd had a shave that morning or not. You know, there's no person more fond of a kiss than I am, between meals; but if you'd heard that kiss, you'd have lost your eyesight. It sounded for all the world like a man, who had a train to catch, trying to eat a plate of hot tripe and onions with a fork. But, in a minute, out came my camera, and I'd got 'em [shows picture of gentleman kissing girl]. Well, the other morning, an old gent came up to me with eyes in his tears, and said, 'Sir, there's a boy running down the street with my watch.' Out came my camera – I saw the boy. I said, 'Right! – got 'em.' I gave the old man the photo, and said, 'There you are! When you see him again, you'll know him.' Well, look what I did. I went into a house, the other morning, and what did I find? You don't know, of course you don't. I found a *sock*. That evidence? Why, simply because I've only got to find the man that it fits, *and I've got 'em.*

In 1903 Dan suffered bouts of a mysterious illness, which may have been a lethal cocktail of depression and alcohol. He was unable to attend his daughter's wedding in the autumn having suffered a 'mental relapse'. He began to stalk Sir Herbert Beerbohm Tree's leading lady, Constance Collier; on one occasion he turned up unannounced and waited in the dark in her sitting room until she arrived home with her mother at one o'clock. It was the first time they had met. She described his eyes as 'beautiful, like the eyes of a wounded animal or a great tragedian. They were deep-sunken and looked as if they would fill with tears at any moment.'[8]

There were rumours that Marie would take over from Dan in panto and he started to behave with inexplicable spitefulness to his friends such as his long-term pantomime partner Herbert Campbell, whose new coat he cut up.[9] In July 1904 Herbert, who had been appearing at the Hackney Empire with Marie, hurt his leg falling into a carriage. The wound became inflamed and the nineteen-stone comic, who had started his career at the Grecian and who had appeared with Marie in three Drury Lane pantomimes, died of a heart-attack at the age of fifty-seven (some accounts say sixty). Dan died in October the same year, aged forty-three, also from a heart-attack. Sir Max Beerbohm said of him, 'so little and frail a lantern could not harbour so big a frame. Dan Leno was more of a spirit than a man.'[10]

Like Constance Collier, Marie was struck by Leno's gaze. After his death she said of the music-hall performer who had wanted to play Mark Antony, 'Ever seen his eyes? The saddest eyes in the whole world. That's why we all laughed at Danny. Because if we hadn't laughed, we should have cried ourselves sick. I believe that's what real comedy is, you know. It's almost like crying.'[11] His ghost is still said to haunt Drury Lane.

A year later George le Brunn, the architect of so many of Marie's successful songs, died aged forty-two from meningitis. It soon became apparent that the man the *Daily Mail* described as the 'most prolific popular melodist of the time', and who had written over a thousand songs for most of the top singers, had died almost penniless. His music publishers, Francis, Day & Hunter, said he was owed £1. 0s. 7d. (£51) in royalties earned during the last year. The paper blamed music pirates, rather than that songwriters were paid a pittance.

The three deaths, and the way that Bella's life had been crushed overnight, shook Marie and she found it harder to right herself in a landscape that was becoming less familiar. Although its population was expanding, central London was becoming smaller. The Bakerloo, Piccadilly, Hampstead and District underground lines, with the distinctive red glazed tiles of their stations, made travelling to, from and within London easier.[12] The Piccadilly line even boasted the capital's first railway escalator and a man with a wooden leg was hired to travel up and down it all day to reassure the public of its safety. Better transport, together with improved street lighting, also revolutionized the entertainment industry by persuading people to travel further for leisure. These developments were not lost on Oswald Stoll, who became convinced that a newly mobile, upwardly aspiring audience was receptive to a different form of entertainment.

He planned the London Coliseum – a great Matcham palace, which finally opened in December 1904 in St Martin's Lane – after standing at Charing Cross station watching the waves of people descending on London from the outskirts. Stoll believed they wanted something midway between serious theatre and racy music hall so for this new audience he built the stately pleasure dome that could hold nearly 3,500 people and which beamed out the letters of its name in the night sky through a giant, revolving globe – until this was deemed illegal advertising. Visitors to the Coliseum were welcomed by *Salve* picked out in a mosaic on the floor and physicians were told to leave their seat number with the box office so that they could be informed of any urgent message. Following the American model of 'continuous variety' there were to be four shows a day, starting at noon. The Coliseum, with its tearooms, telephones and electric lifts, claimed to combine the elegance of a club and the comfort of a café with a luxurious theatre and family resort.

Among the Coliseum's special features was a stage made up of three segments that could each rotate independently at twenty miles per hour. Stoll made use of this gadget, which required a ship's bridge of controls to work it, to stage huge military and sporting spectacles, which usually led to several casualties. The most notorious of these was a re-creation of the Derby, which involved twelve horses who ran in the opposite direction from the revolving floor to give the illusion of speed. On the thirteenth day after the Coliseum opened one of the horses fell into the orchestra pit and flung its rider, Fred Dent, against the side of the proscenium arch. He later died from head injuries, his fate helping the theatre to earn the nickname, Morgueseum.

The refined, if lethal, atmosphere of the Coliseum was no place for the teasing innuendo of Marie and she was never asked to appear on its unpredictable stage. Her views on this are not recorded, but it is likely that she was hurt. Although the Coliseum had a rocky ride financially, and Stoll took desperate measures to attract audiences, it was still the most talked-about theatre of varieties in London. It was also typical of a new strain of buildings in which a performer like Marie struggled for intimacy with her audience: it had been designed, after all, to accommodate extravagant shows such as the London Hippodrome's water spectacles, which featured cavorting elephants, or the tragic posturing of opera singers.

Marie's one consolation over the snub came when a proud Stoll showed Edward VII around his new theatre in April 1905. When they reached the royal box Stoll unveiled the special electric carriage designed to glide smoothly along rails and sweep the royal personages out through the theatre's exit. When the carriage refused to budge, the King, who had been squeezed into it, broke the embarrassed silence by singing, 'Eh, what – what – what – what – what!'[13]

Chapter 15

TROUBLE BREWING

(1 9 0 6 – 7)

~*~

I was never one to interfere a lot
With other folks and their particular affairs,
Certain people see a lot and hear a lot . . .
And interfere in what is no concern of theirs.
Lor, if I liked to let my tongue wag,
Well, there might be revelations
That would spoil some reputations . . .
'She Doesn't Know That I Know What I Know' by
Orlando Powell and Fred W. Leigh

In October 1906, Marie was elected first president of the Music Hall
Ladies Guild. Ostensibly, the main purpose of this organization was to
help the wives of artists who became ill or lost their jobs. The Guild
provided food, coal and medicine and lent baby clothes. It also helped
poor families or orphans by finding young boys jobs as programme-
sellers, messengers or call-boys. This last job involved knocking on
dressing-room doors to remind the performer when they were due on
stage. Shouts of 'Five minutes, Miss Lloyd!' were part of the familiar
backstage soundtrack of every hall. Although right at the bottom of
the music-hall pecking order, the call-boys were a vital cog in the
clockwork precision that kept the evening going. It was their call that
ensured an act was not left floundering on stage while the next performer was found. The call-boy also saw and heard things to which
others were not privy: arguments between performers, illicit love affairs
and scheming among managers and artists. The institution continued
until loudspeaker systems were introduced into most dressing rooms by
the 1940s.

Although the Guild's defined aims were altruistic, there was also a
strong element of social one-upmanship in their efforts. By drawing up
formal lines between the needy and their bounteous benefactors, the
ladies reinforced their own social standing. The Guild also offered useful

networking opportunities for any who wanted to climb a few rungs higher up the social ladder.

Marie had no need or inclination for such social engineering, but she was always a soft touch when it came to a good cause. Her reckless generosity and regular support of charitable events, together with her position as the most well-known female in music hall, made her an obvious choice for the role of Guild president. In reality she abhorred the social pretensions of the group of overdressed women, whose monumental hats bobbed away as they exchanged gossip. The guild enjoyed organizing carefully stage-managed events that did as much for its own self-promotion as it did for charity. Marie preferred to depart from the script, persuading people (usually men) to forget their manners and indulge in a bit of fun as she cajoled and teased them from the sidelines. At one stuffy event she divided half the men into horses, while the rest were jockeys in a race in which bets raised cash for charity. On another occasion she 'warmed up' the crowd by staging a 'caterpillar' race.[1] Men were ordered to lie on the floor and propel themselves towards a five-pound note by using only the palms of their hands and their toes to shuffle and wriggle across the room in a race that left their expensive suits ruined by the chalk used to protect the wooden floor. If they had stopped to think about it, they might have been concerned at the evident enjoyment that Marie took from their humiliation.

Marie particularly disliked the Guild's treasurer, the lumpish American singer Belle Elmore, who was married to a homoeopathic doctor called Hawley Harvey Crippen. Belle's real name was Kunigunde Mackamotzki, and she grew up in New York where she was nicknamed the Brooklyn Matzos Ball after her size and her Polish father. She was Crippen's second wife and, in 1897, the difficult economic climate persuaded them to move to England, where American acts were popular. In her début at Marylebone Music Hall she was billed as Cora Motzki but soon changed her stage name to the more pronounceable Belle Elmore. Belle fancied she bore a strong resemblance to Marie and her choice of pseudonym is suspiciously similar to Marie's earlier stage name, Bella Delmeyer.

The comic singer Clarkson Rose described her as a 'blowsy, florid type of serio':[2] she wore too much make-up and liked to drape herself with gowns and furs that she could not afford. Dr Crippen was a 'quiet, meticulously mannered little man', balding with a bristling moustache and a slightly embarrassed air. Marie called him the 'Half-crown King', because he was always borrowing money to buy a drink.[3] Crippen numbered several music-hall performers among his patients and enjoyed attending the halls himself, but his life was a constant battle to fund his wife's desire for the lifestyle of the successful music-hall singer she never became.

Belle entertained members of the Guild at her home, 39 Hilldrop Crescent in Holloway, north London, which she had decorated with pink velvet bows and *objets d'art* picked up at auction rooms for their capacity to impress rather than please. She became friendly with the well-known mime artist Paul Martinetti and his wife, and with Lil and John Nash (Lil was half of the Hawthorne Sisters) whom she asked over for games of whist on a Sunday afternoon. Marie had no desire to play card games in a pretentious little household in north London — especially not with someone who endeavoured to be a watered-down version of herself. Her uneasy relationship with the parvenu treasurer was strained to the point of collapse by events in the last months of 1906 and early 1907.

Music-hall performers always rallied round to support one of their own in times of need. When the profession's most prolific songwriter George le Brunn died, leaving a widow who could not even afford to erect a gravestone to his memory, a special matinée was organized that raised six hundred pounds, and a fund was started in his name. Such funds usually worked by printing a list of performers and how much they had donated; the combination of public shaming and competitive generosity proved an effective way to swell the coffers. Marie kept secret as long as she could that she had donated over a hundred guineas: she did not want other performers to feel there was no need to make a donation. When the figures were finally published Marie was at the top of a list that hardly shone with generosity: evidently music-hall performers believed that they were the ones who made a song, rather than the man who had written it. Alec gave £10. 10s., and other members of the Lloyd family were in the top twenty or so donations: Tom and Fred McNaughton came up with £5. 5s., Alice £3. 3s. and Rosie £2. 2s.[4]

But, while they responded to individual appeals, as a single body of professionals music-hall performers were not usually to be relied upon.

The very nature of their work made it difficult to gather them in one place for meetings and to ensure that sensitive egos stayed in check for long enough to achieve anything. The Music Hall Artistes' Railway Association (MHARA) worked because it had one guiding principle: cheaper fares for all artists. But it was an unwieldy beast with eleven thousand members, most of whom were unwilling to extend the organization's role because they feared this would jeopardize the cosy arrangement with the railways. In the years immediately following Queen Victoria's death, music-hall performers needed more than an informal charitable machine that would crank into action in moments of extreme need. Halls were increasingly concentrated in the hands of a few mighty magnates, who were unapproachable accountants rather than grandfatherly caterers like Charles Morton. As the stranglehold of the most powerful impresarios tightened, their competitors, the dwindling number of independent operators, came under greater pressure to squeeze as much as possible out of their turns.

Stoll was the most ruthless of the new breed of impresario, and the London Coliseum, opened on 24 December 1904, rose like a monument to his power. He did not smoke, drink or swear and, although he married twice, his mother remained the main influence in his life. He was the proud author of books on finance and approached everything with careful consideration. His idea of exercise was a drive round Putney Heath (where he lived), of violent exercise, a drive twice round Putney Heath. Only his immediate family called him by his first name and he rarely smiled, sitting stony-faced through rehearsals. He spoke in a disconcertingly quiet voice, pausing between sentences to make sure his words had been absorbed. The audience were errant children who needed to be taught how to behave. When he spotted a man stubbing out a cigarette on the carpeted floor of his beloved Coliseum Stoll approached him and asked him in schoolmasterly tones whether he would do the same thing in his own home.

Every anecdote about him hinges on his business acumen. Once he was marching along the pavement to the Coliseum, wearing his customary top hat, frock coat and pince-nez, when a beggar asked him to buy some matches. Stoll ignored him, but when the beggar pleaded that he had sold very few matches recently, Stoll's commercial curiosity was aroused and he paused to quiz the man about how this compared with the previous year's turnover. His research completed, he continued on his way leaving the beggar's sales figures unchanged.

With most of the halls in the hands of a powerful few, Stoll and his rivals started to introduce practices that forced artists to work harder and harder. Performers were expected to play extra matinées for the same money (one had previously been the norm) and in some halls twice- or even thrice-nightly shows were introduced. It became common for acts to be transferred to far-away halls at short notice and some managers started to cut the agent's commission to cover nebulous costs such as 'office expenses'; the agents then passed on this expense to the performers. Other unscrupulous agents would sign up an act for, say, five pounds a week, then trade them to music-hall managers for fifteen pounds in a practice known as 'farming', which caused a great deal of resentment.

Most damaging of all was the 'barring system'. This varied from contract to contract, but the general principle was to prevent a performer from appearing, during a given period, at a rival venue within a certain radius of the hall he or she was contracted to play. At its very worst, the barring clause could stop a performer from working within a seven-mile radius of one hall over twelve months. Stoll argued that the barring system was necessary to offer performers the previously unheard-of security of long periods of continuous employment, but in reality there were gaps during which the artist could not supplement the lean periods by working for other halls. As Alec said, 'The beginning and the end of the whole affair [the dispute] is the barring clause.'[5]

It was also a cause close to Marie's heart, and as early as 1899 she had taken a manager to court about his over-enthusiastic interpretation of her contract.[6] Her triumph was recognized at the Grand, Clapham Junction, when she was presented by colleagues, including Dan Leno, Herbert Campbell, Henry Randall, Eugene Stratton, Alec and Tom, with a framed, illuminated testimonial and dressing-bag fittings featuring her initials. The presentation marked her 'generosity' in defending artists' rights on 'time and distance'. In her reply, Marie acknowledged that if she had lost the case she would have almost certainly been forced to give up her home to pay the lawyers' fees.

In 1903 the MHARA put forward a reasonable six-point contract, which attempted to address the worst of these abuses: barring was limited to three months and one mile in London, and extra performances had to be paid for. But the contract was no more than a token gesture without the signatures of the biggest operators: in London, Stoll, Walter Gibbons, who controlled theatres such as the Empress, Brixton, the Holborn Empire and the Palladium, and George Adney Payne, whose halls included the South London, the Oxford, the Canterbury and the Paragon; and in Scotland, Richard Thornton and Edward Moss.

Marie wrote to the *Era* in support of the MHARA's attempt at a model contract, but her letter also seemed to chide the hapless music-hall performer for lacking business sense, although it may be her convoluted style that gives this impression:

> I know from experience that music hall artists would never have had to sign one-sided contracts if they were at all businesslike, and took an interest in what was really being done for them. I am, and always have been ready and willing to help my brother and sister artists by every means in my power in anything that is for their good. I write to show that I agree with all the Music Hall Artists' Railway Association is doing and in the hope that, in doing so, it may make others lend a hand.[7]

Stars like Marie had greater clout than the humbler performer and were not pushed around as much as the smaller turns, but they still had to contend with the barring system. Stoll and other managers had good lawyers and were not afraid to use them, even if a big name was involved. Both Marie and Alec had been in court several times and knew how expensive legal proceedings could be. They also knew that playing the halls was not the cheap profession the managers made it out to be. Anyone other than a soloist had to share their wages, and every turn had to pay for props, scenery and costumes, tips to stagehands, travel and accommodation. As Alec started to perform more 'scena', he encountered all these costs. His 'Coster's Beanfeast', which was popular in 1906, consisted of a three-scene sketch including a charabanc and two horses. Marie's biggest expenses were her costumes, her dresser and transport.

Concern at the creeping introduction of these new management ploys eventually led to a backlash. The MHARA called a meeting on 18 January 1906 at the Grand Order of Water Rats' headquarters, the Vaudeville Club in Charing Cross Road, to which the main groups representing music-hall performers were invited: the Water Rats, an élite, male-only society founded in 1890 whose aims were social and philanthropic, the Terriers, a more democratic version of the Water Rats, and the International Artistes' Lodge, a highly organized group that offered performers legal advice and even had an office in Berlin. The meeting agreed to form a new organization, the Variety Artistes' Federation to defend performers' rights. One of the first members to join, no. 98, was Tom Major, a comedian, whose son, John, later became prime minister.

The impetus for a new weapon with which to fight the managers came from men such as Joe O'Gorman, Frank Gerald and Wal Pink, but as the year wore on it became obvious that this was one industrial dispute in which female workers had as much at stake as men. Marie Kendall, a doe-eyed singer who had performed as a teenager next to Alice Lloyd and stole hearts with songs such as 'Just Like The Ivy, I'll Cling to You', showed that it took ruthlessness to be a sweet-faced singer of romantic songs and sued a manager who tried to bar her. The judge found in her favour, but his ruling was eventually overturned on appeal.

By June the VAF called a meeting for 'all interested, even ladies'[8] and by the autumn Marie's rather distant concern turned into something more immediate as she found herself caught in the cross-fire. She was due to appear at the Paragon, an intimate, old-fashioned music hall on Mile End Road, Stepney, when only a few hours before the show's start the manager, Charles Beecham, received an injunction preventing his biggest star from setting foot on the stage. He was forced to appear in front of the footlights himself to inform an expectant audience that six turns, including Marie and the Poluski Brothers, could not appear. Moreover, the injunction had arrived at such short notice that there was no hope of securing replacements.

The move was the latest spat between the London Music Hall in Shoreditch High Street, a Matcham theatre that could hold a thousand people, and the Paragon, barely one and a half miles away. Only a week before, the Paragon had served an injunction preventing artists, including the Scottish singer Harry Lauder, from appearing at the London. Marie was fully aware that technically she was breaking her contract but she did not like being told what to do – especially not on her 'home turf' in the East End of London. If she had been wavering about taking action over barring and other iniquities the Paragon experience helped to make up her mind. When the call to action came she was in the mood to respond.

Marie's anger and inflamed pride were briefly dissipated by her marriage in October 1906 to Alec, which helped to smooth her ruffled feathers and reassure her of her standing in her profession. That she should consider marriage after a ten-year courtship is best explained by the string of tragedies that led up to her decision and made her conscious, at the age of thirty-six, of her own mortality. George le Brunn, Dan Leno and Herbert Campbell – three long-standing friends and pillars of the music-hall establishment – had died in the last two years and she had seen her best friend, Bella, robbed of happiness when her new husband was sent to prison. Middle age was creeping up fast, of which she was reminded nightly through the success of songs that cast her in matronly, and sometimes haggish, roles. In 'You're A Thing Of The Past' she was a faded, gin-drinking old woman, and in 'She Doesn't Know That I Know What I Know' she portrayed the sort of gossipy harridan who had been the butt of many earlier songs.

There was much curiosity about Marie's age, partly because she had lied about it at the start of her career, making out that she was older than she really was, and partly because she was now a *grande dame* of the music-hall world. A strange conundrum circulated that suggested her age was as difficult to guess as the weight of the average fox.[9] She eventually published an advert in several papers to end the controversy: 'To set the matter at rest once and for all, "our Marie" first saw the light in 1870.'[10]

Percy had kept a low profile since starting divorce proceedings in 1894. He had lived in France for a while, although it is not known where or what he did there. In January 1904 he petitioned again for divorce, naming Alec as co-respondent. Although Marie had been quite open about her relationship with Alec she denied the allegations of adultery. She may have been advised to adopt this approach because the law took a dim view of adulterous women when it came to granting custody rights. It is unclear as to whether Marie or Percy had custody of their child – it was normal for the father to be granted custody, although often this was merely a technicality and the child lived with its mother. Marie's daughter was sixteen and, in the eyes of the law, would remain a child until she was twenty-one. Should Percy decide to make a stand about Marie Junior's education, religion, or even whether she should leave the country, her mother would be in a better position to put her foot down if she had not been tarred officially as a woman with an adulterous past.

The decree nisi was granted in November. By this time Percy was living at 66, Galveston Road in East Putney, and described himself as 'of no occupation'. From this point he disappeared from Marie's life.[11] The only clue to what may have happened to him is that a Percy Charles Courtenay died, aged seventy, at 26 Brunswick Terrace, Hove on 22 September 1933 from an accidental drugs overdose. His death certificate describes his occupation as of 'independent means'. The correct spelling of his unusual name, the age, the place of death (the south coast is a favourite retirement place for people with theatrical connections) and the 'occupation' all point to this having been Marie's ex-husband.

Marie's second wedding took place one Saturday morning at Hampstead Town Hall. Her choice of costume made her look like a visiting queen from an obscure, far-off island determined not to let her ignorance of the local dress code put her in danger of being outshone by the people around her: she was a plump, upholstered figure in ermine and feathers, struggling under the weight of immense headgear. She wore a pearl-grey corselet skirt, a fur cape and stole with matching muff decorated with pink carnations. Her head was adorned with an ermine toque that had a panache of grey feathers sprouting from it like an exotic animal and a long, white curtain veil framed her chubby face. Alec looked quietly understated, with polished shoes, slicked-back hair and immaculate suit.

From the very start, when crowds began to gather outside the register office, the wedding felt like a burlesque show. After the service, thirty motor-cars took the guests to the reception at the Gaiety restaurant in the Strand, with members of the Boys' Brigade running alongside for part of the journey. Outside, crowds cheered the two hundred guests, many of them music-hall stars in their own right, as they arrived and the bride and bridegroom struggled to make their way through the masses. Inside, Tom McNaughton and Sam Poluski, who considered themselves bridesmaids, wiped away imaginary sweat from Alec's face with clown-sized gestures that made the party giggle.

The newlyweds received over a thousand telegrams, and a statuesque wedding cake, supplied by Romano's and weighing a hundred pounds, was decked with sugar sprays of convolvulus, geranium, azalea and phlox, and was cut amid much cheering. Tom and Sam made speeches, as did the veteran comedian Arthur Roberts. Another guest posed the riddle: 'Why was Alec Hurley?' The answer: 'In order to Marie Lloyd.'

The new Mrs Hurley made a sentimental speech in which she said she was proud of her husband and hoped to remain on the stage for a few years longer. She continued in a reverie about retirement which, given her reputation, could be read in two different ways: 'Then we shall settle down at one of those roadside hostelries where the motor-cars pass by and never stop, and I shall say to my old man, "Put up the shutters, and we'll go out on horseback . . ."

'And now, ladies and gentlemen, I thank you very much for turning up here today to wish us good health. I'm not going to invite you again, so don't worry yourselves.'[12]

The contrast with her first 'walking wedding' in Hoxton could not have been greater. She had made that marriage as a struggling, pregnant young performer and it threatened to smash her fragile career. Her second, to an established figure from her own profession, confirmed her standing.

Chapter 16

STRIKE
(1906−7)

~❧

Oh, Mr Karno, what are you trying to do,
Make more money from the sketches, if what they say is true,
All your lads are winners, not one's an also-ran,
Oh, Mr Karno, don't be a silly man.
Anon.

Soon after her wedding Marie was taken ill with another unspecified complaint and her sister, 'dainty' Alice, stood in for her at the Oxford and Euston music halls. She was too ill to attend the Music Hall Ladies Guild charity matinée in December and later that month went to recuperate among 'the pines at Bournemouth'. Her doctor ordered her to delay returning to work for a week, but by the new year she was topping the bill at the Tivoli and the Metropolitan where she was given a warm welcome but was reported as being 'exceedingly nervous'.

Her illness may have been exhaustion, or it may have been an excuse. If she was really ill then it could not have done her much good to spend bitterly cold January nights picketing selected London music halls. But this is exactly what she did. War had broken out between the management, represented by Walter Gibbons, and the VAF, now dubbed 'Very Awkward Fellows' by proprietors.[1] In October 1906 Gibbons bought the Brixton Theatre with the intention of transforming it into a hall, even though he already owned the Empress in the same part of south London. He decided to make the acts at the Empress repeat their show at his other theatre, and vice versa, thus doubling their workload. The VAF saw its moment and ordered a strike. A mixture of musicians, stagehands and performers took to the picket lines. As news of the dispute spread, the antics outside the theatres became more appealing than the entertainment inside. The pickets marched up and down with placards and handed out leaflets to curious passers-by.

After intensive negotiations Gibbons eventually agreed to close the second theatre, to operate the Empress on a once-nightly basis and to pay for matinées. The agreement was celebrated with a pre-christmas lunch at the Café Royal given by Gibbons and attended by members of the VAF, including Tom and Fred. But the strikers did not trust Gibbons and their mistrust was well-founded: he was discussing tactics with Stoll and other London managers on the very morning of the celebratory Café Royal lunch. Although the battle had been won in Brixton there were skirmishes at Gibbons's other halls: the Empires in Islington and Holborn, the Croydon and Ealing Palaces, the Duchess in Balham and the Clapham Grand.

On Sunday afternoon, 20 January, the VAF, now joined by the National Association of Theatrical Employees and the Amalgamated Musicians' Union in a group known as the National Alliance, met at the Surrey Theatre to discuss tactics. The mass meeting drew up a charter that was sent out to theatre managers demanding they sign up; failure to do so would leave them open to picketing. Alec and Tom attended what seems to have been an all-male gathering (one of the speakers even mentioned the difference between straight-cut and twist tobacco in making a point), but Marie was working behind the scenes. She called a meeting of VAF members at the Bedford Head pub in Tottenham Court Road to support the new Alliance.[2] Roused by her words the charter was delivered to Adney Payne, who refused to countenance it. As a result, some of the halls most closely linked to Marie's name joined the blacklist: the Tivoli, the Oxford, the Euston and the Paragon, as well as the Canterbury, the Walthamstow Palace, the East Ham Empire and the South London Palace. At its height, twenty-two London theatres were affected and over two thousand performers took to the streets.[3] Bigger names started to join the ranks, with Marie leading the way. She entertained the crowds that gathered by performing swathed in furs and standing in her motor-car adding topical words to familiar songs: 'Rule, Britannia, Britannia rules the waves, Four shows every night and two matinées.'

It was by no means a foregone conclusion that Marie would become

so involved in the strike. She was not a politically motivated person –
but, then, to her the strike was not about politics.

When the MHARA was set up in 1896 the *Era* had asked why there
were no ladies on its committee and, in particular, why no Marie Lloyd.
The answer was twofold: as in her stage act, Marie did not like anything
that constrained her, and she found meetings and committees stultify-
ingly dull. She recognized unfairness when she saw it but her quick
temper and impetuousness meant that she normally did something about
it there and then, without waiting for a committee meeting. As a
teenager in the East End she had witnessed the early twitchings of
workers' demands: there had been the riots of London's unemployed in
Trafalgar Square in 1886 and 1887 and the dock strike in 1889, but more
immediate were the protests at Bryant and May's match factory in 1888
where girls worked in such hazardous conditions that their bodies were
permanently polluted by the chemicals they handled. A favourite trick
of reformers was to turn out the lights to see the girls' jaws glow in the
dark. The tale has been handed down within Marie's family that she
went to hear the reformer Annie Besant speak on the girls' behalf at
Mile End. This was the sort of uncomplicated politics she understood,
where right and wrong were clearly defined.

The music-hall dispute fell into this category and Marie threw her
energy into it; she was genuinely shocked to discover how little
stagehands and lesser performers earned. She enjoyed being at the centre
of events and she and Alec invited members of the Water Rats and Joe
O'Gorman, chairman of the VAF, to their Hampstead home for secret
strategy meetings.

She also enjoyed performing on the picket lines where she was as
close to her public as she had been in the chaotic early days of music
halls – and as free from managerial censure. The demonstrations had a
funfair feel to them: men paraded up and down wearing sandwich
boards bearing the slogan 'Music Hall War' and the public came to
gawp at their idols, who had briefly alighted from their pedestals.
Picket-line duty was an extension of Marie's stage act and she behaved
like a star. She burst through the gloomy winter's evening, which was
so cold you could see your breath and beggars were dying on the
streets, to thrust union leaflets on bewildered members of the public.
She dazzled them with her jewellery, her sumptuous gowns and a

constant stream of cheery patter that lit up the dark London pavements. Policemen, loitering ready to step in if the picketing became heated, found themselves helpless in the face of an insurgent who had two deadly weapons: a voice trained to project clearly across milling crowds and a store of acerbic one-liners honed through years of dispatching persistent hecklers. Marie, as catty as she could be seductive, was left untouched by the perplexed police who had to deal with violent outbursts from stagehands with far more at stake than big-name performers. When Marie Kendall was arrested by an over-zealous officer she was quickly released when the publicity implications of his action became obvious.

R. G. Knowles, George Robey and Little Tich joined the strike, adapting their own songs in support of the struggle. Marie's most memorable contribution was aimed at Fred Karno's practice of 'farming', whereby he creamed off large profits for himself by selling sketches, which were becoming increasingly popular now at music halls after intensive negotiations with 'legitimate' theatre owners about their legality. Marie sang, to the tune of 'Oh, Mr Porter':

> Oh, Mr Karno, what are you trying to do,
> Make more money from the sketches, if what they say is true,
> All your lads are winners, not one's an also-ran,
> Oh, Mr Karno, don't be a silly man.[4]

The strike split the music-hall world along fault-lines of scabs and pickets. Ancient performers were dragged out of retirement, managers dusted down routines from their own days on the halls and even enticed their wives to rejoin a world they had left behind several years before. Orchestras were ravaged: often only a conductor or pianist turned up and managers resorted to recitations and tableaux that did not require musical accompaniment. Some artists were persuaded to break the strike because they needed the money; others were enticed by the prospect of their only chance to play the top of the bill – although it was sadly depleted. Yet others, like Lockhart's Elephants, had no say in the matter – at the South London, Adney Payne was forced to stand before the audience and offer his customers a stark choice: 'You have had the elephants on once and the pictures once. Would you care to have the pictures again, or the elephants? What will you have, pictures or elephants? Pictures?'

Shouts of 'No!'

'Elephants?'

'Yes! Yes! Yes!'

'Very well, we will put on the elephants again.'[5]

For Belle Elmore the attractions were manifold. Her allegiance was firmly with the establishment and the voluntary removal of some of the top female singers was a dream come true. She also needed the money. The sight of her waddling towards the picket line also fulfilled a dream for Marie. Unrestrained by the petty politeness of the Music Hall Ladies Guild, she was unable to conceal any longer her resentment at the pretentiousness that had infiltrated the profession. As Belle attempted to find a chink in the picket line Marie shouted, 'Don't be daft. Let her in. She'll empty the theatre.'[6]

There was no respite from the barrage of abuse even for those performers who braved the picket line and made it into the theatre. A few strikers positioned themselves strategically inside and did their best to disrupt the performance by batting rude comments around the sparsely occupied auditorium. One blackleg, known as Mrs Brown-Potter, specialized in recitations and one of the strikers, Millie Payne, would start to cry as soon as Mrs Brown-Potter's act began. Her sobbing and wailing grew in volume until she was asked to leave the theatre. She did so, very noisily, explaining between sobs, 'I can't help it. The lady's beautiful reciting m-makes m-me c-cry.'[7]

As the strike continued into February the enthusiasm of some performers, who had expected only to make a token display of solidarity, faltered. Bitterness erupted at those who broke the strike, but open warfare provided cover for old scores to be settled while festering jealousies went unchecked. Some performers were beaten up on the pretence that they were scabs and, even after the strike, there were rumours that certain artists had offered to act as strikebreakers. The illusionist Chung Ling Soo was accused by *Conjurors' Magazine* of doing just this.[8] Vesta Tilley kept a low profile until the end appeared to be in sight when she urged reconciliation.

Another casualty of the propaganda war was Mr Datas. His act, which centred on his phenomenal memory, was re-created in the character of Mr Memory in the film *The Thirty-Nine Steps*, and was so famous that he agreed that his head could be sold after his death to a hospital for £300. He had originally backed the strikers but when, with Arthur Roberts and Marie, he was sued by the proprietors for £1,800 over breach of contract he changed sides amid much publicity. His was one of the names that appeared when the *Performer*, the official publication of the VAF, published a list of 'strike-breakers'; VAF members like Datas carried a black cross next to their names. The bitter attacks continued in a mock play-bill that lampooned blacklegs like Datas, Lockhart's Elephants and the Kinetoscope: 'Nitas – The Human Gasbag, Lockouts Elephants, the Wantascope (to enable the turns to escape under cover of darkness).'[9]

Publications ranging from *Punch* to the *Daily Telegraph* and the *Daily Express* followed the regular episodes of street theatre, and the managers and unions did their best to manipulate the coverage. Gibbons printed a broadsheet highlighting how much some of the big names earned: it claimed that Arthur Roberts and Marie both received £80 a week at a time when a skilled man could expect to earn on average £96 a year. But he failed to point out that an orchestral player was earning barely £1 a week and that many performers had to share their earnings if they were part of an act that included several artists. The *Daily Telegraph*, which provided its readers with regular bulletins on the strike, took a remarkably measured and modern approach to the dispute. In an editorial it argued that, while stars like Marie earned as much as a cabinet minister, their salaries were not excessive compared to opera singers, surgeons and barristers.

Punch took up the theme of music-hall pay in a letter, which mocked the efforts of Arthur Roberts, Joe Elvin, Little Tich and Marie, headed, 'The Brotherhood of Art':

> Dear Mr Punch, – My blood boils for my poor downtrodden colleagues who are being starved in order that popular artistes like myself may roll in motors on a salary of £7,500. Cruel, cruel Managers!
> Yours cordially,
> Arthur Elvin Lloyd Tich[10]

In the same issue *Punch* took full advantage of the comic potential of the strike. Its special correspondent wrote:

Miss Marie Lloyd is ready to start at any moment on a tour through the country in a motor-car of a vivid red colour. Her purpose is to address roadside meetings from her car, in the hope of arousing the people of the country to a sense of their duty in this great struggle. (Costumes by WORTH, wigs by CLARKSON. Parish and Borough councils interested should apply for terms to Miss Lloyd's manager).

The piece went on to point out that male impersonator Vesta Tilley had been annoyed by a famous serio-comic, who had addressed a meeting of ladies and told them to stand firm and play the man. Miss Tilley 'feels that the competition in her line of business is already great enough'. The Cockney singer Gus Elen was said to be peeved that he had not been asked to draw upon his knowledge of London dialect to address the working-class man, adding: 'If yer ain' got no wurk, yer cawn't git the sack.' This, *Punch* pointed out, was the dialect that cost managers £40 (£1,817) a week.

Performers hit back with high-profile snubs at the managers whose investments in music halls had paid handsome dividends. Marie and Little Tich, reunited as conspirators against authority, sent telegrams to Adney Payne: 'I am busy putting a new flounce on my dress so I can not appear tonight – Marie Lloyd' and 'I am learning a new coronet solo. Cannot tear myself away – Little Tich.'[11] But public humiliation was a dangerous tool when used against the pride and long memory of a powerful music-hall manager.

Alec and, especially, Marie became unofficial spokespeople: 'No, I don't think the managers will be able to carry on very long with "scratch" turns. It is the public who make the "stars" and they cannot be gulled by inferior "talent",' Alec told the *Daily Telegraph*.[12]

Marie added:

'A wrong impression has got abroad . . . as to the position of the "star" artists. It is said that they are quarrelling with the managers on their own behalf. That is not so. We can dictate our own terms. We are fighting not for ourselves, but for the poorer members of the profession, earning 30/- to £3 per week. For this they have to do double turns, and now matinées have been added as well. These poor things have been compelled to submit to unfair terms of employment, and I mean to back up the federation in whatever steps are taken.'

She was photographed in the offices of the VAF in Wellington Street, sitting in the background, looking regal in furs and a lightly veiled hat.[13] Arrangements were made to have her photograph taken outside the Tivoli but police had to be called in to deal with the crowds that gathered to watch, and eventually her car swept her off to Maiden Lane, where she was photographed amid much cheering.

Marie, though, did not make a terribly good spokesperson: she found it impossible to express anything other than her own views, which were not consistent. In her shiny new cars she made a tempting target for newspapers eager to stress the hypocrisy of stars defending a system from which they benefited. She was never able to abandon her links with the powerful managers, either, and was troubled by Stoll's biting comments about her: 'Have you noticed the statements of Miss Marie Lloyd? – Oh, yes. Her utterances are so grossly exaggerated that it is to be hoped they are due to an innate partiality for dramatic effect, rather than to the truth which constitutes her value as an artist. It is, however, gratifying to a manager to find that she is fairly satisfied with her contracts and is really engaging in the fight for the sake of others.'[14]

Leaflets and adverts were printed with the heading 'Miss Marie Lloyd's Appeal' and the dictum, 'The managers are fighting us with shareholders' money. We are giving our own to win this fight.'[15] But she tempered her stance after a stinging letter appeared in the *Era* pointing out how accommodating Adney Payne had been in releasing her from engagements due to ill-health, but that now she was repaying that kindness by spending the winter nights distributing leaflets.

Her own insecurity meant she would never be fully happy about a confrontation with authority. Writing to the *Era* she said:

Sir, – There has been so much controversy re the music hall strike, and I have been credited with making so many mis-statements during the conflict . . .

What we are fighting for are better terms and conditions for the smaller turns re the barring clause.

I do not think the barring clause makes one iota of difference to the star turns, as their engagements extend for a long period at each West End hall. Not so with the smaller turns. They only get six nights, and very likely barred from other halls for twelve months or more. Now, is this fair? My suggestion to proprietors would be, by all means bar your drawing power, but let the smaller turns get a living when and where they can within a reasonable radius.

Re the leaflets distributed called 'Marie Lloyd's appeal to the Public'. I did not mention anything about 'using shareholders' money etc. What I did say, I said on the stage of the Empress Music Hall, and London Shoreditch, was:

'I want it to be roughly understood that I and the other stars are not fighting to come forward and help every charitable cause ... We do not ask for money; we have helped you, now we want you to help us in this fair and just cause.'

I should like to see a speedy settlement, 'Peace with Honour' to both sides —

Marie Lloyd[16]

Marie's confused approach to the conflict contrasts sharply with the intransigence of more earnest members of the National Alliance, who had plans to transform the strike into something more lasting. The Alliance had signed a lease on the Scala, a Matcham theatre in Charlotte Street, London, which they planned to use to run their own, alternative music-hall performances. Stoll responded by threatening to sue anyone who appeared in the Scala's *Night with the Stars*. Marie was at the party thrown on Sunday, 3 February to celebrate the Scala's opening for the Alliance, but she was becoming uneasy about the aggressive stance that some of the Alliance members were adopting. The strike had been going on in some form or another for nearly a month; she was losing a lot of money and there was the constant threat of legal action from Stoll. She and other key figures, such as Wal Pink and Arthur Roberts, felt that some members of the Alliance had hijacked the strike for their own ends. Again, Marie held secret meetings at Granville Lodge, but this time with members of the Water Rats to try to decide how best to reach a settlement with the proprietors.

On Monday, 4 February, Joe Lyons arranged a meeting at the Trocadero with Marie, Alec, Arthur, Wal, Joe Elvin, Joe O'Gorman, Paul Martinetti and other performers and managers, including Stoll. Wal, Paul and the two Joes walked out as soon as the managers said they would recognize the performers only individually and not as a body. Marie and Alec were among those who stayed put for the discussions, which lasted six hours. Following the meeting, Henry Tozer, a proprietor whose halls included the London and Collins's, issued a statement:

A definite and satisfactory agreement between the chief 'stars' and the managers has been arrived at.

Certain clauses in contracts were open to misinterpretation and gave the idea that the management held a giant's power of the artiste. By agreement the clauses have been modified and refined.

The question of the stage hands and musicians was mentioned at the meeting, but nothing was done with regard to their position. Their case will be considered separately and individually later on.

So far as the 'stars' are concerned, the matter is now at an end. The agreement which I have in my pocket will be signed tomorrow by all of them, and they will recommend their brother artists to accept it. Until it is signed we cannot publish the terms.[17]

The meeting seemed even more of a betrayal by Marie since only three days earlier, on the Friday, she had seconded a motion of confidence in the union officials at a war conference held at Frascati's restaurant. But her words at the Scala mass meeting on the Sunday hinted that she was contemplating capitulation: 'Whatever peace is concluded, I will never go back upon the music hall stage until the wants of every musician and stage-hand are satisfied.'[18] Like others, she may have felt uneasy at the presence of Ben Tillett, a notorious union leader and orator who had led the dockers' strike of 1889.

On the face of it, Marie and Alec had played right into the managers' hands. They had been seduced by a separate agreement for stars and lip-service had been paid to the plight of the stagehands and other minions. A more accurate version, though, was that the managers had manipulated Marie, Alec and Arthur into helping break the strike. Immediately after the statement a desperate Arthur Roberts rang the VAF offices: 'Please tell the committee on behalf of Miss Marie Lloyd, myself and others that the report that is all over London that we have settled affairs with the managers is a lie. We only went to listen to the proposal, and signed and settled nothing.'[19]

In the same week Marie's name appeared, alongside other stars' signatures, on a statement urging performers to stay true to the Alliance. On Monday, 11 February, she and Alec took a box at the opening of *A Night with the Stars* at the Scala, but decided it was too risky to appear in the musical comedy and face legal action from Stoll.[20] She was not alone: there were no big names in the cast and the theatre was reduced to the humiliating recourse of using entertainers to give impersonations of stars. Arthur Roberts, Joe Elvin and Tom were also in the audience, and Alice and Daisy helped distribute free programmes.

The cause had become muddied by too many conflicting interests. Many of the small performers themselves felt it was time to call it a day. The strikers had made a well-publicized stand and it was now necessary to reach an agreement. Their ranks were splintering; the strike could not go on for ever. The only way forward was to hand the halls back to the people capable of running them: the managers. Marie knew this and she also knew that, as one of the biggest names in the business, she could play a part in forging a compromise. She was not good at politics, she was not a profound thinker, neither was she a schemer. Her own logic allowed her to urge her fellow performers to support a cause she still believed in while, at the same time, she was talking to 'the enemy' about resolving a dispute in a way that would answer the original grievances. This was treachery to militant members of the Alliance, but to Marie it was pragmatism. This sort of behind-the-scenes manoeuvring is often the only way that the most bitter disputes are settled. And Marie's insecurity meant that she was always susceptible to compromise.

The day after *A Night with the Stars* opened, the Board of Trade, under its president Lloyd George, appointed an arbiter to the dispute, George Ranken Askwith, QC. Askwith, who was leading counsel for HM Works and Public Buildings, was the most experienced negotiator of his day. He was forty-six at the time of the dispute, but had been involved in industrial negotiations for a decade. Although he came from a privileged background (he was educated at Marlborough and Oxford), he was patient and fair, and well respected by both sides in the music-hall dispute. He immediately passed an interim award: the strikers must return to work, managers must suspend all legal proceedings against artists and picketing had to stop. Then Askwith set himself up at St Bride's Institute, just off Fleet Street, on 12 February to hear a hundred witnesses, from lowly musicians to household names and mighty managers over a period of three weeks. He was accompanied by counsels from each side, representatives from the VAF, Stoll and two other managers, a stenographer and a map of London with the main music halls plotted like a general's plan of campaign.

Askwith recalled that the strike and subsequent arbitration aroused great interest: 'The reports were followed by the whole of Great Britain with more interest than those of an international football match where the odds were doubtful; and the strike appeared to succeed. Why should not others do likewise?'[21] He also noted that the public referred to it as the 'Music Hall Strike', whereas the performers themselves used the term 'theatre of varieties'. At the Tivoli, Arthur Roberts mimicked Askwith in a sketch in which artists were shown bickering among themselves. In reality those who filed in to give evidence were subdued, cowed by the court-like atmosphere. Only Marie gave value for money to the audience of eleven men when she appeared on Wednesday, 10 April.

She was due to give evidence first thing in the morning but eventually had to be sent for at 11.30 a.m. When she arrived, she complained that she had been forced to skip breakfast although, Askwith noted, 'She had had time to don a most dainty gown.' She was cross-examined by Walter Payne, as counsel for the managers, who asked her how much she earned. Marie replied that her wages had risen from £4 a week per hall in 1889 to £25 in 1895, £40 in 1900, £60 in 1903 and £80 at present. Her current earning power meant she could command £10 a hall more than Little Tich and £55 more than George Robey.[22] Marie made sure that the tribunal knew that her expenses came to about £149 a week and that she was not paid if, as had happened frequently in 1906, she was ill.[23]

The cross-examination succeeded, momentarily, in lifting her mask of bravura: 'But you see, we are here today, and gone tomorrow. You may get a little song tonight and you are a star tomorrow; then you may not get another song, and what are you going to do then?'[24] When she had finished giving evidence she thumped her counsel on the back in relief at having finished her 'turn'.

Soon afterwards she left for a holiday in Madeira to try to recover her health. As her advert said, 'Could not go before on account of strike but now happily peace is tending. Au revoir; Yours always, MARIE.'[25]

Alice, too, felt free to leave the country once the strike was settled and set off with her husband and Fred for New York. By the time Marie returned the war was over, and VAF, the *Era* said joyfully, now stood for Variety, Amity, Fraternity, although it could not help worrying that the public might have got out of the habit of going to music halls. The Walthamstow Palace was decked with bunting and a banner, 'The strike is ended. Peace with honour, All stars will appear'; the Canterbury carried the notice 'Peace Night' in gigantic letters.

It was not until 14 June that Askwith made his recommendation. There was to be payment for matinées, barring would be limited to one mile and four months in the centre of London, two miles in Outer London and ten miles in the provinces for a period of five months. But there was no mention of extra performances; timing and billing was still up to the manager; and the settlement failed to address agents' fees.

The wedding of Marie Junior in March 1907 provided an opportunity to start to heal the rift that the strike had wrenched open. Marie Alice Victoria Courtenay was eighteen when she married and her life so far had been lived in the shadow of her famous mother. She had accompanied her to South Africa, where she had made her stage début at the age of nine, and had then been sent to boarding-school in Kent. Mother and daughter had always had an uneasy relationship. Marie Junior was too similar in looks and temperament to her father to offer anything other than a constant reminder of that unhappy marriage. No photos of Marie Junior as a child have survived and only a handful of her as a young woman. She is slightly taller than her mother, and does not have her trademark protruding teeth.

Although she spent much time with her aunts and grandparents, Marie Junior was never viewed as a 'Lloyd'. She had a habit of saying the wrong thing at the wrong time, and she lacked her mother's ability to put strangers at ease. Born into a family of performers, she was not a natural entertainer. Impersonations of fellow artists, in particular her mother, which, as a child, had been charming, became embarrassing as she grew older. Her style of performance was stilted and she had no sense of timing.

Marie sent her to school at Clarence House in Brighton,[26] which some of the child's younger aunts had also attended, but – like many children of entertainers – she saw performing as the only way of proving her worth to her mother. The 'Marie Courtenay' who appeared at the Oxford in December 1910 may have been Marie's daughter, but she soon dropped her surname to capitalize on her famous mother. She became known as 'Little Marie' and 'Marie Lloyd Junior' and built her act around an impersonation of her mother.[27] Film of her shows an immobile woman, going through the gestures she had studied in her mother, but without any of the subtlety or animation.

The more famous Marie was embarrassed by her daughter, whom she recognized lacked talent. In choosing to copy her, Marie Junior also homed in on one of Marie's pet hates: copycats. The coolness between mother and daughter became well known, and crops up in several stories handed down about Marie. In one she is reported as overhearing her daughter singing and commenting in her customary direct style: 'That one will never make a star as long as she's got a hole in her arse.'[28]

Marie's attitude to her daughter was similar to Little Tich's relationship with his only son, Paul.[29] Like Marie, Little Tich suffered from bouts of insecurity: he was sensitive about his size and began to resent the big-boot routine that had made him famous and that caused increasing physical pain as he grew older and it became harder to balance on the tips of the gigantic shoes. He wanted his son to continue the family's upward mobility and sent him to the élite Dulwich College, hoping that he would either become a priest or go into business. In the event, Paul, who stammered, began training as a watch-maker but eventually abandoned this to join the Fred Karno Company. Father and son had a stormy relationship: Paul frequently asked for money and, after Little Tich's death, he made a living from impersonations and was billed as 'Son of a Famous Father – Dancing in Big Boots'.

Marie Junior married a twenty-two-year-old jockey, Harry (known as Tubby) Aylin from Newmarket at St Stephen the Martyr church in Hampstead. Her father, Percy, although only forty-five, was described as 'retired'. He was still on such poor terms with the Wood family that it seems he did not attend the wedding; Brushie, erect and immaculate as ever, gave away his granddaughter. Marie's aunts Annie, Rosie and Maudie, acted as witnesses with Bella.

The wedding was a grand affair, stage-managed by the bride's mother. Marie designed her daughter's dress, an Empire-line gown of Valenciennes lace with a silk sash secured at the back with a large pearl butterfly, and the outfits worn by the six bridesmaids, who included Maudie, who was two years younger than the bride. The bride wore a pearl and diamond necklace and pendant given to her by her mother, and diamond earrings supplied by the bridegroom. Marie Senior, wearing lace and chiffon, had a high profile in the service, leading a procession of guests into the church.

As well as some of the top performers of the day, the guest list included names that only a few months ago had been spoken with real bitterness by artists: Mr and Mrs Stoll and Mr and Mrs Adney Payne. The reception was held at Granville Lodge, and the couple's health drunk on the lawn as the sun shone and a light breeze stirred the orchestra's music. Champagne flowed and the cake bore two flags, one inscribed 'Marie' the other 'Harry'. Amid the crowd who waved the couple off on their honeymoon to Brighton, then Germany, was the best man, Bernard Dillon, who was also a jockey. Bernard, known to his friends as Ben, was an Irishman who, the previous year, had won the Grand Prix de Paris and had appeared as a sporting pin-up in *Vanity Fair*. He was a shy twenty-year-old, who became more voluble as the drink flowed. Marie Senior did not need an excuse to talk to this intense young man from Tralee, with his piercing gaze and long eyelashes.

Chapter 17

ALICE LLOYD'S SISTER GOES TO NEW YORK
(1907)

~A

'Oh, naughty, naughty, Marie Lloyd!
How you do shock us puritanical New Yorkers!'
Cartoon in New York newspaper, 13 October 1907

In the months after the strike Marie gave the managerial egos she had bruised a chance to heal and performed mainly outside London. In June she appeared at the Folies-Marigny, a theatre on the Champs-Élysées in Paris that had presented music-hall-style entertainment since 1896. The city was then in the throes of its own traumas: theatregoers were scandalized by a production of Oscar Wilde's *Salome* and café waiters had recently staged a lightning strike demanding the right to join trade unions, keep all their tips and grow moustaches.

It was not Marie's first trip to France. She had been to Paris in 1893 and appeared at the casino in Deauville the same year. Any association with the city was good for her image, adding yet another suggestion of raunchiness. At the turn of the century Paris had 264 café-concert rooms that offered music-hall-type entertainment, and Parisians had a relaxed approach to theatre: they relished jokes about bodily functions and breasts. British performers whose acts did not depend on words received a warm welcome: Chung Ling Soo's magic went down well, as did the slapstick of Charlie Chaplin performing in Fred Karno's company and Little Tich's big-boot clowning. Although it was not strictly necessary for his act, Little Tich took pains to learn French and became a proficient Gallic swearer. His popularity eventually earned him Les Palmes Académe in 1910 and he felt so at home in Paris that he kept an apartment in the city.

Marie's grasp of French only went as far as recognizing the words 'salt' and 'toothpick' on a menu – still no mean feat for a poorly educated woman from the East End of London.[1] When bombarded by cries of '*Bis, bis*' at the Marigny – 'More, more' – she was convinced that the audience was shouting, 'Beast, beast,' at her.[2] Although the quintessentially English lyrics of Marie's songs meant nothing to Parisians, they appreciated her sumptuous gowns and sensual movements. She was fortunate in that she followed a Spanish singer on the bill who was a great success for her melodramatic songs and flamboyant dancing: Marie's 'The Spanish Señora' was a perfect vehicle with which to lampoon her precursor.

After eight performances in Paris Marie spent most of that summer in the provinces, visiting Plymouth, Eastbourne, Norwich, Ipswich, Goodwood, Southampton, Margate, Portsmouth and Derby. East Anglia, isolated from the cosmopolitan south-east and still a predominately rural community, was a particular challenge. At Norwich, the manager of the Hippodrome took her to one side after the afternoon band practice and suggested she should tone her act down in keeping with a cathedral city. Her response was to ask for a timetable so that she could catch the next train home. Eventually, she performed her usual routine with no complaints.[3]

Marie enjoyed a huge send-off for her fourth trip to America in late September 1907. She and Alec threw a farewell party at Romano's and crowds of fellow performers, managers, journalists, authors, composers and friends gathered to see her off at Euston station. Marie's parents, Rosie, Marie Junior and Bella were also there. Annie, who acted as Marie's dresser, secretary and housekeeper, was to accompany them to America. Alice rushed down from Birmingham to kiss her sister goodbye before heading back for a matinée in the Midlands. Liveried servants, commissionaires and messenger boys zigzagged between the crowds delivering flowers and messages to the departing pair. Marie wore a sober dark blue travelling costume, while Alec looked his immaculate best in suit and bowler hat. A deafening cheer went up as the train pulled slowly out of the station.

Eugene Stratton met them at Liverpool, where he delivered a few words of welcome to Marie in front of a group of local actors and music-hall performers. On behalf of the local branch of the VAF he presented her with a huge floral arrangement, whose central white flowers had been arranged to read 'Our Marie's Heart'. The group paused while a photo was taken with the elegant White Star liner *Cedric* as a backdrop: Marie and Alec are pictured surrounded by men in bowler hats, boaters and flat caps, while the women are in their Sunday best, one even wearing a feather boa. The cheery, confident group looks like a scene from J. P. Priestley's *The Good Companions*.

There was a more muted reception in New York. Percy Williams, the quiet, balding impresario who had signed up Marie and Alec, was there to meet them. It was ten years since Marie had last set foot in the USA and there were no crowds to greet her. She told custom officials she had nothing to declare but a cough.[4]

Percy immediately took his British stars on a tour of his theatres: the Colonial, the Alhambra (on Seventh Avenue and 126th Street), the Orpheum in Brooklyn and the Gotham in East New York. At Park Avenue and 34th, their chauffeur was stopped for speeding and fined ten dollars.

Percy had decorated Marie's dressing room at the Colonial on Broadway and 62nd Street especially for her, painting the ceiling baby blue and decorating it with cherubs. She appreciated the gesture and began to warm to him. With his small stature, moustache and quiet demeanour, he reminded her of her father. Percy's father had been editor of a Sunday newspaper in Baltimore, but Percy himself had started as an actor. He moved into property, buying up sites in Long Island and running theatres in Manhattan.[5] The glasses he wore gave him an academic air, but he was a shrewd businessman.

He was continually shocked by Marie's apparently relaxed attitude to her work, which she exaggerated to tease him. When Percy decided to take a few days' break to visit the coast Marie insisted on seeing him off at Manhattan's Pennsylvania railway station despite his entreaties that she would be late for her performance. 'Tra-la!' she replied. 'They can put on the funny man, Cliff Gordon, in my place and that would make everything OK as you say over here.'[6]

Their subsequent exchange of telegrams reads like an exasperated father trying to control a spoilt teenager. Marie: 'All well. Hard time to make it, but did it so I was right.' Percy: 'Had severe attack of nerves. Glad all was well. Admire your nerve. Be a nice child.'

However, Marie's confidence in her standing on the New York vaudeville scene was misplaced. Audiences had changed in the decade since she had last visited New York and, worse, Alice had made her own American début a year before and had proved a stunning success. For the first time in her life Marie was someone else's sister.

The irony was that Alice had originally been booked to appear at the Colonial because Percy had wanted a British star to rival the New York success of Vesta Victoria and Vesta Tilley. His British agent had cabled: 'Can send Lloyd by next steamer. Am confident she will make big success.'[7] Percy had naturally assumed that he had secured the services of Marie and had started to prepare the bills, erroneously announcing Marie's *first* American visit. They had been hastily put away when Alice sent a cable from Liverpool explaining that it was she and not her elder sister who was heading for Manhattan. A different version of events has it that the McNaughton Brothers had secured a booking, but Tom insisted that his wife should also be given a place on the bill. Either way, Alice was an instant hit. Originally she was billed fifth in line and was due to perform for fifteen minutes; but the audience kept her on stage for three-quarters of an hour, forcing her to sing seven numbers. Overnight she was promoted to top billing and her weekly salary increased from $200 to $1,500 (£13,998).[8] Alice became the biggest female British performer on the other side of the Atlantic, second only to the Scottish singer Harry Lauder in the overall pecking order.

Before she had finished her first visit the American agents Klaw and Erlanger had signed her up for forty weeks at $2,000 (£18,664) a week over a five-year contract. By the time Marie arrived in New York Alice was back in England to fulfil a pantomime commitment but her new contract was due to start in March 1908, and the ghost of her success followed Marie wherever she went.

New Yorkers liked Alice's gentle, English rose appeal. She was not a classic beauty but had the homely attractiveness of the girl next door. She had a mass of shiny hair, pretty eyes, and the flowing, dainty Edwardian style of dress suited her figure, which she had kept in better shape than Marie had hers. Alice could be saucy but she did not wriggle and wink like her sister, and New Yorkers saw in her the genteel vaudevillian that many of them wanted. She was a 'dainty girl' and 'winsome'. Several Americans fell in love with her and when a Boston journalist went to interview her she showed him a row of visiting cards strung together by red ribbon; trophies of the hearts she had won. 'These have come to me with mash [flirtatious] notes and flowers,' she told the reporter.[9]

Alice was also better at 'reading' the American market. Initially, she chose songs similar in tone to her sister's: brash tales of showing too much lace while climbing on to the top deck of a bus, or of being spied upon by 'some Johnny' while bathing at the seaside. However, as she found the measure of the New York audience, she began to alter her approach and her songs became gently seductive numbers such as 'Splash Me', or 'Looking For The Love-light In Your Eyes' by J. P. Harrington and Orlando Powell. In the latter, she studied her face in a delicate hand mirror, which she used to deflect a spotlight so that its rays landed on the pate of an unfortunate man in the audience:

> I'm a lone little thing: with no beau to my string;
> I might, p'r'haps, get left on the shelf;
> So, excuse me for speaking, a spouse I am seeking.
> A girl must look after herself!
> Oh, there's a nice boy there! He, with the curly hair.

The audience loved her combination of vulnerability and gentle teasing and, it has been claimed, the mirror trick became the first piece of vaudeville 'business' to be protected by a US patent.[10]

No one knew quite what to expect from Alice's elder sister. Marie arrived with fifty gowns, the same number of hats and a medicine chest. The publicity mill was grinding out quaint stories to make her sound more glamorous. The pink shawl she wore while singing her Spanish number was said to be more than four hundred years old and worth over $4,000: maids guarded it when it was out of her sight. Asked why its colour never faded Marie replied, with the disingenuousness of a Hollywood starlet, 'Because it is never in the sun, always in the limelight, you know.'[11]

She had to confront a less than flattering story as soon as she arrived in New York: it was said that last time she had visited the city she had seen an astrologer and beauty consultant, Agnes Charcot.[12] This woman, who ran her business from 606 Fulton Street, Brooklyn, claimed Marie had agreed to pay her $500 a year in return for tips to help her preserve her beauty and figure. Charcot said that although Marie had already made a down payment for her horoscope she was suing her for $4,500. Marie admitted that she had considered visiting the astrologer, but Charcot's five beauty tips hardly seem tailor-made for a music-hall star:

(1) Stand on head for fifteen minutes a day;
(2) Use an ounce of rare Turkish perfume, 'Flowers of the Harem', and rose-water;
(3) Walk six miles a day;
(4) Never, under any condition, use powder or paint on the face;
(5) Gaze at the stars every evening.

The case was quietly dropped. It might even have been a bizarre publicity stunt. However, Marie may have wished she had kept up the payments as she had put on a substantial amount of weight and the American press, more brutal than its British counterpart, had no qualms about pointing this out. The *New York World* said she was 'broader in size, if not in song',[13] and the *Boston Transcript* commented, 'It is true that apparently she ignores the possibility of a waistline, at times, and regards corsets as the enemies of the supple and sinuous dancer.'[14]

The journalist Acton Davies, who visited her in the Astor Hotel, found there was 'nothing affected' about Marie Lloyd, but that she was nervous at appearing in New York again.[15] Marie lectured him on her belief that women should not smoke in public and how she was glad the Queen had made riding astride – presumably horses and bicycles – illegal. Since Marie occasionally smoked and Queen Victoria had been dead for six years she must have been teasing the unsuspecting journalist. 'In bringing Miss Lloyd to America again, Manager Williams has exploded the biggest bomb of the vaudeville season,' Davies concluded.

In the event, though, the bomb went off with more of a whimper than a bang. Youngsters in the audience did not know who she was and found songs such as 'Customs Of The Country', 'The Tale Of The Skirt', 'The Coster's Wedding', 'Something On His Mind', 'Eh, What, What, What', 'Tiddly-om-pom' and 'Spanish Burlesque' tame. *Variety* described her act as 'sedate'; adding, in a biting comment, 'The thing lacking with the sister of Alice Lloyd is songs.'[16]

On the other hand, middle-class women expected to be shocked by what the papers described as Marie's 'stag humour'.[17] She brought with her a reputation for coarseness, which was confirmed in that she had recently appeared in Paris. An unidentified newspaper cartoon (in the Billy Rose Collection) published just after her arrival shows a cross-section of the audience with the men smiling secretly and knowingly at Marie as a Spanish dancer, while the female customers look cross. The caption reads: 'Oh, naughty, naughty, Marie Lloyd! How you do shock us puritanical New Yorkers!' It goes on to suggest that wives with long memories should not allow their husbands to drop in at a theatre where Marie was playing.

There were favourable reviews, too, and Marie was so stung by *Variety*'s verdict that she took a whole page in the *Era* to reproduce her best notices.[18] One report spoke of her 'ingrained London face', her 'bawly voice that the London music-hall artist acquires after shouting for years at the low foreheads of the London 'alls'. It continued that she 'gets at her ditties and worries the very life out of them. She looks you straight in the eye. She is quite embarrassingly confidential.'[19]

British newspapers, at least, ignored claims of jealousy between Marie and Alice, but one American journalist made his readers acutely aware of it in this melodramatic account of his interview with Marie:

> 'Have I sisters? Well, yes and then some. When it comes to a family jar it takes sisters to do you up. Why, there was a time when, except for father and mother, I hadn't anything but sisters [Johnny is overlooked]. There's Gracie and Daisy and Alice.' (When she spoke the word 'Alice' a frozen note crept into her voice and tarried a bit until she turned and introduced a pretty little girl in the next chair). 'This,' she said, 'is Anne, the youngest of the lot and the pick of the Lloyd basket. But as far as education goes, they're all fine ladies, compared to poor me. I've been a mother to them all, haven't I, Annie?'[20]

The journalist suggested – wrongly – that it had been Marie who had paid for Alice to come to America in the first place, that she had fitted her out with costumes, given her songs and coached her through her act, but that once Alice had made a success of herself in the USA she had tried to persuade Marie not to come over, saying that her work would not be understood by Americans. When Alice returned to the United States in March 1908 there were rumours, too, that she had allowed people to believe that Marie was her mother.[21]

All this may have been spiteful hearsay, but it was inevitable that an element of jealousy found a crack in the close, sisterly bond between Marie and Alice and needled away until it became a painful gap in their friendship. Of all her sisters, Marie was closest to Alice, both in age and emotionally. Alice was just three years younger than Marie and, as the second oldest sister in the family, she had been Marie's second in command when they were planning Sunday-school performances or trips out with the troupe of seven siblings. Even from their earliest days in the Fairy Bell Minstrels Marie had coached and stage-directed her sister.

As in most families, the eldest child paved the way for her siblings. If she was a success at what she did, her chosen way of life became more acceptable to parents and made the road easier for the offspring who followed. Matilda and Brushie Wood had been wary of their daughter taking to the halls but once Marie made a success of it, it was hard for them to forbid their other children to follow her lead. In practical ways, too, Marie had given her sisters the name 'Lloyd' as an 'Open Sesame' in the highly competitive music-hall world.

It takes a secure, contented personality to enjoy being overtaken by their protégé, and Marie was neither. She had chosen to work in the halls because she thrived on being centre-stage; being pushed out of the limelight was difficult to cope with, especially now that she was an accepted star and the name edging her to one side was Lloyd.

Marie found her own mixed reviews and the constant talk about her sister enervating, but at least she had the comfort of her husband and little sister. While Alec was still performing in New York they found time to sightsee. They visited Chinatown, an area that visitors still liked to believe was full of opium dens and victims of the white slave trade, but which to Marie resembled the densely packed alleyways of Hoxton. But even this tourist trip was spun into a publicity yarn: it was revealed that, during her visit to Chinatown, Marie had been wearing a jade amulet given to her by the Chinese ambassador to England, which had been taken from a Peking temple and was viewed by the Chinese as sacred. As a result everywhere she went she was greeted by deferential bows.[22]

She also suffered her usual string of mishaps and minor irritations. An over-zealous hotel porter at the Astor burnt an ostrich plume that she had had sent over from South Africa and which was worth £50.[23] In November she was dashing in full make-up and costume from Hammerstein's to watch Alec at the Colonial when the cab she was travelling in, with Annie and two others, was stopped for speeding by a – presumably fairly nippy – policeman on his bicycle. She was taken to the local police station but soon released.[24]

Alec was worried about his brother Alfred, who had taken over the George IV pub in Haggerston, north London. Alfred was the only one of the four Hurley sons not to go on the stage and Alec had agreed to act as surety for a loan of £109 when Alfred took over the pub and the firm of distillers had taken Alfred to court to recover the money. They had agreed to delay the prosecution until Alec returned from America but the signs were not good. The distillers' solicitor had commented ominously that Alec 'had the good fortune to belong to a profession in which the artists were said to be rolling in gold ...' For Alec, who worried about money more than his wife, the financial burden lay heavy on his shoulders.[25]

As Christmas approached Marie was feeling homesick and ordered her cook to send her some English plum puddings. Her sense of isolation grew when she left New York for a tour of north-eastern cities. Alec had embarked on a similar tour but, typically, their itinerary rarely coincided. Their paths crossed briefly in Boston: a photograph captures Marie, immense in a fur coat, like a great bear, as Alec lifts his bowler politely to shake hands with her. 'Haven't we met before?' the caption asks.[26]

Boston had a reputation as a difficult city for performers. Audiences could be cold and indifferent; they felt they were superior to New Yorkers and were loath to laugh. Risqué material did not generally go down well. Edward Franklin Albee and Benjamin Franklin Keith brought 'polite' vaudeville to Boston when they became partners in the late 1880s. Both, like Tony Pastor, had started their career in the circus and Keith had run a 'museum' featuring exhibits such as a mermaid and a chicken with a human face. They were tough operators, who insisted on 'clean acts' to attract a better class of clientele: vulgarity and *double entendre*, as well as such words and phrases as 'liar', 'sucker', 'slob', 'holy glee', 'son-of-a-gun' and 'devil' were banned, as a notice in theatres warned all performers.

As the two expanded their vaudeville circuit Keith became the financial brains of the partnership, while Albee acted as general manager. A year before Marie performed at Keith's theatres in Philadelphia, Pittsburgh and Boston, the two men set up the United Booking Office. Every act had to go through the UBO, which charged a 5 per cent commission for the privilege. Managers were also required to file reports, providing detailed information on each act: the precise length of the performance, costumes, material and how well it was received.

Carl D. Lothrop was a fastidious manager of Keith's in Boston. In the report he compiled for head office of Marie's first – afternoon – performance in Boston on Monday, 2 December 1907 he agonized over whether the Worker and Ower comedy act, at six minutes, was too short and whether he should tell 'Our Boys In Blue' to cut out early parts of the act and start with the lights up showing the soldiers in action. The fact that he found the 'Tunny Fisheries In Sicily', a kinetograph show, 'rather an entertaining picture' gives some indication of his tastes and it is not surprising that he was nervous of how Bostonians would respond to Marie. Lothrop noted that she stepped on stage at 3.32 p.m.

> A string of interrogation points would best express my opinion of Miss Lloyd. She is undeniably a great artist and had she made her appearance before [Vesta?] Victoria and her sister [Alice Lloyd?], she would undoubtedly have made a much stronger impression than she did in New York. Of course, to the pure all things are pure, so I found that some of her audiences today could find nothing in her songs at which they took offence. Some others, with more worldly experience, thought that she was absolutely the limit, that every verse she sung was full of suggestiveness. She did not sing the 'Eh, what, what' song, and I made one cut in 'Customs of the Country'. I am anxiously awaiting the verdicts of the different critics in tomorrow's papers. I feel quite confident that we will find the same differences of opinion as I found existing among our patrons today. With Lloyd it is practically a case of all or nothing, for if you start to cut it is almost impossible to stop. Boston would rather have one Millie Lindon than all of the Lloyds and Victorias that can be found.[27]

Several performers suffered from Lothrop's anxiety that day. He ordered one act to cut a reference to ' "company's coming" and subsequent scratching' and another to remove the line 'she slept alone in the garret'. Marie was asked to remove a verse from 'Customs Of The Country' that dealt with scantily clad foreigners:

> In far-away Samoa,
> They ought to wear *some more*
> It's so very warm, the ladies go half bare;
> Now, *our ladies*, thin or fat,
> Wouldn't walk about like *that*,
> No, they save their bare-back show for evening wear!

Lothrop's final comment shows just how touch-and-go he felt Marie's chances of success were: 'I consider this a very good show indeed, but feel that the business will depend largely on whether or not Lloyd catches on with the Bostonians.'

A week later Lothrop's tone had changed completely. She had capitulated to Lothrop's requests to 'tone down her act', as his comments, effusive in their sense of relief, show:

> Much to our delight Miss Lloyd has proven an extremely strong attraction. Our patrons think her the cleverest artiste in her line that has ever been on our stage. She is very easily handled, being extremely anxious to make good. The turn that she is doing for us is as clean as a whistle and I do not think it would be possible for the most prudish person to take exception to any of her lines.

Lothrop made no further cuts and concluded: 'I do not think we have had many stronger shows in this house.'

Touring in America was even more gruelling than in England, due to the vast distances performers had to cover. It was not uncommon for a singer to come off stage at 10.30 p.m., catch the midnight sleeper and be ready the next morning for rehearsal at ten thirty. By Christmas Marie had doubled back to Philadelphia, a town with a reputation for being as puritanical as Boston but without the metropolitan sophistication. She arrived tired and in low spritis, feeling a bit like 'The Little Girl Who Didn't Believe In Santa Claus' – a kinetograph that followed her on the bill. The theatre manager's report shows him willing to make allowances for her, given that she was obviously attracting audiences:

Advance hand [applauded before she appeared?]. Monday afternoon and evening did not sing, arriving in Philadelphia very much under the weather. In order to keep faith with the public, however, she appeared in the afternoon, being introduced by Mr George Abel [the previous act], who made a nice little speech, telling the audience of Miss Lloyd's indisposition. Miss Lloyd made her apologies and showed very plainly that she was very unwell. The crowd gave her a good strong hand. Tuesday afternoon Miss Lloyd appeared, and although it was plain to be seen that she was not up to form, she gave a very good show. In the evening her work was still better and promises to improve for the balance of the week. Lloyd is certainly drawing many to the house.[28]

On Christmas Day her frustration and loneliness reached a peak. The unkind reviews were still festering at the back of her mind and, sitting in her hotel room, she decided to pen a contorted letter defending her reputation to the founder and editor of *Variety*. It reads as if she was straining to prove her intellectual capacity, but we are left with an impression of confusion. The reference to the *Era* may have been because she believed *Variety*'s poor reviews were due to her refusal to advertise in the publication:

Dear Sime,

Being Christmas Day, I address you familiarly, knowing full well such action breeds contempt, though that contempt emanates from me. I am sending by same post a copy of the world's greatest variety paper, the Era, wherein you will see I reproduce a copy of your well conceived criticism, my one object being that, should the circulation of your paper fail to have reached all whom you desired it to (my friends being far greater than yours), the Era would reach them quicker and have more effect, hence I have given your remarks the most prominent position in my advertisement.

In conclusion, let me remind you that 'criticism' is wholesome, at least for the critics, as it helps to relieve the pains of journalistic dyspepsia. Yours, with kind thoughts, Marie Lloyd.

P. S. My sister Alice and Tom McNaughton send their LOVE.[29]

The postscript is particularly curious. Is she implying that Tom and Alice are in league with Sime, or that they too despise him?

After Philadelphia she appeared in Toronto, where she was presented by the city's nautical club with a solid silver punch-bowl. Then she appeared in Chicago before travelling back to New York to perform at the Colonial and the Orpheum. At the Colonial she sang a number called 'The Hag' and was billed as 'England's Most Popular Comedienne'.

Marie was at the quayside to greet another member of the Lloyd family who had come over to capitalize on the family's American success. She was desperate to see Rosie after a gap of six months and, with Annie, tried to board the ship before it had been passed by Customs and Immigration staff. 'I'm Miss Lloyd. Rosie's just come, and I'm all over shakes to see her. Let me pass, there's a good man,' she said to an official.[30] Eventually the two sisters made a dash for the gangplank while his back was turned and were safely in the purser's office; meanwhile, the official had slipped and fallen into the sea.

Rosie, now twenty-nine, arrived with forty gowns and a reputation that owed much to her two sisters. Marie coached her in the ways of American audiences and took a box to watch her first performance at the Colonial, which had now played host to three of the Lloyd sisters. Rosie borrowed songs from both Marie and Alice, 'When The Leaves Began To Fall' from Marie and 'Never Introduce Your Bloke To Your Loidy Friend' from Alice, but was gawky by comparison, with her long nose and flaring nostrils. One paper described her as 'the girl with the long-distance face'[31] and went on to say that she looked like a horse 'and not a very nice horse at that'. This was a particularly unfortunate jibe since, later in the tour, Rosie found herself appearing in the same theatre as an equine act. The horse had higher billing.

Variety criticized her relentlessly. She was accused of ignoring the gallery[32] and of hiring a 'claque' to cheer her on,[33] that her voice was not suited to ballads and that she had 'an uncertain quaver in her notes where her tones are forced'. In its third damning article on her *Variety* dealt a blow that hit both her and Marie: 'Miss [Rosie] Lloyd is unsuccessfully attempting to imitate her sister, Marie, without approaching at any time her sister, Alice, whom she might better copy.'[34] Comparisons between the sisters were inevitable. They all had the same 'half-lisp that makes the letter S an almost unknown quantity'[35] and they had similar protruding teeth, although Rosie's were bovine rather than alluring.

Rosie tried elaborate costumes – gypsy dress for 'Lady, Lady' and a cowboy outfit with Colt revolver for 'Midnight On The Prairie' – and eventually she started to win a following, if only for her staying power and the fact that the critics found her hard to pigeonhole. Also, notwithstanding her gawkiness, she had a certain exuberance: she loved driving cars and would rise at 7 a.m., despite having worked late, to race through Central Park, fulfilling what she described as her 'madness for motoring'.[36] Yale students, curious about this quirky English singer who had more spirit than talent, waited for her at the stage door and swept her off to dinner.[37]

Rosie was still finding her feet when it was time for Marie to return home. Percy gave a farewell supper for her in a private dining room at the Astor, and Marie returned the compliment with a beefsteak and kidney pudding lunch at Keen's English Chophouse. She also presented Percy's wife with a diamond ring. At her last performance Percy came on stage to give her a loving cup. Marie swooped down on him, her arms raised like a swan's wings, and said, with a pointed glance at the box, 'I'm going to kiss you, yes, even though Mrs Williams is watching us.' The audience howled with delight and Percy glowed with embarrassment.[38]

Alec had already returned to England by the time Marie set sail for home and an engagement at the cavernous Hackney Empire. She arrived in London just as Alice was preparing to return to America for the start of her five-year engagement. The American experience had shaken Marie's belief in her ability and her relationship with her public. With the tension and jealousy between herself and Alice it had also dented her vision of herself as the supreme head of a family of performers, who constantly looked to her for guidance and leadership. A few family get-togethers on home territory might have been enough to restore the sisters' closeness, but this was not to be. However, at least Marie had the comfort of returning to a country whose entertainment terrain she knew intimately.

Chapter 18

MARRIAGE PROBLEMS

(1908–11)

It's warranted to knock a male thing silly;
First time I put it on,
And sailed out like a swan,
I stopped the traffic all down Piccadilly.
'The Directoire Girl' by Orlando Powell and J. P. Harrington

Marie had been away from England for almost six months and had missed her home. During that time she may have clung to a romanticized view of her country as homesick people do. The reality was that tastes were changing.

The American dancer Maud Allan arrived in London a few weeks before Marie's return to perform her 'Vision of Salome' with a sensuousness and lack of clothing previously unimaginable in a respectable London theatre. She had already appeared privately before Edward VII the previous September in Marienbad, despite warnings from his advisers. Alfred Butt, one of the new breed of theatrical impresarios, had booked her for his Palace Theatre where Marie had performed a decade earlier before Kitchener. Dripping with beads and clothed only in a low-slung, diaphanous skirt and breastplates held together by a spider's web of gold and pearls, Maud cavorted in front of audiences who included luminaries such as Sir Arthur Conan Doyle and minor royals. Where Trilby's bare feet had been sensational, Maud's naked flesh caused uproar. While Trilby had been hypnotized by Svengali, Maud was said to use her huge dark eyes to mesmerize her audience so that some people believed they were watching an entirely naked woman. And Maud set a new fashion trend: Salome's classical sandals and beaded jewellery became all the rage among society women.

Marie's *double entendres* and winks were tame compared to Maud's display, but Maud had the pretence of art, and even religion, on her side and stayed at the Palace Theatre for over a year. She managed to annoy moral campaigners but generally won over the Establishment: Archdeacon Sinclair changed his mind about her when they took tea together at St Paul's Chapter House and she was even a bridesmaid when Sir Edward Moss's youngest daughter got married.[1] Her success was as much about a greater sophistication among London audiences as about changing public morals. Marie, though, found it difficult to gauge what her audiences wanted.

Although she was only thirty-seven, people commented on how her American trip had aged her and she had to temper her songs to this more matronly image. Glamour was sacrificed as she began to sing about women like the old maid who 'lives in hope if she dies in despair'. Harry Day, who operated from an office in Arundel Street off the Strand, took over from Hugh Didcott as her agent but lacked a sure hand when it came to spotting songs that matched current taste.

'Tiddley-om-pom!' by Fred W. Leigh and Orlando Powell (1908) tried to strike a note of playfulness. It explains how the Spanish have overtaken the French as the continent's most enthusiastic lovers. In style it is the sort of nonsense song Marie had used before as the chorus shows:

> Tiddley-om-pom! tiddley-om-pom!
> Tiddley-om-pom-pom-pom pay!
> Oh! the dainty dancing donah
> Sends you off your 'bar-ce-lo-na'
> The contortions they are cautious!
> Well, the best thing I can say,
> Is pom tiddley-om-pom-pom-pom-pom!
> Tiddley-om-pom-pom-pom-pay!
> Tiddley-pay!

Marie relied on older hits such as 'Hulloah, Hulloah, Hulloah' until she found in 'The Directoire Girl', by Powell and J. P. Harrington, a song that matched the decadence of the time and showed her back at her confident, flirting best. The song poked fun at the latest fashion craze, the directoire dress, and Marie wore a daring silver-trimmed black outfit with a long slit that revealed a gartered leg. Using a cane that was nearly as tall as she was, she sashayed along, making the most of what the Lloyd sisters prided themselves on – a neat bottom:

The New Directoire Girl
Has set the world a whirl.
Her costume is so very well, directoire,
Divided down one side,
Each time she takes a stride,
It shows enough to make the men expect more.
'Twas over in Paree,
That they built mine for me.
It's warranted to knock a male thing silly;
First time I put it on,
And sailed out like a swan,
I stopped the traffic all down Piccadilly.
Chorus
When they saw me in Directoire Dress,
Fellows nearly had a fit.
Um, yes; They all followed up behind,
In dozens, all the London
Johnnies and their Country Cousins,
And they all said, 'Yum, yum!' [slang for both male and female
   sex organs]
I really was a big success,
For I showed the fellows more than I ever did before
When I put on my Directoire Dress! Dress!

The first edition of the sheet music, published in the Monte Carlo Company's 'Sixpenny Successes' series, sold out quickly and Anna Held was so taken by the song that she ordered an Americanized version to be written for her to perform in a Ziegfeld production.[2] During the summer of 1908 Marie made the song the mainstay of a seaside tour.

But the 'Directoire Dress' was a rare burst of life in an otherwise fallow period. Unfortunately for Marie's self-esteem, the period of low productivity coincided with a string of successes by the other Lloyds and she could read almost weekly episodes in the *Era* of Alice's progress through America. While Marie had to be content with the compliment that Americans wanted to hear 'Directoire', Alice cabled her songwriter in Britain that she needed new numbers for a musical that she and her husband had been asked to perform in and which would be produced in New York by Florenz Ziegfeld Junior.[3] With Tom acting as manager she extended her influence across America; in Spokane, Washington, demand was so great that she had to give an extra performance.[4]

Even Rosie seemed to be doing well. She was the headliner at the Orpheum in Boston, and her initial ten-week contract had been extended indefinitely. When she returned to England in the late summer of 1908 she was engaged by the agent George Foster, who had introduced Marie to her first husband. George increased Rosie's salary and launched her on a provincial tour. By the autumn she had fallen in love with fellow performer Will Poluski. They married at the end of October, by special licence, at what had become the routine church for the sisters' weddings, St Mary's in Primrose Hill. It was a quiet affair: only close friends and family were invited and little sister Annie was the bridesmaid. Unusually, the reception was held at the bridegroom's parents' home in Brixton. Perhaps Marie was feeling too tired or ill to cope with a wedding breakfast, or perhaps she was not in the mood for a blast of young love at close quarters. Ironically, Rosie's fame was now such that Marie was able to trade on it with a new song, 'Rosie Had A Very Rosie Time', that alluded to the recent nuptials.

Daisy, who had retired from the stage to marry Donald Munro, decided in 1908 to return to the halls. She had played beside Alice in one of the Lloyds' traditional pantomimes at Peckham in the Christmas of 1907 and had received such encouraging reviews that she wanted to rekindle her variety career. She was still under thirty, sweet-faced with luxuriant hair that reached to her knees, and had lost none of her ability to make an audience fall in love with her from across the footlights. Her new songs such as 'Willie, You Are Slow' (Harrington and Powell) and 'Will You Be My Valentine?' carried on where she had left off before her marriage.

In September she and Donald left for New York where she was met by Alice and Tom. Sid and Maude, the youngest members of the Wood family at twenty-three and eighteen respectively, had also headed for America where they performed as a double act – which, naturally, made the most of their elder sisters' reputations.[5]

Tom and Alice had taken an apartment in West 66th Street and were treating America as their home.[6] As each new Lloyd arrived, the older couple reassured them, showed them round and coached them in the niceties of winning over an American audience. It was the sort of role Alec and Marie usually fulfilled. Tom and Alice took Daisy to see a local comedienne, and Alice helped Daisy refine her act with the sort of 'business' she knew audiences at Blaney's Lincoln Square Theater would love.

In 'I'm Fishing For A Sweetheart' Alice suggested Daisy dangle a circular landing-net attached to a six-foot pole over the audience for admirers to fill with tokens of their appreciation: dollar bills, cigars, calling cards and boxes of candy.[7] She paused in the middle of a song to pop a chocolate in to her mouth and munched her way seductively through it. For 'Paddling' she wore a white muslin dress with a pink hat and sash, and ended the number by slowly removing her tiny boots and blue silk stockings to finish in bare feet.[8] While *Variety* praised her shapely legs it demanded that she shed her skin-coloured stage tights: 'Since "Salome" New Yorkers want theirs bare, so Daisy had better get down to the pelf.'[9]

Americans described her as 'winsome' and 'charming',[10] and she was asked to sing at a millionaire's dinner party.[11] Brooklyn Rowing Club made her a life member, presenting her with a brooch and promising to name their next boat after her.[12] There was even a rumour that she was to marry a detective and member of the Rowing Club, although, of course, she already had a husband.[13]

Daisy, who usually performed in Britain as Wood, rather than Lloyd, enjoyed the best of both worlds in America by calling herself Daisy Lloyd Wood. She was compared to Alice and Marie and described as 'having something of the roguishness of one and daintiness of the other',[14] the roguishness presumably of Marie. New Yorkers were enthralled, as this poem, published in the *New York World*, after Daisy had left for Britain, suggests:

> Oh, Mrs Pankhurst, what have we done to you,
> To bring you sailing to our shores across the ocean blue?
> We hope that you'll have lots of fun and leave US overjoyed,
> But many here would much prefer to welcome Daisy Lloyd.[15]

Daisy returned to England to appear in Aladdin at the Prince's Theatre, Bristol. Marie tracked her success, knowing that her sister's songs were the sort of playful, little-girl-lost numbers she herself had performed so successfully at the beginning of her career. Now she was searching for a new stage persona as she approached forty, dogged by ill-health and legal problems.

Alec had won the case against the distillery company who owned his brother's pub, but lost against the MacNaughton vaudeville circuit (no relation to Tom).[16] He had claimed a week's salary when the circuit withdrew his contract to perform a scena, 'The Coster's Beano', because he had not submitted the script in advance. The manager said that this was vital to comply with LCC rules.

Marie was in trouble with the important Moss Empire for playing the Glasgow Pavilion when her contract forbade her to appear within an eleven-mile radius of a Moss music hall.[17] Moss's lawyer said that Marie was 'playing fast and loose with her contract', and the proceedings were seen as a test case. The action dragged on for over a year and was postponed in July 1909 when Marie was taken ill. She was unable to appear at the Empire in Southend and had an operation at home, the nature of which remains a mystery but it may have been concerned with her nasal passages, which gave her constant problems.

Marie decided to take a week's holiday at Felixstowe and was well enough to attend her brother Sidney's wedding in Brixton to Ouida McDermott, granddaughter of the music-hall star J. H. Milburn. The summer turned into a rare family reunion when Alice finished at Young's Pier Theater in Atlantic City and set sail for a holiday in England, leaving Tom in New York. As Marie was performing during the summer in London halls it gave the sisters a chance to spend time together in a setting where Marie was indisputably the main attraction. Her predominance was confirmed at the end of July when she and Harry Lauder were asked to perform at the Lord Mayor's dinner at the Guildhall in London, an honour which, the Era claimed, had not been given to a performer for seven hundred years. Another worry disappeared when Moss lost its legal claim against her.

There was further cause for celebration that year when Dick Burge was unexpectedly released from prison after saving the life of a prison warder who had been attacked by another inmate. Soon after leaving gaol he took over an old chapel in Blackfriars and opened the Ring, a venue for boxing. Dick's own boxing record, together with his spell in prison, meant that he commanded considerable respect and was able to operate the business with a tight discipline that ensured violence was confined to the fighting ring. He helped to bring a degree of respectability to the sport and the frequent visits of music-hall friends, like Marie and Alec, boosted its glamour.

In September Marie allowed herself a second short break, this time with the artist Claire Romaine at Margate, a seaside town she was particularly fond of. Marie was spending increasing amounts of time with young female friends, most of whom were fellow performers, and together they indulged in the latest fads, single-minded in their determination to have a good time. Marie also did her best to fill the void in her house left by the departure of her siblings to their own homes. She even 'adopted' a 'piccaninny' boy who had been dancing at the Oxford Music Hall, taking him on as a servant.[18]

She was photographed with Victoria Monks, a vivacious artist who had a reputation similar to her own, indulging in 'rinking' and looks unsteady, if not drunk, on her roller skates. Cars, which offered the combination of freedom and showing off, always attracted Marie; Bella and an American newspaper woman were with her when hers broke down on the Scottish moors as they motored between Edinburgh and Newcastle. They waited four hours until a passer-by fixed it for them, but as soon as he had gone the lights failed and they had to continue in the dark.[19]

Marie found great comfort in her female friendships, but the plight of the suffragettes failed to move her. Like most music-hall performers she saw this group of passionate women, who occasionally interrupted an evening's entertainment by unfurling banners and waving the tubes with which female prisoners were force-fed, as misguided.[20] However, Marie once took a walk-on part in the suffragist play *How The Vote Was Won* when it was performed at the Oxford Music Hall.[21] It was a farce about the day women went on strike and opened with the Prime Minister being forced to make his own bed. Marie enjoyed its absurdity, but generally she preferred to champion individuals rather than causes. The only other occasion when she helped the cause was when she assisted the militant suffragette Annie Kenney to outwit the police. Marie allowed her to hide in a theatrical hamper marked 'Marie Lloyd, Pavilion', which was then smuggled through the police cordon surrounding the theatre and on to the stage. Annie emerged triumphant, to make her speech.[22] This was the sort of action Marie understood: helping someone out who was in a tight corner and simultaneously hoodwinking the police. The music-hall dispute had struck a chord with her because she knew the real hardship an extra matiné or the barring system caused, but she failed to see the relevance of having the right to vote.

While four hundred actresses, including Ellen Terry and Mrs Kendal, who were both in their sixties, met at the Criterion Restaurant in December 1908 to form the Actresses' Franchise League, most music-hall performers were unmoved by their campaign. A lone exception was Kitty Marion,[23] who was originally from Germany but came to England at the age of fifteen. She appeared in the chorus line of *Robinson Crusoe* in 1889 and toured the provinces as a comic singer. A speech by Mrs Pankhurst converted her to the cause and she became an enthusiastic hurler of bricks through windows. She was repeatedly imprisoned, once devising a way of communicating with a fellow inmate by scribbling notes on toilet paper.

An issue closer to Marie's heart was her marriage, which was beginning to buckle under the strain of her growing insecurity, her loneliness and her need for constant flattery and reassurance. Marie had been attracted to Alec for his no-nonsense approach to life and their shared background, but these two attributes were no longer enough. She wanted to be seen as just as glamorous and attractive as she had been in her youth. The dream she had expressed at their wedding of living together in a roadside hostelry that motor-cars passed without stopping now represented a nightmare of obscurity. She wanted someone with more gusto than a man who sang self-effacing songs with titles such as 'I Ain't Nobody In Particular'.

Also Alec was rarely at home to banish his wife's anxieties. He was now running his own company, which performed the 'scena' based around his songs. He and Marie were often in different parts of the country, unlike Tom and Alice, who arranged their work schedules so that they coincided as much as possible. Whenever Alec and Marie met it was usually in somewhere like Romano's where Alec had to share his wife with her coterie of hangers-on. Alec enjoyed his own circle of male friends but, perversely, Marie resented him spending time with them, which soured the precious hours they did spend together.

They had bitter fights followed by reconciliations, and both Alec and Marie heard the insidious whisperings in the music-hall world that its most famous marriage was on the rocks. There had always been rumours about Marie's private life but Alec had treated them with his customary levelheadedness. Now, worn down by her verbal abuse, he allowed doubts to take shape and made the fatal mistake of voicing them. Marie retorted with one of her favourite sayings: 'Well, if I've got the name, I might as well have the game!' Both were too proud to back down.

They started to lead separate lives. Alec embarked on a tour of South Africa, to give him time to think, and by his return he had resolved to try for a reconciliation with his wife. When he arrived at Waterloo station his brother and family met him, and he proudly showed them a pendant inset with a large diamond that he had bought for Marie.[24] He was eager for news of her, but silence fell on the group until someone found the courage to tell him that Marie had left him. Alec gave the pendant to one of his nieces and set off for Granville Lodge. When he opened the front door he found the house empty except for the hallway, which was neatly stacked with his trunks and all his other possessions. Marie had made up her mind and moved with a ruthlessness that took her husband's breath away.

By Christmas 1910 Marie was 'lying dangerously ill of acute rheumatism'[25] having fallen sick in Liverpool and been brought back to London by her own doctor. All her engagements were cancelled and she booked herself and Bella on the next sailing for South Africa. Her rheumatism was so debilitating that she had to be carried on board by stretcher, her stout little body muffled in blankets. The departure was as inauspicious as her last trip to South Africa when Percy had tried to kidnap Marie Junior. She was again running away from marriage, but this time she was leaving behind a man she still loved.

She was also abandoning Alec in his moment of greatest need. In January 1911, he was declared bankrupt.[26] Alec cited 'keen competition' in the halls, gifts to friends, the high costs of running a company and betting as the main reasons for his insolvency. He admitted that in the last three years he had earned up to £600 a year, but had lost several hundred pounds in betting. His many court appearances over the last few years had also eaten into his income as had keeping up with Marie's social life. Alec was a naturally generous man and, like most of his colleagues, he saw open-handedness as representing proof that he had 'arrived'. On the tenth anniversary of Fred Higham's position as Alec's sole agent, for example, Alec presented him with a magnificent diamond ring at Simpson's in the Strand.

In the same month that he was declared bankrupt Alec filed for divorce, citing Marie Junior's best man, Bernard Dillon, as co-respondent.[27] When the case was due in court, though, neither he nor Marie had the heart to pursue it and the proceedings were dropped.

The Crippens' marriage was also suffering, although Belle kept up the pretence of a happy private life. At the Music Hall Ladies Guild Annual Dinner at the Hotel de Boulogne in Gerrard Street, she was presented with a gold bangle inscribed 'To the hustler', in recognition of her work as treasurer. In her acceptance speech she commented, 'Knowing this lovely compliment is paid me in appreciation of my work for the Guild, I can only say that as long as I am permitted I will do in the future as I have done and further the interests of the Guild to the best of my ability.'[28] She was to be 'permitted' much less time than she realized when making the speech.

In February 1910 Crippen appeared at the MHRA's annual dinner at the sparkling Criterion with a young woman on his arm who, the *Era* remarked, was 'very showily dressed' and was definitely not Belle. Some people recognized her as his secretary, Ethel Le Neve. Her 'showy dress' included a sealskin coat similar to one of Belle's and a distinctive brooch, with a central cluster of diamonds designed to depict the rising sun, that also looked uncannily like one of Belle's. Marie was out of town on the night of the Criterion ball, but the brazen appearance of Crippen and his paramour did not go unnoticed by members of the Music Hall Ladies Guild.

Crippen cancelled his wife's subscription to the *Era* and the *Stage*, and made it known that she had returned home to America to visit a sick relative in California. The Guild's secretary, Melinda May, was horrified that Belle had left without saying goodbye and without allowing her to provide a proper send-off with flowers and tears at the railway station. She was further shocked when a package containing

Belle's passbook, paying-in and cheque books arrived at the Guild's headquarters. The mystery deepened when Ethel Le Neve delivered a letter in Crippen's handwriting, saying that Belle had resigned as treasurer and been forced to go to America because a relative was ill. Elmore was spelt with two Ls.

In March Crippen called on his wife's friends, Paul and Clara Martinetti, to say that Belle had a lung problem; a few days later he wrote to say that the condition had become double pneumonia – but ignored Clara's request for her friend's address in America. Then, suddenly, a notice appeared in the births, deaths and marriages section of the *Era*: 'ELMORE – March 23 in California, USA, Miss Belle Elmore (Mrs H. H. Crippen).'[29]

Clara and other members of the Guild hounded Crippen with questions about his wife's death. Where was his wife's final resting place? Where should they send flowers? Was it decent that a Catholic had been cremated? Unhappy with his replies, the Guild swung into action. One member's husband tailed the doctor and watched his house, while two ladies interviewed neighbours in Hilldrop Crescent. Isabel Ginnett, the Guild's president, who was in New York while her husband toured with an equestrian act, wrote to the Los Angeles police, who told her that they had no record of Belle's death. This was enough for the Guild to call in detectives who eventually discovered Belle's body in the cellar of 39, Hilldrop Crescent. She had been poisoned, but in the heat of the moment, Crippen had doused her body in a type of lime that acted as a preservative rather than promoting decay.[30]

Before leaving for South Africa Marie, like other music-hall perform-ers, had been questioned about Belle's disappearance.[31] Now the whole country became obsessed with finding Crippen and Ethel, who were known to have visited Willy Clarkson's wig shop in search of a disguise, saying they wanted to play a practical joke on some friends.

Eventually the captain of the *Montrose*, which was on its way to New York, wired Scotland Yard: 'Have strong suspicions that Crippen London Cellar Murderer and accomplice are among saloon passengers. Moustache taken off, growing beard. Accomplice dressed as boy. Voice manner and build undoubtedly a girl. Both travelling as Mr and Master Robinson. Kendall.'

The message marked the first time the wireless was used to catch a criminal. What followed must have been one of the first big transatlantic media stories. Unbeknown to Crippen and Ethel, Captain Kendall sent regular reports about his famous passengers back to the newspapers, who printed details of how Le Neve's trousers had split and were being held together by a safety-pin, and how a ship containing detectives was gradually gaining ground on the *Montrose*. A ratpack of reporters was at New York to greet the poisoner.

Music halls marked the chase in song:

> Oh, Miss Le Neve, Oh, Miss Le Neve,
> Is it true that you are sittin',
> On the lap of Dr Crippen,
> In your boy's clothes,
> On the *Montrose*,
> Miss Le Neve?[32]

Little sympathy was wasted on Belle, and music-hall references to her murdering husband were commonplace for years after he was hanged. If a comedian was describing his lodgings he might say: 'You ought to see the landlady – what a face! Crippen was innocent!'[33] Number 39 Hilldrop Crescent became theatrical digs but failed to prosper: music-hall performers were superstitious and persistent reports of scraping sounds from the cellar did not help trade.

Chapter 19

HORSE-RACING

(1911)

~*~

I at the races shone,
With my Directoire on,
They said that I was warmer than the weather;
No bookie had the grace
To look me in the face,
No they were looking elsewhere altogether.
'The Directoire Girl' by Orlando Powell and J. P. Harrington

The Derby of 1 June 1910 was a sombre occasion. Edward VII, who through his patronage had done so much to bring respectability and excitement to horse-racing, had died on 6 May and the sport was in deep mourning. The racegoing public had been unaware of his illness, and his death came as a shock that still hung in the air at what became known as the 'Black Derby'.[1] During his reign the cigar-smoking, sybaritic king had given racegoers leave to enjoy themselves after the dreary last years of his mother's reign and there was genuine sorrow at his passing.

The usual carnival atmosphere was missing and the Derby crowd, estimated at around a quarter of a million, was subdued in both dress and temperament. Gentlemen wore mourning bands on their silk hats, the race-cards were edged with black, and the blinds on the royal box were drawn. Bernard Dillon was riding Lemberg, the 7–4 favourite, but allowed a horse called Greenbank to dominate the race until two furlongs from the end. When Lemberg finally staged a challenge Greenbank responded with a sudden sprint forcing Dillon to sit down and ride hard for the finish. Lemberg won by a neck in a record time of 2 minutes and 35.2 seconds.[2]

It has been said that Marie was there to cheer on Dillon, but there is no proof that she witnessed his biggest triumph. She had been there for him at other meetings, scandalizing the crowd by reaching up to kiss him on his way to the starting-post.[3] Later she said that they had been living as 'man and wife' since 1907 or 1908, which would set the beginning of their relationship at around the time of Marie Junior's wedding and only a year or two after she had married Alec.

It is easy to see why she found Ben attractive. Marie had just turned forty when he won the Derby; he was seventeen years younger, and good-looking in an intense, Celtic way, with thick dark eyebrows, long eyelashes and freckles scattered over his broad face. Marie expressed his appeal more bluntly when she introduced him to a friend. After pointedly looking him up and down she said, with her best stage-sideways glance, 'This is my third husband. He's got more than the other two put together.'[4]

To be seen with someone who was nearer her daughter's age than hers was a boost for Marie, especially a man who was a pin-up and a star in his own profession and who looked even more handsome in his racing silks high up on the best horseflesh money could buy. Ben was different from the music-hall types with whom she usually socialized: he was taciturn, which gave him a brooding, sensual air. *Vanity Fair* featured him in its 'men of the day' series in September 1906, commenting, 'When on duty Dillon presents a sphinx-like expression to the curious; off duty he can unbend.'

According to his family, Ben had been more interested in Marie's younger sister, Maude, who was half Marie's age and in December 1912 married the twenty-six-year-old champion jockey Elijah Wheatley.[5] He was so small that he was nicknamed 'Whippet', soon abbreviated to Whip. But Ben was more than a trophy lover. Although their characters were quite different – he was as shy as Marie was brash – there were similarities in their backgrounds. He was one of seven children and had spent much of his early adult life on the move. At the age of fourteen he was plucked from his home in rural Tralee, County Kerry, to become a stable jockey for the highly secretive racing syndicate of wealthy businessmen called the Druid's Lodge Confederacy. Towards the end of his career he also rode for the trainer Peter Gilpin, who set up the Clarehaven Stables on the Bury Road in Newmarket. It was probably while Ben was living in a pretty cottage among the gently rolling hills of Suffolk that he got to know Marie Junior's future husband, Tubby Aylin.

Marie had always loved horse-racing and she relished the Edwardian delight of dressing up for meetings, especially the elegance of Ascot.[6] More than once she had been late for a performance because she had been delayed on her way back from a fixture, and in Australia and South Africa horse-racing had been her main form of relaxation. 'Going racing' to Marie was equivalent to a performance on stage: she dressed in her finest clothes, extravagant hat and tantalizing veil, and strutted up and down, twirling her parasol and enjoying the whispers of recognition from other spectators. She had many jockey friends, such as Danny Maher, who, like her, enjoyed dancing and rollerskating, which helped to keep his weight down. Like several jockeys he was a regular at Romano's, which was also popular with racehorse owners, many of whom had theatrical interests.

Jockeys and music-hall stars belonged to different strands of the same newly formed entertainment business that allowed individuals from poor backgrounds to earn huge amounts of money. The two worlds were close enough for someone like George Formby to make the transition from one to the other. Before he picked up his ukulele Formby originally trained as an apprentice jockey and raced in Lord Derby's colours when he was ten years old, weighing 3 stone, 13 pounds, one of the youngest jockeys ever to compete professionally.[7] Marie's sister Grace married the jockey George Hyams, and two of their daughters married jockeys: Alice wed Charlie Smirke[8] and Bessie's first husband was George Duller;[9] her second was Walter Nightingall, who trained horses for Winston Churchill.

The poor and the wealthy had enjoyed horse-racing in the nineteenth century; the middle classes had distrusted racecourses, as places of riot, theft and prostitution, in the same way that they worried about music halls. Jenny Hill, like Marie, had her own racehorse, and one of the reasons why Bessie Bellwood got on so well with the Duke of Manchester was their shared love of the sport. Many of the early music-hall managers displayed betting lists at their bars and bookies shouted odds during performances, but it was not until the end of Victoria's reign that the sport began to accumulate social cachet. In 1875 Sandown

Park became the first course to have a members' enclosure that segregated the upper classes and respectable women from the *hoi-polloi*. The patronage of the Prince of Wales, who registered his racing colours in 1875, elevated horse-racing from a sport into an entertainment. He built Sandringham in East Anglia so that he could be near Newmarket, and in 1909 he became the only reigning monarch to win the Derby. Newly wealthy men had enjoyed betting when they were poor, and now that they were wealthy they wanted to own horses and mingle with royalty. Jockeys and trainers became less like servants and more like talented performers, who earned a lot of money in prizes, gifts and bribes.

The technological advances that had helped make Marie a star were widening the appeal of horse-racing. Before the advent of railways, horses had to be walked to races, which limited the number of events, and their geographical spread. Now the trains that allowed Marie to take her songs to Edinburgh, Newcastle, Bristol and Glasgow transported horses and jockeys around the country. A new mass media, which publicized music-hall songs and disseminated Marie's image and her worldwide adventures, did the same for horse-racing and its stars, while the sport, like music hall, made life more comfortable for its audiences through larger, more lavish settings.

Towards the end of the nineteenth century, American jockeys, owners and trainers headed for Britain in a bid to escape the onerous betting laws in their own country. They brought with them a new approach to the sport, which was now measured by the stopwatch and weights rather than by a well-practised eye. American trainers kept their horses in properly ventilated stables and watched their diet as much as jockeys did theirs, but the most fundamental change was a startling new way of riding the horse: instead of the traditional English huntsman's erect, long-stirruped seat, American jockeys crouched over the horse's neck giving the animal greater freedom to run. The revolutionary approach, known as the 'monkey up a stick', was made popular by the American Tod Sloan, whose name gave rise to the cockney rhyming expression for being alone: 'On your tod [Sloan]' – on your own – due to his habit of 'waiting in front' during a race.

The Druid's Lodge Confederacy were among the first British owners to use this more scientific approach to the sport. The syndicate, which included the West End impresario and Romano's stakeholder Wilfred

Purefoy, known as Pure, built Druid's Lodge in Wiltshire and ran the stable with a combination of secrecy and science to train horses to bring home huge winnings. One reason why the site was chosen was that the wide-open spaces of Salisbury Plain made it difficult for betting touts to study the horses in training without being spotted.

This paranoia spilt over into the stable lads' dormitories, where mail was censored. Also riders were made to sit with their backs to the scales when they were weighed so they were ignorant of what the horse was carrying, and, therefore, unable to judge how it was performing. The stables took on the worst aspects of the public-school system: bullying was rife and there was a daily curfew. Unlike most public schools the boys were locked into their dormitories at night. Ben Dillon entered this hot-house environment at the age of fourteen. He was slightly better off than his peers because his older brother, Joe, was already working for Pure and because he himself had been singled out to race for the Confederacy; most of the lads were simply 'gallop fodder', used to train the horses. Perhaps it was being marked out as special from an early age that gave Ben his propensity for arrogance and a low tolerance of his own failures.

In the early years of the century he notched up a series of impressive wins including the Cambridgeshire, the Lincolnshire, the One Thousand Guineas, the Grand Prix de Paris and the Coronation Cup. But he was an unpredictable rider and the darker side of his character would emerge when he was either drunk or on a horse. Although he liked to sing Irish songs and play the accordion, and is remembered by members of his family as someone who always had sweets for them when they were children, he had a cruel streak that surfaced when he did not get his own way. He was known as 'Butcher Ben' because of his easy resort to the whip, and a story told by the Duke of Portland reveals his obsession with being in control and in the limelight. The Duke remembers how Ben bet the other jockeys that a particularly bad-tempered horse, who had thrown many experienced riders, would not unseat him. Ben asked to ride it with long stirrups. As soon as the horse bucked Ben 'gave him a good rib-binder', which forced him into submission.[10] The story also spotlights Ben's love of gambling, which meant he was never quite above suspicion of being influenced by betting touts. Rumours about his honesty circulated when he failed to win a race he should have won.

When the much loved 'Peerless', Pretty Polly, lost the Ascot Gold Cup in 1906, one of only two races in her distinguished career that she lost, the defeat was treated with something close to national mourning among the racegoing public: 'Alas!, and again Alas! Pretty Polly beaten! Lamentations as sincere as they were loud were heard on every hand after the race was over,' wailed one newspaper.[11] Ben was accused of disobeying orders and of taking too relaxed an approach to the race. Ben's experience with Pretty Polly – just as his Derby Day victory was black-edged – showed that he never quite got things right. He was prone to bad timing all his life.

Druid's Lodge jockeys frequently celebrated their victories at Romano's, where Marie had her own table by the door so that she could see and be seen by everyone as they entered. The chances are that she knew Ben long before he was best man at her daughter's wedding in March 1907. Their affair started when Marie was experiencing a roller-coaster ride in both her private and her public life.[12]

Music hall was becoming more and more refined, and in April 1910 the burning issue of the moment was the 'matinée hat question': how to persuade women to remove their headgear so that those behind them could see. On Boxing Day 1910 the Palladium opened – another great Matcham palace that could hold nearly 3,500 people. The theatre in Argyll Street, just off Oxford Street in London's West End, was built on the site of the old Hengler's circus ground and aimed to rival both the Hippodrome and the Coliseum with its palm gardens, its 'boudoirs' and its hairdresser. It cost a reported £250,000 (£11 million) and its stage was one of the biggest in the country.

Marie was rarely mentioned in the *Era* during 1910 and when her name did appear it was to say that she was 'temporarily indisposed'. Arnold Bennett went to see her at the Tivoli on New Year's Eve 1909 and was not impressed:

Little Tich was very good, and George Formby, the Lancashire comedian, was perhaps even better. Gus Elen I did not care for. And I couldn't see the legendary cleverness of the vulgarity of Marie Lloyd. She was very young and spry for a grandmother. [Bennett was wrong on this count.] All her songs were variations of the same theme of sexual naughtiness. No censor would ever pass them, and especially he wouldn't

pass her winks and her silences. To be noted also was the singular
naïveté of the cinematograph explanation of what a vampire was and is,
for the vampire dance . . .[13]

Marie's only significant success of 1910 was 'When I Take My
Morning Promenade', by A. J. Mills and Bennett Scott, but it became
an enduring hit. It has a slow but catchy tune and Marie performed it
with a stateliness that conveyed the knowingness of an older, experienced woman revelling in the attentions of a younger generation:

> Since Mother Eve in the Garden long ago
> Started the fashion, fashion's been a passion,
> Eve wore a costume we might describe as brief,
> Still ev'ry season brought its change of leaf,
> She'd stare . . . if she could come to town,
> Oh! What would Mother Eve think of my new Parisian gown?
>
> *Chorus*:
> When I take my morning promenade
> Quite a fashion card, on the Promenade.
> Oh! I don't mind nice boys staring hard
> If it satisfies their desire,
> Do you think my dress is a little bit,
> Just a little bit – well, not too much of it,
> Tho' it shows my shape just a little bit,
> That's the the little bit the boys admire.

The second verse brings the traditional theme up to date:

> Fancy the girls in the pre-historic days
> Each wore a bearskin covering her fair skin,
> Lately Salome has charmed us to be sure,
> Wearing some rows of beads and not much more.
> Fancy me dressing like that too,
> I'm sure the *Daily Mirror* man would want an interview . . .

She returned from South Africa in March 1911 with renewed vigour
and marked her reappearance with a raunchy number, 'Put On Your
Slippers, You're Home For The Night', by J. P. Harrington and

Orlando Powell. The tempo was faster than that of her previous hit, reflecting the new fascination with ragtime. The words paint a picture, unusual for its time, of a sexually domineering woman who enjoys keeping her man at home. As the chorus puts it:

> Put on your slippers, you're here for the night,
> Stir up the fire and turn down the light.
> There's no need for you to roam.
> You've quite enough to do at home.
> So put on your slippers, you're here for the night.

The song is laced with *double entendres*. In the first verse, Gertie's father is stung by the rising cost of his fuel bills as she and her sweetheart, Bertie, sit courting by the gas fire. Father pops his head into the parlour and calls sarcastically to them:

> Put on your slippers, you're here for the night.
> Stir up the fire but turn down the light.
> Don't let me spoil your yummy-yum.
> Call me when the milkman comes.
> Put on your slippers, you're here for the night.

For most of the audience 'yummy-yum' would have been just another silly music-hall term, funny for no particular reason – just as words like 'grouting', 'haddock', and 'polyester' can sound hilarious in the mouths of today's comedians. But some of Marie's audience, especially the men, would have recognized another meaning. Even without this knowledge, the image of a fire being stoked and of an unmarried couple staying up together until the milkman arrives is daring. And just in case there was any doubt that the lyrics were risqué, the orchestra interrupted her in mock-indignation at the words thus drawing attention to them.[14]

The innuendo is driven home in the third verse when Bertie, now married to Gertie and working as a fireman, is forcibly kept at home.

> You'll help them with the hose machine?
> I know the sort of hose you mean!
> Put on your slippers, you're here for the night.

'I Haven't Had A Cuddle For A Long Time Now', a title posed as an invitation rather than a plea for sympathy, followed in September

1911. 'Every Little Movement Has A Meaning Of Its Own', which Marie introduced at the beginning of January 1912, is jaunty and playful, a return to the opaque social codes of the nineteenth century. The first verse tells of Miss Maudie Brown, a country curate's daughter, whose gaucheness slowly dissolves as she becomes accustomed to West End life. The chorus gave Marie a chance to flaunt her figure:

> When she walks in dainty hobble
> At the back round here, there's a kind of wibble wobble.

In the next verse Maudie allows herself to be saved by Reggie as she pretends to drown in the sea. The final verse abandons Maudie and returns to Gertie and Bertie on their honeymoon night: Bertie is obviously anxious about what will happen when the guests depart but is reassured by the little movement Gertie makes with her wedding ring. The final verse cannot help but sound charming compared with the blatant innuendo of Gertie and Bertie's previous encounters.

> When alone no words they utter,
> But when midnight chimes, then their hearts begin to flutter.
> And she yawns like this,
> And stretches out her arms so frail,
> And the hubby full of love,
> Looks at her and points above,
> Every little movement tells a tale.

This song came after a year of emotional upheaval for Marie. In September 1911 Marie Junior was taken ill and diagnosed with an extreme form of ptomaine poisoning, an illness which at that time was believed erroneously to be caused by eating contaminated food.[15] For a while the worst was feared and her mother cancelled several performances. Just as she seemed to be recovering Marie herself was taken ill with a poisoned arm. At the end of a wretched month of illness and worry, Daisy's husband, Donald Munro, died of consumption at a sanatorium in Bournemouth.[16] He had been sick for a long time and Daisy had been forced to perform throughout his illness, singing romantic, cheerful songs like 'Come Again Through Lovers' Lane' to provide for their two children, Dorothy and Donald. Shortly after his death Daisy was back in harness at the Regent, Salford, with 'the year's biggest principal boy chorus number', the morbidly appropriate 'I Don't Care What Becomes Of Me', which she rendered 'in sparkling fashion'.

Marie's little sister, who was thirty-four but still looked like a girl, had lost her husband and Marie had traded in hers for a much younger version. Her daughter had nearly died and she herself was in poor health. This series of unsettling events made Marie crave domestic security. The obvious place to look for it was in her new home in Golders Green and – since she was too proud to ask Alec to return – to try to create it with Ben.

Chapter 20

DISGRACE

(1912-13)

~乛

See 'em strolling all up and down
With a pretty little girl, what, what, what!
It's a trifle hot, Great Scott!
But it's fine, fine, simply divine,
Grab yourself a girlie and go right into line.
That's the Pic-Pic-Piccadilly Trot.

'The Piccadilly Trot' by Worton David and George Arthurs

Marie's nesting instincts found an outlet in the home she had built on the northernmost reaches of the Finchley Road in Golders Green. The area was sleepy and suburban, and felt almost rural in its distance from the West End. The move represented a clean break with the past and from the house to which she had returned from her tours of America and Australia, and from which she had hosted the weddings of her daughter and several of her sisters.

Her new home, on the corner of Finchley Road and Wentworth Road, was to be bright and cheerful, and she supervised its construction from her temporary home in nearby Armitage Road. From the start she was deeply involved with the design of the house, which was granted planning permission on 14 December 1911. Its seventy feet of frontage looked out on to the Finchley Road and had a doll's-house neatness: there were two tall chimneys and shuttered windows, and the four bedrooms (there were five in total on the top floor) that faced the road each had access to a long balcony. Upstairs there was a bathroom, boxroom, a WC and a large landing. Downstairs there was a dining room, morning room, drawing room, 'green room', kitchen, scullery, various storage rooms and a large billiard room. The house became Marie's project and she visited it regularly, often changing her mind about key parts of the layout. The builders quickly became used to her foibles and as soon as she appeared the foreman would order his men to down tools, since her arrival meant there was likely to be a major change in plan. Marie found it particularly difficult to make up her mind where she wanted the stairs. By July 1912 she still had not moved into the house – to be called Oakdene – and had decided to add a 'motor garage' to the rear.

Ben was finding it difficult to accommodate his lifestyle as a jockey, and essentially an athlete, with Marie's role as a star and performer. He had not had a big win since the Derby of 1910 and was waging a constant battle with his weight: it was too great a temptation not to emulate Marie's heavy drinking for he liked a drink himself and he could hardly be outdone by a woman. Marie's topsy-turvy lifestyle – her socializing began when most people were in bed – wrecked his attempts at a disciplined life and he spent hours in Turkish baths, attempting to sweat away the offending pounds of flesh. Food became an obsession and when Ben was interviewed for an article entitled 'Round the Clock with a jockey' he could talk of little else, bitter about the sacrifices he had to make as his teenage physique deserted him:

> 'It isn't pleasant – especially when one has an appetite like a hunter – to see other people feeding on the fat of the land, while one has to breakfast off a couple of pieces of dry toast and a cup of coffee, and lunch off half a dozen grapes or a wineglassful of soda-water, to say nothing of spending a morning sweltering in a Turkish bath to get weight off, or else tramping a good ten miles on a hot summer day in thick sweaters.'[1]

He started to resent the demands Marie's friends made on her, and that the two of them were rarely alone. Often he would come home to find the windows of their home thrown wide open so that the sound of music and revelry assaulted him before he had even opened the front door. Yet while Ben was desperate to get away from the sort of communal living he had been forced to endure as a teenage boy it was the only way of life Marie knew.

As Marie tried to create some semblance of a stable home life, the wider music-hall world was trying to cement its growing respectability with the ultimate seal of social acceptance: a royal command performance. The music-hall establishment had craved public recognition by the Royal Family for the last twenty years. There had been no chance of royal patronage from Victoria, who had enjoyed the circus, horse spectacles, ballet and opera, but who, towards the end of her life, rarely visited the theatre. In 1894 the *Era* complained gently that the only performers asked to appear privately before the Queen at Windsor tended to be foreign singers. However, her son enjoyed both theatre and music hall. The Prince of Wales was keen to see the boxing kangaroo at the Aquarium in 1894 and paid several visits, some clandestine, to the Empire and the Alhambra in Leicester Square, Evan's Music Hall and the London Pavilion. It was he, too, who after his accession to the throne had awarded the profession its greatest honour so far by inviting Dan Leno to perform at Sandringham on 26 November 1901 to mark the birthday of Prince Charles of Denmark. The future George V recorded in his diary that Leno was very funny and 'talked most excellent nonsense'.[2]

Bella always maintained that she had shooed the Prince of Wales out of Marie's dressing room by mistake, and his burst of 'Eh? what – what – what – what – what!' when he was trapped in the Coliseum's royal 'carriage', suggests that he was familiar with her songs. He may also have been a guest of Marie if, as local legend has it, he used the Albion Hotel at Hastings for illicit rendezvous.

The grand new theatres made a trip to the music hall less likely to raise eyebrows and it soon became acceptable for a queen to accompany her spouse. In 1905 the King and Queen Alexandra visited the Palace Theatre to see operetta[3] and in 1908 the Princess of Wales was said to laugh 'heartily' when she saw Harry Tate's 'Motoring' sketch at a charity gala in 1908.

The music-hall world finally received the royal recognition it craved when George V agreed to a royal command performance in July 1911. Moss's favourite theatre, the Empire in Edinburgh, was chosen for the honour but a month before the long-awaited date disaster struck. In May a thirty-eight-year-old illusionist and animal trainer, the Great Lafayette, was performing his speciality, 'The Lion's Bride', when the scenery was suddenly engulfed with flames. The fire was caused either by an electrical fault or by Lafayette's burning torch setting light to the stage curtain then licking up the backdrop in a stunt that the audience initially assumed was part of the performance. Lafayette, who was from Los Angeles, escaped initially but rushed back into the burning theatre to rescue his favourite lion, Arizona, and horse. He perished, with several other performers. The published descriptions of those who died reflected the strict adherence to rank with which the deceased artists had lived throughout their careers. It included: Alice Dale, 17, 'played a teddy bear'; Joseph Coast, 14, 'played a midget and understudied Dale'; John Wheelan, 40, 'trombonist'; James Baines, 46, 'double bass'; Walter Scott, 'cornet player'; Alexander Joss, 'temp'; James Watt, '(about 63), sceneshifter'; 'Man, believed to be the negro with who Lafayette duelled'.[4] However, we are left to wonder which was the greater humiliation: to have played a teddy bear or a midget, or to be nameless and 'believed to be a negro'?

Lafayette was buried in Edinburgh with his dog, Beauty, whom he had treasured to the extent of giving him his own room and a compartment in the car. Beauty wore a gold and diamond collar engraved with the name of every manager who had ever employed them and when this was full, a bracelet to carry on the tradition.

The horrific fire seemed like a return to the bad old days of dangerous Victorian theatres, and the disaster made music-hall managers even more anxious that, when it happened, the first royal command performance should be worthy of the profession. However, Sir Edward Moss died in November 1911, before he could see his dream fulfilled, and the baton of responsibility for the night's success was handed to Alfred Butt. The performance was set for June 1912 at Butt's elegant, turreted Palace Theatre on Cambridge Circus in London.

News of the date and venue set up a flurry of speculation about who and what were fit to present to the King and Queen. Would ragtime be appropriate? Should the list of performers be entirely British? The tension was heightened by postponement, due to the death of the King of Denmark, until 1 July.

Finally the list of performers was published:

Charles Aldrich 'the most versatile of American entertainers – an actor, a quick change artist, and comic conjuror'

Boganny's 'Lunatic Bakers', acrobats

Wilkie Bard comic singer

G. H. Chirgwin the 'white-eyed Kaffir', one of the oldest music-hall artists

Ida Crispi and Fred Farren 'eccentric dancers, from the Empire' [in the event they did not appear]

Cinquevalli   juggler
David Devant   conjuror
Happy Fanny Fields   'American Deutscher girl, comedienne'
Barclay Gammon   'humorist at the piano'
Alfred Lester   sketch artist and comedian
Cissie Loftus   mimic
La Pia   dancer
Harry Lauder   'Scotch comedian'
Clarice Mayne   comedienne, with her pianist
Pipifax and Panilo ('Humpsty Bumpsty')   acrobats and clowns
Arthur Prince   ventriloquist
Palace girls   dancers
Anna Pavlova   the Russian dancer
George Robey   comedian
Vesta Tilley   male impersonator
Harry Tate   in one of his sketches
Little Tich   comedian[5]

The committee's worries that their selection was likely to upset several fragile egos became evident in their choice of the item that was to complete the evening's entertainment. This was to be a 'tastefully arranged tableau with a special setting', which would give the opportunity for a large number of artists to appear. In other words, the committee hoped to be able to appease the wrath of all those performers not asked to appear before the King by offering them the chance to do what most of them hated: stand absolutely still and share the stage with their rivals. A statement tried to pre-empt the furore that the selection was bound to cause:

> It is obvious that there are many artists whom the committee would gladly have seen in the programme, but it would clearly be impossible to include everyone with an artistic claim to selection, in an entertainment of limited length. The honour, after all, is not only to those artists who will appear, but to the entire music hall profession.[6]

Whom did the committee think it was fooling? If the bill was designed to represent the best of British music hall there were several glaring omissions: Gus Elen, Arthur Roberts, Harry Randall, Albert

Chevalier, Marie Kendall, Joe Elvin, Vesta Victoria – but the most obvious was Marie Lloyd. Her absence was even more marked because each of the above was to appear in the final tableau. It was left to Albert Chevalier to defend her name:

> The whole arrangement as it stands is really extraordinary. Take the case of Miss Marie Lloyd. Who is there more representative of the variety profession? Miss Lloyd is a great genius, she is an artist from the crown of her head to the sole of her foot. You know the range of my theatrical experience, the actors with whom I have been associated, and the parts I have played. Well, I say deliberately that no woman alive can 'read' a song like Marie Lloyd – can get so much out of the lines. It is an education to hear her.
>
> As for myself, I should indeed be ungrateful if I did not feel keenly the extraordinary unanimity of the press and the public in their resentment at the omission of my name. I am so overflowing with gratitude for all the kind things which have been and are being said and written about me and my work that I almost want to write and thank the Selection Committee, whose incomprehensible action has called forth so much enthusiastic sympathy on my behalf. I dare say Miss Lloyd feels the same.
>
> As I have said, I am convinced that my name was never submitted to the King. Why not? I have already appeared by Royal Command at Sandringham. But when I ask the Committee for an explanation I am declined information.
>
> I should like to say in conclusion that I think I may claim without egotism that my work has helped to purify the music halls and has assisted to produce a condition of things which has made the Command Performance possible.[7]

So why was Marie excluded from this first royal command perform-ance? It has been said that the managers saw their chance of revenge for the part she played in the music-hall strike, but the bill included several performers who took an active part in the dispute. Little Tich, after all, was 'practising his coronet', he said, during the strike while Marie was sewing on her flounce. However, the venom Oswald Stoll directed at Marie during the strike showed that he felt especially bitter at her involvement – perhaps more so because he did not like being mocked by a woman, and one with her roots firmly in the East End.

Another theory was that Marie's private life made her unsuitable: she was a divorcee who was currently in cahoots with a jockey nearer her daughter's age than her own. There may be something in this, but again, Little Tich makes a useful 'control' test case since his private life was just as complicated as Marie's. His first wife had run off with a Frenchman and Little Tich's money. When Little Tich found a new lover he pretended to be married to her, even though this was impossible because his first wife was still alive and not divorced. He also fathered a child out of wedlock by a woman who became his third wife. Little Tich, though, was highly discreet: then the facts were not widely known. And he was male.

A more pragmatic suggestion is that the bill was already top heavy with comedy and female comics. Although, as one outraged member of the public countered in a letter to the *Era*, 'Marie Lloyd must ever be our representative comedienne on the halls'.[8] However, it is most likely that Marie's personality was the main reason why she did not appear. As countless managers had found to their cost, she was a victim of her own spontaneity. Would she have been able to resist ad libbing or tipping a wink to the royal box? She was not so much a loose cannon, as a loose, bouncing cannon. On a night when every facet of the evening's performance was to be controlled, with the most minute attention to detail, Marie was too great a risk. She might over-run her six-minute slot – far too short for her to do herself justice – deviate from the script or hog the limelight.

However, the following, previously unpublished correspondence between Sir William Carington and Alfred Butt shows that Marie's name appeared on a provisional list of performers drawn up by the command committee. Sir William was Keeper of the Privy Purse and conveyed the King's wishes to Butt about the royal command performance. The letter is dated 10 May 1912.

> The Palace Theatre Ltd
> Shaftesbury Avenue,
> WC

Dear Sir William Carington,
    Following your admirable suggestion that the programme should be revised so as to include more comedy acts, in addition to singing turns,

I have carefully made out the enclosed, and propose to-day communicating with all these artistes with a view to finding out whether they are willing to perform in accordance with the wishes of the Committee as regards place in progamme, length of turn, and the particular item to be presented out of their repertoire.

Immediately I have their replies I will send you on a final programme for approval, when we can delete any items that you think advisable.

Kind regards,

Yours faithfully,

Alfred Butt

The following list, which is, again, published for the first time, shows that Marie's name was included in this provisional bill just six weeks before the performance.

1. Jackson Troupe	Cyclists	5 minutes
2. Chirgwin or Eugene Stratton in Coon songs	Burlesque Musician	7 minutes
3. Marie Lloyd or Ella Retford or Gertie Gitana or Wish Wynne	Comedienne	6 minutes
4. Tom Hearn – Lazy Juggler – or Sam Elton, Chas Aldrich	Plate Juggler Comedy or Juggler	8 minutes
5. George Robey	Comedian	8 minutes
6. Crispi & Farren	Dancers	6 minutes
7. Albert Chevalier	Singer	6 minutes
8. Riogoku Troupe	Japanese Acrobats	8 minutes
9. Little Tich	Burlesque Comedian	8 minutes
10. La Pia	Dancer, with lighting effects	7 minutes
11. Arthur Prince	Ventriloquist	7 minutes
12. David Devant	Illusionist	7 minutes
13. Selection		12 minutes
14. Cinquevalli	Juggler	8 minutes
15. Fanny Fields	Dutch Comedienne	5 minutes
16. Harry Lauder	Scotch Comedien [sic]	7 minutes
17. Henriette de Serris	Living Pictures	7 minutes
18. Wilkie Bard	Comedian	8 minutes
19. Vesta Tilley	Male Impersonator	8 minutes

20. Anna Pavlova	Dancer	16 minutes
21. Barclay Gammon	At the Piano	8 minutes
22. Pippifax [sic] & Panlo	Comedy Acrobats	6 minutes
23. Clarice Mayne	Comedienne & Mimic	6 minutes
24. Harry Tate	'Motoring'	8 minutes
25. 'POPULARITY' [tableau]		5 minutes

Albert Chevalier, who suspected his name had not even been submitted to the King, was also in this programme. All in all, eight of the acts mentioned in the first list were not transferred to the final bill. In some cases their exclusion must have been as much to do with creating a balanced bill as it was with choosing acts who would behave in front of royalty.

There was a straight choice between Chirgwin and Eugene Stratton to represent what was now 'old-fashioned' music hall. Chirgwin, who was then sixty-eight, won hands down. He had become known as the 'white-eyed kaffir' when he accidentally wiped away part of his black make-up to leave a lozenge-shaped white area around his right eye. Similarly, it was a matter of picking the best jugglers. The Riogoku Troupe may have been cut in favour of home-grown talent and, besides, acrobats were already represented in the form of Pipifax & Panlo, who had the advantage of performing a comic version of the art. The Living Pictures may have been lost for brevity's sake, which leaves a question mark over Albert, Marie and the three alternative names for her provisional slot as number three 'comedienne' on the bill.

Albert's omission is even more of a mystery than Marie's. As an ex-character actor who had turned to coster songs, who performed at afternoon recitals and in fashionable drawing rooms, he had proved that he was unlikely to offend delicate sensibilities. The bill was also short on male 'serios', which makes the snub all the more curious. Perhaps the content of his sentimental Cockney songs was deemed too lower class.

It is easy to forget just how great and rare an honour it was in 1912 to appear before the King. Today the queen is pictured daily with an indiscriminate mix of celebrities and members of the public, while the heir to the throne not only commands showbiz stars to perform before him but has several as close friends. The Royal Family's voices and mannerisms are now so familiar that they provide easy fodder for the professional impersonators whose very existence was unthinkable in 1912. At the time of the first royal command performance the Royal Family was surrounded by a potent mystique: few people had seen royalty in the flesh, and before the arrival of the wireless, the King's voice was recognizable only to his immediate circle of friends, family and servants. To be excluded from the first ever formal chance to appear before him dealt a rabbit punch to a star's ego.

At the time, it appeared that Marie absorbed the blow with dignity and restraint; the truth was that it sent her into a blinding rage. So great was her wrath that Carington and Butt had cause for concern, as the following handwritten letter, again previously unpublished, shows:

From
Alfred Butt,

Palace Theatre
W.
June 8/12

Dear Sir William Carington
As we anticipated there have been one or two people who have not approved entirely of the programme and think certain artistes should have been included but on the whole it seems to have given general satisfaction. Marie Lloyd is I understand writing to H. M. The King, regarding her omission. Should you have occasion to write me regarding the programme may I ask you to be good enough to give instructions for your letter to be marked 'private' as I should prefer opening them myself in case you wished the contents treated as confidential. Glad to say everything is now going forward splendidly.
Yours very truly
    Signed . . . Alfred Butt
    Lt Col. The Rt. Hon. Sir Wm. Carington, K.C.V.O., C.B.
    Buckingham Palace.'

We do not know whether Marie carried out her threat to fire off a complaint to George V but it seems unlikely. Many of the King's personal papers were destroyed, at his own request, after his death, so we cannot be certain. She threatened frequently to write to people, but as her few surviving letters show, she was out of her depth on paper. It is more likely that she fumed in private, her injured pride smarting with every mention of the command performance and the accompanying publicity that built up into a crescendo as the day approached.

Every detail of the evening was tightly controlled and choreographed. Each performer who had agreed to appear in the tableau at the end of the performance had to submit details of exactly what they would wear so that it could be checked for suitability. Artists were told to dress in the sort of costume they were known for on stage, with the exception of acrobats or swimming acts who, in the interests of decency, had to wear 'modern afternoon dress and hat'. Since the Palace Theatre's dressing rooms were overflowing, elaborate arrangements were made to house the tableau participants round the corner at the Queen's Theatre, Shaftesbury Avenue, and drive them over when they were needed.

The well-known sculptor Albert Toft was called in to arrange the twenty-eight men and women in the most pleasing artistic tableau. They included female stars who had not been invited to appear on the main bill: Kate Carney, Florrie Forde, who became famous for 'Down At The Old Bull And Bush', Marie Kendall, Victoria Monks, the male impersonator Ella Shields and Vesta Victoria. Among the men were Tom and Fred McNaughton, Gus Elen, Joe Elvin, Lupino Lane, Harry Randall, and Wee Georgie Wood. The group was to remain still until a given signal when the ensemble would turn and face the footlights; men would remove their hats and when one of the group, who was dressed as a white knight, sang 'God Save the King' everyone would join in the chorus. The highly controlled finale was the nearest music hall ever came to the television representation of it in *The Good Old Days*. It seems likely that Marie was invited to join in the tableau but that she would not countenance this stilted mockery. The list of star names who did take part, though, shows how anxious performers were to be associated with the first royal command performance, no matter how great a sham their participation was.

As the day approached, excitement among the public and performers reached fever pitch. The audience queued from midnight on the day before the performance, sitting patiently in their best clothes on camp stools in the hope of securing good seats and huddling under umbrellas when it started to rain at about 2 p.m. Inside, the theatre resembled an overstocked florist's. On the way to their seats the audience was dazzled by three hundred tiny lightbulbs hidden inside yellow roses, which trailed along the staircase and into the dress circle. Elsewhere, the theatre was decorated with pink hydrangeas, variegated maple leaves and lilies, and the proscenium arch was submerged in red and pink rambling roses. The stage backdrop was a copy of a Beauvais tapestry, including a picture of the gardens of Versailles. Smoking was banned, making the smell of flowers almost overpowering.

Despite all the planning, the performances that night were tame and lacklustre. Little Tich dusted down the big-boots dance for which he had become famous but which he now resented for its freakishness. He was sick with nerves and failed to appear for the grand finale. Harry Lauder sang 'Roamin' In The Gloamin'' and Arthur Prince, in full naval uniform, performed his speciality of drinking a glass of claret while his dummy, Jim, dressed as a cabin boy, chatted away. Vesta Tilley sang 'Jolly Good Luck To The Girl Who Loves A Sailor' and 'Algy, The Piccadilly Johnny With The Little Glass Eye'.

Legend has it that Queen Mary was so shocked by the sight of Vesta's legs in men's trousers that she ordered her ladies-in-waiting to avert their eyes, but this seems unlikely: in the first place, the painstaking thought and preparation that had gone into the performance would have taken into account the Queen's feelings, and if there had been even the shadow of a doubt that Vesta's limbs would cause offence she would have been ejected from the line-up. British queens, too, are not known for such dramatic gestures, which would have appeared both rude to the performers and have drawn attention to the cause of the offence.

While what the *Era* described as 'the cream of variety' was going through a parody of music hall, Marie was on stage at the London Pavilion in nearby Piccadilly. It has been said that she threatened to put up placards saying, 'Every performance by Marie Lloyd is a command performance – by command of the British Public', or that notices to this effect actually appeared. At the Pavilion she sang jolly songs, like the 'Piccadilly Trot', whose jaunty tune capitalized on the growing popularity of ragtime.

Ben was proving less of a support than Marie might have hoped. He had been taken to court by a trainer, George Aston, who claimed that he owed him £660 from gambling.[9] The judge decided it was a case for the Jockey Club, who 'warned off' both Aston and Ben, effectively banning both men from having anything to do with horse-racing. Apart from the disgrace, the ruling robbed Ben of his livelihood and Marie once again found herself with a man in tow who relied on her for financial support. Like Percy Courtenay, Ben resented having to rely on a partner who made her money from public display. He was also jealous that Marie remained in the public spotlight while he had been consigned to obscurity.

Immediately after the royal command performance, Marie left London for a three-week stay in Paris, where the audience was less judgemental than the pretentious command performance committee. The visit gave her the chance to introduce a new song, 'I'd Like To Live In Paris All The Time' or 'The Coster Girl In Paris', about a Cockney who becomes enamoured of the French capital and its daring ways, but who retains an affection for the ''Ackney Road'.

On her return she encountered another reminder that the entertainment world was changing. There was much talk about whether music halls, in an attempt to compete with the growing popularity of cinemas, should open on Sundays but most artists were keen to preserve a rare day of rest when they could see their families or travel home after a far-off booking.

Marie spent much of the second half of the year darting in and out of the provinces. In August she was at the Hippodromes in Margate, Southend, Boscombe and Exeter. September saw her back in London, in the West End, Willesden and the Hippodromes of Ealing and Woolwich. For the rest of the year she yoyoed up and down the country; travelling north to the Pavilion, Glasgow, down to East Ham, up to the Palace, Manchester, then returning to London before travelling to the Olympia in Liverpool and the Empire, Sunderland, before finishing the year back in London.

It was not just cinema she was competing with: audiences were finding other distractions in their free time, as a journalist's first experience of ragtime reveals:

The musical nonsense got into our blood and we found ourselves suddenly as merry as children. The American girl seemed to have joy at her finger-tips, the beauty of her joy was its freedom fron sentiment or passion or thought. It was the pure joy of heartless youth – the kittenishness of the kitten, the puppyishness of the puppy, the kiddishness of the kid . . . And now ragtime has swept over us like a prairie fire. It dominates our dances. It reigns in our restaurants. It rollicks through all our pantomimes. It frolics in our music halls. We live to ragtime.[10]

Entertainment was becoming more susceptible to American influence and there was a growing emphasis on having a carefree good time. Songs had playful cosmopolitan titles such as 'When The Midnight Choo-Choo Leaves For Alabam', 'Snooky Ookums', 'On The Mississippi' and 'Oh, You Beautiful Doll'. Marie's songs of the time, such as 'The Coster Girl In Paris' and 'One Things Leads To Another' began to seem parochial and old-fashioned.

By 20 August 1913 *Hullo, Ragtime*, which combined the popularity of the new music craze with the equally successful performance vehicle of revue, had celebrated its four-hundredth performance at the Hippodrome in London's West End. J. M. Barrie wrote a scene for *Hullo, Ragtime*, and the Empire and the Alhambra soon followed the Hippodrome with their own revues. Daisy, Rosie and Alice were all singing 'Popsy, Wopsy', a song that had been a hit for the revue *Step This Way*.

The Coliseum had already tried revue as early as 1906 in a bid to increase takings, and in the summer of 1913, amid much publicity, Stoll persuaded Sarah Bernhardt to appear on his stage. Later Alice recalled how Marie's friend, the costumier and wig-maker Willy Clarkson, had introduced her to Sarah and the classical actress had told Marie she was the 'greatest living comedienne' (some versions even say actress).[11] Charming though this story is, it is probably inaccurate. It has been suggested that Sarah's comments were made as a slight to her rival Ellen Terry, but what seems more likely is that if she ever made such a comment she was referring to the French Marie Lloyd. Marie's Gallic namesake was a classical actress.

Ragtime provided the theme for Marie's birthday in February 1913, which she celebrated in her new home in Golders Green. She invited friends like Gus Elen and his wife, and received over two hundred telegrams from well-wishers. The party was a prelude to an extensive provincial tour that wound its way around the country with typical disregard for Marie's constitution:

February
Finsbury Park; Empire, Nottingham; Palace, Plymouth; Empire, Edinburgh.

March
Empire, Shepherd's Bush; Hippodrome, Norwich; Hippodrome, Ipswich; Hippodrome, Exeter; Empire, Croydon.

April
Hippodrome, Lewisham; Hippodrome, Woolwich; Hippodrome, Ilford.

May
London: Tottenham, Tivoli, Metropolitan, Oxford, Chelsea.

June
London: Tivoli, Euston and Hackney Empire; and Brighton.

July
Portsmouth Empire; Wellington Pier Pavilion, Great Yarmouth; Southend; Margate Hippodrome.

August
Grand Theatre, Birmingham; Empire Sheffield; Leeds; Ardwick Empire, Manchester.

September
Tivoli, London; Palace Theatre, Luton.

By the time she was due to sail for New York at the end of September the thought of nearly a week's rest in a comfortable suite was an enticing prospect. She had secured a twenty-five-week tour with the Orpheum and United Booking Offices at a salary of $1,750 (£14,970) a week.[12] At least someone recognized her worth.

Chapter 21

MORAL TURPITUDE

(1913 – 14)

~

I have begun to wonder recently
Why I am so misunderstood, poor me.
If with a simple wink I greet some friend,
Somebody's bound to think I mean something I didn't intend.
Well, it's wrong – it's a shame – and you probably think the same.
'The Twiddly Wink' by Fred W. Leigh and Orlando Powell

RMS *Olympic* was one of the most luxurious liners of her day, and at 27,000 tons she was also one of the biggest. First-class passengers like Marie and Ben could saunter through rooms decorated in a heady mixture of styles plundered indiscriminately from around the world and history. Cabins were furnished with themes ranging from Jacobean and Georgian to Dutch and Louis XIV. Travelling was almost too comfortable, and when Joseph Bruce Ismay, chairman of the White Star Line, which owned the ship, travelled on her maiden voyage to New York he was dismayed to find that the mattresses in first-class were so soft that they amplified the vibrations of the ship's engines.

For the *Olympic*'s 735 first-class customers, the vessel was more like a sumptuous hotel than a means of crossing the Atlantic. They could relax in the elegant reading and writing room or the mahogany-encased lounge with its carved wooden ornaments. The darker, more Victorian smoking room had a male intimacy with its tables arranged like conspiratorial islands and its Norman Wilkinson painting, *The Approach of the New World*, above the large open fireplace. There was a sweeping oak staircase between decks that had intricate banisters and the statue of a nymph lighting the way with a lantern held aloft. Alternatively, passengers could use the three, new-fangled lifts.

The less stuffy veranda cafés, with their wicker seats and palms, were

236

more to Marie's taste. The huge restaurant, easily the largest afloat, also suited her: it offered the innovation of an *à la carte* menu and the opportunity for passengers to dine at times that suited them. Ben was also well catered for: the *Olympic*'s swimming-pool, at thirty feet long, was the largest to be found on a ship, and there was also a gymnasium and a squash court. The Turkish baths broke records for their size, but were remarkable, too, for their seventeenth-century Arabian-style cooling room and the elaborately carved *faux* Cairo curtain in wood that masked the portholes. The lavatories even had cigar and cigarette holders.

Yet the *Olympic*'s main claim to fame was that she was the elder sister of the *Titanic*, which had sunk only eighteen months before Marie and Ben made the same journey. A third sister ship, the *Gigantic*, was hastily renamed the *Britannic* after the disaster. The *Olympic* had attracted much attention when it docked in New York on its first voyage from Southampton since the *Titanic* had gone down, but confidence grew in her with every safe Atlantic crossing. Captain Haddock was in charge of the *Olympic* when it received the *Titanic*'s distress signal, but was too far away to help the stricken vessel. He was still at the helm in September 1913, by which time the *Olympic* had been filled with extra lifeboats. When Marie, who was superstitious, and Ben boarded her, her reputation for speed and comfort outweighed her unhappy connections.

The crossing was a sort of honeymoon for Marie and Ben. Marie enjoyed the luxury of the first-class apartments and the ship's amenities, but she also liked showing off to her fellow first-class passengers and shocking them occasionally by dipping into the maelstrom of the 675 second class and 1,030 steerage passengers swarming beneath the upper decks. By the time the Statue of Liberty appeared, she was well rested and ready for an onslaught on a market that had never been kind to her.

As the *Olympic*'s elegant four-funnelled profile slid into the Lower Bay of New York harbour medical inspectors climbed aboard from their waiting cutters to carry out their quarantine examinations on first- and second-class passengers. These were routine, and usually cursory, searches for contagious diseases such as cholera and smallpox. A more thorough examination was reserved for steerage passengers, who were 'processed' in the forbidding red-brick and limestone-trimmed buildings on Ellis Island, which the *Olympic* passed on her way to Manhattan.

Once the ship had docked, the third-class passengers, wearing a name-tag with their manifest number, were herded across a pier into a waiting area before being transported by barge to Ellis Island. The first- and second-class customers were free to continue their journey within the United States.

Alice, who had arrived in New York a week before on the *Mauritania*, was there to greet her sister and Ben; and the group was soon engulfed in a wave of reporters. There is confusion about what happened next, but the most probable version is that an English reporter arriving late told Marie that he had scoured the list of passengers arriving on the *Olympic* but could not find her name in the Ls. Marie, with her usual lack of guile, explained that this was because the reporter should have been looking under the Ds, for Dillon. As if to underline that she had been sharing a cabin with Ben, she was standing with her trunks under a huge letter D.

An immigration official arrived to whom Marie admitted that she had been travelling with Ben 'as man and wife'. The official said that she could stay in the United States but that Ben would have to return to England. After much swearing, Marie burst into tears at this latest public humiliation. She drank a glass of champagne with Alice on the quayside then felt strong enough to gather her thoughts. Further discussions took place in Captain Haddock's cabin. Marie and Ben were allowed to stay overnight on the *Olympic* on condition that Alice put up a bond for $1,500 (£12,831) while their case was referred to the Commissioner General of Immigration in Washington. The next morning they were transported to what Alice called 'that ghastly hole, Ellis Island'.

Marie was being held because her cohabitation on board the *Olympic* left her open to charges of 'moral turpitude', a clause in the immigration laws of the United States that still exists today and is most commonly invoked to prevent rapists and other sex offenders from entering the country. In 1913 it was open to broader interpretation and the decision to use it was left up to the discretion of the official handling the case. Marie's furious, foul-mouthed response to her detention did not help her. Officials may also have felt that they had to take a tougher line since 1913 saw a flood of immigrants: 1.2 million people poured into the country that year, the largest number since Marie's previous visit in 1907.[1] Ben's position was more clear-cut: he was held under the White

Slave Traffic Act of 1910, which had been introduced in response to a growing fear at the spread of loose sexual morals.

Ellis Island was an archipelago of three plots strung together to form a complex of around eighteen acres of low-lying land that housed one of the biggest brick buildings in New York. The vast, echoey institution, with its four cupola towers, felt like a prison or lunatic asylum. Hopeful immigrants from around the world, tired and frightened, formed endless queues in and around the building as they waited to see whether they would be deemed suitable to enter the United States. Often they were dressed in their Sunday best, or the national costume of the country they had left behind: little Scottish boys in kilts, West Indian women in long dresses with elaborately twisted headgear and old ladies from Eastern Europe with scarves knotted tightly under their chins. These dispossessed people staggered under the weight of trunks, wicker baskets and boxes or clutched their most precious possessions, whether a featherbed, a ripe cheese or a family photograph. They were herded past doctors, who examined their face, hair, neck and hands and chalked a letter on their coat if they were not in good health: B for back problems, C for conjunctivitis and so on. If they passed the health check, they faced an inspector seated on a tall stool who fired questions at them, often via an interpreter, to verify their details as stated in the ship's manifest.

The islands were a place of heightened emotions: a no man's land between the open sea and the metropolis. It was here that families were split up if one member failed the medical, and here that long-separated relatives were reunited. Its atmosphere of desperation, and of milling, exotic humanity, gave it the air of a Hieronymus Bosch painting and Marie became hysterical. In less than twenty-four hours she had been hurled from the ultimate luxury of the *Olympic* to a cheerless place of basic amenities. She was surrounded by people who came from a similar, desperately poor background to herself and she was now at the mercy of the same authority that the steerage class faced.

Marie and Ben went before an inquiry board and it was agreed that they should stay on Ellis Island overnight. Ben shared the cell-like conditions, so reminiscent of his time at the Druid's Lodge Confederacy, of the other immigrants, while Marie was allowed, as a special concession, to stay in the governor's quarters with her maid available to run errands for her – although she was locked in and watched over by a wardress. For Marie this represented her own personal nightmare of solitary confinement. She was surrounded by the eerie cries of the seagulls that swooped around the islands, and her quarters gave her a view of the Statue of Liberty, an irony that was not lost on her. Furious at its mocking stance she slammed the blinds shut and demanded to be taken back to the *Olympic* and home to England.

Alice believed this humiliation had a profound impact on her. 'The indignity of the subsequent experience there I am sure went to Marie's heart in a way she never survived. She could not bear to talk of that awful twenty-four hours.'[2]

Ellis Island was an uncomfortable reminder of what it felt like to be without money or influence. Marie told the *New York Sun*: 'The United States is the only country on earth that would treat a professional woman, and an utterly defenceless one, as I have been treated. I shall never forget the humiliation to which I have been subjected and I shall never sing in America again, no matter how high the salary offered. I requested my counsel to withdraw my appeal and that is why I am going back with Mr Dillon.'[3]

Her subsequent protestations about privacy have a very modern ring. She seems suddenly to have realized that she was public property, which fuelled her insecurity:

I have always supposed and considered that my private life was my own affair. I have never tried or wished to obtrude it upon the public. My divorce case in all its details is well known over there, and I never realised how many friends I had over there until I was obliged to abide by its conditions. [It is unclear what she means by this – perhaps Alec had dropped divorce proceedings on condition that she stopped seeing Ben?] However, that is a personal matter, my own business – or rather it would be if I did not happen to be an actress, why heavens knows I've been in America – which until now I loved, mind you! – long enough to know that frequently when a drunken woman gets hauled into court she calls herself an actress, and you see the headlines to that effect in the newspapers, next morning.[4]

She made no attempt to hide the chip on her shoulder:

The same heartless ruling, if applied to some of the grand opera singers, to some of your millionaires, to many of the greatest stars which shine in the theatrical firmament, would bar a number of the greatest artists of the world from your country. That is the reason why both Mr Dillon and myself withdrew our appeals from Washington today and decided to go home.[5]

Even her employers, the Orpheum Circuit, washed their hands of their latest star and later commented snootily: 'Miss Lloyd's remarks are the lamentations of a disgruntled artist, who blames us because we cannot control the United States Immigration Laws which forbid the entry of a certain class of women to this country.'[6]

Marie's lawyers compared her to George Eliot, who in the last century had lived with a married man.[7] The comparison with a Victorian intellectual best indicates how unfamiliar New Yorkers were with Marie's character and reputation. After intense negotiations, Marie was finally released and she made her way back to Manhattan, although it was still not certain whether she would be allowed to stay in the country. Marie, wearing a plum-coloured coat with matching toque, met reporters at Battery Park. She was subdued, but angry, and told them she would rather go home than spend another night on Ellis Island – to prove the point she waved a sheaf of cables from managers in England offering her work. A mere thirty minutes before the *Olympic* was due to set sail with her and Ben on it, a permit arrived allowing her to stay in the country. The conditions were that she and Ben must live apart and leave the USA the minute her tour was over.

The anger she felt at such treatment set the tone for this, her fifth, tour of America. From the moment she was questioned about her sleeping arrangements she fell into a black mood that never quite left her: every mishap that befell her only added to her fury. In November she tripped while hurrying on her way to perform at the Orpheum Theater and was unable to perform for a week. She hated the cold weather and ill-health dogged her. At the start of the tour she lost her voice and Alice, unwilling to be seen as her understudy, refused to take her place. Marie tried to treat her indisposition with humour: 'He was a cruel doctor. He took some kind of a probe and rammed it down my throat. It struck the pit of my stomach and went on down to my toes.

"Did I hit the spot?" he asked. "Yes, Doctor," said I, "you hit everything I've got." '[8]

Her experience on Ellis Island had made headline news in New York papers, but her tribulations did not always generate sympathy. In some instances, her complaints, and the way the story was handled in London newspapers, provoked anti-British feelings. 'The *Daily Mail* jeers at us,' one insulted American paper protested,[9] while others described Marie's incarceration as a publicity stunt that had gone wrong. Only a few papers were sympathetic. One commented, 'Outside of Siberia there is not a blacker stain on the name of any country than this same Ellis Island . . .'[10] and another added, 'We may all have to pin our marriage certificate to the cab-door when we travel.'[11]

Initially, at least, her trials on Ellis Island boosted her appeal, and 'People who have been in seclusion or retirement for years were in evidence' when she made her first appearance at the Palace in New York, looking 'a trifle stouter than before'.[12] Her songs included 'Every Little Movement'; 'The Twiddly Wink', 'I'd Like To Live In Paris All The time (The Coster Girl In Paris)', 'Woman Knows How Far She Can Go', 'The Ankle Watch' and 'The Aviator', a song written especially for America.

The first three were catchy tunes but the lyrics must have mystified the audience. Although Marie Americanized them to some extent, there was only so much she could do with a song based on life in the East End of London. What would New Yorkers have made of lines such as these?

> But don't think I've done wiv good old England, not likely,
> Bred and born down 'Ackney Road – ah! and proud to own it too.
> (I'd Like To Live In Paris All The Time')

Or 'In a flash, what a joke! He's forgotten he's 'earts of oak [stony broke]!' from 'The Twiddly Wink'.

If she was relying on affection for Britain to see her through, she was badly mistaken: her audiences were too ethnically diverse for that, and the United States was still a young enough country not to feel nostalgia for a nation it viewed as a competitor.

Even the innuendo of 'The Ankle Watch', in which Marie lifted her skirt to show the timepiece and commented, 'As soon as they want to wind it up it's time to take it off,' hit the wrong note with an audience who now enjoyed the uninhibited movements of the tango and ragtime. Her old adversary *Variety* commented, 'Her first costume, a sort of rakish harem dress, needed time to figure out.' It added, 'Miss Lloyd's songs which four years ago would have been termed suggestive are really very mild when one recalls the daring (and worse) "rag" songs, the lewd dances, the tainted sketches and everything unclean big-time vaudeville has stood for of late to hold up the box office.'[13]

On her previous visit to America, Alec had been by her side offering professional advice about the audiences and theatres he was experiencing. In comparison Ben was a dead-weight. He was left kicking his heels, with no real role or function and with Marie again at the centre of attention. Soon he started to take out his frustration on her. She missed several important first-nights and some theatres cancelled her bookings after she received a warning note from Edward Albee, the influential business manager who ran a circuit of theatres across America through his United Booking Office, when she failed to appear at the Orpheum Theater, Brooklyn. Her excuse was that she was ill and did not like her position on the bill. Others thought there was a more sinister reason for her non-appearance. One paper suggested, 'In vaudeville circles her domestic relations are thought to be at the bottom of her attacks of disposition.'[14]

She failed to appear at a matinée at the Colonial in New York because of 'domestic difficulties', and the manager was forced to ask vaudevillians he spotted in the audience to fill her place in their 'street clothes'. When she eventually turned up for the evening performance, staff had a replacement ready in case she let them down again. Newspapers had no qualms now about voicing the reasons for her non-appearance. 'Dillon is exceedingly jealous of any attention paid to Miss Lloyd, and it was because of his emotional disposition that Miss Lloyd found it impossible to keep her engagement . . .'[15]

Marie also missed the personal touch of Percy Williams and never fully realized how powerful the UBO was: when she found herself in a lift with her booking agent, Pat Casey, and a few others whose names she did not catch she launched a tirade against vaudeville management, the UBO and Albee in particular. When she had finished Mr Albee calmly introduced himself to her. As one newspaper put it, Pat Casey 'indulged in his first blush since he attended an undress rehearsal at the *Ziegfeld Follies*.'[16]

An early excursion outside New York was not a success. At B. F. Keith's Hippodrome in Cleveland, Ohio, in the first week of November the manager sent back a despondent report to his masters at head office: 'Marie Lloyd flopped at both shows Monday,' he wrote, adding that he had agreed to her request to be shifted further up the bill after the matinée.[17] 'Only four of the acts on this week's bill speak United States,' he continued. 'A stranger in town might imagine that he was on Piccadilly Circus or the Strand, if he judged his location by the dialect. After the four acts had handed out the English conversation for nearly an hour, the audience was quite ready to leave without waiting for the finish of the last act. Miss Lloyd was billed like a circus and I have never known a headliner to fall as hard and quickly as she did.'

Marie appeared after a group of trick cyclists, the Three Arthurs, and a female violinist who specialized in classical pieces. They were received warmly. Marie's act lasted thirty minutes and, as the manager reported:

> Outside of Miss Lloyd's gowns, she fell flat on the opener and couldn't get over hard as she tried. Her reception, while not a frost, was decidedly unresponsive and in two of her songs she did not get a hand. Miss Lloyd herself has a charming manner and should be a big hit, but her songs are entirely too slow, and not the kind expected of her. Works hard but seems to be unable to warm up the house. The act closed to subdued applause and did not please.

Marie was not even allowed to escape back to New York as a blizzard held her captive in Cleveland for four days, during which she was caught in a classic slapstick routine when a great blanket of snow plummeted off a rooftop and on to her.

She fared better in the more cosmopolitan city of Chicago, which she visited in December, although the audience definitely did not view her as a glamorous woman about town:

> Marie Lloyd is a plump little person who cuts plump little capers as she sings, wearing pretty gowns and making the most of a fetching smile and a jolly wink. She impresses one somehow as a contented, capable

matron who has just put a large family of children to bed and has come
back to have a regular good time with the folks.

Miss Lloyd herself seems to like them [the songs] so much that you
are ashamed not to like them with her — and you do.[18]

It was while she was in Chicago that she heard news of Alec. Since
Marie had left him he had been lodging at Jack Straw's Castle, near
Hampstead Heath, with his dog, Mike. Alec had been drinking heavily
and neglecting his health. On 28 November he was taken ill between
appearances in Glasgow and ordered home, a long journey that exacer-
bated his condition. In London a doctor diagnosed pleurisy, and
pneumonia followed. It may simply be romantic fancy, embellished after
the event, but he was said to have told a friend: 'Tell Marie, because
you'll see her again and I shan't, that I love her as much as I did the
first day I saw her. She knows how much that is.'[19] Alec died at Jack
Straw's Castle on Saturday, 6 December at 2.35 a.m. He was forty-two.

Marie's response to the news, which Bella cabled her, was astonishing.
She told a newspaper: 'With all due respect to the dead, I can cheerfully
say that's the best piece of news I've heard in many years, for it means
that Bernard Dillon and I will marry as soon as this unlucky year
ends.'[20]

There was always, of course, the possibility that Marie did not say
these words, or that their hardness masked her true emotions. Her
relationship with American newspapers had never been good and had
deteriorated during this tour. But, if accurate, her comment on the death
of a husband she had known for over twenty years, who had been the
closest she had come to finding a soul-mate and who had treated her
with kindness and gentleness, is beyond callous. It smacks of someone
in shock. She had not known that Alec was ill and had not seen him for
several months. Far away in a foreign land it must have been difficult to
take in his death; she missed the funeral and she had no immediate
reminder that he was no longer there for her. Alec's death was the latest
in a string of setbacks and disappointments; if she had crumpled now
without her family around her for support, but with a menacing, erratic
lover in tow and employers who were constantly snapping at her heels,
she might have been unable to go on. Her bravura statement sent a
message to the world that she was not about to give in.

A generous obituary in *The Times* gave a detailed critique of Alec's contribution to music hall and only briefly mentioned his role as Marie's husband. A long procession accompanied his body from Jack Straw's Castle to Bow cemetery; the wreaths were so numerous that they filled three landaus and a hearse. Several music-hall stars, such as Gus Elen, Arthur Prince and Eugene Stratton, attended and Marie's family was out in force: Annie, Rosie and Will Poluski, Maude and Whip, Bella and Dick, Marie Junior, Daisy and Johnny. Tom and Alice sent a telegram of regret.

There was no wreath from Marie – she claimed she did not want yet more publicity – but, and again this may be music-hall romanticism, Bella was said to have secretly placed Alec's favourite flowers, red roses, inside the coffin with a note from Marie saying, 'Until we meet again'.[21] Bella and Dick, anxious that Alec should not be remembered as someone who failed to honour his commitments, paid his debts.

Alice and Tom were in no mood to counsel or console Marie because they had their own problems to contend with. Tired of hanging around backstage waiting for his wife and being called 'Mr Lloyd', 'Alice's dresser' and the 'band-part carrier', Tom had decided to carve out a career for himself as an English comedian in musical comedies.[22] He did this with some success and starred in *The Spring Maid*, a production by Werba & Luescher, which toured the country from 1911.[23] In 1913 he appeared in another comedy, *Sweethearts*, as a villain bent on destroying the happiness of a baby found in a tulip garden and brought up by a laundryman, who later discovers that his adopted child is a princess. Tom was the main comedian in the cast and the script gave him plenty of scope for comic asides. Observing a couple locked in an ardent embrace with their backs towards him he murmured pensively, 'I wonder if they know each other.'[24]

But disaster struck at the end of 1913 when Tom was forced to file for bankruptcy.[25] He was a 'sleeping partner' in some of Werba & Luescher's companies and when the theatrical production company collapsed in October he knew it was only a matter of time before he would be forced to follow their lead. He acknowledged debts of $157,024; to add insult to injury, Alice was on a long list of Werba & Luescher's creditors and was owed $13,909. Tom and Alice, who had spent the last six years making a name for themselves – both socially and professionally – now had to figure a way out of the financial mire they had plunged into. Typically, they decided to saddle themselves with as dense a workload as they could manage which allowed them no time to support Marie.

From Chicago Marie went on to St Louis, Missouri and Milwaukee then over the border to Canada, which she found a freezing, parochial country. She was well received in Winnipeg, although she had to suffer possibly the most unpleasant episode in the whole tour: her face was badly burned by carbolic acid mysteriously mixed into the cold cream she applied when removing her make-up.[26] She was in great pain, but it was never discovered who was behind it. A jealous performer was the most likely candidate: only a fellow artist would have thought of something that would be so hurtful both physically and emotionally. It would not have been the first time, either, that a performer had done something like this to a colleague: there are stories of ground glass placed in face creams by a 'turn' with a score to settle.

In Regina Church leaders and officials took offence at Marie's songs. There was a similar response in Vancouver: audiences loved her, and she was asked to be godmother to a local child, but the mayor and several newspapers thought her material too suggestive and tried to cut her act. When she attempted to explain herself on stage she ended up in tears. On another occasion she marched into the offices of a local newspaper, produced a horsewhip from her muff and beat the editor with it over the head.[27] Marie was also peeved that, by entering Canada, she had unwittingly forfeited the conditions of her immigration bond. More negotiations followed and she was eventually allowed back into the USA, although Ben had to follow her later.

Her first stop in the USA was Seattle and she met up with Ben in Portland, Oregon. They married quietly at the British Consulate, Marie giving her age as twelve years younger than she was. It appears she married Ben because she was tired of all the red tape and kerfuffle. A comment she made to the *Morning Oregonian* indicates that she was trying to reconcile what she had thrown away in her failed marriage to Alec: 'I do not see how marrying Mr Dillon is going to make any difference, only that I might like him less. I know that the quickest way to lose your pal and friend is to marry him. I lived with my second husband for ten years before I married him and in two weeks after we trailed up the altar he was smiling at another.'[28]

She had a mixed response from audiences on the West Coast. On the whole San Franciscans liked her, but the *Los Angeles Inquirer*, 31 March 1914, took offence at her songs and, again, the ghost of Alice's fame came back to haunt her: 'There is not the touch of real wit to them that made some of us think out loud yesterday: "Oh, don't we remember sweet Alice – with her dress that was just a little bit, and her wooing invitation to 'splash me'." ' Marie was also 'quite touched by *embonpoint*'.

By the time she and Ben were back on board the *Olympic* Marie was disillusioned with both America and her new husband. She told a reporter bitterly: 'But there's one consolation I have, although I've had everything since I came over here except the smallpox and a strait-jacket, my husband has turned out to be a hero. He went out the other night and had a mix-up and knocked down two big burly Irish-American policemen. Only a real hero could do that. I may have had my troubles, but, anyhow, I'll leave the country married to a hero.'[29]

Since she was returning to a country on the brink of war, there would be more than enough scope for heroics.

Chapter 22

WAR

(1914−18)

⟶

I always hold in having it if you fancy it,
If you fancy it that's understood!
And suppose it makes you fat?
I don't worry over that,
'Cos a little of what you fancy does you good!
'A Little Of What You Fancy Does You Good' by
Fred W. Leigh and George Arthurs

By June 1914 Marie and Ben were back in London and Marie's summer engagements took her round the country to Liverpool, Birmingham, Aldershot, Southend and Margate. By the time war was declared on 4 August she was at the London Pavilion, a theatre with which she had long been associated, wearing a pink gown 'blazing with diamonds' and carrying a matching parasol to perform 'The Dress Of The Day', which analysed the various techniques of attracting a man. For 'The Ankle Watch', she changed into a white gown with emerald green sash, then sang, 'I'd Like To Live In Paris All The Time'. As an encore she performed 'The Next Best Thing − Being Careful If You Can't Be Good'. A young soldier, and future occult novelist, Dennis Wheatley was among the soldiers who flocked to the Pavilion to listen to Marie and to forget about the constant rumours of banks calling in overdrafts and shops running out of food.[1] The audience was fired up with emotion at the recent news of hostilities and was reported to have sung the French, Russian and British national anthems, although it would have taken a highly educated crowd to know the words to the foreign ones − perhaps they hummed along to the orchestra.

The war threw the music-hall world into a dilemma. Even before the outbreak of hostilities performers had been faced with lower takings; now competition from the ever popular revues in theatres, as well as halls, and from the cinema was strengthening. Performers' salaries fell, halls were closing and the number of unemployed turns was increasing. Even the stars were accepting only a proportion of their former salaries. Managers feared that the war would present yet another body-blow for business, but they could not afford to appear unpatriotic. As fuel and food shortages grew more acute, they trod a thin line between advocating music hall for its morale-boosting properties and appearing self-serving in promoting its attractions.

Uncertain times bred fear and suspicion. Maud Tiffany, who was due to appear at the Holborn Empire on the day war broke out, played two houses, left her theatrical baskets and props in her dressing room and was never seen again.[2] The Bishop of Kensington and others worried about the white slave trade, that the Germans had a list of Britain's most sexually depraved men and women whom they intended to blackmail and that revues were weakening Britain's moral fibre. The Defence of the Realm Act, passed in August, introduced censorship and, for the first time, passports.

Anti-German feeling sprang up almost immediately, and for the unemployed performer proved an outlet for anger and resentment, as well as a way of flushing out Teutonic performers whose places they could fill. Paul Cinquevalli, the juggler who had been included in the royal command performance, was ostracized when it became known that his real name was 'Kestner' and that, although Polish, he had spent his early years in Germany.[3] In every walk of life, the remotest connection with the enemy country became a handicap. Even the Saxe-Coburg-Gotha family felt it wise to become Windsor and the magician Carl Hertz was so worried about his surname that he made a public announcement that he was, in fact, American.[4] Exotic-sounding names lost their veneer of glamour and sophistication overnight and wholesome, Anglo-Saxon ones became fashionable. The comedian George Mozart let it be known that his true name was David John Grilling and that he had been born in Great Yarmouth.[5] Music by the composer Edward German was rarely played until he eventually admitted that he had been born Edward German Smith but that he had dropped the surname because he thought it too common.[6] Even animals could not escape the xenophobia: at the Coliseum a sketch featuring Lipinski's performing dogs in a canine play called *Everyday Life in a German Town* was hastily renamed *A Day in Dogville* and performed in front of a backdrop almost entirely covered by a huge Union Jack.[7]

German musicians were regarded with great distrust and Belgians were suspected of being Germans in disguise.[8] It was seen as treason to use Leichner's greasepaint which, until the war, had been regarded as the best. It soon became the enemy within. One performer, who had run out of an English brand and was forced to rely on Leichner's, was reported to have woken one morning with his nose swollen to twice its normal size. He had blood poisoning, which caused him to take a week off work losing £200 in fees.[9] The Hun was everywhere – even hiding in a pot of face paint. Patriotic performers used British products such as Clarko greasepaint, endorsed by Marie and the glamorous young actress Gladys Cooper. It concluded its advertisement with 'God Save the King'.

Music-hall songs were romantic ballads such as 'Take Me Back To Dear Old Blighty', chirpy numbers to whistle to like 'Pack Up Your Troubles In Your Old Kit Bag' or gung-ho calls to action as typified by 'We Don't Want to Lose You But We Think You Ought to Go'. When recruitment faltered at the end of 1914 the halls did their best to help with rousing sketches such as 'The Slacker'; 'The Enemy', 'Saved by the British' and 'The Coward'.[10] J. M. Barrie wrote a one-act play about the German emperor called *Der Tag*, which was performed at the Coliseum. Virginia Woolf, who regularly went to the halls and picture palaces, was not impressed by it: she preferred to see comic singers, 'men imitating Prima Donnas' or jugglers. *Der Tag*, she wrote in her diary, was 'sheer balderdash of the thinnest kind'.[11]

Individual artists helped to stoke the patriotic fervour: Vesta Tilley appeared as a young Tommy to sing, 'The Army Of Today's All Right' during which she tempted on to the stage with her men old enough to enlist. In her memoirs she boasts of how she managed to recruit three hundred young men during one performance and that one group of soldiers was known as the Vesta Tilley platoon. The *Era* began to run a regular column, 'The Profession with the Colours', which listed artists who had signed up and those who had fallen. Tom's brother Fred and Marie's ventriloquist friend, Arthur Prince, were recruited in 1915.

In January of that year Marie entertained ten thousand soldiers at Crystal Palace, but it was not until the end of 1915 that she produced her only war song, 'Now You've Got Yer Khaki On' by Charles Collins and Fred W. Leigh. The jaunty song preached the message that a uniform was sexy, it got you noticed, and life in the army transformed a 'Derby Kell' (short for Derby Kelly, which was rhyming slang for belly) into a hard-as-iron torso. Dancing round her brother Johnny, dressed as a soldier, Marie made clear the rewards of enlisting:

> Now, I do feel so proud of you, I do, honour bright!
> I'm going to give you an extra cuddle tonight,
> I didn't like yer much before yer join'd the army, John,
> But I do like yer, cocky, now you've got yer khaki on.

The soldier tries to persuade her to marry him but she wants to wait in case their haste gives rise to gossip. She finally relents – adding a typical *double entendre*:

> Then on me word, the honest truth to speak,
> He told me that his furlough might be cut short any day.
> So I says, 'Then I'll be ready in a week!'

Marie's second big hit of 1915 'If You Want To Get On In Revue' poked fun at young actresses desperate to do anything to further their careers, but it also had soldiers in mind. It told the story of 'Flossie the Flapper' who was courting a sapper but who was tempted by a ride on the back seat of a car:

> The night may be 'parky'
> When a nice young man in khaki,
> Says 'Come in my Lotus for a mile or two'.

Her third new song that year was 'The Three Ages of Woman (Woman's Opinion Of Man)' by Orlando Powell and George Arthurs, a rather cynical look at the female approach to the opposite sex. It was particularly cruel about the 'new woman':

> What is woman's opinion of man
> When she's twenty-five – now a young lady?
> She's one of the lads of the village, her fads
> Are advanced and a little bit shady.
> She understands man, or she thinks so at least.

She's read the six novels, and calls him a beast
She vows she won't marry, but when she is tough,
Oh, she's fearfully certain she won't get enough.
Dear, dear! – Hm, hm – don't fret.
If a fellow says, 'Wilt?' will she wilt? You bet!

The song reflected the new attitudes of young women who, like the suffragettes, could threaten to kidnap Lloyd George; or, because of wartime necessity, were working as nurses, going to the cinema or music hall alone or dressing in the provocative fashion of the 'flaunting flapper'. Since nearly one in ten men under forty-five was killed in the war, and another one in five wounded, there was a great need for workers to replace them and, by necessity, many of them were women.[12] About a quarter of all domestic servants switched to work in munitions and other factories, transport and the land; and there was an influx of women to the civil service. With the shortage of men and the circumstances of war, there was more scope for the sexes and classes to mix in their leisure and work time. Women grew in self-assurance: lipstick became popular and hem lengths climbed.

Such freedoms had long been available to music-hall performers like Marie, but even her milieu was changing because of the war. Women were playing a greater part in running music halls and at the Lyceum in Ipswich, Suffolk, the entire staff, including the manager, was female.[13] It became common for a music-hall bill to include a note explaining that men in the cast were either too old to enlist, or had been deemed unfit for military service.[14] There were more female musicians, although there was still some scepticism about whether they were up to the job. Those musicians who were not in the trenches were feeling threatened as the principal of the Guildhall School of Music revealed, in an article in which he argued that women were incapable of playing wind, brass or wood, instruments – with the sole exception of the flute. He explained: 'This, I might say, is due almost to physical disability that dates back to the era of the caveman.'[15]

Marie made two major provincial tours in 1914, but as the war progressed touring became more problematic and performers had to journey further afield to find audiences. Rail travel was unpredictable and expensive, and trains were filled with troops. Trucks were in short supply and performers were urged not be extravagant with costumes and scenery.

By 1915 the war was truly having an effect on music halls. Managers, terrified that an entertainment tax would push up ticket prices and keep customers away, stressed the recuperative attractions of music hall. The capital, once a rich seam of bookings for a star like Marie, was transformed by Zeppelin raids into a menacing place of darkened streets and electric globes muffled in blue paint. Moonlight, shining a guiding path for enemy bombers, was to be feared and drew waves of people out of the centre of London as surely as it drew the tides around the planet. Sitting in a West End music hall at night now seemed risky. Alfred Butt, convinced that audiences were staying away from the Palace Theatre through fear, offered the lame comfort that the building was safer than most since several gallons of water were stored in its roof.[16] The Criterion claimed that, since it was underground, it was bomb-proof. However, when a fifty-kilo bomb was dropped near Swan & Edgar's department store on Piccadilly Circus the theatre's boast seemed empty: the huge crater in the pavement provided a reminder that being underground during an attack was no guarantee of safety.

An unaccountable dipping of electric lights signalled the prelude to a raid, followed by the sound of guns returning fire, the whistle of shells and, finally, the all-clear of the bugle blown by Boy Scouts. At home, servants huddled side by side with their employers wherever seemed safest – under the stairs or in the coal bunker. A raid during a theatre performance could spark panic, as Marie discovered when playing the Woolwich Hippodrome. During the interval the nearby naval guns barked into action and the audience looked set to stampede. Marie stepped in front of the curtain and said: 'If some of us are going to get it then let's all get it together. Meanwhile, if you will take your seats again I will sing you a song or two.'[17]

By 1916 Marie stayed close to home, only leaving London for brief jaunts to Northampton, Nottingham and Watford. By September the reason for her less frenetic schedule was clear: she had had a nervous breakdown. She had been unwell after appearing at the Palladium and was reported to be 'lying seriously ill' at her home in Golders Green. She had barely stopped working since arriving back from America, dashing around the country with no time for a holiday or to come to terms with Alec's death. She took the rest of that month off, and October.

It was not simply her consuming workload that had caused her collapse. She had planned Oakdene as a sanctuary, and when Bella and Dick moved into the house opposite with their bull terrier, Betty, Marie's home seemed to fulfil its potential in this respect – but not for long. Ben was drinking heavily and racing through the money he had earned as a jockey, as well as Marie's. He had reluctantly joined the army, but it soon became clear that military life was not for him.[18] In July 1916, aged twenty-eight, he applied for exemption from military service, saying that he had to support his parents and four brothers.[19] In his defence he argued that he had once earned a good deal of money as a jockey, but had not taken part in flat racing for four years, due to his increased weight. He added that his main work now was as a 'dealer in horses', a sufficiently vague job description as to be almost meaningless. His case failed, and an appeal in September was withdrawn.[20]

Dick, who was almost fifty when war was declared, became a sergeant in a Surrey regiment and threw himself into the role of military policeman, often helping to restore order after a Zeppelin attack. He was as self-disciplined, reliable, brave and popular as Ben was lax, cowardly, volatile and loathed by the Lloyd family. A bitter enmity grew up between the two men, especially when Ben hit Marie, who would run across the road in her nightdress to Bella for comfort.

Now that Ben no longer had the excitement of a race in which to vent his aggression and frustration and was out of the limelight he found consolation, like many sportsmen after him, in proving that he could still exert power over the woman in his life. Bella urged Marie to leave him, while Dick, unable to control his anger at the way his dead friend's wife was being treated, rushed over the road to threaten him. Eventually the strain between the two couples became intolerable; Dick felt it was dangerous for him to live so close to Ben, and he and Bella moved to a flat off the Marylebone Road, near Madame Tussaud's.

Marie's nerves were in tatters, and she looked back with regret to the confident days of her youth. She told a newspaper, 'You see, I had no nerves in those days. I did not know what fear was. I was stage-struck certainly, but stage-fright I did not know. Now I am ill a week before I sing a new song. I used to be able to sing three new songs in one evening without a shiver. But now it takes me days and days to pluck up courage to sing one. It is one of those things not easily explained.'[21]

And Ben was a liability in another way: he was not good for Marie's image. Having a violent and unstable husband when performers were meant to be presenting a united front to the world was bad enough, but a husband who had been born in Ireland, which was still ruled from London, and was reluctant to serve king and country was a double blow. So why did she stay with him? Probably because she did not have the energy to leave.

Her husband's wayward ways also deprived Marie of the establishment recognition she craved. The war provided music-hall managers and artists with the means to acceptance; it was a period when an élite class of performer emerged and when future knighthoods were secured. Marie did her fair share of fund-raising and morale-boosting appearances, but she did not receive the recognition her efforts deserved. In June 1915 she made a collection at a Lingfield Park race meeting for an ambulance that was to be named after her, and later that year she visited injured soldiers at the Ulster Volunteer Force Hospital in Belfast. Newsreel footage shows her in a fur coat kicking off a charity football match with great gusto and in 1918 she appeared in a matinée at the Palladium for a Welsh prisoner-of-war fund, and headed a cast at Collins's for wounded soldiers celebrating Empire Day. Ironically, she was particularly popular with American soldiers, known then as Sammies. She also made private visits to ammunition factories and paid for ten lorry-loads of soldiers to be brought from Hammersmith to a hotel at Thames Ditton where they were entertained by the orchestra of the Oxford Music Hall.

These low-profile contributions paled into insignificance against the recruitment drive of Vesta Tilley, the £40,000 George Robey raised, or the 36,000 miles Harry Lauder travelled to address two million people and collect £60,000 for his own Harry Lauder War Fund. Marie had no close relatives at the front – although Rudyard Kipling's 'A Recantation (To Lyde of the Music Halls)' is supposed to have been based on Marie and on the false assumption that she had lost a son in the war:

> Therefore, I, humble, join the hosts,
> Loyal and loud, who bow

To thee as Queen of songs – and ghosts –
For I remember how.

Never more rampant rose the Hall
At thy audacious line
Than when the news came in from Gaul
Thy son had – followed mine.

But Marie failed to capture the wartime spirit in the way that performers like Harry Lauder managed. Harry had entertained soldiers at the front and visited his son's grave, commenting, with heartbreaking stoicism, 'I had only one prayer and desire, and that was that God would allow the grave to open for one minute so that I could kiss him on each cheek and thank him for what he has done for his country.'[22]

Not every soldier appreciated the forced joviality of the music hall. Siegfried Sassoon expressed his disgust in his poem, 'Blighters', which was written in February 1917:

The House is crammed: tier beyond tier they grin
And cackle at the Show, while prancing ranks
Of harlots shrill the chorus, drunk with din;
'We're sure the Kaiser loves our dear old Tanks!'

I'd like to see a Tank come down the stalls,
Lurching to rag-time tunes, or 'Home, sweet Home',
And there'd be no more jokes in Music-halls
To mock the riddled corpses round Bapaume.

As the war progressed Marie's image changed as she endured a physical battering at home and professional snubs in public. She had become someone's mother, rather than their sweetheart. James Agate's friend Ernest Helme remembers her on stage in Norwich, making a farewell speech to soldiers from the South Wales Mounted Brigade: 'Now, boys, I know you will all remember our girls and write to them. And I, Marie Lloyd, beg and pray you to remember your mothers, to whom you are more than anything else in all the world.'[23]

In 'A Little Of What You Fancy!' Marie was the experienced woman more interested in allowing the younger generation to enjoy themselves than indulging herself. The song, which for many people summed up

Marie's life, tackled familiar subjects but from a slightly different standpoint. When Marie stumbles into a railway carriage containing a couple who have honeymoon 'stamp'd all over 'em', she feels sorry for them and confides, 'Excuse me, if you want to have a cudddle, *Have* a cuddle, 'cos I'm going to have a nap!' And while they enjoy themselves she takes comfort in her own fond memories of past times:

> I'll be dreaming while you spoon
> That I'm on *my* honeymoon
> 'Cos a little of what you fancy does you good!

'I Can't Forget The Days When I Was Young', by Sam Mayo and Worton David, which she sang in 1917 carrying a parasol and wearing an old-fashioned crinoline-style dress made clear that she was now from another age.

> I can't forget the days when I was young.
> And it don't seem so very long ago,
> Since I used to twist my feet to the organ in the street,
> I can't forget the days when I was young.

Her experience on Ellis Island still haunted her, and in May 1915 she was awarded $1,250 damages when a cinema displayed an almost life-size picture of her with the words 'White Slave Trade' across it.[24] The cinema claimed that the caption referred to another picture being shown at the time. In earlier years she might have laughed it off but her position at home and in the music-hall world turned the incident into something sordid and unpleasant. She still offered a teasing wink, but it was the wink of a middle-aged woman who was reminding you that she had once led a daring life. However, her position as a national treasure was unchanged: she was known affectionately as 'our Marie' or 'the one and only'.

Marie was never very good at sticking to rules and at times seemed unaware of the extreme hardship that most of the country was suffering. Food prices were soaring and queues became a music-hall joke in themselves. Sugar was rationed and there were frequent crowd distur-bances by frustrated women angry about shortages. Theatre staff again complained about their wages. Just round the corner from Oakdene, at the Golders Green Hippodrome, the stage hands went on strike over pay in August 1916 and some of the wings and scenery collapsed, 'with considerable noise', during a rendition of 'When Irish Eyes Are Smiling'. The *Era* reported loyally that 'beyond the mishap, little of noticeable importance happened'. There were similar disputes among musicians at the Coliseum and some of Stoll's other theatres.

By 1917 paranoia was such that there were rumours that theatres were to cut their shows to one and half hours and that matinées would be scrapped. One whisper suggested that theatres were to be burned to the ground so that their ashes could be used as fertilizer to tackle turnip blight.

Amid the austerity Marie decided to have Oakdene painted.[25] Shortly after the outbreak of hostilities she had built an extension to the house that included 'rustic posts' supporting a veranda, new doors, window and gate to the garage and rooms for storing trunks and wine. By 1917 she was ready to spruce up the front of the house. It was an odd decision to make when people were cutting back, making do, getting by as best they could and a new government Department of Food was urging housewives to be frugal. Marie's attitude reflected perfectly the first lines of 'A Little Of What You Fancy': 'I never was one to go and stint myself, / If I like a thing, I like it, that's enough.'

The decorating backfired, though, when the painter, Arthur Smith, from nearby Child's Hill, made off with an electric stove and five pounds in cash. Anyone else might have preferred not to draw attention to the unfortunate incident, but Marie took him to court. As she had shown in the past, she did not want to be thought of as someone who was easily taken advantage of – although, or perhaps because, this was exactly what was happening in her private life. She complained that Smith had left paint pots all over the house and ruined the property, making it look like a patchwork quilt. In court Smith had the cheek to demand payment for the work. Marie's reply revealed her hardened approach to life: 'You don't get paid until the work is finished, at least, I don't.'

Her brush with the law, though, looked insignificant when compared with Ben's antics. During 1917 he appeared regularly in court; his tribulations were reported fully in the press under headlines that often read 'Miss Marie Lloyd's husband'. In June he was remanded in custody charged with assaulting a policeman, PC Lewis, and while the case was being heard a telegram arrived from his commanding officer asking for him to be arrested for being absent without leave.[26] Details of the assault charge that emerged painted Ben as a man whose cowardice stretched beyond a mere reluctance not to serve for his country.

The court heard how PC Lewis had been called to Oakdene by Marie's friend, Claud Wilson, who had pleaded with him, 'For God's sake, come in, Bernard is threatening to murder Mrs Dillon.' When the policeman arrived he found Marie and her maid crouched in a corner of the room with Ben standing over them, threatening to batter them with a soda siphon. According to PC Lewis, Ben was 'mad drunk' and started to attack him so badly that he was later put on the 'sick list' at work. Marie was too unwell to attend the court.

When the case continued, a few days later, alcohol emerged as the main catalyst for the violence. Claud said Ben was 'a good man when sober, but when he was drunk he was very violent'. The trainer Robert Sievier, for whom Ben had ridden in the past, was called as a character witness. He claimed that he had sent his secretary to see Ben in Brixton prison where Marie's husband had promised to give up drink and to 'attend to his duties as a soldier'. He was ordered to do one month's hard labour after which he was to be handed over to the military authorities.[27]

Ben was in trouble again in October 1917 when he was accused of hitting a waiter, Antoine Prete, at the Café Royal also with a soda bottle after Prete told him he had taken a table that was already occupied.[28] At the trial Prete appeared with his head dramatically swathed in bandages. Ben was bound over for two years and the court heard that the military authorities wanted him to return to his regiment where he should be available to be drafted abroad.[29] The judge added that he was glad to hear there was the possibility of Ben going to a place where violence was permitted.

Nineteen eighteen was a year of reckoning. The war had been going on for long enough for the music-hall world to feel it could indulge in some mutual back-slapping at its efforts during the struggle. In February a lunch was thrown at the Criterion for George Robey in honour of his fund-raising efforts, and other self-congratulatory celebrations followed. Marie was invited to few and at one she did attend she was not asked to speak. The snub was mentioned in the press and Marie was deeply hurt.

In June it was announced that Alfred Butt was to be knighted. Although he was from the management class the honour opened a door for music hall through which its performers could see a path to a higher level of recognition.

Despite talk of a ceasefire, working conditions were still grim. Opening hours were cut – although the *Era* argued, implausibly, that everyone who lived in town should be forced to go to a music hall rather than sit at home wasting coal and electricity. Paper and paste shortages meant even advertising became difficult and there was talk of an Anti-amusement Society whose sole aim was to wipe out public entertainment. Conspiracy theories continued. Chung Ling Soo, the Chinese magician, whose real name was Billy Robinson, was fatally wounded during his act at the second house at the Wood Green Empire in March. He was originally from America but, like Marie, had performed around the world. His most famous trick was to catch bullets – actually blanks – in his teeth fired by a 'volunteer' from the audience. That night the stunt went wrong and he died in hospital of his wounds. The inquest reported a verdict of 'death by misadventure' but speculation surrounded the tragedy when the coroner received a letter, written in capital letters, which said that a man in the audience had stood up and shouted at the top of his voice at the moment of the fatal gunshot. Marie was performing a few miles away at the Finsbury Park Empire and was appalled by the incident.

Dick Burge's death the same month was just as unsettling, if less dramatic. He had caught double pneumonia while spending the night searching for survivors through the rubble left by an air-raid in Piccadilly. He was given a military funeral and Tom, with Betty by his side, led the cortège that followed the gun carriage to the crematorium. The crowd of mourners, estimated at three thousand, included jockeys, boxers, actors, music-hall stars and workers from Billingsgate and Covent Garden. Dick's death robbed Marie of the only man who had shown he was willing to stand up to Ben, and, of course, left Bella alone again.

That year Marie had a new song, 'My Old Man Said Follow The Van' or 'Don't Dilly-Dally On The Way' by Charles Collins and Fred W. Leigh. Marie dressed as an old woman in a shawl, carrying her 'old cock linnet' in a cage, to tell the story of a family doing a moonlit flit to avoid the rent man. The words were entirely appropriate to her feelings of isolation:

> Lost the van and don't know where to roam
> I stopp'd on the way to have the old half-quartern
> And I can't find my way home.

Chapter 23

A CROWDED HOUR OF LIFE

(1918–21)

~✢

I'm very, very fond of ruins, ruins I love to scan
You'd say I'm very fond of ruins if you saw my old man . . .
'It's A Bit Of A Ruin' by
Harry Bedford and Terry Sullivan

Initially, the end of the war provided a boost for business: people wanted an outlet for their euphoria and the transitory nature of music hall seemed to meet that need. The increase in ticket sales, though, was a temporary blip since, even before the ceasefire, another lethal threat had replaced enemy bombs: the flu epidemic, which now swept the world.

Once again, music hall was seen as a dangerous folly at a time of national emergency. Just as managers had used far-fetched arguments to defend entertainment against the frugality of wartime Britain, so Oswald Stoll and others launched a campaign to protect the halls in the face of mounting hysteria about the risk of contagion and any activity in which the public were allowed to mingle in close proximity with each other. When there was talk of closing the halls to prevent the flu from spreading, Stoll, now posing as a health expert, claimed, 'To keep warm in a well-aired theatre is a safeguard against infection because it helps to maintain vitality.'[1]

The flu viciously attacked the army, and in some towns troops were banned from music halls in a bid to reduce the risk of soldiers spreading the illness beyond their own. Theatre managers became obsessed with germs and hygiene, and all over the country threw themselves into a frenzy of cleaning, disinfecting, spraying and vacuuming, in the intervals and between performances. Sliding roofs, which normally opened only in the summer, became a selling point in icy November when improved ventilation was seen as helping to dispel the menace. The London Palladium bragged about its 'wonderful ozone ventilating system' and of the theatre's ability to clear the house in a few minutes so that it could spray the auditorium and stage with the 'strongest known germ killer' in the interval.

Marie, with her weak constitution and propensity for colds and flu even in non-epidemic years, was a prime candidate for the illness, which struck down several music-hall performers, but she continued with her punishing schedule. As well as her London dates, 1918 saw her perform in Swansea, Newport, Bolton, Manchester, Glasgow, Newcastle, Sheffield, Mansfield, Nottingham, Birmingham, Blackpool, Halifax and Hull. She was in Liverpool when peace was declared. Nineteen nineteen was no less stressful and her itinerary hurled her around the country. She rested briefly in April but spent a humid June in London at the Palladium and Holborn Empire.

As well as the physical exhaustion of touring, Marie was eaten up with bitterness at the praise lavished on her colleagues for their contribution to war charities while her own efforts were ignored. Early in 1919 George Robey was made a CBE and in April Harry Lauder and Oswald Stoll were knighted. Walter de Frece was also knighted that year and elected to Parliament in 1920. London's idol, Vesta Tilley, became Lady de Frece. Marie's image may have been as a woman of the people who did not stand on ceremony, but she resented being left out. She was scornful of the speeches and dinners, the kowtowing and watching of Ps and Qs that enabled people from humble backgrounds to transform themselves into dignitaries, but she wanted the recognition that rewarded such behaviour.

When, in July 1919, it was announced that the King had commanded variety artists to perform for him again, the omission of Marie's name from the list went largely unremarked. The evening was a recognition of ostentatious charity work during the war so Marie had no part to play in it. The cast included stalwart war workers such as Arthur Prince and George Robey, and the show was held at the London Coliseum.

Marie was no longer an obvious choice because she represented older times and audiences wanted to look forward rather than wallow in nostalgia. Instead, the line-up included people like Harry Tate, who had perfected sketches such as 'Motoring'. Ironically, his trademark 'St Vitus moustache', which cavorted across his face, had been first suggested by Marie during a weekend trip to the countryside. When he emerged from the river in his swimming costume, two pieces of weed twitching on his upper lip, she pointed out how funny he looked and suggested he included a similar moustache in his act.

When they did notice her, reviewers treated her with condescension, like a still talented old aunt who must be allowed to have her turn at the piano even though all everyone really wants is jazz or to go to the Picture Palace. 'When Marie comes on to the stage a sense of security pervades you. You have the comfortable knowledge that she will "deliver the goods" without fail and there will be no questioning the quality.'[2] And: 'One would miss her remarkable Paris gowns, but I confess I always prefer Marie when she is quite English and a little shabby.'[3] The reviews are more telling for what they leave out. They praise her professionalism, but there is no sense of excitement; the main merit in her performance appears to lie in comforting familiarity.

In October 1919 she stayed close to London as the national railway strike made touring difficult. Bella had more time to spend with Marie and kept her company in her dressing room while she waited to go on. As Marie's anxiety about performing grew, she insisted that Bella stood in the prompt corner to help her out if she faltered over her words.

There was no respite from the tension that now engulfed her life, both private and professional. When she returned to Oakdene Ben was often drunk and looking for a fight. The house was no longer a symbol of Marie's success, instead it had become a magnet for gossip and rumour. It was said that Ben had taken a lover, a Frenchwoman called Yvonne Granville, and that Marie had found them in bed together at Christmas 1919 when Ben had asked his wife to join them.[4] Whether this was true or not, Ben's violence to Marie and members of her family and household is well documented and Marie sometimes had to wear a veil to hide the bruises he gave her. It was said that Ben had knocked out one of her front teeth.

For her fiftieth birthday in February 1920, Marie was at the Bedford, Camden Town. It was a maudlin occasion, rather than one of the riotous celebrations she had enjoyed so often in the past. It was the first time she had performed at the theatre for twenty-eight years and both houses were packed. She was handed flowers and fruit over the footlights, and Joe Elvin and Arthur Roberts emerged from the audience to embrace her and make speeches of praise. She was visibly moved, according to the *Era*, and remembered how she had first earned fifteen shillings a week at the Bedford. She said she hoped to spend a few more years 'pleasing the public and helping the poor'. She admitted that she had had her 'fair share of knocks' and concluded that she had to keep on working to pay the income tax. Her father, Brushie, was introduced to the audience, and Arthur, with typical hyperbole, told them that Sarah Bernhardt had described Marie as the best actress in the world.

Reaching her half-century increased bitterness that had established itself in her during the war years. While in the past she had been able to exorcize any dark demons through bursts of anger, she was now falling into a profound depression. She was unable to hide her feelings and in an article, in which she thanked the public for the 'super touring years of strenuous starring', she could not resist a swipe at her recently decorated colleagues: 'Well, I have had a crowded hour of life, work and worry, sorrow and joy. People don't always get the credit for the good they do, and some get more than they deserve, but the wounded Tommies know what I did for them and the gratitude which I know they feel is more to me than diamonds and decorations.'[6] Despite her protestations that she felt no need to defend herself, she then went on to recount a story of the time she had hit a German officer in 'Fred reich Street' (*sic*) in Berlin for insulting Britain.

Her friends tried to cheer her up with a parody of a popular song of the time, 'Where Do Flies Go In Winter Time?' – Marie's home had long been known as 'The Flies' after the theatrical term for the area above the stage:

> They all go round to Marie Lloyd's in the summer time.
> And tickle a tune upon her ticolee
> There's something nice, always on ice,
> And you never have to ask her twice
> For a drink of her kickolee
> Her front door is never known to lock,
> It's always standing open so you never have to knock,
> Nobody knows what time it is, for the hands are off the clock

And we don't go home till morning
At good old Marie Lloyd's.

Most of her friends, and many of her public, though, knew that Marie's private life had turned into a nightmare and that she had nowhere to run. In March Ben overheard Marie Junior criticizing him to Brushie and Marie's cook, Mary Brady; Marie said she could not understand why her mother did not divorce Ben and that her own father had treated Marie much better.[7] Ben burst in and started swearing at her and, when Brushie tried to intervene, Ben spat in his face and knocked him to the ground. Brushie, in his seventies, hit Ben so hard that the cook had to mop up the blood from his face with a towel. Ben was charged with assault on 18 March; the case was adjourned until 30 March because the cook, a vital witness, was ill. The outburst of violence against their elderly father was the turning point for Marie's siblings who now refused to have anything to do with Ben.

While the case was waiting to be heard, Ben was accused of hitting Marie, and, on a separate occasion, of punching Yvonne Granville in the mouth in Piccadilly.[8] Yvonne did not attend court and he was discharged. Later in July he was fined for 'using insulting behaviour' in Camberwell when a policeman stepped in and told him to release a woman with whom he was having an argument.[9] Ben let her go, but as he was walking away he muttered that he wished he had the policeman in Ireland. It required three officers to take him into custody.

When the case involving Ben and Brushie came to court, Mary testified that Brushie had hit Ben first.[10] Ben was bound over on the sum of £100 to be of good behaviour for twelve months. Marie refused to have anything to do with the case and sent a statement through her solicitor that she knew nothing of the incident. She may have been too frightened to appear in court, or simply did not want to face facts. Shortly before the court case Ben had climbed through her bedroom window at dead of night, spat at her and thrown beer in her face.[11] Confused by sleep, and all too aware of her husband's wild temper, she initially mistook the various liquids for vitriol and assumed Ben had tried to blind her. He dragged her out of bed, beat her up and threw a jug of water over her.

Marie was ill in April and removed from the bill at the Kilburn Empire.

In July she took Ben to court; a brave action given his violence and the fact that a court appearance would lay bare her private life for all to see. Due to her nervous disposition, she was allowed to sit while giving evidence that catalogued the numerous beatings she had received at her husband's hands and which had caused her to miss several performances. Her statement, at Hendon Magistrates Court, was corroborated by her doctor, Graham Hargreaves, who said he had been called to Oakdene several times during the last few years and had treated Marie for nervous collapse, bruises and black eyes. Marie's loyal maid, Maud Wilson, her cook and the local police sergeant all confirmed Ben's violence. Maud added that Marie often could not go out because of her bruises. Ben was bound over to keep the peace for twelve months; which the magistrate said was lenient but had been granted at Marie's request.

During the court case Marie said that she had been divorced twice – perhaps she was trying to rewrite history to expunge the Ellis Island episode or perhaps it was her way of dealing with the guilt she felt at abandoning Alec: if she had really divorced him then she had not let him down by her subsequent actions. In the Hendon courtroom she said she did not want to divorce Ben – which was more an indication that she hated being alone or being seen to be alone, than a triumph of romantic love. She also revealed that she had borrowed a thousand pounds (£16,690) from Ben during her first nervous breakdown, but claimed she had repaid it several times over since then.

Despite her protestations, Marie had financial problems and she became obsessed with work, refusing to go on holiday to Scotland with her sister Annie and Bella.[12] Economic conditions for performers were growing ever more onerous: rail concessions disappeared in April 1920 and unemployment rose throughout the country. The miners' strike that autumn again threatened music hall, whose brilliantly illuminated interiors were seen as an extravagance. Marie's fears that she was an antique caught in a timewarp were brought into sharp focus when Vesta Tilley, now Lady de Frece, announced her intention to retire. She was given a huge send-off at the Coliseum, where she was presented with flowers by Ellen Terry. There was a sense that she was leaving a sinking ship: Little Tich penned an article defending music hall and the *Era* wrote an editorial on 'The Cinema Invasion' – although the warning came years too late.

On the other side of the Atlantic Alice and Tom were finding the going tough. They were still working hard to pay off their debts and to maintain their privileged Long Island lifestyle, with friends like Charlie Chaplin. Tom was in a show called *Melody Maker*, but he suffered headaches and was gripped by an overwhelming nervousness before he went on stage.[13] One evening, rather than appear in the Grand Pasha costume that the part required, he wandered on-stage, seemingly bewildered and wearing a loosely secured bathrobe over 'abbreviated underwear and no shoes'. He was hustled off and taken to his hotel where he collapsed. Doctors at a private sanatorium diagnosed a nervous breakdown and ordered him to return to Europe for a complete rest.

During this difficult period Marie's brother, Johnny, assumed the role of agent. He had fulfilled several small-time management roles, such as running the Loughborough Hotel in Brixton, and, most recently, the bar at the Empress, Brixton. Although he was hardly overburdened with business acumen, he had the advantage of being a member of the Lloyd family and someone Marie could trust. They had been partners of a sort since the early days of her career when Johnny had waved his handkerchief during 'The Boy I Love Is Up In The Gallery'.

Johnny suggested that she entered a sharing agreement with provincial managers so that she would be given 50 per cent of a provincial hall's takings, out of which she had to pay the other turns on the bill and the hire of the theatre. Since her wages had been falling, it made good business sense and was reported as a 'comeback'. Some of Johnny's figures for 1920 are preserved, jotted down in an old diary that was already out of date when he started using it.[14] The following examples show the economics of her new way of working:

Venue	*Date*	*Duration*	*Gross takings*
Empire, Swansea	February 1920	one week	£858.15.5 (£14,337)
			TR£279 (£4,657)
Empire, Cardiff	8 March 1920	one week	£1,645.12.5 (£27,472)
			TR£622 (£10,382)
Hippodrome, Southampton	19 July 1920	one week	£657.11.1 (£10,982)
			TR£250 (£4,172)
Coliseum, Glasgow	6 December 1920	one week	£1,076.0.9 (£17,958)
			TR£337 (£5,625)

TR: amounts reported to the tax authorities as gross salary, including matinées.

Johnny's figures, compared with the gross figures presented to the tax authorities and assuming that Marie was telling the truth, show the considerable expense involved in running a music-hall bill. The official gross figures also failed to take into account Marie's own expenses such as her dresser, costumes, accommodation and travel – the last two would have been especially high since she was travelling further afield in search of audiences.

The tax returns reveal huge swings in her earning power and also that she seems to have been playing just one hall a night against the four or five of earlier years. The Palladium, where she became a firm favourite, brought in £250 a week in 1920; Sheffield brought in £90 and New Cross a mere £8.10. Cardiff was her biggest earner, bringing in £622. The decline in music hall is reflected in the figures: in 1907 at the arbitration hearings she had told Askwith she was earning £150 a hall each week.

The new way of operating seems to have boosted her confidence and by the end of the year she had a hit: 'It's A Bit Of A Ruin' by Harry Bedford and Terry Sullivan. When she sang the song, about a 'half-muddled and elderly female', early in 1921 at the Palladium, the audience took up the chorus 'with gusto'. The portrayal of an old woman robbed outside a country pub allowed Marie, who was still only fifty-one, to hide the increasing pain she was suffering from a number of long-term ailments, in addition to the bruises supplied by Ben. She had rheumatism in her back and legs and, as the condition worsened, she found it excruciatingly painful even to raise her arms to allow her dresser to change her costumes. Her appetite disappeared and she began to sip champagne or sweet white wine to dull the habitual pain in her stomach. Gradually the busty, matronly figure disappeared.

In 1921 she was called to jury service, which meant a long trek from the Cardiff Empire. Her selection caused much hilarity, which spread as far as New York where a newspaper article was headlined, erroneously, 'Marie Lloyd, Triple Divorcee, is a Juror'.[15] Marie had tried to avoid serving by claiming that she was ill, which did not carry much weight since she was well enough to perform. She endured two days in court, after which it became obvious that sitting still for hours on end was causing her agony. Johnny reckoned the episode cost her £300 (£6,015) in lost earnings, although it generated welcome publicity: one newspaper man pursued the story by hitching a lift on the back of her car as it sped to Oakdene.[16] The escape from court was incorporated into 'My Old Man', in which she ran through a list of items she had mislaid: 'I've lost my puff, and I've lost my jury summons'.

As a star turn, Marie was becoming less and less reliable. At Cardiff she performed for only six minutes, rather than her scheduled twenty-eight,[17] and the curtain was brought down abruptly as she floundered: she forgot her words, looked confused and stumbled. Marie knew she had become a liability and was frequently in tears in her dressing room. Performing was a trial, and she would sit quietly, playing patience, while she waited to go on. She left it until the last minute to leave her dressing room, and nervous managers took to having a stand-in turn loitering in the wings in case she came off early or looked as though she might collapse.[18] Sometimes the manager asked a stagehand to stand behind the curtain and support her if she seemed unsteady.

Most of the audience knew the true story behind the charade they were watching. Virginia Woolf saw Marie at the Bedford Music Hall and described her in her diary on Friday 8 April 1921 as, 'a mass of corruption – long front teeth – a crapulous way of saying "desire", & yet a born artist – scarcely able to walk, waddling, aged, unblushing. A roar of laughter went up when she talked of her marriage. She is beaten nightly by her husband. I felt that the audience was much closer to drink & beating & prison than any of us.'

On 12 August 1921 Marie failed to appear at the Palladium and instead spent the day writing her will. The document provides a snapshot, not so much of where her friends and family stood in the pecking order of her affections, but of who might need her help. There was no mention of Ben. Johnny was left £300, her maid, Maud Wilson, £100. The rest went to Marie Junior and, on her death, to Hoxton charities. Presumably she felt that other members of her family were well taken care of: all of her siblings were married and most were doing well financially. She knew that they would never allow her parents to suffer, but she was not so sure that Johnny could make it alone – ironically the star performer was bailing out her business manager.

Marie's absence set the rumour mill into a flurry of activity, the *Era* suggested that 'the Queen of Comediennes had been taken seriously ill and that some time would elapse before she returned to the halls'.[19] Johnny did his best to play it down, saying that Marie was taking a brief rest on doctor's orders and that she would reappear at the Holborn Empire the following week. She did, indeed, appear at the Holborn and was recalled three times after 'It's A Bit Of A Ruin'.

By early September, though, she had gone to Boscombe to try to regain her health. A week later the *Era* reported that she was making 'good progress' and hoped to be at the Hammersmith Palace in a week's time. She failed to appear. By the end of November she was 'much better' and expected to be back at work for the Christmas season. When she appeared at the Kilburn Empire in December, on the same bill as Jimmy Jewell, the audience sensed the supreme effort involved and demanded that she make a speech.

For much of 1922 Marie was on tour. She spent her Easter holidays at Brighton, but was not comfortable as a spectator: she could not resist stepping out of the audience to give an impromptu performance. Her summer tour took in the Midlands and Sheffield, but by August she was back in London. A gossip item at the end of the month gave the impression of a tidy-minded woman who was entirely in control of her life:

> Tired of keeping an open house for everybody; and sighing for that more compact cosiness which so often conveys the true homely touch, Marie Lloyd has given up her spacious residence 'Oakdene', Finchley Road, NW, and settled into a smaller house. 'Oakdene' and its magnificent 'household goods', will go under the hammer at the London Auction Mart, Queen Victoria Street on Tuesday, September 5th.[20]

The reality was that Marie needed the money and she also needed to get away from Ben. Rate books for the period show that she had moved into Walstead, 37 Woodstock Road, where she lived with Daisy, although the house was owned by Alice. The new address was less than half a mile away from her beloved Oakdene, but it was cheaper to run and a place to which Ben had no claim. It was also handy for many of her autumn dates, such as the Willesden Hippodrome and Islington Empire in September. The house was most convenient of all for the Edmonton Empire, which she was to play in October.

The theatre was built on a former rubbish tip, and when it opened in

1908 its audience was concerned that the site's original use would render it unable to withstand the troupe of elephants hired for the music hall's first night. From the outside it was ugly, utilitarian rather than grand, and built directly opposite Lower Edmonton railway station. It was made of red brick and white stone, with an awning that ran along its length to protect the queuing crowds from the weather while a blind accordion player entertained them. Inside, the theatre was much grander than the exterior suggested. The plush and gilt auditorium boasted tip-up seats and private boxes, and bicycles were stored free of charge. The stage was built with an exit that opened directly on to the yard outside so that large pieces of scenery could be manoeuvred in and allow for spectacular shows.[21] The building could hold 1,525 people and had standing room for a further five to six hundred. Performers were also well served: there were seven dressing rooms, each with hot and cold running water.

Like most music halls in 1922, the Empire was struggling. The Bernstein family, who owned the site and whose family dynasty went on to found the cinema-and-leisure giant Granda, had just bought back the lease of the building to try to restore its fortunes. The hall had originally been let to Mae Rose, an American-born 'sand' dancer: she performed a comic shuffling dance on boards covered with sand. She had once made a living by dressing up in a Little Lord Fauntleroy suit and performing under the name of 'My Fancy'. Her husband, Harry Bawn, was charming and good-looking but not particularly hard-working. One of his economies had been to reduce the number of lightbulbs the theatre used so that from the outside it appeared to be almost in darkness. Sidney Bernstein spruced it up then enticed some big names to the Empire – Marie was one of the first and biggest he attracted – in a bid to make it pay.

The Empire's new manager, Leon Pollock soon realized, though, that stars needed special handling. On Monday, 2 October he was forced to ring Sidney and warn him that Marie was unwell. She refused to go home because she did not want to lose the night's pay. Sidney said he would pay her, whether she appeared or not, but that she must go home to bed. Marie refused and Johnny, who had spoken to her specialist and knew just how ill she was, had to support her as she struggled from her dressing room to the back of the stage. He stood in the wings watching throughout the performance and told a newspaper reporter standing next to him that she had eaten practically nothing for five days and that medicinal tonics alone were keeping her going.

Marie normally liked to use the entire stage in her act, but as she sang her first song, 'The Cosmopolitan Girl', she hardly moved. During 'It's A Bit Of A Ruin', she hitched up her skirts and made a feeble attempt to dance, but the effort was too much for her: she stumbled to the wings, lost her footing and crashed into the scenery.

On Tuesday Sidney attended the first house at six thirty and found Marie huddled over a stove in her dressing room. She complained of a pain in her stomach and her teeth were chattering.[22] He tried to persuade her to go home but she laughed at him saying, in a comment that sounds as though it may have been exaggerated in the reporting, 'Ten minutes in the footlights will do me more good than ten days in bed.'[23] He later told a newspaper, 'So it really seemed, for upon coming under the limelight of the stage her appearance changed. We were struck by her recovery, but when she returned to the wings she was exhausted and faint.'

Sidney summoned Marie's doctor and asked him to give her an injection to calm her.[24] Norman Benjafield[25] later told a newspaper, 'I did not want her to go on the stage, but she insisted that she could not let her fans down, so I just kept on drugging her.'[26]

During the interval Sidney overheard one of the audience say, 'She's wonderful, but she's very drunk.'[27] In the second house her voice was noticeably different, although the audience cheered her just the same. Those who knew how ill she was looked on in horror. For 'I'm One Of The Ruins' she wore a long, ill-fitting dress and crushed hat with a plume and carried a large handbag. Her body was so shrunken inside the costume that she looked only half human: her face was so drawn that she looked like a man in drag and her voice was weak and unfamiliar.[28]

The audience, who knew of her marital problems, listened intently for her usual nuances and inflections as she sang:

> I went out in the country for a stroll the other day
> Cos I like to study history . . .
> And the pubs along the way.

I came across an abbey
That was tumbled all to bits
It seemed a relic of a bygone day.

A gentleman said, 'What is this?'
I said, 'Excuse me, sir,
I'll tell you all about it, if I may . . .'

It's a bit of a ruin that Cromwell knocked about a bit
One of the ruins that Cromwell knocked about a bit
In the gay old days, there used to be some doings
No wonder that the poor old abbey went to ruin.

Those that study history
Sing and shout a bit
And you can bet your life there isn't a doubt of it
Outside the Oliver Cromwell, last Saturday night
I was one of the ruins that Cromwell knocked about a bit . . .

At one point she staggered and fell. The audience, thinking this was part of the act, shrieked with laughter. She recovered momentarily, but collapsed backstage. There was no encore.

She was taken home, still unconscious, and her maid phoned the Empire to say she would probably not make the next performance. Dan Harlow, a local comic who had been on the bill with Marie three times during the previous twelve months, sang a parody of 'It's A Bit Of A Ruin' on the Friday night in which he made frequent allusions to the local football rivals, Spurs and Arsenal. It brought the house down amid cries of 'Good old Marie.'

Marie Lloyd died at 11.20 a.m. on Saturday, 7 October, at 37 Woodstock Road. She had not regained consciousness. Harlow immediately dropped the parody from his act and Marie's dressing room at the Empire, room 108, was kept locked in her memory for ten days. The Empire's programme the following week carried a tribute bordered in heavy black: 'We are honoured to remember that the last performance of England's greatest comedienne was on the stage of the Edmonton Empire. In all humbleness we offer this, our last tribute to that exquisite artiste who won the hearts of millions.'

WHO KILLED MARIE LLOYD?

Marie's public image was remoulded almost as soon as she died. Those who had been closest to her in life jockeyed for pole position as keepers of her image in death. It was even disputed as to whose arms she had died in. Arthur Roberts claimed that her last words were, 'I shall work soon again,'[1] which is highly unlikely given that when she collapsed she fell instantly into a coma. Just as implausibly, it was claimed that she made a final charitable donation of ten shillings while lying on her deathbed. It was also said that she died in Rosie's arms of a broken heart,[2] and with a tear on her cheek; or that she was simply 'worn out'. Her friend and early biographer, Walter Macqueen-Pope stated, 'She was going down hill of her own volition. The complaint was incurable, some might call it heartbreak, perhaps a less sentimental diagnosis is disillusionment.'[3]

The death certificate is prosaic, stating that Ben was present and giving the cause of death as 'mitral regurgitation 14 months, nephritis 14 months and uraemic coma three days'. But even these facts were disputed. Ben's detractors said that he managed to slip his arm under Marie's head at the very moment she died so that he could claim his position on the death certificate.

Apart from the list of medical terms that appear on the certificate, what exactly killed her has remained a mystery. 'Mitral regurgitation', referring to a faulty valve in the heart, is given as the primary cause of death. This frequently leads to heart and kidney failure, which would tie in with 'uraemic coma' and 'nephritis'. But Marie had been ill for several years and Macqueen-Pope hints at 'medical treatment', adding, 'There was nothing tangible that medicine or treatment could cure.'

There was a rumour that she died of syphilis and, consistent with Ben's track record, that she had caught it from him. Daniel Farson was assured by an unnamed friend of Marie that she had attended the Lydia Ward of St Thomas's Hospital for treatment, but no medical records survive to shed any light on this theory.[4] Apart from providing another opportunity to place the blame for Marie's unhappiness squarely on Ben, the rumour may have sprung from the appearance of Marie's teeth, which in some later photographs appear heavily stained. Mercury, which was at one time used as a common treatment for syphilis, frequently turned the sufferer's teeth black – it did Oscar Wilde's.[5]

More convincing is the theory that Marie was suffering from stomach cancer, one of the commonest and most feared killers in the 1920s. Fred McNaughton's granddaughter Lindy remembers being present at several family gatherings at which Marie's stomach problems were discussed. Lindy heard how Marie survived on seltzer, tonic water and sweet sparkling wine, and how occasionally she could take a little egg white mixed with sugar, milk and seltzer, but very little else. Towards the end of her life, Marie was barely able to digest any food, or even water. Marie made Lindy's father – who was eighteen when she died – and her three aunts swear on the Bible never to mention the illness. According to Fred, Marie was well aware of her illness, but she wanted the public to think she was suffering either from a broken heart or from a 'fast' life of champagne and parties. 'Let them think I died of good living – don't leave them crying,' she told her family.

Cancer was an even greater bogey then than it is today, and treatment was hopeless. Marie was worried that her condition would make her unemployable, since audiences would feel awkward laughing at a dying woman, especially if she had the most feared disease of her day. Instead, she portrayed herself, through her songs, as someone who struggled against everyday problems like wayward husbands and money difficulties but who still had a good time.

Marie's early life made her a prime candidate for an illness that thrived on poor diet and overcrowding and which killed a third of all cancer victims in the early part of the century. Earlier treatments of food – salting, pickling and smoking – have all been linked to the illness because of the nitrate in food preservatives, which forms carcinogenic compounds when mixed with gastric juices. A lack of fresh fruit and vegetables, together with alcohol, is thought to be a contributory factor. The cancer's incidence has fallen dramatically throughout most parts of the world because of the increased use of refrigeration and improved food preservation.

The circumstantial evidence of Marie's lifestyle backs up the cancer theory. She grew up in a family of eleven children in one of the most overcrowded parts of London. She loved pickled and salted fish, and drank heavily. Relatively few cases are detected in sufferers under the age of fifty – Marie was fifty-two when she died – and the illness is normally only detected at an advanced stage. Marie also suffered several of the symptoms of stomach cancer: indigestion, tiredness, poor appetite, vomiting, pain and weight loss. There would have been no obligation to mention stomach cancer on her death certificate if, technically, it did not cause her death even though it may have contributed to it.

Ignorance about just how ill she was contributed to the shock of her death. When a comedian dies suddenly and prematurely fans feel a sense of betrayal: how could someone who was so successful at generating laughter leave them callously. To her public, Marie's death was akin to a national tragedy. People remembered vividly where they were when they heard the news of her death. James Agate recalled being rooted to the pavement in Tottenham Court Road when he caught sight of a newspaper placard that announced it.[6] Macqueen-Pope spoke of her death as a 'deep personal loss' to millions.[7] T. S. Eliot was surprised by the depth of his feelings at her death, which he described as a 'significant moment in English history'.[8] People behaved as if they had known her personally. They associated her with events in their lives or places and, because they knew the story of her life so intimately, they felt they 'owned' a part of her. The novelist Storm Jameson, writing in 1933, looked back at a time when she had lived in south London. The place and time were inextricably linked to Marie: 'the whole of it rank with life, life oozing between the bricks, strong, ugly, bitter, nasty, beautiful and unabateable. That was Marie Lloyd.'[9]

In a BBC broadcast following Marie's death, Sir Max Beerbohm commented: 'It is strange that of all the women of the Victorian era the three most generally remembered are Queen Victoria herself, and Miss Florence Nightingale, and – Marie.'

They made a curious trio: a queen who was famously not amused, a nurse who had little time for amusements and a performer who made her living by making people laugh. Of the three Marie was the only one who spanned the Victorian and Edwardian eras and the Great War. Her changing image, which circulated round the country on picture postcards and Ogden's cigarette cards, represented a comforting bridge between the two centuries. Like a modern celebrity, the vicissitudes of her private life were well known, and added an extra depth to her songs. Unlike other performers such as Vesta Tilley, who was presented at court, and George Robey, who took up collecting Chinese porcelain and claimed he had been to Jesus College, Cambridge, Marie stayed true to her roots.

She might have won greater Establishment recognition if she had been more circumspect. Ellen Terry, who died six years after Marie, also married three times – the last time, like Marie, to a man nearly twenty years her junior – and had two children out of wedlock. Although her position as a Shakespearean actress gave her a head start over Marie, the main difference between them was that she did not flaunt her 'transgressions' and became a dame.

Marie did not fit easily into the categories defined by her time. Just two days after her death, the *Daily Mail*, uncertain how to pigeonhole her, described her as 'a splendid housewife spoiled by the footlights'.[10] Friends and family were anxious to prove that her material had never been 'dirty', which was to miss the point entirely. Marie was a master of timing and innuendo, and an important link to a technique and tradition that stretch back to Shakespeare's time. George Orwell believed that *double entendres* helped to unite an audience by expressing a common background, but he also believed that 'women cannot be low without being disgusting, whereas a good male comedian can give the impression of something irredeemable and yet innocent, like a sparrow'.[11] He was wrong: Marie could appear innocent. As T. S. Eliot said: 'There was nothing about her of the grotesque; none of her comic appeal was due to exaggeration; it was all a matter of selection and concentration.'

Today, innuendo is still popular and still unites an audience. Ironically, it has become one of the more coded forms of comedy in an age when jokes can be as explicit as the teller wants. The *double entendres* and bittersweet characterizations of Victoria Wood are closer to Marie as, for example, when a clumsy canteen worker falls awkwardly while practising a curtsy for a visiting dignitary. 'I'll just go and check my *dried goods*,' she says, in an echo of Marie's old woman, who sits down heavily on the wide slats of a park bench and explains, with a pained expression, 'I've been nipped in the bud.'[12]

Marie proved that women could be funny, and funny about risqué subjects, but her greatest dramatic achievements were her characterizations. It is impossible to know how good they were because success depended on their pinpoint accuracy at a fleeting moment. The annoyingly manipulative young girl of 'Johnny Jones' still exists today, but characters like a late-nineteenth-century barmaid or a streetwise East End girl have long since disappeared. Similarly, in a few years' time the comic creations of the 1980s, such as Harry Enfield's 'Loadsamoney', may be incomprehensible to a world that has moved on to other odious stereotypes. Given their transitory nature, it is surprising that so many of Marie's songs are still heard. Some have taken the place of playground rhymes while others crop up in even more unusual places: 'My Old Man Said Follow The Van' is sung by – mainly Arsenal – football fans in a terrace version that might make even Marie blush.

Probably the nearest I will ever come to seeing a ghost was in a dimly lit front room in Norwich. I was sitting on the sort of settee that welcomes you with the promise of cosiness then swallows you whole when I saw my first moving image of Marie Lloyd. The flickering black-and-white film lasted only a few minutes and showed a tiny woman in an ill-fitting dress, carrying a handbag nearly as big as she was. She was singing 'It's A Bit Of A Ruin', and she skipped and pranced with the lightness of a teenager, defying the age written across her face. I was entranced by the woman I had imagined a thousand times but whom I still found surprising – surprising for her almost Garboesque cheekbones, for the wink, which I was prepared for and which she had been flashing at audiences for decades but which still felt as though it was directed solely at me.

More tangible evidence of her life than this fleeting celluloid memento quickly disappeared after Marie's death as her possessions became as sought after as holy relics. The Second World War performer and great-niece of Marie Mary Logan believes she has the diamanté-topped cane Marie used in her 'Directoire' act. It has also been suggested that Norman Wisdom's silver-topped stick, which was given to him by another performer as a good-luck charm, may once have belonged to Marie. Other accounts claim that her cane was buried with her. The cage with the old cock linnet that she used for 'My Old Man' disappeared after her death too.

One artefact that remains is an empty champagne bottle, which sits above the fireplace in the saloon bar of the Warrington pub in Maida Vale, north-west London. The pub is said to have been one of Marie's regular haunts, perhaps on her way home from the Metropolitan in Edgware Road, and the bottle one of the many she emptied during a life that she wanted her public to believe was measured by champagne glasses.

NOTE ON SOURCES

Of the four existing Marie Lloyd biographies, the first two, by her friends Walter Macqueen-Pope and Naomi Jacob in 1936 and 1947 respectively, present a romanticized picture of both Marie and music hall. It is probably not putting it too strongly to say that Naomi Jacob, who was known as 'Mickie', was infatuated with Marie. She was also, by her own admission, hazy about several parts of Marie's life.

Daniel Farson, writing in 1972, was fortunate enough to be able to interview many of the people who had played a key part in Marie's life and to view his subject with greater dispassion. By the time Richard Anthony Baker wrote his biography in 1990 there were fewer survivors of the music-hall era, but his book chronicles Marie's life in an accurate and entertaining way.

I have been wary of the information in the two earliest biographies and only quoted them when I considered that the authors were likely to have had inside knowledge of Marie's life. Farson's biography is most useful for its first-hand interviews with contemporaries and I have made it clear in the text when I have quoted these sources.

It would be impossible to attempt a biography of any music-hall star without thorough reference to the *Era*, a weekly publication that covered theatre, music hall and, later, cinema. As well as detailing which halls a performer was playing, the *Era* provides an insight into the main issues and gossip concerning the music-hall world, although it frequently took the managers' side. As a balance to the *Era* I have drawn on several other music-hall and theatrical publications including the *London Entr'acte*, the *Stage* and the *Performer*.

Music-hall artists were not great letter writers, nor did they leave behind them diaries. A series of articles written by Alice Lloyd for *Lloyds Sunday News*, in the weeks immediately following Marie's death, offer an interesting perspective on her life but, again, are not always to be trusted for accuracy.

The following museums, theatres and collections have been invaluable in my research for this book and I am most grateful to their staff for their help: African Studies Centre, Cambridge University; Bibliothèque de l'Arsenal, Paris; Billy Rose Theater Collection, the New York Public Library for the Performing Arts; London Borough of Barnet; British Library; British Library Newspaper Collection at Colindale; Cambridge University Library; Central Reference Library, Westminster; Ellis Island Museum, New York; Local History Archives, Enfield; Family Records Centre, Islington; Guildhall Library, London; Hackney Archives; Harvard Theater Collection, Harvard University; Hastings Public Library; Local Studies and Archives, Hendon Library; Keith/Albee Collection, Special Collections, University of Iowa Libraries; University of Iowa; Liverpool Record Office; Mander and Mitchenson Collection; Museum of the City of New York; Museum of London; National Maritime Museum, Greenwich; Performing Arts Museum, Victorian Arts Centre, Melbourne, Australia; Public Record Office; Racing Collection, Newmarket Library; the Royal Collection Trust, Windsor Castle; the Salvation Army, International Heritage Centre; Reference Department, South African Library; Theatre Museum, London; Trade Union Congress Library; Wellcome Institute Library; Zentral und Landesbibliothek, Berlin.

Note
The Bank of England's *Equivalent Contemporary Value of the Pound: A Historical Series 1270 to 1998* has been used. The equivalent 1998 value has been given in brackets immediately following the historical value.

Dollar to Pound Conversion Rates
A pound in 1894 was worth US$4.862.
A pound in 1897 was worth US$4.839.
A pound in 1907 was worth US$4.867.
A pound in 1913 was worth US$4.868.
A pound in 1915 was worth US$4.748.

Source: Bank of England.

NOTES

Full bibliographical details of publications mentioned in these notes appear
in the Bibliography, pages 304–12.

Prologue: The Funeral of Marie Lloyd
  1. *Era.* 19 October 1922.
  2. *Era,* 19 October 1922.
  3. *Hampstead and St John's Wood Advertiser,* 19 October 1922.
  4. *Daily Mail,* 13 October 1922.
  5. A. France & Son is still run as a family business and operates from
     discreetly old-fashioned premises in London's Lamb's Conduit Street
     where an enlarged copy of a newspaper report of 1804 'advertises'
     France's involvement in Nelson's funeral. Marie Lloyd remains their
     most famous customer of modern times.
  6. Alice Lloyd, *Lloyds Sunday News,* 5 November 1922.
  7. Later Marie was joined at Hampstead Cemetery by her friend Arthur
     Prince, the first ventriloquist to perfect the art of drinking and
     talking at the same time. His dummy, Jim, is buried with him. Other
     notable residents of Hampstead Cemetery include Grand Duke
     Michael of Russia; George Careless Trewby, who built the largest
     gasworks in the world at Beckton, East London; Samuel Palmer, one
     of the founders of the biscuit company, Huntley and Palmer;
     children's writer and illustrator Kate Greenaway; Florence Upton,
     creator of the golliwog; Laszlo Biro, inventor of the pen; and actors
     Fred Terry, Dame Gladys Cooper and Rex Harrison's wife Lilli
     Palmer.

1: Early Life in Hoxton (1870–85)
  1. From Marie Lloyd, 'How I became a serio', in Park and Stuart,
     Variety Stars, p. 6.
  2. The School Board for London, Inspector's Report, Finsbury Division,

Bath Street School, quoted in Baker, *Marie Lloyd – Queen of the Music-halls*, p. 12.

3. See the *Era*, 28 October 1893, and 6 February 1904.
4. Jacobs, *Our Marie*, p. 47.
5. 'How I Became a Serio', *Variety Stars*, p. 6.
6. According to Marie's 'How I Became a Serio', Matilda Wood had also been on the stage before she was married. But Marie told a reporter in 1893: 'If my mother had gone on the stage she'd have shown 'em something. But she didn't, you see. She contented herself with bringing us up and bringing us out. She's always suggesting and criticizing, is Ma' (*Era*, 28 October 1893).
7. In *Green Room Gossip*, page 161, by Archibald Haddon, Marie said she made her début at a free and easy at the Eagle. In interviews in the *Era*, 28 October 1893 and 11 February 1899, Marie said she preferred to date her career from her first appearance at the Falstaff.
8. The Salvation Army had several close encounters with music hall and General Booth, who was reported to have said, 'Why should the devil have all the best tunes?', capitalized on the popularity of music-hall songs by adopting their lyrics for Christian purposes. Charles Coborn's 'Two Lovely Black Eyes' became 'My Jesus Has Died'; Alec Hurley's 'I Ain't A-going To Tell' was transformed to 'I Ain't A-going To Hell' and 'Champagne Charlie Is My Name' became 'Bless His Name, He Sets Me Free'. See the *Call Boy*, summer 1998.
9. Seamus Cassidy, 'L is for Laughter', *Guardian*, 23 May 1997.

2. Playing the Halls (1885–7)

1. *Era*, 21 January 1893.
2. *London Entr'acte*, 15 August 1885.
3. *London Entr'acte*, 26 September 1885.
4. *Era*, 10 October 1885.
5. Jerome K. Jerome, 'Variety Patter' in the *Idler*, March 1892.
6. *Era*, 16 January 1886.
7. Robinson, *Chaplin*, p. 7.
8. *London Entr'acte*, 23 October 1886.
9. *Era*, 9 July 1887.
10. Foster, *The Spice of Life*, p. 58.

11. *Era*, 24 December 1887.
12. *Era*, 7 January 1888.
13. *Era*, 19 September 1891.
14. Fields and Fields, *From the Bowery to Broadway*, p. 247, and Louvish, *Man on the Flying Trapeze*, p. 174.
15. *Era*, 30 November 1901 – a cast of his body was taken.

3: Developing an Act (the late 1880s)
1. *Era*, 2 August 1890.
2. Marie Lloyd, 'How I Became a Serio', in Park and Stuart, *Variety Stars*, p. 6.
3. George Foster, *The Spice of Life*, p. 59.
4. 55, Graham Road has since been divided into flats, and in 1977 a blue plaque was erected bearing the inscription, 'Marie Lloyd (1870–1922), music-hall artiste, lived here'.
5. Alice Lloyd, in *Lloyds Sunday News*.
6. *The Uncommercial Traveller*, p. 33.
7. Barry and Stanley Lupino's nephew, Lupino Lane, took his great-aunt's surname and became a star of musical comedy, most notably as Bill Snibson in *Me and My Girl* in which he created the dance known as the Lambeth Walk.
8. *Era*, 1 September 1888.
9. *Era*, 26 September 1896.
10. *Era*, 15 August 1885.
11. 'Variety Patter', in the *Idler*, March 1892.
12. *Era*, 12 January 1889.

4: A Proper Pantomime (1890–91)
1. From Fred Stone, *Rolling Stone* (1945), quoted by Zellers, *Tony Pastor, Dean of the Vaudeville Stage*, p. 72.
2. *London Entr'acte*, 23 May 1891.
3. *Era*, 3 January 1891.
4. *Era*, 11 January 1890.
5. *London Entr'acte*, 24 January 1891.
6. *London Entra'acte*, 14 February 1891.
7. *Vanity Fair*, September 1889.
8. *Strand*, February 1912.

9. *The Times*, 28 December 1891.

10. *Era*, 2 January 1892.

11. *Era*, 2 January 1892.

12. *Saturday Review*, 2 January 1892.

13. *London Entr'acte*, 2 January 1892.

14. *The Times*, 28 December 1891.

15. *Saturday Review*, 2 January 1892.

16. *Dwarf*, 5 January 1892.

17. The reference to Compton Mackenzie is from *My Life and Times* (Octave 1, 1883–1891). He erroneously dates his visit to *Humpty Dumpty* as January 1891 but in a later volume of his memoirs, *My Life and Times*, Octave 2 (1891–1900) concedes that he must have got the date wrong.

18. Ernest Shepard, *Drawn from Memory*, p. 172.

5: Celebrity Status (1891–2)

1. *Era*, 12 September 1891.

2. 'Music Hall Melodies', in Park and Stuart, *Variety Stars*, p. 36.

3. *Manchester Empire*, quoted in *London Entr'acte*, 25 July 1891.

4. For description of the masked ball see *Dwarf*, 26 January 1892.

5. *The Times*, 19 January 1892.

6: Twiggy Voo, My Boys? (1891–2)

1. See *The Piano: A History*, Cyril Ehrlich, p. 10.

2. Ibid., p. 91.

3. *Era*, 13 March 1886.

4. *Music in London*, 19 October 1892.

5. See *The Piano*, p. 96.

6. For the early history of the *News of the World*, see *The News of the World Story*, Cyril Bainbridge and Roy Stockdill, and *Tickle the Public* by Matthew Engel.

7. *Era*, 20 February 1904. For another example, see, 'P.S. Many thanks to Mr E Hyman for stopping artistes singing my songs previous to my opening in Johannesburg. Have been asked especially to sing "Johnny Jones" song to let the public there see the way it should be sung – not murdered, as it was by a certain artiste out there.' *Era*, 30 January 1897.

8. *Era*, 3 September 1892.

9. Cyril Ehrlich, *The Music Profession in Britain Since the Eighteenth Century*, p. 56.

10. In 1900 Oswald Stoll merged his interests with Moss and Thornton to become Moss Empires.

11. *Theatre*, 1 February 1893.

12. *Athenaeum*, 31 December 1892. The *Saturday Review* (31 December 1892) followed a review of *Little Bo-Peep* by praising *Dick Whittington* at the New Olympic Theatre: '... The variety element is, happily, entirely unrepresented at the New Olympic, the management of which is, to that extent at least, entitled to our hearty thanks.'

13. Max Beerbohm to Reggie Turner, January 1893, *Letters to Reggie*.

7: Maid of London (1893–6)

1. *Sketch*, 30 August 1893.

2. *Era*, 28 October 1893.

3. Farson, *Marie Lloyd and Music Hall*, p. 53.

4. Ibid.

5. De Frece, *Recollections of Vesta Tilley*, p. 19.

6. Boardman, *Vaudeville Days*, p. 88.

7. Roberts, *50 Years of Spoof*, p. 88.

8. H. G. Hibbert, *Playgoers' Memories*, p. 205, and the *Westminster Budget*, 16 February 1893.

9. *Sketch*, 3 January 1894.

10. Naomi Jacobs attributes this story to Dan Leno. See *Our Marie*, p. 82.

8: The Battle for the Empire (1894)

1. *Era*, 20 January 1894.

2. From *The Referee*, date unknown, quoted in Mrs Ormiston Chant's *Why We Attacked the Empire*.

3. *Era*, 16 June 1894. The attack was reported in full.

4. *Era*, 29 September 1894.

5. *New York Mail and Express*, quoted in the *Era*, 20 October 1894.

6. *Era*, 20 October 1894.

7. *Liverpool Review*, 29 December 1894.

9: Charges of Immorality (1895–6)

1. See Max Tyler, 'Looking for Trilby', in the *Call Boy*, (spring 1995) vol. 33, no. 1.
2. As early as 1886 Oscar Wilde's wife, Constance, attended a meeting about rational dress at Westminster Town Hall. In 1893, the sixteen-year-old Tessie Reynolds caused consternation by cycling from Brighton to London and back in eight and a half hours wearing baggy trousers.
3. *Sketch*, 25 December 1895.
4. Ibid.
5. *Era*, 1 March 1890.
6. *Era*, 18 April 1891.
7. *Era*, 3 September 1892.
8. Naomi Jacobs says that Alice and Tom married on 16 January 1905, but on 14 March 1896 the *Era* reported that Alice and Tom had married two years previously. On 9 November 1901 the *Era* referred to Alice and her husband.
9. *New York Telegraph*, 10 May 1909.
10. *Variety*, 22 July 1911.
11. *Era* 13 February 1908. Lawyer: 'What time was it?' Tom: 'It struck twelve and we struck the lamp-post.'
12. See Tracy Davis, in Foulkes (ed.) *British Theatre in the 1890s*, p. 124.
13. Alice Lloyd in *Lloyds Sunday News*.
14. The Norton case was reported in the *Era*, 21 March 1896.

10: Taking the Empire Abroad (1897)

1. *Era*, 30 January 1897.
2. *Era*, 30 January 1897.
3. At a benefit held at the Middlesex for the United Costermongers' Society in 1895.
4. *South Africa*, 27 March 1897.
5. *Lloyds Sunday News*.
6. *South Africa*, 22 May 1897.
7. Swaffer, *Fleet Street Goes Racing*, p. 21.
8. *South Africa*, 8 May 1897.
9. *South Africa*, 29 May 1897.
10. *Era*, 16 October 1897.

11. Reproduced in the *Era*, 16 October 1897.
12. The Billy Rose Theater Collection of the New York Library for the Performing Arts.

11: Alec Hurley and the Family Years (1898–1900)

1. For Alec's early life see *Music Hall*, issue 9, and Logan, *Bring on the Dancing Girls*, p. 8.
2. When actor Robert Lister devised a one-man show in the 1980s about Alec, called *Mr Marie Lloyd*, he felt compelled to leave out several hits because he sensed today's audience would be unable to stomach them.
3. Quoted in Fisher, *Funny Way to be a Hero*, p. 51.
4. *Era*, 29 June 1895.
5. *Era*, 22 February 1896.
6. *Era*, 18 March 1899.
7. *Era*, 1 January 1898.
8. Description of Royal Cambridge Music Hall from the *Era*, 1 January 1898.
9. *Era*, 2 April 1898.
10. See Jacobs, *Our Marie*, pp. 95 and 98.
11. *Era*, 29 April 1899.
12. *Hastings Standard*, 5 April 1899.
13. *Era*, 12 November 1898.
14. 'Jingoism': from a popular music-hall song performed by G. H. MacDermott during the Russo-Turkish War of 1877–8 – 'We don't want to fight, but by Jingo if we do . . .'
15. When Edwin Samuel Barnes, the manager of Collins's, was accused by the owners of financial impropriety – including keeping for himself Marie's salary – he claimed she had been unable to arrive at the hall because the streets were so crowded with people celebrating the relief of Mafeking. See *Era*, 14 December 1901.
16. *Era*, 9 June 1900.
17. See *London Town*, p. 13 for anthill story.

12: A Measure of Indistinctness – Australia (1901)

1. The farewell party and her preparations for the tour were reported in minute detail; see, in particular, the *Register, Adelaide*. It devoted

several column inches to descriptions of the dresses she was bringing to Australia and which were expected to create a 'furore'. It added: 'There is a perfectly exquisite Geisha dress, in pale eau-de-Nil satin and rose pink, made, of course, in approved Japanese fashion and worn with chrysanthemums. The satin of which it is composed is most beautifully embroidered with figures, flowers, and birds worked in coloured silks. There must be hours and hours of work in it' (2 March 1901).

2. *Era*, 16 February 1901.
3. Ibid.
4. Alice Lloyd, in *Lloyds Sunday News*.
5. Ibid. Alice does not say which of Alec's brothers went with them to Australia.
6. Ibid.
7. *Register, Adelaide*, 26 March 1901.
8. *Man on the Flying Trapeze*, Simon Louvish, p. 112.
9. Quoted in Lacour-Gayet, *A Concise History of Australia*, p. 272.
10. *Sydney Morning Herald*, 8 April 1901.
11. *Australasian*, 25 May 1901.
12. From scrapbooks, Performing Arts Museum, Victorian Arts Centre, Melbourne.
13. *Argus*, 20 May 1901.
14. *Age*, 20 May 1901.
15. *Australasian*, 25 May 1901.
16. *Argus*, 20 May 1901.
17. *Australasian*, 25 May 1901.
18. *Sydney Morning Herald*, 8 April 1901.
19. *Register, Adelaide*, 26 March 1901.
20. Alice Lloyd, in *Lloyds Sunday News*.
21. *Era*, 19 October 1901.

23: Bella's Troubles (1901–2)
1. *Daily Chronicle*, 18 February 1902.
2. *Era*, 30 November 1901.
3. *Daily Express*, 26 November 1901.
4. *Era*, 23 November 1901.
5. *Daily Mail*, 18 February 1902.

6. Bell, *Bella of Blackfriars*, p. 57.
7. Farson, *Marie Lloyd and Music Hall*, p. 107.

14: Changing Tastes (1902–5)

1. *Era*, 16 August 1902.
2. In 1903 Marie produced three single-sided records for the Gramophone and Typewriter label. She also recorded 'Every Little Movement Has A Meaning Of Its Own' and 'I'd Like To Live In Paris All The Time' on the Regal Zonophone; 'A Little Of What You Fancy Does You Good', 'The Three Ages Of Women', 'Now You've Got Yer Khaki On' and 'If You Want To Get On In Revue' on the Regal Gramophone; and 'The Twiddley Wink', 'When I Take My Morning Promenade', 'The Piccadilly Trot' and 'Put On Your Slippers' on the Zonophone label. See the CD, *'A Little of What You Fancy' – the Marie Lloyd Record*, LC 1836/GEMM CD 9097, Pearl, Pavilion Records Ltd. There may have been more recordings, which were lost during the Second World War.
3. *Era*, 3 January 1903.
4. Marie's niece, Tomme Thomas, gave me this anecdote.
5. Quoted in Chanan, *The Dream that Kicks*, p. 144.
6. Hibbert, *Fifty Years of a Londoner's Life*, p. 56.
7. Fisher, *Funny Way to Be a Hero*, p. 98.
8. Quoted in Brandreth, *The Funniest Man on Earth: the Story of Dan Leno*, p. 85.
9. Disher, *Winkles and Champagne*, p. 50.
10. Quoted in Cheshire, *Music Hall in Britain*, p. 69.
11. Quoted in *The Funniest Man on Earth*, p. 46.
12. Porter, *London, a Social History*, p. 316.
13. Hibbert, *Fifty Years of a Londoner's Life*. p. 137.

15: Trouble Brewing (1906–7)

1. Jacobs, *Our Marie*, p. 142.
2. Rose, *Red Plush and Greasepaint*, p. 29.
3. Baker, *Marie Lloyd, Queen of the Music-halls*, n. 16, p. 185.
4. See *Era*, 20 January 1906, for list of donations to George le Brunn's fund.
5. *Era*, 2 February 1907.

6. *Era*, 6 May 1899. Details of which manager or hall were not given.

7. *Era*, 26 September 1903.

8. *Stage*, 4 June 1906, quoted in Walsh, *A Lost Leader*, p. 19.

9. Booth, *Master and Men, Pink'un Yesterdays*, p. 299.

10. See the *Era*, 25 April 1908 for advert concerning her age.

11. A search of the record of deaths in the Family Records Office in Islington produced the Charles Percy Courtenay mentioned here, but a letter to the local newspaper the *Brighton Argus* asking for information drew a blank, as did another to the local history society. It seems that Percy did not want to be remembered as Marie's first husband.

12. *Era*, 3 November 1906.

16: Strike (1906–7)

1. Honri, introduction to *Music Hall Warriors*.

2. Walsh, *A Lost Leader*, p. 43.

3. Marsh and Ryan, *Historical Directory of Trade Unions*, vol. 1, p. 224. The *Daily Telegraph*, 15 February 1907, confirmed that twenty-two halls were affected. Lord Askwith said that, at the height of the strike, twenty-two London theatres were picketed and 2,500 performers took to the streets – Askwith, *Industrial Problems and Disputes*, p. 104.

4. R. A. Leeson, *Strike*, p. 48. A year after the strike ended Karno reluctantly signed up Charlie Chaplin, at the insistence of Charlie's brother, who was already working for him.

5. *Era*, 26 January 1907.

6. Farson, *Marie Lloyd and Music Hall*, p. 84.

7. *Call Boy*, autumn 1996, vol. 33, no. 3.

8. Dexter, *The Riddle of Chung Ling Soo*, p. 72.

9. *Performer*, 31 January 1907.

10. *Punch*, 30 January 1907.

11. Honri, *Working the Halls*, p. 127.

12. *Daily Telegraph*, 24 January 1907.

13. *Sphere*, 2 February 1907.

14. *Daily Telegraph*, 25 January 1907.

15. *Performer*, 7 February 1907.

16. *Era*, 2 February 1907.

17. *Era*, 9 February 1907.

18. *Performer*, 7 February 1907.

19. *Era*, 9 February 1907.

20. *Era*, 16 February 1907.

21. Askwith, *Industrial Problems and Disputes*, p. 103.

22. Arbitration-hearing transcript, quoted in Honri, *Music-hall Warriors*, p. 72.

23. Ibid., p. 73.

24. Ibid., p. 71.

25. *Era*, 16 February 1907.

26. Jacobs, *Our Marie*, p. 225.

27. Ibid., p. 62.

28. Farson, *Marie Lloyd and Music Hall*, p. 169. The story loses some of its impact as Marie is said to overhear her singing on the theatre PA system and they were both on the same bill.

29. For more detail of Little Tich and his complicated private life see Tich and Findlater, *Little Tich: Giant of the Music Hall*.

17: Alice Lloyd's Sister Goes to New York (1907)

1. Alice Lloyd in *Lloyds Sunday News*.

2. Boardman, *Vaudeville Days*, p. 45.

3. Baker, *Marie Lloyd: Queen of the Music-halls*, p. 109.

4. *Morning Telegraph*, 13 October 1907.

5. *New York Star*, 7 November 1908. Percy also managed the Orpheum in Boston and the Novelty in Williamsburg.

6. *New York Telegraph*, 20 October 1907. Cliff Gordon was on the same bill as Marie at the Colonial and appeared as 'The German Senator'.

7. *Brooklyn Daily Eagle*, 8 March 1907, quoted in Baker, *Marie Lloyd, Queen of the Music-halls*, p. 109.

8. Quoted in Honri, *Music Hall Warriors*, p. 71.

9. *Boston Traveller*, undated cutting in the Robinson Locke Collection, Billy Rose Theater Collection.

10. Obituary, probably in *Variety*, 23 November 1949.

11. *New York Telegraph*, 29 October 1907.

12. *New York Evening Telegraph*, undated cutting, Billy Rose Theater Collection, and *New York Telegraph*, 2 October 1907.

13. *New York World*, undated cutting, Billy Rose Theater Collection.

14. *Boston Transcript*, undated cutting, Billy Rose Theater Collection.

15. *Morning Telegraph*, 13 October 1907.

16. *Variety*, 12 October 1907.

17. *Variety*, 19 October 1907.

18. *Era*, 7 December 1907.

19. Alan Dale, in *New York American*, 9 October 1907.

20. *Pittsburgh Leader*, 24 January 1904.

21. *Vanity Fair*, March 1908.

22. *New York Telegraph*, 26 October 1907.

23. *New York Mirror*, 2 November 1908.

24. *New York Telegraph*, 24 November 1907.

25. *Era*, 14 December 1907. According to Logan, *Bring On the Dancing Girls*, p. 13, Alfred eventually emigrated to Australia, returning home ten years later a rich man.

26. *Boston Herald*, 15 December 1907.

27. Keith/Albee Collection, Special Collections Department, University of Iowa Libraries.

28. Ibid.

29. *Variety*, 4 January 1956. Marie and Sime later became good friends.

30. *Era*, 14 March 1908.

31. Unidentified cutting, 20 March 1908, Billy Rose Theater Collection.

32. *Variety*, 28 March 1908.

33. *Variety*, 22 February 1908.

34. *Variety*, 29 February 1908.

35. *New York Mirror*, 29 February 1908.

36. *New York Telegraph*, 22 March 1908.

37. *Pittsburgh Leader*, 19 July 1908.

38. *New York Mirror*, 11 April 1908.

18: Marriage Problems (1908–11)

1. *Era*, 9 June 1906.

2. *Era*, 11 July 1908.

3. *Era*, 30 May 1908.

4. *Era*, 5 February 1910.

5. Sid and Maude Lloyd, the youngest members of the Wood family at twenty-three and eighteen respectively, were already in America when they arrived. *Era*, 8 August 1908.

6. *New York Telegraph*, 27 June 1908.

7. *New York Mirror*, 10 October 1906. For a description of the act see *Variety*, 3 October 1908.

8. *Morning Telegraph*, 27 September 1908.

9. *Variety*, 26 September 1908 and 14 November 1908.

10. Unidentified cutting, Billy Rose Theater Collection.

11. *New York Telegraph*, 6 June 1909.

12. *New York Telegraph*, 6 June 1909.

13. *New York Telegraph*, 15 November 1908.

14. Unidentified cutting, Billy Rose Theater Collection.

15. Reproduced in the *Era*, 20 November 1909.

16. *Era*, 12 October 1907.

17. *Era*, 23 May 1908.

18. *Era*, 24 October 1908. The boy was appearing at the Oxford and was nicknamed 'Piggy'. He seems to have worked as some sort of domestic servant for Marie, although little more was heard of him and he may have returned home to America.

19. *The Green Book*, Billy Rose Theater Collection (1910); *Era*, 31 October 1908.

20. *Era*, 15 November 1909.

21. Holledge, *Innocent Flowers: Women in the Edwardian Theatre*, p. 67.

22. Kenney, *Memories of a Militant*, p. 237; and Richardson, *Laugh a Defiance*, pp. 72–3. I am indebted to Vivien Gardner, of the Department of Drama at Manchester University, for drawing my attention to these references. She also pointed out that a Marie Lloyd appears on the list of early members of the Actresses' Franchise League. This could not have been Marie's French namesake, who died in 1897.

23. *Innocent Flowers*, pp. 56–9; Rowbotham, *A Century of Women*, pp. 8, 12 and 113.

24. Farson, *Marie Lloyd and Music Hall*, p. 87. Farson does not supply a date for this story, which Alec's niece, Joan, told him.

25. *Era*, 24 December 1910.

26. *Era*, 7 January 1911.

27. For details of divorce proceedings see *The Times*, 27 January 1911 and 13 July 1911.

28. *Era*, 2 October 1909.

29. *Era*, 24 March 1910.
30. Hitchcock was said to have based *Rear Window* on the Crippen case; Cullen, *Crippen — the Mild Murderer*, p. 30.
31. Bell, *Bella of Blackfriars*, p. 83.
32. Cullen, *Crippen*, p. 134.
33. Rose, *Red Plush and Greasepaint*, p. 29.

19: Horse-racing (1911)

1. *Daily Express*, 2 June 1910.
2. Moorhouse, *The History and Romance of the Derby*, pp. 26–7.
3. According to the *Era*, 11 June 1910, Marie was performing at the Empire Palace, Edinburgh, that week with a rehearsal at 1.30 a.m. In *Queen of the Music Halls*, Macqueen-Pope says Marie kissed Ben in public on his way to the starting post.
4. Farson, *Marie Lloyd and Music Hall*, p. 109.
5. Elijah Wheatley (1886–1951) won the St Leger on Night Hawk in 1913. Ten years later he went to Egypt where he trained horses until just before he died.
6. The early photojournalist Horace Nicholls captured the atmosphere of Edwardian horse-racing through his stunning photographs – including one of Marie at Ascot – which inspired Cecil Beaton when he designed the set and costumes for *My Fair Lady*.
7. Fisher, *Funny Way To Be A Hero*, p. 98.
8. Charlie Smirke was born in Lambeth, the son of a fruit and fish salesman. He was retained intermittently by the Aga Khan over a thirty-year career before being barred from racing for allegedly 'pulling' a horse. He married three times and ended his career selling ice-creams on the sea-front at Brighton.
9. George Duller (1892–1962) dominated National Hunt hurdle racing in the 1920s. He was also an expert motor-racer.
10. Portland, *Memories of Racing and Hunting*, p. 72.
11. *Sporting Life*, 22 June 1906.
12. In October 1913 Marie told the *Pittsburgh Post* that she had been living with Ben for five years. In the same year she told the *Morning Telegraph* that they had been a couple for six years. This would mean their affair started in 1907–8, a year or two after she had married

Alec. Both undated cuttings are from the Billy Rose Theater Collection.

13. *The Journal of Arnold Bennett*, 1896–1910.
14. *Era*, 27 May 1911.
15. *Era*, 7 September 1911.
16. *Era*, 30 September 1911.

20: Disgrace (1912–13)

1. Unidentified press cutting, probably from *Fry's Magazine*, date unknown.
2. Royal Archives.
3. *Era*, 16 May 1908.
4. *Era*, 13 May 1911.
5. *Era*, 8 June 1912.
6. Ibid.
7. Printed in the *Daily Graphic* and reproduced in the *Era*, 22 June 1912.
8. *Era*, 29 June 1912.
9. *The Times*, 6 June 1913.
10. James Douglas, in the *Daily News*, quoted in the *Era*, 18 January 1913.
11. In *Lloyds Sunday News*, 26 November 1922, Alice later recalled how Marie's friend, the costumier and wig-maker Willy Clarkson, had introduced her to Sarah. This may have been in 1902. Marie Lloyd-Vibert, born Marie-Emilia Jolly (1842–97) was a member of the Comédie Française.
12. Baker, *Marie Lloyd: Queen of the Music-halls*, p. 124.

21: Moral Turpitude (1913–14)

1. Figures on immigration from Statue of Liberty historic resource study, vol. 1.
2. Alice in *Lloyds Sunday News*, 10 December 1922.
3. *New York Sun*, 4 October 1913.
4. Ibid.
5. Ibid.
6. *New York Telegraph*, 27 June 1914.
7. *Toledo Daily Blade*, 3 October 1913.
8. *New York Telegraph*, 17 May 1914.

9. Unidentified cutting, Billy Rose Theater Collection.
10. *Dramatic Mirror*, 8 October 1913.
11. *Dramatic News*, 11 October 1913.
12. *Morning Telegraph*, 14 October 1913.
13. *Variety*, 17 October 1913.
14. *New York Telegraph*, 26 November 1913.
15. Unidentified cutting, Billy Rose Theater Collection.
16. *New York Telegraph*, 26 November 1913.
17. Manager's report from Keith/Albee Collection, Ohio, Iowa University.
18. *Chicago Record Herald*, 11 December 1913.
19. Jacobs, *Our Marie*, p. 165.
20. *Morning Telegraph*, 1913 (day not given).
21. Bell, *Bella of Blackfriars*, p. 115.
22. *Variety*, 5 November 1910.
23. *Vanity Fair*, 18 February 1911.
24. *Chicago Record Herald*, 10 February 1914.
25. *New York Telegraph*, 20 and 22 December 1913.
26. Two unidentified newspaper cuttings, Billy Rose Theater Collection, one headlined 'Poison Paste Jack Dopes Marie Lloyd's Face Cream With Acid'.
27. *Lloyds Sunday News* and the *Era*, 11 February 1914. Alice said the victim was a prominent local man.
28. *Morning Oregonian*, quoted in Baker, *Marie Lloyd: Queen of the Music-halls*, p. 129.
29. *New York Telegraph*, 17 May 1914.

22: War (1914–18)

1. Dennis Wheatley, *Officer and Temporary Gentleman*, p. 36. I am indebted to Robert Gillies for drawing my attention to this reference.
2. Mander and Mitchenson, *Lost Theatres of London*, p. 185.
3. Scott, *Early Doors*, p. 196.
4. *Era*, 23 September 1914.
5. *Era*, 21 October 1914.
6. *Era*, 19 July 1916.
7. Barker, *The House That Stoll Built*, p. 118.
8. *Era*, 17 February 1915.

9. *Era*, 13 September 1916.
10. *Era*, 2 December 1914.
11. *Virginia Woolf Diaries*, 3 January 1915.
12. Thompson, *The Edwardians: The Remaking of British Society*, p. 252.
13. *Era*, 31 May 1916.
14. *Era*, 31 May 1916.
15. *Era*, 1 November 1916.
16. *Era*, 22 September 1915.
17. Alice, in *Lloyds Sunday News*, 24 December 1922.
18. Like other First World War soldiers, Ben's army records do not seem to have survived, but when he appeared in court in 1920 his defence lawyer claimed that Ben had served for two to three years in Mesopotamia. See *Daily Telegraph*, 28 May 1920.
19. *The Times*, 29 July 1916.
20. *The Times*, 14 September 1916.
21. *Era*, 26 September 1917.
22. *Era*, 11 July 1917.
23. Quoted in Agate, *Ego 5*, p. 223.
24. Unidentified newspaper cutting, dated 13 May 1915, Billy Rose Theater Collection.
25. *Era*, 29 August 1917.
26. *The Times*, 5 June 1917.
27. *The Times*, 8 June 1917.
28. *The Times*, 13 October 1917.
29. *The Times*, 21 November 1917.

23: A Crowded Hour of Life (1918–21)

1. *Era*, 30 October 1918.
2. *Era*, 10 December 1919.
3. *Era*, 10 September 1919.
4. Farson, *Marie Lloyd and Music Hall*, p. 110.
5. Ibid., p. 122. Farson says that a freelance journalist, George Godwin, saw her in her coffin and that Alice explained the reason for the missing tooth.
6. *Era*, 10 March 1920.
7. *The Times*, 19 March 1920.
8. *Marie Lloyd and Music Hall*, p. 111.

9. *The Times*, 3 July 1920.

10. *The Times* and *Daily Telegraph*, 28 May 1920.

11. *Marie Lloyd and Music Hall*, p. 112.

12. Bell, *Bella of Blackfriars*, p. 156.

13. *New York Times*, 15 September 1920.

14. I am grateful to Johnny's grandson, Dick Mott, for allowing me to see this notebook and to Alec Hurley's great-nephew, Colin Devereaux, for showing me Marie's tax figures.

15. Unidentified cutting, Billy Rose Theater Collection.

16. Jacobs, *Our Marie*, p. 272–3.

17. *Bella of Blackfriars*, p. 155.

18. Brough, *Educating Archie*, p. 11.

19. *Era*, 17 August 1921.

20. *Era*, 23 August 1922.

21. During a performance of *Mr Tower at London* at the Empire, Edmonton, in 1926, a double-decker Tilling bus was wheeled on to the stage bearing, among others, Gracie Fields. The Empire was later bought by Gaumont, but leased to Sidney Bernstein of Granada. It was completely rebuilt in 1933, and sound equipment installed to enable 'talkies' to be shown. The gilt and plush were ripped out in favour of sleek new greys, silver and blues, but the canopy that had sheltered queues of patient music-hall customers was retained. Dwindling cinema audiences led to its closure on 13 July 1968. A brief period as a bingo hall followed before it was finally demolished in 1970.

22. *Era*, 12 October 1922.

23. *Tottenham and Edmonton Herald*, 13 October 1958.

24. Moorehead, *Sidney Bernstein, a Biography*, p. 18; and *Hendon Times*, 13 October 1922.

25. According to his son Dr Benjafield never spoke of the incident to his family although she must surely have been the most famous patient he treated.

26. *Tottenham and Edmonton Herald*, 3 October 1958.

27. *Sidney Bernstein*, p. 18.

28. *Tottenham and Edmonton Weekly Herald*, 13 October 1922.

Epilogue: Who Killed Marie Lloyd?

1. Roberts, *Fifty Years of Spoof*, p. 92.
2. *Our Marie*, p. 240.
3. Macqueen-Pope, *Queen of the Music Halls*, p. 166.
4. Farson, *Marie Lloyd and Music Hall*, p. 121.
5. Ellmann, *Wilde*, p. 89.
6. Agate, *Ego 2*, p. 189.
7. *Queen of the Music Halls*, p. 170.
8. Eliot, *Selected Essays*, p. 458.
9. Jameson, *No Time Like the Present*, p. 74.
10. *Daily Mail*, 9 October 1922.
11. *Time and Tide*, 7 September 1940.
12. Gielgud, *Backward Glances*, p. 201.

BIBLIOGRAPHY

Aaron, Charles D. *Diseases of the digestive organs with special reference to their diagnosis and treatment*, H. K. Lewis & Co. Ltd., London, 1921

Agate, James. *Alarums and excursions*, Grant Richards Ltd., 1922

Agate, James. *Ego*, Hamish Hamilton, London, 1935

Agate, James. *Ego 2*, Victor Gollancz, London, 1936

Agate, James. *Ego 5*, G. G. Harrap & Co. Ltd., London, 1942

Agate, James. *Ego 9*, G. G. Harrap & Co. Ltd., London, 1946

Agate, James. *Here's Richness!* G. G. Harrap & Co. Ltd., London, 1942

Anderson, Roy. *White Star*, T. Stephenson & Sons, London, 1964

Askwith, George Rankin. *Industrial Problems and Disputes*, Introduction by Roger Davidson, The Harvester Press, Brighton, 1974

Bailey, Peter. *Leisure and Class in Victorian England, Rational Recreation and the Contest for Control 1830–1885*, Methuen, London, 1987

Bailey, Peter (ed.), *Music Hall: The Business of Pleasure*, Open University Press, Milton Keynes and Philadelphia, 1986

Bainbridge, Cyril, and Roy Stockdill. *The News of the World Story. 150 Years of the World's Best-selling Newspaper*, HarperCollins, London, 1993

Baker, Richard Anthony. *Marie Lloyd, Queen of the Music-halls*, Robert Hale, London, 1990

Barker, Felix. *The House That Stoll Built, the Story of the Coliseum Theatre*, Muller, London, 1957

Baron, Wendy. *Sickert, paintings, drawings and prints of Walter Richard Sickert, 1860–1942*, Arts Council of Great Britain, London, 1977

Baron, Wendy and Richard Shone (eds). *Sickert: Paintings*, Royal Academy of Arts, London; Yale University Press, New Haven, 1992

Barry, Margaret and Nimmo Law. *Magnates and Mansions – Johannesburgh 1886–1914*, Lowry: Thorold's Africana Books, Johannesburg, 1985

Beerbohm, Sir Max. *Letters to Reggie Turner*, Rupert Hart-Davis, London, 1964

Beerbohm, Sir Max and William Rothenstein. *Max and Will, Their Friendship and Letters (1893–1945)*, John Murray, London, 1975

Behrman, Samuel Nathaniel. *Conversation with Max*, Hamish Hamilton, London, 1960

Bell, Anne Olivier. *The Diary of Virginia Woolf*, Hogarth Press, London, 1978

Bell, Leslie. *Bella of Blackfriars*, Odhams Press, London, 1961

Bennett, Arnold. *The Journal of Arnold Bennett, 1896–1910*, Viking Press, New York, 1932

Blow, Sydney. *Sydney Blow Presents: Through Stagedoors, or Memories of Two in the Theatre*, W. & R. Chambers, London, 1958

Boardman, William (Billy). *Vaudeville Days*, Jarrolds, London, 1935

Bonynge, Richard. *A Collector's Guide To Theatrical Postcards*, BT Batsford, London, 1988

Bonsor, N. R. P. *North Atlantic Seaway*, T. Stephenson, Prescot, 1955

Booth, Charles. *Life and Labour of the People in London*, vol. III, Macmillan, London, 1903

Booth, J. B. *A Pink'Un Remembers*, Werner Laurie, London, 1937

Booth, J. B. *London Town*, Werner Laurie, London, 1929

Booth, J. B. *Master and Men, Pink'Un Yesterdays*, Werner Laurie, London, 1926

Booth, J. B. *The Days We Knew*, Werner Laurie, London, 1943

Brough, Peter. *Educating Archie*, Stanley Paul & Co., London, 1955

Brandreth, Gyles. *The Funniest Man on Earth: the Story of Dan Leno*, Hamilton, London, 1977

Bratton, J. S. (ed.). *Music Hall: Performance and Style*, Open University Press, Milton Keynes and Philadelphia, 1986

Briggs, Asa. *Victorian Cities*, Pelican Books, London, 1968

Brinnen, John Malcolm. *The Sway of the Grand Saloon, A Social History of the North Atlantic*, Macmillan, London, 1971

Brisbane, Katharine. *Entertaining Australia – an Illustrated History*, Currency Press

Buckland, Gail. *The Golden Summer – The Edwardian Photographs of Horace W. Nicholls*, Pavilion, London, 1989

Busby, Roy. *British Music Hall – an Illustrated Who's Who from 1850 to the Present Day*, Paul Elek, London, 1976

Camden History Society. *The Streets of West Hampsted*, Camden History Society, London, 1992

Camden History Society. *The Streets of Belsize*, Camden History Society, London, 1991

Camden History Society. *Hampstead Cemetery Tomb Trail*, Camden History Society, London, 1994

Chanan, Michael. *The Dream That Kicks, the Pre-history and Early Years of Cinema in Britain*, Routledge, London, 1996

Chant, Ormiston. *Why We Attacked the Empire*, L. Marshall & Son, London, 1895

Cheshire, D. F. *Music Hall in Britain*, David & Charles, Newton Abbot, 1974

Chilvers, Hedley A. *Out of the Crucible*, Cassell, London, 1929

Churchill, Winston. *My Early Life*, Macmillan, London, 1930

Coborn, Charles. *The Man Who Broke the Bank*, L. Hutchinson, London, 1928

Cook, Arthur E. *Immigration Laws of the United States*, vol. I, 1915–1919, and vol. II, 1920–24, Callaghan and Company, 1929, Chicago

Cullen, Tom. *Crippen – the Mild Murderer*, Penguin, Harmondsworth, 1977

Davis, Rob, Sipho Dlamina and Dan O'Meara. *The Struggle for South Africa*, Zed, London, 1984

Davis, Jim (ed.). *The Britannia Diaries of Frederick Wilton*, Society for Theatre Research, London, 1992

Davis, Tracy C. *Actresses as Working Women*, Routledge, London and New York, 1991

De Frece, Lady. *Recollections by Lady de Frece*, Hutchinson, London, 1934

De Moubray, Jocelyn. *Horse-racing and Racing Society: Who Belongs and How It Works*, Sidgwick & Jackson, London, 1985

Dexter, Will. *The Riddle of Chung Ling Soo*, Arco Publishers, London and New York, 1955

Dickens, Charles. *Sketches by Boz*, Macmillan & Co., London, 1958

Dickens, Charles. *The Uncommercial Traveller*, T. Nelson & Sons, London, 1925

Disher, Maurice Willson. *Winkles & Champagne*, BT Batsford, London, 1938

Dixon, Roger, and Stefan Muthesius. *Victorian Architecture*, Thames and Hudson, London, 1978

Ehrlich, Cyril. *The Music Profession in Britain Since the Eighteenth Century: a Social History*, Clarendon Press, Oxford, 1985

Ehrlich, Cyril. *The Piano, A History*, Clarendon Press, Oxford, 1990

Eliot, T. S. *Selected Essays*, Faber and Faber, London, 1951

Ellmann, Richard. *Oscar Wilde*, Hamish Hamilton, London, 1987

Emmons, Robert. *The Life and Opinions of Walter Richard Sickert*, Lund Humphries, London 1941

Engel, Matthew. *Tickle the Public: One Hundred Years of the Popular Press*, Victor Gollancz, London, 1996

Era Almanack, 1899

Farson, Daniel. *Marie Lloyd and Music Hall*, Tom Stacey, London, 1972

Fields, Armond and Marc. *From the Bower to Broadway, Lew Fields and the Roots of American Popular Theater*, Oxford University Press, 1993

Fisher, John. *Funny Way To Be a Hero*, Frederick Muller, London, 1973

Foulkes, Richard (ed.). *British Theatre in the 1890s*, Cambridge University Press, 1992

Furbank, P. N. *E. M. Forster: A Life, vol. 1*, Cardinal, London, 1977

Gardner, Viv (ed.). *Sketches from the Actresses' Franchise League*, Nottingham Drama Texts, 1985

Gelatt, Roland. *The Fabulous Phonograph 1877–1977*, Cassell, London, 1977

Gibbon, Sir Ioan Gwilym, and Reginald Bell. *History of the London County Council (1889–1939)*, Macmillan, London, 1939

Gielgud, John. *Backward Glances*, Sceptre, London, 1993

Glasstone, Victor. *Victorian and Edwardian Theatres*, Thames and Hudson, London, 1975

Glover, J. M. *Jimmy Glover and his friends*, Chatto & Windus, London, 1913

Green, Benny (ed.). *The Last Empires*, Pavilion, London, 1986

Green, Jonathon. *Slang Down the Ages: the Historical Development of Slang*, Kyle Cathie, London, 1993

Grossmith, George Weedon. *The Diary of a Nobody*, Penguin, Harmondsworth, 1983 (first published 1892)

Haddon, Archibald. *Green Room Gossip*, Stanley Paul, London, 1922

Haill, Catherine. *Fun Without Vulgarity – Victorian and Edwardian Popular Entertainment Posters*, HMSO, London, 1997

Haill, Catherine. *Victorian Illustrated Music Sheets*, HMSO, London, 1981

Harding, James. *George Robey and the Music Hall*, Hodder & Stoughton, London, 1990

Hartnoll, Phyllis (ed.). *The Oxford Companion to the Theatre*, Oxford University Press, Oxford, 1993

Hatton, Joseph. *In Jest and Ernest, a Book of Gossip*, Leadenhall Press, London, 1893

Haws, Duncan. *Merchant Fleets in Profile*, Stephens, Cambridge, 1978–80

Hibbert, H. G. *Fifty Years of a Londoner's Life*, Grant Richards, London, 1916

Hibbert, H. G. *Playgoers Memories*, Grant Richards, London, 1920

Hislop, John, and David Swannell, *The Faber Book of the Turf*, Faber and Faber, London, 1990

Holledge, Julie. *Innocent Flowers, Women in the Edwardian Theatre*, Virago, London, 1981

Hoare, Philip. *Wilde's Last Stand*, Gerald Duckworth, London, 1997

Honri, Peter. *Music Hall Warriors*, Greenwich Exchange, London, 1997

Honri, Peter. *Working the Halls*, Saxon House, Farnborough, 1973

Howard, Bannister J. *Fifty Years a Showman*, Hutchinson & Co. London, 1938

Howard, Diana. *London Theatres and Music Halls 1850–1950*, Library Association Publishing, London, 1970

Howell, Michael, and Peter Ford. *The True Story of the Elephant Man*, Penguin, London, 1980

Jameson, Margaret Storm. *No Time Like the Present*, Cassell, London, 1933

Jacob, Naomi. *Me, Yesterday and Today*, Hutchinson, London, 1957

Jacob, Naomi. *Our Marie*, Hutchinson, London, 1936

Jenkins, Roy. *Gladstone*, Papermac, London, 1996

Kenney, Annie, *Memories of a Militant*, Routledge, London, 1994

Kift, Dagmar. *The Victorian Music Hall: Culture, Class and Conflict*, Cambridge University Press, 1996

Kubicek, Robert V. *Economic Imperialism in Theory and Practice: the Case of South African Gold-mining Finance, 1886–1914*, Duke University Press, Durham North Carolina, 1979

Lacour-Gayet, Robert. *A Concise History of Australia*, Penguin Books, Harmondsworth, 1976

Leeson, Robert Arthur. *Strike*, Allen and Unwin, London, 1973

LeRoy, George. *Music Hall Stars of the 90s*, British Technical and General Press, London, 1952

Lloyd, Ann and David Robinson (eds). *The Illustrated History of the Cinema*, Orbis, London, 1986

Logan, Mary. *Bring on the Dancing Girls: a Showgirl's Life in World War II*, Book Guild, Sussex, 1998

Longrigg, Roger. *The History of Horse Racing*, Macmillan, London, 1972

Louvish, Simon. *Man on the Flying Trapeze: the Life and Times of W. C. Fields*, Faber and Faber, London, 1997

Mackenzie, Compton. *My Life and Times, Octave 1 (1883–1891)*, Chatto and Windus, London, 1963

Mackenzie, Compton. *My Life and Times, Octave 2 (1891–1900)*, Chatto and Windus, London, 1963

Maclean, Hugh. *Modern Views on Digestive and Gastric Disease*, Constable, London, 1925

Macqueen-Pope, Walter. *Queen of the Music Halls*, Oldbourne, London, 1947

Maitland, Sara. *Vesta Tilley*, Virago, London, 1986

Mander, David. *More Light, More Power: an Illustrated History of Shoreditch*, Sutton Publishing, Stroud, 1996

Mander, Raymond, and Joe Mitchenson. *Lost Theatres of London*, Rupert Hart-Davis, London, 1968

Marsh, Russell. *The Jockeys of Vanity Fair*, March, Tunbridge Wells, 1985

Marsh, Arthur, and Victoria Ryan. *Historical Directory of Trade Unions*, vol. I, Gower, Farnborough, 1980

Matthew, H. C. G. (ed.). *The Gladstone Diaries*, vol. 14, Clarendon, Oxford, 1986

Mathieu, Paul. *The Druid's Lodge Confederacy*, Mandarin, London, 1990

McGurn, James. *On Your Bicycle: an Illustrated History of Cycling*, John Murray, London, 1987

Mills, Simon. *RMS Olympic*, The Old Reliable, Waterfront Publications, Launceston, 1995

Moorehead, Caroline. *Sidney Bernstein, a Biography*, Jonathan Cape, London, 1984

Moorhouse, Edward. *The History and Romance of the Derby*, Biographical Press, London, 1908

Mortimer, Roger. *The History of the Derby Stakes*, Michael Joseph, London, 1973

Mortimer, Roger. *Twenty Great Horses*, Cassell, London, 1967

Mortimer, Roger, Richard Onslow and Peter Willett. *Biographical Encyclopaedia of British Flat Racing*, Macdonald and Jane's, London, 1978

Napier, Valantyne. *Glossary of Terms Used in Variety*, The Badger Press, Westbury, 1996

Nicholson, Nigel. *Mary Curzon – A Biography*, Phoenix Giant, 1977

Orchard, Vincent. *The Derby Stakes: a Complete History from 1900 to 1953*, London, 1954

Orwell, George. 'The Art of Donald McGill' in *The Collected Essays: Journalism and Letters of George Orwell*, vol. II, Secker & Warburg, London, 1968

Park, A. J. and C. D. Stuart. *Variety Stars*, The Variety Publishing Company, London, 1895

Parris, Matthew. *Great Parliamentary Scandals*, Robson Books, London, 1995

Pearsall, Ronald. *Victorian Sheet Music Covers*, David and Charles, Newton Abbot, 1972

Pepper, Terence. *High Society Photographs, 1897–1914*, National Portrait Gallery, London, 1998

Plumptre, George. *Back Page Racing: a Century of Newspaper Coverage*, Macdonald/Queen Anne, London, 1989

Plumptre, George. *Edward VII*, Pavilion, London, 1995

Plumptre, George. *The Fast Set, the World of Edwardian Racing*, Deutsch, London, 1985

Portland, Duke of. *Memories of Racing and Hunting*, Faber and Faber, London, 1935

Porter, Roy. *London: A Social History*, Penguin, London, 1996

Potter, Paul. *Trilby and other plays*, Oxford University Press, 1996

Railton, Keith. *Books on Music Hall, a Personal Selection with Commentary*, published by the author, Coventry, 1994

Rearick, Charles. *Pleasures of the Belle Epoque*, Yale, London, 1985

Richardson, Mary. *Laugh a Defiance*, Weidenfeld & Nicolson, 1994

Ritchie, J. Ewing. *The Night Side of London*, William Tweedie, London, 1857

Roberts, Arthur. *Fifty Years of Spoof*, John Lane, London, 1927

Robey, George. *Looking Back on Life*, Constable, London, 1933

Rose, Clarkson. *Red Plush and Greasepaint*, Museum Press, London, 1964

Rowbotham, Sheila. *A Century of Women*, Viking, London, 1997

Saint, Andrew (ed.). *Politics and the People of London: The London County Council, 1889–1965*, Hambledon, London, 1989

Salberg, Derek. *Once Upon a Pantomime*, Cortney, Luton, 1981

Sandall, Robert. *The History of the Salvation Army*, Nelson, London, 1947

Sante, Luc. *Low Life*, Granta, London, 1991

Scott, Harold. *The Early Doors*, Nicholson and Watson, London, 1946

Senelick, Laurence, David F. Cheshire and Ulrich Schneider. *British Music Hall, 1840–1923: A Bibliography and Guide to Sources, with a Supplement on European Music Hall*, Archon Books, Hamden, Connecticut, 1981

Sheehan, James Vincent. *The Amazing Oscar Hammerstein*, Simon & Schuster, New York, 1956

Shepard, Ernest. *Drawn from Memory*, Methuen, London, 1971

Snyder, Robert W. *The Voice of the City: Vaudeville and Popular Culture in New York*, Oxford University Press, 1989

Souhami, Diana. *Mrs Keppel and Her Daughter*, Flamingo, London, 1997

Swaffer, Percy. *Fleet Street Goes Racing*, Hutchinson, London, 1939

Symonds, F. Addington. *The Johannesburg Story*, F. Muller, London, 1953

Temperley, Nicholas (ed.). *The Lost Chord – Essays on Victorian Music*, Indiana University Press, Bloomington, 1989

Tich, Mary, and Richard Findlater. *Little Tich – Giant of the Music Hall*, Elm Tree Books, London 1979

Thompson, Francis and Michael Longstreth. *Hampstead: Building a Borough, 1650–1964*, Routledge and Kegan, Paul, Boston and London, 1974

Thompson, Paul. *The Edwardians, the Remaking of British Society*, Routledge, London, 1992

Tomalin, Claire. *Katherine Mansfield – A Secret Life*, Viking, London, 1987

Tomalin, Claire. *The Invisible Woman*, Penguin, Harmondsworth, 1990

Walker, Brian Mercer (ed.). *Frank Matcham, Theatre Architect*, Blackstaff, Belfast, 1980

Walsh, Beatrix. *A Lost Leader: Frank Gerald's Role in the Music-hall Strikes, 1906–1907*, Theatre Studies Publications, Glasgow, 1997

Wearing, J. P. *The London Stage*, Scarecrow, Metuchen, New Jersey, 1976

Wheatley, Dennis. *Officer and Temporary Gentleman (1914–1919)*, Hutchinson, London, 1978

White, James Dillon. *Born to Star – the Lupino Lane Story*, Heinemann, London, 1957

Willis, Frederick. *101 Jubilee Road, A Book of London Yesterdays*, Phoenix House, London, 1948

Wilmut, Roger. *Kindly Leave the Stage! The Story of Variety, 1919–1960*, Methuen, London, 1985

Worger, William H. *South Africa's City of Diamonds: Mine Workers and*

Monopoly Capitalism in Kimberley, 1867–1895, Yale University Press, New Haven, 1987

Wynn, Michael Jones. *The Derby – a Celebration of the World's Most Famous Horse Race*, Croom Helm, London, 1979

Zellers, Parker. *Tony Pastor, Dean of the Vaudeville Stage*, Eastern Michigan University Press, Michigan, 1971

Miscellaneous

Who Was Who (1916–1928), vol. II, Adam and Charles Black, London, 1929

The Oxford History of South Africa

Ordnance Survey map of Shoreditch, 1872

A Little Of What You Fancy: The Marie Lloyd Record, LC1836/GEMM CD 9097, Pearl CD, Pavilion Records, includes an introduction by Tony Barker and note on the text by Richard Bebb.

Equivalent Contemporary Values of the Pound: a Historical Series 1270 to 1998, Bank of England Press Office

Articles

(In addition to those mentioned in Notes)

Anstey, F. 'London Music Halls' in *Harper's New Monthly Magazine*, January 1891

Bailey, Peter, 'Theatres of Entertainment/Spaces of Modernity: Rethinking the British Popular Stage 1890–1914', in *Nineteenth Century Theatre* (summer 1998) vol. 26, no. 1.

Bailey, Peter, 'Conspiracies of Meaning: Music-hall and the Knowingness of Popular Culture', in *Past and Present* (August 1994), no. 144

Carter, Alexandra, 'Blond, bewigged and winged with gold: ballet girls in the music halls of late Victorian and Edwardian England' in *The Journal of the Society for Dance Research* (autumn 1995) vol. xiii, no. 2

Joseph Hatton, 'On Music with a "K"' in *Idler*, April 1892

Jerome, Jerome, K., 'Variety Patter' in *Idler*, March 1892

'The State of the London Theatres' in *Saturday Review*, 30 July 1887

Senelick, Laurence, 'Politics as entertainment: Victorian music-hall songs', in *Victorian Studies* (December 1975) vol. XIX, no. 2

Sketch, 15 November 1893

WHO'S WHO

Edward Franklin Albee
Started in the circus before joining forces with Benjamin Franklin Keith to introduce polite vaudeville. They were tough operators who insisted on clean acts to attract a better class of clientele: words such as 'liar', 'sucker', 'slob', 'Holy glee', 'son-of-a-gun' and 'devil' were banned. They eventually built up a chain of vaudeville theatres. (*See* Keith.)

Maud Allan
Dancer who mesmerized and shocked London audiences in 1908 with her 'Vision of Salome' at the Palace Theatre.

Louisa Archer
Marie's mother's sister, who performed as Madame Louise Patti.

Matilda Caroline Archer
Marie's mother. She married Brush in 1869 and was still illiterate at Marie's wedding eighteen years later. A headstrong woman and talented seamstress, she helped make many of Marie's costumes.

Barney Barnato
South African millionaire, who started life as an East End music-hall artist. He invested in the Johannesburg Empire and became friendly with Marie. He died after falling overboard on his way back to England, although rumours persisted that he was worried about his collapsing business interests and committed suicide.

Bessie Bellwood (Elizabeth Mahony)
Born in Ireland, she began as a rabbit-skinner in Bermondsey and earned a reputation as a comic singer who was adept at putting down hecklers. She is often quoted as having sung, 'What Cheer, Ria!' She carried on a long-

standing affair with the Duke of Manchester and there were rumours that she planned to sue him for the £4,165 (£195,089) she claimed he owed her. Rumours of her financial affairs prompted audiences on both sides of the Atlantic to hurl coins at her. Her frequent carriage accidents left her face badly bruised and may have been a cover for an explosive private life. She died an alcoholic, aged thirty-nine, in a flat in West Kensington in 1896, leaving estate valued at £63 (£3,256).

George Belmont

Ran Sebright's Music Hall in Coate Street, Hackney, and claimed to have given Marie one of her first bookings, only to discover she had broken the contract by appearing at a nearby rival, Hoxton Theatre of Varieties.

Albert Bial

Half of the team that created Koster & Bial's Theater in New York. Marie appeared there in 1890.

Belle Bilton

One of the Sisters Bilton, serio-comic vocalists and dancers, she is a rare example of a music-hall star who married into the aristocracy. She wed Viscount Dunlo, eldest son of the Earl of Clancarty, much to her new father-in-law's disgust. He kept the couple apart while he tried to find grounds for a divorce. They were eventually reunited, and Belle became a countess and retired from the halls.

Bessie Bonehill

Early male impersonator who appeared in New York several times.

Bella Burge (née Orchard)

Alice and Grace befriended her when all three were in panto at the Pavilion in the Whitechapel Road, Stepney. Her stage name was Ella Lane. She moved in with the Lloyds, and over the next few years appeared as one half of the Sisters Lloyd and as a solo turn called Bella Lloyd. She acted as a dresser to Marie but returned to the halls after her marriage to the boxer Dick Burge. When he was sent to prison for his part in the Goudie financial scandal she reverted to her original stage name, Ella Lane. After Dick's death she ran the Blackfriars' boxing ring, which he had founded.

Dick Burge
Married Bella after they appeared on the same bill.

Alfred Butt
Took over the Palace Theatre (previously the Royal English Opera House) in 1904. Keen to make music hall more respectable, he helped to arrange the first royal command performance. He was knighted in 1918.

Herbert Campbell
His nineteen-stone bulk made a perfect foil to Dan Leno when he played next to Dan's pantomime dame.

Kate Carney
Coster comedienne who sang songs such as 'Are We To Part Like This, Bill?' She died in 1950.

Laura Ormiston Chant
The fiercely bonneted Mrs Chant blocked the renewal of the licence of the Empire, Leicester Square, until a screen was erected between its promenade and the auditorium. This, she argued, would protect customers from the prostitutes who plied their trade there. The screen was torn down in a demonstration in which the young Winston Churchill was heavily involved.

Frederick Charrington
Anti-music-hall campaigner, who renounced his family's brewing fortune. As a supporter of the National Vigilance Association, he was also a member of the music-hall licensing committee of the London County Council.

Albert Chevalier
An ex-character actor who took up coster songs, and helped to make them acceptable to the middle classes. He was born in Notting Hill but had French and Italian ancestors. His most popular songs were 'Knocked 'Em In The Old Kent Road', about receiving an unexpected legacy; 'The Future Mrs 'Awkins' and 'My Old Dutch', an unbearably sad song about an elderly couple who are separated when they enter the workhouse. He was involved in the music-hall strike and omitted from the first royal command performance.

George H. Chirgwin

Singer known as the 'white-eyed kaffir' after he accidentally wiped away part of his black face makeup to leave a white lozenge-shaped area around his right eye. One of the very early music-hall performers to carry on into this century, he was included in the royal command performance.

Paul Cinquevalli

A juggler and acrobat who was born Paul Kestner in Poland. He was supple enough to play billiards on his own back. His German-sounding name ruined his career during the xenophobic war years.

Willy Clarkson

Wig and costume maker, and friend to the stars.

Charles Coborn

His biggest hit was 'The Man Who Broke The Bank At Monte Carlo', the chorus of which he sang ten times on its first outing until the audience was eventually persuaded to join in.

Lottie Collins

She made her name with her frenzied dance, 'Ta-ra-ra-boom-de-ay', which became popular in the 1890s. She died of a heart-attack in 1910.

Percy Charles Courtenay

Introduced to Marie by her unofficial fiancé George Foster. He was variously described as a 'stage-door johnny', 'racing agent' or 'racecourse tout'. Percy first started divorce proceedings in 1894. He had lived in France for a while, although it is not known where or what he did there. In January 1904 he petitioned for divorce again, naming Alec Hurley as co-respondent. A Percy Charles Courtenay, of 'independent means', died of an accidental drugs overdose in Hove in 1933.

Cora Crippen

American singer who performed as Belle Elmore and fancied she bore a striking resemblance to Marie. She was married to Dr Crippen, and crossed the picket line during the performers' strike.

Mr Datas
Famous for his phenomenal feats of memory, he offered to sell his head to a London hospital after his death. He changed sides during the performers' strike when proprietors threatened to sue him for breach of promise.

Bernard Dillon
Marie's third husband. Born in Tralee in 1887, he came to England to race for the highly secretive Druid's Lodge Confederacy. He won the Derby in 1910, but was warned off in 1913. In 1935 he was charged with hitting a woman he was living with. At the start of the Second World War he worked as a night porter at Africa House in Trafalgar Square. He died in 1941 and, due to wartime paper shortages, his death attracted little notice.

Gus Elen
A genuine Cockney, one of his early songs, 'Never Introduce Your Donah [sweetheart] To A Pal!' was prompted by Marie switching her affections from George Foster to his friend Percy Courtenay. His other songs include ''E dunno Where 'E Are'.

Madge Ellis
A serio-comic with whom Marie fell out in 1894 when she found she had been copying one of Marie's songs in New York. Later they became friends, and Madge successfully won costs, damages and an apology when a reformer suggested she had appeared on stage without tights.

Joe Elvin
Cockney comedian.

Florrie Forde
A buxom singer who was hugely popular during the First World War. Her repertoire included 'Hold Your Hand Out, You Naughty Boy' and 'Down At The Old Bull And Bush'.

George Foster
One of Marie's earliest suitors. He later became a successful music-hall agent and his clients included Rosie Lloyd.

Walter Gibbons
Powerful manager who controlled theatres such as the Empress, Brixton, the Holborn Empire and the Palladium.

The Great Lafayette
Illusionist and animal trainer who died returning to the Empire, Edinburgh, to save his favourite lion after scenery was engulfed in flames from a torch used in his act.

Oscar Hammerstein
Grandfather of Oscar Hammerstein, the composer of musicals such as *Oklahoma!* and *The Sound of Music*. His early money came from an invention for a cigar-making machine before he moved into property investment and became an eccentric theatre impresario. He managed Koster & Bial's music hall when Marie appeared there in 1894.

Augustus Harris
Drury Lane theatre manager who staged extravagant pantomimes, which featured elaborate special effects, parades of actors wearing spectacular costumes and music-hall stars. He was known as 'Druriolanus' and when he died in 1896, *The Times* described him as 'the greatest showman on record'. The paper also delivered a back-handed compliment: 'He accurately gauged the tastes of particular sections of the playgoing public, and would incur any expense to gratify them.' (*The Times*, 23 June 1896)

Jenny Hill
'The Vital Spark' emerged from a desperately poor background to become one of the most famous serio-comics of her day. Her dances included 'The Cellar Flap' and her songs 'The Coffee Shop Girl'. She had a keen eye for characterization, and performed in New York.

Alec Hurley
Marie's second husband. He started his working life in the London docks before moving on to the halls to specialize in sentimental coster songs. By the end of the century he was specializing in 'scena', involving specialist

scenery and a chorus of 'supers' in Cockney dress. He toured Australia and America with Marie.

Edgar Hyman
Manager of the Johannesburg Empire.

Solly Joel
South African millionaire, horse-racing enthusiast and nephew of Barney Barnato.

Fred Karno
Started working in a Nottingham lace factory before going on to perform as a gymnast. He produced a series of comic sketches for his group of performers, who later included Charlie Chaplin.

Benjamin Franklin Keith
Started his career in American circus and dime museums. He joined forces with Edward Franklin Albee to bring 'polite' vaudeville to Boston in the late 1880s. In 1906 they set up the United Booking Office, which dominated the eastern part of America, and in the 1920s merged with a western chain of vaudeville theatres to form the Keith-Albee-Orpheum Circuit. In 1928 this joined with Joseph P. Kennedy's Radio Corporation of America (RCA) to become Radio-Keith-Orpheum (RKO), which concentrated on movies. (*See* Albee.)

Marie Kendall
A lifelong friend of Marie, she was most famous for 'Just Like The Ivy I Cling To You' and 'If I Could See This For 1s. 6d. What Could I See For A Quid?' She was heavily involved in the music-hall strike.

Richard G. Knowles
Quick-fire American comedian and early friend of Marie.

John Koster
An immigrant from Hamburg, he formed a joint venture with Albert Bial to run restaurants, and a beer-bottling business in New York, before moving into variety and setting up Koster & Bial's in Manhattan. Marie appeared there in 1890.

Sara Lane
Ran the Britannia pub in Hoxton after the death of her husband, Sam. It became famous for its elaborate pantomime in which Sara appeared in tights until well into her seventies. She ran her theatre with a maternal air and employed several music-hall stars. When she died, following a stroke in 1899 at her home in St John's Wood, she had a huge East End funeral and an obituary in *The Times*.

Harry Lauder
Scottish singer who originally worked in a coal mine. He became famous for songs such as 'Roamin' In The Gloamin', 'I Love A Lassie', 'Stop Your Ticklin' Jock' and 'Keep Right On To The End Of The Road'. He was an enthusiastic fund-raiser during the First World War, which claimed the life of his only son, and was knighted for his efforts. His act was immensely popular abroad.

Katie Lawrence
Sang 'Daisy, Daisy, Give Me Your Answer Do'. At the turn of the century she sometimes replaced Marie if she was too ill to perform.

George le Brunn
The author of many of Marie's songs; he also wrote for countless other performers but died penniless, aged forty-two, from meningitis.

Dan Leno (George Galvin)
He had a quicksilver, surreal sense of humour and genuine feeling for language. He created characters such as the Shopwalker and the orator in 'The Midnight March'. Playing next to Herbert Campbell, he became the most famous pantomime dame and got to know Marie through several Drury Lane appearances. He performed in front of Edward VII at Sandringham, but shortly afterwards lost his mind.

Alice Lloyd
Began performing with her sister Grace as the Sisters Lloyd in the late 1880s. She married Tom McNaughton and both became highly successful in America.

Grace Lloyd
Part of the Sisters Lloyd with Alice until she married the jockey George Hyams and went to live in Austria where he trained horses.

Marie Lloyd Jr (Myria Matilda Victoria Courtenay)
She started imitating her mother from an early age and continued to make a living from a pale reflection of her act. She died, childless, in Hove, at the age of seventy-eight in 1967.

Maude Lloyd
Performed in a double act with her younger brother Sidney and toured America.

Rosie Lloyd
From 1893 she appeared in the Sisters Lena with her cousin Alice Archer and later teamed up with Bella Burge as the Sisters Lloyd. Once described as having 'a long-distance face', she lacked the true Lloyd charm. She married another performer, Will Poluski.

Marie Loftus
Principal boy in pantomime.

Paul Martinetti
Mime artist.

Frank Matcham
Theatre architect who brought glamour, as well as safety and comfort, to music hall. Between 1879 and 1912, 'Matchless Matcham' designed 150 theatres, twice as many as his closest professional rival. His major triumphs were the Empire Palace at Leeds, the Hackney Empire, the London Hippodrome, the Coliseum and the Palladium. His assiduousness eventually proved his downfall when he died in 1920 from heart failure caused by blood poisoning brought about by over-vigorous trimming of his fingernails.

John McDougall
Staunch Methodist and member of the music-hall licensing committee of the London County Council. His hardline stance earned him the nicknames MuckDougall and the Grand Inquisitor.

Fred McNaughton
The 'straight' half of the McNaughton Brothers. His son, Fred, went on to play the part of the mayor in the television comedy *Dad's Army*.

Tom McNaughton
One half of the McNaughton Brothers – a quick-fire double act. He married Alice Lloyd and, after acting as her manager in America, went on to appear in several musical comedies. He lost most of his fortune in unwise theatrical ventures.

Victoria Monks
Vivacious singer best known for her songs 'Won't You Come Home, Bill Bailey' and 'Take Me Back To London Town'. She died in 1927 from influenza at the age of forty-three.

Charles Morton
Known as the 'father of the halls', he opened the Canterbury in 1851 in South London.

Edward Moss
An entrepreneur who began his career in Edinburgh and gradually expanded south. He eventually joined forces with Oswald Stoll to form the giant Stoll Moss empire. (*See* Oswald Stoll)

Donald Munro
Handsome young director of the Crown Theatre and the Pavilion in Whitechapel, who married Daisy Wood.

Tony Pastor
Founding father of American vaudeville, he managed to attract respectable middle-class customers to the new form of entertainment and enticed many British performers to New York. When Jenny Hill (*q.v.*) first appeared at one of his theatres he was so worried that the audience would not understand her that he issued Cockney dictionaries.

Will Poluski Jr
Son of a famous music-hall family, he began his career in the Poluski Brothers and went on to perform in Fred Karno's Football Company. He

married Rosie Lloyd in 1908. After the First World War he appeared in a double act with Joe Mott, the son-in-law of Marie's brother Johnny.

Arthur Prince
Ventriloquist and friend of Marie. He perfected the act of drinking and talking at the same time and his dummy, Jim, is buried with him in the same cemetery as Marie.

Harry Randall
Pantomime dame, who also specialized in character songs.

Harry Rickards
A comic singer who left England when he was declared bankrupt, he set up the Tivoli music halls in Adelaide and Sydney and the new Opera House in Melbourne. He became known as 'the Napoleon of Vaudeville'.

Arthur Roberts
Comedian and friend of Marie. Played an active part in the music-hall strike.

George Robey (George Edward Wade)
Comedian known as the Prime Minister of Mirth. Although lower-middle class, he claimed he had studied at Cambridge and liked classical music.

Clarkson Rose
Comic singer, revue actor and writer.

Eugene Sandow
Strongman over whom women swooned. He had his own fitness club and a corset named after him. He died of a stroke in 1925, aged fifty-eight, after trying to lift a car out of a ditch.

Ella Shields
Originally from America, she became famous as a male impersonator and sung songs such as 'Show Me The Way To Go Home' and 'Burlington Bertie From Bow'.

Chung Ling Soo
American illusionist who died from a gunshot wound after one of his tricks apparently went wrong.

Oswald Stoll
Australian-born impresario who started at the Liverpool Parthenon where as a fourteen-year-old boy he helped his widowed mother to run the business. He expanded into Wales, the Midlands and finally London, building the Coliseum in St Martin's Lane in 1904. In 1900 he merged his interests with Moss and Thornton to become Moss Empires.

Eugene Stratton
Began his career as the Dandy Coloured Coon and later became popular for songs such as 'Lily Of Laguna'.

Harry Tate
Marie was credited with 'inventing' his trademark 'St Vitus' moustache when she saw him swimming in the river with two strands of weed clinging to either nostril. Famous for his comic sketches such as 'Motoring'.

Little Tich (Harry Relph)
So-called because his chubby features as a baby resembled the 'Tichborne Claimant' – the twenty-eight-stone butcher from Wagga-Wagga in Australia who claimed to be the heir to the Tichborne family inheritance. Little Tich was only four feet tall, had an extra finger on each hand and slightly webbed digits. He and Marie became friends after starring together in several Drury Lane pantomimes. His most famous routine was his big-boot dance, an acrobatic feat in which he balanced on the tips of boots that were nearly as long as he was tall. He was awarded Les Palmes Academie for his performances in France and had a highly complicated private life. He died in 1928 after he was hit on the head by a mop during his act.

Vesta Tilley
'London's Idol' was the most successful male impersonator of her day and the highest-earning female music-hall star in the 1880s. She did her best to distance herself from her humble background as one of twelve children born to a china painter in Worcester. She was meticulous about her

costumes, which frequently sparked fashion crazes. She married a music-hall manager and became Lady de Frece.

Henry Tozer
London proprietor whose halls included the London Shoreditch and Collins's.

Vesta Victoria
Made a name for herself with 'Daddy Wouldn't Buy Me A Bow-Wow'.

George Ware
Composer of 'The Boy I Love' and Marie's first agent from 1885. He was responsible for changing her name from Bella Delmeyer to Marie Lloyd, and remained her agent for ten years.

Percy Williams
New York impresario whose halls included the Colonial, the Alhambra, on Seventh Avenue and 126th Street, the Orpheum in Brooklyn and the Gotham in East New York.

Annie Wood
The only member of the Wood family not to appear on stage, which may have been why Marie described her as the sibling with the best voice. She accompanied Marie on many tours and acted as her personal assistant.

Daisy Wood
The prettiest of all the sisters, she was the only one to retain the Wood name professionally. She was particularly successful as principal boy in pantomime.

John 'Brush' Wood
Marie's father was born in Bethnal Green, the son of a willow-cutter and willow-weaver. He became proficient in making artificial flowers for hats and was also a popular barman. His nickname was Brush, or Brushie, because of his meticulous appearance. A quiet man, he was good at mental arithmetic, a talent honed through a lifelong devotion to horse-racing. The family attributed his death to a reduced racing programme during the war, which deprived him of the regular cerebral exercise.

Sidney Wood
Performed in a double act with his sister, Maude.

Zaeo
Young acrobat whose armpits, displayed on posters, caused a scandal in 1890. London County Council inspectors were later criticized for demanding to examine her back, which they claimed was being damaged during the course of her act on the flying trapeze.

INDEX

Abel, George, 196
Acton, Jessie, 18
Actresses' Franchise League, 206
Agate, James, 257, 278
Albee, Edward Franklin, 193–4, 243–4,
  313
Aldrich, Charles, 224, 228
Alexandra, Princess of Wales (*later* Queen),
  55, 223
Alhambra, Brighton, 71
Alhambra, Leicester Square, 24–5, 31, 40, 41,
  47, 58, 86, 107, 130, 223, 234
Alhambra, New York, 187
Alhambra Music Hall, Shoreditch, 10
Allan, Maud, 199–200, 313
Amalgamated Musicians Union, 171
American Biograph, 117
Anglesey, Marquess of, 118
animal acts, 30–1, 173–4, 250–1
Anstey, F., 87
Archer, Alice, 105
Archer, George, 87
Archer, Louisa, *see* Patti
Ardwick Empire, Manchester, 235
Arthurs, George, 221, 249, 252
Askwith, George Ranken, 180–1, 182,
  270
Aston, George, 232–3
Athenaeum, 75–6
Australasian, 138–9
Australia, 132–40
Aylin, Harry (Tubby), 183, 213
Aylin, Marie (née Courtenay, Marie Junior,
  ML's daughter): birth, 36; childhood, 61,
  82, 111, 124, 167–8, 182, 207; education, 4,
  182; career, 116, 182–3; bridesmaid, 126;
  wedding, 183–4; mother's send-off party,
  186; illness, 219; Alec's funeral, 246;
  criticisms of Ben Dillon, 267; mother's
  will, 271; biographical notes, 321

Baccarat case, 49
Baker, Richard Anthony, 283
ballet, 86–7
Bard, Wilkie, 224, 228
Barnard's Theatre of Varieties, Chatham, 80
Barnato, Barney (Barnett Isaacs), 113–17, 313
Barnum, Phineas T., 44
Barrie, J.M., 234, 251
barring system, 164–5, 177
Bartlett, Daniel, 2, 3
Bateman, Edgar, 132
'Bathing Parade, The' (sketch), 150–1
Bawn, Harry, 273
Bedford, Camden Town, 27, 77, 265–6, 271
Bedford, Harry, 263, 270
Beecham, Charles, 166
Beerbohm, Max, 2, 76, 77, 79, 157, 279
Bellwood, Bessie (Elizabeth Ann Mahony):
  career, 39–40; Shaw on, 68; finances, 94;
  relationship with Duke of Manchester, 94,
  213; cab accident, 108; death, 106;
  biographical notes, 313–14
Belmont, George, 17, 111, 314
Belmont's, 86
Benjafield, Norman, 274
Bennett, Arnold, 79, 216–17
Berlin Wintergarten, 117
Bernhardt, Sarah, 148, 234, 266
Bernstein, Sidney, 273–4
Bernstein family, 273
Berry, Robert, 70
Besant, Annie, 172
Bial, Albert, 46–7, 92–3, 314
Bigham, Mr Justice, 145, 146, 147
Bilton, Belle, 34, 314
Bilton, Flo, 34
Bird, N. (piano teacher), 67
Bird, Sydney, 32
Blanche, Ada, 74, 83, 130
Blaney's Lincoln Square Theater, 203

Boardman, Billy, 81
Bobe, Celina, 137
Boer War, 129–31
Boganny's 'Lunatic Bakers', 224
Bon Accord Music Hall, Aberdeen, 31
Bonehill, Bessie, 45, 118, 314
Booth, Charles, 28
Booth, William, 13
Boston, Massachusetts, 193
Boston Transcript, 190
Boys' Brigade, 168
Brady, Mary, 267
Brassey, Leonard, 144
Brett, Edwin, 151
Brinsmead, John, 66
Britannia Theatre, Hoxton, 10, 37–8
British Women's Temperance Association, 102
Brixton Theatre, 170
Broom, Thomas, 11
Brown-Potter, Mrs, 174
Bryant & May's factory, 172
Burbage, Richard, 11
Burge, Bella (née Orchard, Ella Lane): appearance, 62–3; family background, 63; friendship with ML, 62–3, 142–3, 155, 186, 205, 265, 268; Percy's attacks, 87, 88; ML's South African tours, 109, 111–12, 116, 207; wedding, 141; husband's imprisonment, 141–7, 158, 167; Prince of Wales story, 223; Alec's death and funeral, 245, 246; dislike of Ben Dillon, 255; husband's death, 261; biographical notes, 314
Burge, Dick: background, 143; wedding, 141; financial troubles, 141–2; arrest, 142; trial, 144–6; imprisonment, 146–7; release, 204–5; business career, 205; Alec's funeral, 246; wartime career, 255; dislike of Ben Dillon, 255; death, 261; biographical notes, 315
Butt, Alfred: Maud Allan booking, 199; royal command performance (1911), 224, 227–8, 230; wartime, 254; knighthood, 261; biographical notes, 315

Campbell, Herbert: pantomime performances, 53, 74, 83; 'New Women' song, 89; ML's send-off party, 109; tribute to ML, 164; Queen's death, 132, 167; relationship with

Leno, 156, 157; death, 157; biographical notes, 315
Canterbury, Lambeth, 24, 40, 81–2, 94, 123, 165, 171, 182
Cardiff, 60, 71, 270
Carington, Sir William, 227–8, 230
Carmencita (dancer), 46
Carney, Kate, 2, 127, 231, 315
cars, 155
Casey, Pat, 243–4
Cedric, SS, 187
chairmen, 15, 17, 74
Chang the Chinese Giant, 31
Chant, Laura Ormiston, 88–9, 102, 315
Chaplin, Charles (senior), 45, 46
Chaplin, Charlie, 27, 80, 185, 269
Charcot, Agnes, 189–90
Charrington, Frederick, 50, 315
Chevalier, Albert: career, 60, 123; songs, 56, 60; ML's benefit, 61; US success, 94; royal command performance, 225–6; biographical notes, 315
Chicago, 244–5
Chirgwin, George H., 224, 228, 229, 316
Cholmondeley, Marquess of, 144
Chung Ling Soo, 117, 174, 261, 324
Churchill, Lord Randolph, 69
Churchill, Winston, 89, 129, 213
Cinquevalli, Paul, 117, 225, 228, 250, 316
City of London Theatre, 10
Clancarty, Countess of, 34
Clarence, Duke of, 55
Clarkson, Willy: costumes for ML, 82; wigs for ML, 91; gift for ML, 111; reputation, 176; Crippen case, 209; Ellen Terry story, 234; biographical notes, 316
Cleveland, Ohio, 244
Cleveland Street scandal, 50
Coal Hole, 23
Coborn, Charles, 37, 316
Coliseum, Glasgow, 269
Coliseum, London, *see* London Coliseum
Collier, Constance, 157
Collins, Anne, 38
Collins, Charles, 252, 261
Collins, Lottie, 40, 42, 45, 56, 136, 316
Collins, Sam, 38
Collins's, Islington Green, 21, 22, 27, 29, 36, 38, 47, 131, 144, 179, 256
Colonial, New York, 187, 188, 193, 197, 243

Conjurors' Magazine, 174
Connor, T.W., 58
Conquest, Benjamin, 12
Conquest, George, 12–13
Cooper, Gladys, 251
Cooper, Sydney, 114
Corti, Luigi, 6
Costello, Tom, 58
Cotes, C.G., 119
Courtenay, Myria Matilda Victoria (Marie Junior, ML's daughter), *see* Aylin
Courtenay, Percy (ML's first husband): marriage, 35–6; relationship with wife, 41, 62, 63–4, 87–8, 233; assaults on wife, 64, 87–8; separation from wife, 85; relationship with daughter, 111, 167–8, 183, 207; divorce, 167–8; death, 168; biographical notes, 233
Courtney, Baron, 15
Covent Garden Theatre, 63, 80
Crawford, Donald, 48
Crewe, Lord, 144
Crippen, Cora, *see* Elmore
Crippen, Hawley Harvey, 161–2, 208–10
Crispi, Ida, 224, 228
Criterion, 254, 260
Crown Theatre, Peckham, 126, 144
Cumming, Sir William Gordon, 49
Cunningham, Minnie, 25
Curzon, Lord, 90
cycling, 98–100
Cyder Cellars, 23
Cyrus and Maud, 30

Daily Express, 142, 175
Daily Mail, 106, 129, 157, 242, 279
Daily Telegraph, 89, 175, 176
Dalton, Will, 131
Datas, Mr, 174–5, 317
David, Worton, 221, 258
Davies, Acton, 190
Day, Harry, 200
de Frece, Walter, 264
de Serris, Henriette, 228
Deauville, 185
Defoe, Daniel, 82
Dent, Fred, 159
Devant, David, 225, 228
Dickens, Charles, 12, 37
Didcott, Hugh, 200

Dilke, Sir Charles Wentworth, 48
Dillon, Ben (Bernard, ML's third husband): appearance, 3, 184, 212; career, 211–13, 215–16, 222, 232–3; best man at Aylin wedding, 184; relationship with ML, 212, 216, 220, 222, 232–3, 243, 255–6, 259–60, 265, 268, 271; violence, 215, 248, 255, 259–60, 265, 268; cited in divorce proceedings, 208; US visit, 236–45; wedding, 247–8; wartime career, 255, 259–60; wife's will, 271; wife's death, 276–7; wife's funeral, 3; biographical notes, 317
Dillon, Joe, 215
Doyle, Sir Arthur Conan, 199
Druid's Lodge Confederacy, 212, 214–16, 239
Drury Lane, 52–7, 74–6, 82–4, 111
du Maurier, George, 96
du Maurier, Gerald, 96
Duchess, Balham, 171
Duller, Bessie (née Hyams, ML's niece), 213
Duller, George, 213
Dunlo, Viscount, 34
Dwarf, 56

Eagle Tavern Music Hall, City Road, 10, 11–14, 16–17, 23
Edison, Thomas Alva, 154
Edward, Prince of Wales (Edward VII): scandals, 49; Aquarium visit, 31; pantomime visits, 55; racing, 49, 106, 211, 214; Albion Hotel story, 127; Leno's Sandringham performance, 156; theatre going, 223; Coliseum visit, 159; Maud Allan performance, 199; death, 211
Elen, Gus: songs, 35; friendship with ML, 40, 82, 234; driving, 155; music hall strike, 176; Bennett on, 216; royal command performance, 225, 231; Alec's funeral, 246; biographical notes, 317
Elephant Man, the, 32
Eliot, George, 241
Eliot, T.S., 278, 279
Ellis, Madge, 91, 102, 103, 317
Ellis Island, New York, 238–41, 258
Elmore, Belle (Kunigunde Mackamotzki, Cora Crippen), 161–2, 174, 208–10, 316
Elton, Sam, 228
Elvin, Joe: friendship with ML, 40, 109, 266; music hall strike, 175, 178, 180; royal

command performance, 226, 231;
biographical notes, 317
Empire, Cardiff, 60, 71, 73, 269
Empire, Croydon, 235
Empire, East Ham, 171, 233
Empire, Edinburgh, 73, 223–4, 235
Empire, Edmonton, 272–5
Empire, Hackney, 149, 155, 157, 198, 235
Empire, Holborn, 165, 171, 250, 264, 272
Empire, Islington, 171, 272
Empire, Kilburn, 267, 272
Empire, Leicester Square, 40, 52, 77, 86–9,
223
Empire, Liverpool, 146
Empire, Newcastle, 60
Empire, Nottingham, 235
Empire, Portsmouth, 80, 235
Empire, Sheffield, 235
Empire, Shepherd's Bush, 235
Empire, Southend, 204
Empire, Sunderland, 233
Empire, Swansea, 71, 269
Empire Palace of Varieties, Johannesburg,
112, 114, 115
Empress Theatre of Varieties, Brixton, 165,
170, 171
Enfield, Harry, 280
Era, 2, 21, 28, 34, 41, 42, 51, 52, 82, 85, 87,
102, 106, 118, 123, 127, 128, 129, 132, 133,
140, 146–7, 155, 165, 177, 182, 191, 196,
201, 204, 208, 216, 223, 227, 232, 251, 259,
266, 268, 271–2, 283
Etruria, SS, 90
Euston Music Hall, 170, 171, 235
Evan's Music Hall, 223
Evening World, 119

Fairy Bell Minstrels, 9, 192
Falmouth, Viscount, 144
Farren, Fred, 224, 228
Farson, Daniel, 79, 277, 283
Fields, Fanny, 225, 228
Fields, W.C., 80, 117, 136
Financial Times, 52
Flanagan, Bud, 123–4
Folies-Marigny, Paris, 185, 186
Folly Variety Theatre, Manchester, 80
Foote, Dave, 115
Forde, Florrie, 231, 317
Formby, George, 213, 216

Formby, George (Senior), 156
Foster, George, 29, 34–5, 71, 202, 317
France, A. & Son, 2
Francis, Day & Hunter, 158
Franklin, Irene, 136
freaks, 31–2
Frederick, Professor, 30

Gaiety, 47
Gaiety, Birmingham, 60, 71
Gaiety, Glasgow, 71, 80
Gaiety restaurant, Strand, 168
Gammon, Barclay, 225, 229
Gatti's Palace of Varieties, Lambeth, 15, 47,
143
Geere, Catherine, 4–5
George V, King, 223, 224–32
Gerald, Frank, 166
German, Edward (Edward German Smith),
250
Gibbons, Walter, 165, 170–1, 318
Gilchrist, Connie, 34
Gilpin, Pater, 212
Ginnett, Isabel, 209
Gitana, Gertie, 228
Gladstone, William Ewart, 12, 24–5, 48, 69
Glasgow, 71, 80
Glover, Jimmy, 115
Goff, Detective Sergeant, 141–2
Gordon, Cliff, 187
Gordon, General, 129
Gotham, New York, 187
Goudie, Thomas Peterson, 141, 144–6
Grace, W.G., 148
Gramophone and Typewriter company, 154
gramophone recordings, 154–5
Grand, Clapham Junction, 164, 171
Grand Theatre, Birmingham, 235
Grand Theatre of Varieties, Liverpool, 60, 71
Granville, Yvonne, 265, 267
Grecian Theatre, Shoreditch, 10, 11, 13
Guildhall School of Music, 253

Hackney Empire, 149, 155, 157, 198, 235
Haddock, Captain, 237, 238
Hammersmith Temple of Varieties, 22, 27
Hammerstein, Oscar, 93–4, 318
Hampstead Cemetery, 3–4
Hargreaves, Graham, 268
Harley, Lily, 27

Harlow, Dan, 275

Harold, Lily, 83

Harper's, 97

Harrington, J.P., songwriting, 46, 77, 96, 97, 100, 109, 110, 122, 141, 189, 199, 200, 202, 211, 217

Harris, Sir Augustus ('Gus'), 47, 52–3, 74–5, 84, 106, 318

Harwood's Variety Theatre, Hoxton, 46

Hastings Standard, 127

Haweis, Hugh Reginald, 66

Hawthorne Sisters, 162

Hearn, Tom, 228

Held, Anna, 94, 117, 119–20, 201

Helme, Ernest, 257

Hertz, Carl, 250

Hibbert, Henry George, 156

Hicks, Seymour, 146

Higham, Fred, 208

Hill, Jenny: career, 38–9; racehorse, 39, 213; New York performances, 47; songs, 60; charity events, 61; tribute to ML, 82; death, 106; biographical notes, 318

Hippodrome, Boscombe, 233

Hippodrome, Cleveland (Ohio), 244

Hippodrome, Ealing, 233

Hippodrome, Exeter, 233, 235

Hippodrome, Golders Green, 258

Hippodrome, Ilford, 235

Hippodrome, Ipswich, 235

Hippodrome, Lewisham, 235

Hippodrome, Margate, 233, 235

Hippodrome, Norwich, 235

Hippodrome, Southampton, 269

Hippodrome, Southend, 233

Hippodrome, West End, 159, 234

Hippodrome, Willesden, 272

Hippodrome, Woolwich, 233, 235, 254

Hirsch, Baron, 105

Houdini, Harry, 117, 136

Hoxton Hall, *see* McDonald's

Hoxton Theatre of Varieties, 17–18

Hudson, Robert, 144

Hurley, Alec (ML's second husband): appearance, 123–4; family background, 122; career, 122–4, 133–4, 139–40, 206–7; ML's benefit, 82; ML's South African send-off, 109, 110; relationship with ML, 124, 206–7, 212, 243; Australian trip, 132–40; race-going, 140, 155; friendship with

Burges, 144, 146–7; mother's death, 147; le Brunn donation, 162; management disputes, 164, 165; named as co-respondent, 167; wedding, 168–9; music hall strike, 172, 176, 178–9; US tour, 186–7, 192–3; brother's finances, 193, 204; law suits, 204; bankruptcy, 207–8; divorce proceedings, 208; death, 245–6; biographical notes, 318–19

Hurley, Alfred, 193, 204

Hurley, John, 122

Hyams, George, 105, 109, 213

Hyams, Grace (née Wood, ML's sister): birth, 7; appearance, 29; career, 28, 40, 61, 104–5; friendship with Bella, 62; US tour, 90; marriage, 109, 213; sister's send-off, 109; in Austria, 126; biographical notes, 321

Hyman, Edgar, 110, 319

Imperial Music Hall, 89, 90–2

International Artistes' Lodge, 166

Irving, Henry, 52

Isaacs, Barnett, *see* Barnato

Isaacs, Harry, 113

Isle of Man, 71

Ismay, Joseph Bruce, 236

Jack the Ripper, 25, 28

Jackson Troupe, 228

Jacob, Naomi, 283

Jameson, Storm, 278

Jerome, Jerome K., 25–6, 39–40

Jewell, Jimmy, 272

Joel, Solly, 114–17, 319

Joel, Woolf, 114, 117

Jones, Wilton, 74

Karno, Fred, 170, 173, 183, 185, 319

Keith, Benjamin Franklin, 193–4, 244, 319

Kendal, Madge, 206

Kendall, Marie: friendship with ML, 40, 128; songs, 128, 166; music hall dispute, 166, 173; royal command performance, 226, 231; biographical notes, 319

Kenney, Annie, 205–6

Kinetoscope, 175

Kipling, Rudyard, 256

Kitchener, Lord, 129, 199

Klaw & Erlanger, 188

Knowles, Richard G., 40, 173, 319
Koster, John, 46–7, 92–3, 319
Koster & Bial's Music Hall, 45–6, 93, 94, 121
Kraus, George J., 92–3
Kruger, Paul, 116, 117

La Pia, 225, 228
Labouchere, Henry, 69
Lafayette, The Great, 223–4, 318
Lane, Ella, *see* Burge
Lane, Lupino, 139, 231
Lane, Sam, 37
Lane, Sara, 11, 37, 38, 320
Langtry, Lillie, 134
Lauder, Harry: management dispute, 166; US
   popularity, 188; Guildhall performance,
   204; royal command performance, 225, 228,
   232; war work, 256–7; knighthood, 264;
   biographical notes, 320
Lawrence, Katie, 21, 144, 320
le Brunn, George: career, 46, 157–8; songs,
   33, 46, 49, 58–9, 65, 67, 72, 77, 96, 97–8,
   100–1, 109, 122, 132, 141, 147, 148, 156;
   ML's South African send-off, 111; death,
   157–8, 162, 167; fund, 162; biographical
   notes, 320
le Brunn, Thomas, 58, 72
Le Neve, Ethel, 208–10
Leach, Gus, 34
Leichner's greasepaint, 251
Leigh, Fred W., songwriting, 148, 160, 200,
   236, 249, 252, 261
Leighton, Harry, 58, 59
Lena, Lily, 10
Lena Sisters, 105
Leno, Dan (George Galvin): appearance, 23,
   157; career, 13, 22–3, 27, 155–7; friendship
   with ML, 40, 61, 110, 156, 164, 167; songs,
   46; pantomime performances, 53, 74–5, 83,
   156; imitators, 70; US reception, 118;
   tribute to Queen, 132; royal command
   performance, 156, 223; death, 157, 167;
   biographical notes, 320
Leno, Don, 118–19
Leslie, Fanny, 54
Lester, Alfred, 225
Lewis, PC, 259–60
Licensing Committee, 50, 78–9
Lindon, Millie, 194
Lipinski's performing dogs, 250–1

Little Tich (Harry Relph): appearance, 22, 55;
   career, 22, 27, 183; marriages, 227;
   friendship with ML, 40, 82; North
   American tour, 43; pantomime
   performances, 53, 55, 74–5, 82, 83–4;
   Berlin performances, 117; Tivoli revue,
   148, 149; music hall strike, 175–6; earning
   power, 181; Paris success, 185; Bennett on,
   216; royal command performance, 225–7,
   228, 232; defence of music hall, 268; son's
   career, 183; biographical notes, 324
Liverpool, 17, 60, 71, 95
Liverpool, Bank of, 141, 144
Lloyd, Marie (Matilda Alice Victoria Wood):
   LIFE: birth, 5; childhood, 6–9; education,
   8; first jobs, 9; début, 11, 13–14, 16–17;
   stage name, 18–19, 161; first reviews, 21;
   admirers, 34–5; marriage, 35–6; birth of
   daughter, 36–7; pantomime (*The Magic
   Dragon*), 37; social life, 40–1; stillborn
   baby, 41; in New York, 43, 45–7;
   pantomime (*Humpty Dumpty*), 53–7; first
   provincial tour (1891), 60–1; benefit
   performances, 61, 81–2, 128, 130; lifestyle,
   62; husband's assaults, 64, 87–8; piano
   purchase, 66; second provincial tour (1892),
   71–3; pantomime (*Little Bo-Peep*), 74–6;
   pantomime (*Robinson Crusoe*), 82–4;
   separation from first husband, 85; second
   US visit, 89–94; divorce issue, 90, 94,
   167–8; pantomime (*Pretty Bo-Peep*), 95,
   123; memoirs, 103; jewellery theft case, 107;
   cab accident, 108; send-off party, 109–10;
   in South Africa, 112–16; in Germany, 117;
   third US visit, 117–21; *The ABC Girl*,
   125–6; pantomime (*Cinderella*), 129–30;
   Boer War, 130–1; in Australia, 132–40;
   Burge case, 141–3, 147; revue, 148–9;
   recordings, 154–5; pantomime (*Aladdin*),
   155; Music Hall Ladies Guild, 160–2; law
   suits, 164, 165, 204, 259; second marriage,
   168–9; music hall strike, 170–82;
   daughter's wedding, 182–4; French
   performances, 185–6; provincial tour
   (1907), 186; fourth US visit, 186–98;
   suffragist play (*How The Vote Was Won*),
   205–6; separation from second husband,
   207–8, 240; in South Africa, 207, 217;
   relationship with Ben Dillon, 212, 216, 220,
   222, 232–3, 243, 255–6, 259–60, 265, 268,

271; left out of royal command
performance, 226–31; provincial tour
(1913), 234–5; fifth US visit (1913), 235,
236–45, 247–8; confinement on Ellis
Island, 238–40, 258; in Canada, 247; third
marriage, 247–8; wartime, 249–62;
provincial tours (1918–19), 264; jury
service, 270–1; will, 271; death, 275,
276–9; funeral, 1–4 PERSON: appearance,
16, 21, 28–9, 57, 138, 168, 190, 193, 200,
213, 271, 274, 280; cars, 155, 171, 176, 177,
205, 244–5; clumsiness, 124; costumes,
13–14, 21, 29, 36, 46–7, 56, 61, 73, 82, 99,
111–12, 189, 243, 249; dancing, 28, 47, 56,
83; earnings, 61, 83, 91, 175–6, 181, 266,
269–70; friendships, 205; generosity, 80–1,
162; health, 41–2, 85, 103, 108, 144, 155,
170, 181, 204, 207, 219, 241–2, 254–5, 264,
271–2, 273–5, 276–8; homes, 37, 62, 85,
124, 221–2, 255, 259, 272; interviews, 112,
119, 135; letters, 120–1; musicianship, 59;
personality, 8, 17, 28–30, 70–1; race-going,
115–16, 140, 155, 211–12, 213–14; reviews,
21, 54, 55, 56, 60–1, 91, 120–1, 136–7,
138–9, 190–1, 192, 216–17, 265; sense of
insecurity, 70–1, 112, 120, 206, 255–6;
sexual innuendo, 78–80, 108, 128, 279–80;
speaking voice, 110; speech making, 61, 82,
109–10, 177 SONGS: 'Actions Speak
Louder Than Words', 58, 59; 'After The
Pantomime', 47; 'Among My Knick-
knacks', 112; 'And The Leaves Began To
Fall', 153–4, 197; 'The Ankle Watch',
242–3, 249; ''Arriet's Reply', 60, 61, 137;
'The Aviator', 242; 'The Barmaid', 83, 85,
87, 91; 'Bathing', 128; 'Bird In The Hand',
91; 'The Bond Street Tea Walk', 141,
149–50; 'The Boy I Love', 5, 18, 106; 'Buy
Me Some Almond Rock', 69, 79; 'The
Cosmopolitan Girl', 274; 'The Coster Girl
In Paris', 54, 233, 242; 'The Coster
Wedding', 151, 190; 'The Coster's
Christening', 151–2; 'Customs Of The
Country', 152–3, 190, 194–5; 'The
Directoire Girl', 199, 200–1, 211, 281;
'Don't Laugh', 58; 'The Dress Of The
Day', 249; 'Every Little Movement Has A
Meaning Of Its Own', 219, 242;
'Ev'rything In The Garden's Lovely', 122,
128–9, 139; 'G'arn away', 68–9; 'The
Geisha Girl', 108; 'The Girl In The Khaki
Dress', 130–1; 'Hulloah! Hulloah!
Hulloah!', 127–8, 200; 'I Can't Forget The
Days When I Was Young', 258; 'I Haven't
Had A Cuddle For A Long Time Now',
218; 'I Was Slapped', 49; 'I'd Like To Live
In Paris All The Time', 54, 233, 242, 249;
'If You Want To Get On In Revue', 252;
'In The Good Old Days', 16, 18; 'It Was
A Good Job I Had These On', 99; 'It's A
Bit Of A Ruin', 263, 270, 272, 274–5, 280;
'It's A Jolly Fine Game Played Slow!',
100–1; 'Johnny Jones', 101–2, 103, 280;
'Keep Off The Grass', 77, 91; 'Listen With
The Right Ear!', 47–9; 'A Little of What
You Fancy!', 249, 257–8, 259; 'Madame du
Vann', 58; 'Maid Of London', 77, 80, 108;
'Mischief', 58; 'My Old Man Said Follow
The Van', 261–2, 271, 280, 281; 'My
Soldier Laddie', 16; 'The Naughty
Continong', 77–8, 82, 83, 91; 'The Next
Best Thing', 249; 'No Flies On Me', 49;
'No More Up At Covent Garden Market',
123; 'Not For The Very Best Man', 128;
'Now You've Got Yer Khaki On', 252;
'Oh! Mr Porter', 68, 72–3, 75, 90, 91; 'The
Piccadilly Trot', 221, 232; 'Put On Your
Slippers, You're Home For The Night',
217–18; 'Rosie Had A Very Rosie Time',
202; 'Salute My Bicycle', 98, 99–100; 'The
Same Thing', 77; 'She Doesn't Know That
I Know What I Know', 160, 167; 'She'd
Never Had Her Ticket Punched Before',
78, 119; 'Silly Fool', 77; 'So I Know Now',
101; 'Spanish Burlesque', 190; 'Tale Of A
Pretty Sole', 91; 'The Tale Of The Skirt',
148, 152, 190; 'That Was Before My Time',
43, 58; 'That's How The Little Girl Got
On', 154; 'There They Are – The Two of
'Em – On Their Own', 125; 'There Was
Something On His Mind', 154, 190; 'The
Three Ages of Woman', 252–3; 'Tiddly-
om-pom!', 190, 200; 'Time Is Flying', 16;
'Tricky Little Trilby', 96, 97–8; 'The
Twiddly Wink', 236, 242; 'Twiggy Voo?',
65, 67–9; 'The Wedding March', 151;
'Whacky, Whack, Whack', 49, 56; 'What,
What', 153, 190, 194; 'What's That For,
Eh?', 101; 'When I Take My Morning
Promenade', 217; 'Who'll Buy My

Flowers?', 27; 'Wink The Other Eye', 33, 46–7, 135; 'Woman Knows How Far She Can Go', 242; 'You Can't Stop A Girl From Thinking', 109, 110; 'You Needn't Wink – I Know', 154; 'You Should Go To France', 47; 'You're A Thing Of The Past', 167
Lloyd, Marie (French actress), 234
Lloyd George, David, 180
Lloyds Sunday News, 115, 283
Lockhart's Elephants, 30, 82, 173–4, 175
Loftus, Cecilia (Cissie), 94, 148, 225
Loftus, Marie, 74, 76, 118, 321
Logan, Mary, 281
London and South Western Bank, 142
London Coliseum, 158–9, 163, 234, 250, 259
London County Council (LCC), 50, 89, 135
London Entr'acte, 21, 38, 47, 49, 51, 53, 55, 74, 283
London Music Hall, Shoreditch, 166, 179
London Palladium, 165, 216, 254, 256, 264, 271
London Pavilion, *see* Pavilion
Los Angeles Inquirer, 248
Lothrop, Carl D., 194–5
Lundberg, Ada, 111
Lupino, Barry, 37–8
Lupino, George, 53
Lupino, Harry, 27
Lupino, Stanley, 37–8
Lupino family, 37–8
Lyceum, Ipswich, 253
Lyons, Joe, 109, 111, 178
Lytton, W.T., 33, 101

Macdermott, Ouida, 204
McDonald's (Hoxton Hall), 10–11, 24
McDougall, John, 50, 51, 321
McGuinness, Deputy Sheriff, 93
Mackenzie, Compton, 56–7
McNaughton, Alice (née Wood, ML's sister): birth, 7; childhood, 8, 9; appearance, 29, 188, 248; career, 28, 40, 61, 104–5, 129–30, 170, 246–7, 248, 268–9; friendship with Bella, 62–3, 141; sister's benefit, 82; marriage, 104–5; sister's send-offs, 109, 186; bridesmaid, 126; Queen's death, 132; family outing, 155; le Brunn donation, 162; music hall strike, 180, 182; in US, 182, 188–9, 191–2, 198, 201–3, 238, 268–9;

relationship with sister, 191–2, 238; Alec's funeral, 246; husband's bankruptcy, 246–7; London house, 272; account of sister's life, 11, 35, 66, 149; biographical notes, 320
McNaughton, Charles, 150, 155
McNaughton, Fred: appearance, 104; career, 104–5, 122, 129; Queen's death, 132; le Brunn donation, 162; music hall strike, 171, 182; US tour, 182; royal command performance, 231; wartime, 251; accounts of ML's illness, 277; biographical notes, 322
McNaughton, Tom: appearance, 104; career, 104–5, 122, 129, 246–7, 268–9; marriage, 104–5; ML's South African send-off, 109, 111; Queen's death, 132; friendship with Burges, 141; family outing, 155; le Brunn donation, 162; presentation to ML, 164; ML's wedding to Alec, 168–9; music hall strike, 171, 180, 182; in US, 182, 188, 202–3, 268–9; royal command performances, 231; Alec's funeral, 246; bankruptcy, 246–7; breakdown, 269; biographical notes, 322
McNaughton Brothers, 104–5, 188
Macqueen-Pope, Walter, 276–7, 278, 283
Maher, Danny, 213
Mahony, *see* Bellwood
Major, John, 166
Major, Tom, 166
Mances, James, 141, 145, 146
Manchester, 60, 71, 80
Manchester, Duke of, 94, 213
Mansel, Lady, 102
Marconi, Guglielmo, 81, 106, 148
Marie Lloyd's Blue Book, 103
Marion, Kitty, 206
Marks, Laurence Abraham, 141, 145, 146
Martinetti, Clara, 162, 209
Martinetti, Paul, 162, 178, 209, 321
Mary, Queen, 224, 232
Marylebone Music Hall, 161
Matcham, Frank, 73–4, 321
May, Melinda, 208
Mayne, Clarice, 225, 229
Mayo, Sam, 258
Merrick, Joseph, 32
Metropolitan Building Act (1878), 50
Metropolitan Music Hall, 24, 27, 170, 235, 281
Metropolitan Theater, Broadway, 45

Middlesex Music Hall ('Old Mo'), Drury
  Lane, 22, 27, 30, 40, 86, 94, 123
Milburn, J.H., 204
Miller, Max, 80
Mills, A.J., 217
Monks, Victoria, 205, 231, 322
Montrose, SS, 209–10
Morgan, John Pierpont, 148
Morning Oregonian, 247
Morton, Charles, 24, 163, 322
Morton, Richard, 58, 65, 67, 82
Moss, Sir Edward, 73, 200, 224, 322
Moss, Richard, 165
Moss Empire, 204
Mozart, George (David John Grilling), 250
Munro, Daisy (née Wood, ML's sister): birth,
  7; appearance, 103, 202; career, 61, 103–4,
  108, 202–4, 219–20, 234; sister's benefit,
  82; sister's send-off, 109, 110; illness, 126;
  wedding, 126–7; music hall strike, 180; in
  US, 202–3; husband's illness and death,
  219–20; Alec's funeral, 246; home, 272;
  biographical notes, 325
Munro, Donald, 126–7, 202, 219, 322
Munro, Donald (Junior), 219
Munro, Dorothy, 219
Music Hall Artistes' Railway Association
  (MHARA), 163, 164–6, 172, 208
Music Hall Benevolent Fund, 61
Music Hall Ladies Guild, 160–2, 170, 174,
  208–9

Napol, Felise, 27
Nash, Lil and John, 162
National Alliance, 171, 178–80
National Association of Theatrical
  Employees, 171
National Standard Theatre, 11
National Vigilance Association (NVA), 50, 89
Nelstone, Arthur, 140
New Fourteenth Street Theater, 45
New York, 43–7, 89–94
New York Mail and Express, 91
New York Sun, 93, 240
New York World, 190, 203
Newberry, Pollie, 64
Newland, J., 156
News of the World, 70
Nicholls, Horace W., 129
Nightingale, Florence, 279

Nightingall, Walter, 213
Norton, Herbert, 107

O'Connor, T.W., 43
O'Gorman, Joe, 166, 172, 178
'Old Kate', 2
Olympia, Liverpool, 233
Olympic, RMS, 236–8, 241, 248
Opera House, Melbourne, 136, 137–9
Orchard, Bella (Ella Lane), *see* Burge
Orford, Emmeline, 151
Orkney, Countess of, 34
Orpheum, New York, 187, 197, 202, 235, 241
Orpheum Circuit, 241
Orpheum Theater, Brooklyn, 243
Orwell, George, 279
Oxford Music Hall, 24, 27, 30, 36, 40, 47, 58,
  61, 77, 94, 101–3, 144, 165, 170, 171, 205,
  235, 256

Paine, Harry, 56–7
Palace, Croydon, 171
Palace, Ealing, 171
Palace, Hammersmith, 272
Palace, Manchester, 233
Palace, Plymouth, 235
Palace, Walthamstow, 171, 182
Palace girls, 225
Palace Theatre, Cambridge Circus, 125,
  199–201, 224, 233, 254
Palace Theatre, Luton, 235
Palace Theatre of Varieties, 129
Palace Theatre of Varieties, Manchester, 60,
  71
Palladium, *see* London Palladium
Palmer, Minnie, 150, 151
Pankhurst, Emmeline, 206
Paragon Theatre of Varieties, Mile End, 27,
  40, 73, 77, 86, 165, 166–7, 171
Paris, 185–6
Parnell, Charles Stewart, 50
Parthenon, Greenwich, 27
Parthenon, Liverpool, 17
Pasta, Jean, 38
Pastor, Tony (Antonio), 39, 43–5, 47, 193,
  322
Pathé company, 154
Patti, Louisa (Archer), 10, 16, 313
Paul, R.W., 106–7
Pauline, Princess, 68

Pavilion, Glasgow, 204, 233

Pavilion, Piccadilly, 30–1, 41, 47, 223, 232, 249

Pavilion, Whitechapel, 62, 126

Pavlova, Anna, 225, 229

Payne, George Adney: ML's benefit, 82; ML's South African send-off, 109; influence, 165; music hall strike, 171, 173, 176, 177; Marie Junior's wedding, 184

Payne, Millie, 174

Payne, Walter, 181

Performer, 175, 283

Persico, Emilia, 117

Philadelphia, 195–6

pianos, 65–7

Pike, Captain, 30

Pink, Wal, 166, 178

Pipifax and Panilo, 225, 229

Pollock, Leon, 273

Poluski, Rosie (née Wood, ML's sister): birth, 7, 105; appearance, 105, 197; career, 105–6, 112, 131, 142, 155, 197–8, 202, 234; South African tour, 109, 111–12, 116; bridesmaid, 126, 141; le Brunn donation, 162; Marie Junior's wedding, 183; sister's send-off party, 186; in US, 197–8; wedding, 202; Alec's funeral, 246; sister's death, 276; biographical notes, 321

Poluski, Sam, 155, 168–9

Poluski, Will, 202, 246, 322–3

Poluski Brothers, 166

Polytechnic, Regent Street, 106

Poole, Ellen, 38

Pope, Macqueen, 35

Portland, Duke of, 215

Powell, Orlando, songwriting, 160, 189, 199, 200, 202, 211, 218, 236, 252

Power, Nelly, 18

Prete, Antoine, 260

Prince, Arthur: royal command performances, 225, 228, 232, 264; Alec's funeral, 246; war work, 251, 264; biographical notes, 323

Prince of Wales's Theatre, Great Grimsby, 32

Proctor, Frederick Francis, 91

Punch, 52, 89, 175–6

Purefoy, Wilfred (Pure), 214–15

Queen's Palace of Varieties, 27

racing, 211–16

ragtime, 233–4

railways, 71–2, 163, 214

Randall, Harry, 40, 164, 225, 231, 323

Rational Dress Society, 99

Reed, Carina, 102

Reed, Charles Cory, 102

Reed, Mrs, 103

Register, 135

Relph, Harry, *see* Little Tich

Relph, Paul, 183

Retford, Ella, 228

revue, 148–51

Rickards, Harry, 136, 137, 323

Rickards, Madge, 137

Rickards, Noni, 137

Riogoku Troupe, 228, 229

Ritchie, J. Ewing, 12

Roberts, Arthur: friendship with ML, 81, 169, 266; music hall strike, 175, 178–81; royal command performance, 225; ML's death, 276; biographical notes, 323

Robey, George (George Edward Wade): songs, 70; social life, 115, 279; music hall strike, 173; earning power, 181; royal command performance, 225, 228; war work, 256, 260, 264; biographical notes, 323

Rogers, E.W., 69, 85, 150

Romaine, Claire, 205

Romano's restaurant, 124–5, 169, 186, 206, 213, 214, 216

Rose, Clarkson, 161, 323

Rose, Mae, 273

Rothschild, Lord, 114

Rouse, Thomas, 11, 12

Royal Albion Hotel, Hastings, 81, 127, 223

Royal Aquarium, 31

Royal Cambridge Hall of Varieties (Royal Cambridge Music Hall), Shoreditch, 22, 77, 94, 123, 125

Royal Canterbury, 77

Royal Court Theatre, 148

Royal Forresters, Mile End, 27, 30, 36, 40

Royal Holborn, 21, 30, 40, 105

Royal Standard, Victoria, 40

Russell, George, 50

Sadler's Wells, 26, 86

St Luke's Church, Hampstead, 2

Sandow, Eugene, 32, 67, 109, 136, 323
Sargent, Epes Winthrop, 120–1
Sassoon, Siegfried, 257
Saturday Review, 55
Savoy Hotel, 113
Scala, Charlotte Street, 178–80
Scott, B., 119, 217
Sebright's Music Hall, 17–18, 27, 130
Shakespeare Theatre, Liverpool, 95, 123
Shaw, George Bernard, 67–8, 79
sheet music, 69–70, 201
Shepard, Cyril, 57
Shepard, Ernest, 57
Shields, Ella, 231, 323
Sickert, Walter Richard, 25, 27
Sievier, Robert, 260
Sinclair, Archdeacon, 200
Sir John Falstaff Music Hall, Old Street, 17
Sketch, 77, 83, 97, 99
Sloan, Tod, 214
Smirke, Alice (née Hyams, ML's niece), 213
Smirke, Charlie, 213
Smith, Arthur, 259
Smith, W.H., 50
Somerset, Lord Arthur, 50
Soukes Brothers, 136
South Africa, 109–17, 131, 207
South Africa, 112, 116
South London Palace of Varieties, 15, 27, 36, 38, 40, 47, 49, 123, 165, 171
Stage, 75, 83, 208, 283
Star, Bermondsey, 21
Stoll, Oswald: business career, 73, 163–4; Coliseum opening, 158–9; influence, 165, 234; music hall strike, 177, 178, 180; relationship with ML, 177, 184, 226; wartime disputes, 259; influenza epidemic, 263; knighthood, 264; biographical notes, 324
Stone, Fred, 45
Stormat, Leo, 131
Stratton, Eugene: ML's benefit, 82; career, 131, 139; race going, 155; presentations to ML, 164, 186–7; royal command performance, 228; Alec's funeral, 246; biographical notes, 324
suffragettes, 205–6
Sullivan, Terry, 263, 270

Surrey Theatre, 13
Swaffer, Percy, 116
Symons, Ernest, 43, 58

Tabrar, Joe (Joseph), 58, 60, 61, 69, 77, 109
Tate, Harry: friendship with ML, 109, 111; Mafekinging, 131; in Australia, 136; charity gala, 223; royal command performances, 225, 229, 264–5; biographical notes, 324
Tennyson, Alfred, Lord, 108
Terriers, 166
Terry, Ellen, 2, 206, 234, 268, 279
Theatre Royal, Exeter, 73
Theatres Act (1843), 24
Thornton, Richard, 73, 165
Tich, Little, *see* Little Tich
Tichborne, Sir Roger, 22
Tiffany, Maud, 250
Tiller Girls, 117
Tillett, Ben, 179
Tilley, Vesta (*later* Lady de Frece): career, 118–19; songs, 46, 97; pantomime performances, 53; charity work, 81; marriage, 81, 264; social life, 115, 279; reputation, 91; in US, 118–19, 188; ML's benefit, 130; cars, 155; music hall strike, 174, 176; royal command performance, 225; 228, 232; war work, 251, 256; husband's knighthood, 81, 264; retirement, 268; biographical notes, 324–5
Times, The, 54, 55, 64, 106, 246
Tivoli, 42, 131, 148–9, 170, 171, 181, 216, 235
Tivoli, Adelaide, 136
Tivoli, Sydney, 136
Toft, Albert, 231
Tony Pastor's Opera House, New York, 44
Torr, Sam, 32
Tozer, Henry, 179, 325
Tree, Sir Henry Beerbohm, 157
Trilby, 96–7
Trocadero Palace of Varieties, 40, 68, 109, 178
Turner, Reggie, 76
Twain, Mark, 136

Una the Human Fly, 32
Union Square Theater, 45
United Booking Office (UBO), 194, 235, 243

Vance, Alfred, 31

Vanity Fair, 53, 74, 212

Variety, 190–1, 196, 197, 203, 243

Variety Artistes Federation (VAF), 166, 170–82, 186–7

Variety Theatre, 11

Vaudeville Club, Charing Cross Road, 165

Vauxhall gardens, 23

Victoria, Queen: piano, 66; Windsor entertainment, 223; diamond jubilee, 111, 114; reputation, 279; death, 132, 163

Victoria, Vesta: career, 77, 194; ML's benefit, 82; in US, 188; royal command performance, 226, 231; biographical notes, 325

Vigilance Record, 89

Vincent, Sir Edgar, 144

Wallenda, Mollie, 30

Ware, George: songwriting, 5, 49; ML's agent, 18–19, 20, 61; death, 106; biographical notes, 325

Ware, George (Junior), 111

Water Rats, 165–6, 172, 178

Watkins, John, 15

Webb, Beatrice, 136

Wellington Pier Pavilion, Great Yarmouth, 235

Werba & Luescher, 246

West End, Willesden, 233

Westminster, Duke of, 144

Wheatley, Dennis, 249

Wheatley, Elijah (whip), 212, 246

Wheatley, Maude (née Wood, ML's sister): birth, 40; career, 106, 202; bridesmaid, 126, 183–4; marriage, 212; Alec's funeral, 246; biographical notes, 321

White Brothers of Nottingham, 132–3

Wilde, Oscar, 50, 185, 277

Wilkinson, Norman, 236

Williams, Percy, 187–8, 198, 243, 325

Wilson, Arthur, 49

Wilson, Claud, 260

Wilson, Maud, 108, 268, 271

Wilton's (Old Mahogany Bar), 122

Winkelmeier, Herr, 31

Wisdom, Norman, 281

Wood, Alice (sister), *see* McNaughton

Wood, Annie (sister): birth, 28; career, 106;

bridesmaid, 126, 202; Marie Junior's wedding, 183; ML's US tour, 186, 192, 197; Alec's funeral, 246; holidays, 268; memoirs, 7; biographical notes, 325

Wood, Daisy (sister), *see* Munro

Wood, Grace (sister), *see* Hyams

Wood, John (Brush, Brushie, ML's father): family background, 5; appearance and character, 7, 8, 63–4; career, 5–7, 15, 17, 28, 81; marriage, 5; attitude to ML's career, 10, 192; attitude to ML's suitors, 34–5; relationship with ML's first husband, 63–4; Albion Hotel, 81, 127; Wardour Street pub, 81; Bella's wedding, 141; Marie Junior's wedding, 183; ML's US send-off party, 186; ML's fiftieth birthday, 266; fight with Ben Dillon, 267; ML's funeral, 3; biographical notes, 325

Wood, Johnny (brother): birth, 7, 8; character, 8; childhood, 9; ML's South African send-off, 109, 111; business career, 127, 269–70; Alec's funeral, 246; stage appearances, 18, 252; ML's agent, 269–70, 272; ML's will, 271; ML's last illness, 273–4

Wood, Matilda Caroline (née Archer, ML's mother): family background, 5; character, 7, 8; marriage, 5–7; work, 7, 66, 81; children, 7, 28, 40; attitude to ML's career, 10, 192; relationship with ML's first husband, 63; Wardour Street pub, 81; ML's South African send-off, 109, 111; Bella's wedding, 141; ML's US send-off party, 186; ML's funeral, 3; biographical notes, 313

Wood, Maude (sister), *see* Wheatley

Wood, Rosie (sister), *see* Poluski

Wood, Sidney (brother), 28, 106, 202, 326

Wood, Victoria, 280

Wood, Wee Georgie, 231

Woolf, Virginia, 251, 271

Worth, 176

Wynne, Wish, 228

Young's Pier Theater, Atlantic City, 204

Zaeo (acrobat), 52, 326

Zangwill, Israel, 146

Zeppelin raids, 254

Ziegfeld, Florenz Junior, 201